The Chartered Institute of Marketing

Professional Diploma in Marketing

STUDY TEXT

The Marketing Planning Process

For exams up to December 2010

First edition September 2009

ISBN 9780 7517 6812 1

e-learning ISBN 9780 7517 7685 0

British Library Cataloguing-in-Publication Data
A catalogue record for this book
is available from the British Library

Published by

BPP Learning Media Ltd
Aldine House, Aldine Place
London W12 8AA

www.bpp.com/learningmedia

Printed in the United Kingdom

All our rights reserved. No part of this publication may be reproduced, stored in a retrieval system or transmitted, in any form or by any means, electronic, mechanical, photocopying, recording or otherwise, without the prior written permission of BPP Learning Media Ltd.

We are grateful to the Chartered Institute of Marketing for permission to reproduce in this text the syllabus, tutor's guidance notes and past examination questions. We are also grateful to Superbrands and The Centre for Brand Analysis for their support of our online feature 'A Word From...'

Author: Kate Machattie
CIM Publishing Manager: Dr Kellie Vincent
Template design: Yolanda Moore
Photography: Terence O'Loughlin

Your learning materials, published by BPP Learning Media Ltd, are printed on paper sourced from sustainable, managed forests.

©
BPP Learning Media Ltd
2009

A note about copyright

Dear Customer

What does the little © mean and why does it matter?

Your market-leading BPP books, course materials and e-learning materials do not write and update themselves. People write them: on their own behalf or as employees of an organisation that invests in this activity. Copyright law protects their livelihoods. It does so by creating rights over the use of the content.

Breach of copyright is a form of theft – as well as being a criminal offence in some jurisdictions, it is potentially a serious breach of professional ethics.

With current technology, things might seem a bit hazy but, basically, without the express permission of BPP Learning Media:

- Photocopying our materials is a breach of copyright

- Scanning, ripcasting or conversion of our digital materials into different file formats, uploading them to facebook or e-mailing them to your friends is a breach of copyright

You can, of course, sell your books, in the form in which you have bought them – once you have finished with them. (Is this fair to your fellow students? We update for a reason.) But the e-products are sold on a single user licence basis: we do not supply 'unlock' codes to people who have bought them second-hand.

And what about outside the UK? BPP Learning Media strives to make our materials available at prices students can afford by local printing arrangements, pricing policies and partnerships which are clearly listed on our website. A tiny minority ignore this and indulge in criminal activity by illegally photocopying our material or supporting organisations that do. If they act illegally and unethically in one area, can you really trust them?

Contents

Introduction

• Aim of the Study Text • Studying for CIM qualifications • The Professional Diploma Syllabus • The CIM's Magic Formula • A guide to the features of the Study Text • A note on pronouns • Additional resources • Your personal study plan..v

Chapters

1	Marketing the planning process	1
2	External and internal influences on objectives	33
3	Environmental drivers of organisational change	53
4	The marketing audit process	73
5	Appraising the external marketing environment	87
6	Appraising the internal marketing environment	103
7	Market segmentation	121
8	Targeting	143
9	Positioning	159
10	Implementing marketing planning	181
11	Marketing planning in different contexts	209

Key concept ....?

Index ....?

Review form & free prize draw

1 Aim of the Study Text

This book has been deliberately referred to as a 'Study Text' rather than *text book*, because it is designed to help you though your specific CIM Professional Diploma in Marketing studies. It covers Unit 1 The Marketing Planning Process.

So, why is it similar to, but not actually a text book? Well, CIM has identified key texts that you should become familiar with. The purpose of this workbook is not to replace these texts but to pick out the important parts that you will definitely need to know in order to pass, simplify these elements and, to suggest a few areas within the texts that will provide good additional reading but that are not absolutely essential. We will also suggest a few other sources and useful press and CIM publications which are worth reading.

We know some of you will prefer to read text books from cover to cover while others amongst you will prefer to pick out relevant parts or dip in and out of the various topics. This Study Text will help you to ensure that if you are a 'cover to cover' type, then you will not miss the emphasis of the syllabus. If you are a 'dip in and out' type, then we will make sure that you find the parts which are essential for you to know. Unlike a standard *text book* which will have been written to be used across a range of alternative qualifications, this Text has been specifically compiled for your CIM course.

Throughout the Study Text you will find real examples of marketing in practice as well as key concepts highlighted. The Study Text also aims to encourage you to not only learn the theory but also provides cues and helps you to plan your own project work. You should use the activities to help you to build a portfolio of your own organisation.

2 Studying for CIM qualifications

There are a few key points to remember as you study for your CIM qualification:

(a) You are studying for a **professional** qualification. This means that you are required to use professional language and adopt a business approach in your work.

(b) You are expected to show that you have 'read widely'. Make sure that you read the quality press (and don't skip the business pages), read Marketing, The Marketer, Research and Marketing Week avidly.

(c) Become aware of the marketing initiatives you come across on a daily basis, for example, when you go shopping look around and think about why the store layout is as it is, consider the messages, channel choice and timings of ads when you are watching TV. It is surprising how much you will learn just by taking an interest in the marketing world around you.

(d) Get to know the way CIM write its exam papers and assignments. CIM uses a specific approach which is referred to as the Magic Formula to ensure a consistent approach when designing assessment materials. Make sure you are fully aware of this as it will help you interpret what the examiner is looking for (a full description of the Magic Formula appears later and is heavily featured within the chapters).

(e) Learn how to use Harvard referencing. This is explained in detail in our CIM Professional Diploma Assessment Workbook.

(f) Ensure that you read very carefully all assessment details sent to you from the CIM. It is very strict with regard to deadlines and completing the correct paperwork to accompany any assignment or project. Failing to meet any assessment entry deadlines or completing written work on time will mean that you will have to wait for the next round of assessment dates and will need to pay the relevant assessment fees again.

3 The Professional Diploma Syllabus

The Professional Diploma in Marketing is aimed at anyone who is employed in a marketing management role such as Brand Manager, Account Manager or Marketing Executive etc. If you are a graduate, you will be expected to have covered a minimum of a third of your credits in marketing subjects. You are therefore expected at this level of the qualification to be aware of the key marketing theories and be able to apply them to different organisational contexts.

The aim of the qualification is to provide the knowledge and skills for you to develop an 'ability to do' in relation to marketing planning. CIM qualifications concentrate on applied marketing within real work-places.

The complete qualification is made from four units:

- Unit 1 The Marketing Planning Process
- Unit 2 Delivering Customer Value Through Marketing
- Unit 3 Managing Marketing
- Unit 4 Project Management in Marketing

The CIM stipulate that each module should take 50 guided learning hours to complete. Guided learning hours refer to time in class, using distance learning materials and completing any work set by your tutor. Guided learning hours do not include the time it will take you to complete the necessary reading for your studies.

The syllabus as provided by the CIM can be found below with reference to our coverage within this Study Text.

Unit characteristics

The aim of this unit is to provide an understanding of the nature and scope of the internal and external marketing environment with broad consideration of the impact of international and global marketing.

The unit seeks to provide an overview of the significance of the marketing environment within the confines of the PESTEL model, but with consideration of issues including environmental and economic sustainability.

The unit addresses the key characteristics of the marketing environment and assesses the impact of market forces that are uncontrollable and how an organisation responds to them. At the same time, some consideration should be given in terms of how the factors within the micro- and internal environment can be manipulated to the benefit of the organisation and its customers.

On completion, students should be able to demonstrate a detailed understanding of the internal, micro- and macro-environment. This should include consideration of the key controllable and uncontrollable drivers of change, and the challenges posed to market-oriented organisations in today's volatile and dynamic business and marketing environment.

Overarching learning outcomes

By the end of this unit students should be able to:

- Evaluate the role of the marketing planning process and the marketing plan implementation in a range of marketing contexts including that of the organisation's strategy, culture and broader marketing environment.

- Evaluate the interconnectivity between corporate, business and marketing objectives and consider the impact of the external marketing environment and the organisation's resources on their development and achievement.

- Conduct a marketing audit including a detailed analysis of the internal and external marketing environments.

- Assess the findings of the audit and develop a marketing plan that is responsive to market and organisation changes and underpins the organisation's marketing strategy. Determine the important of segmentation, targeting and positioning and their relative interdependencies and develop effective segmentation, targeting and positioning strategies which are innovative, cost effective, valuable and maximise the potential marketing opportunities successfully.

- Utilise a range of positioning platforms including price, quality, service and brand perception, to establish an organisation's marketing positioning strategy.

- Recognise the significance of retaining existing customers through relationship marketing when developing strategies to achieve marketing objectives.

SECTION 1 – Marketing planning to deliver marketing strategies (weighting 25%)

		Covered in chapter(s)
1.1	Critically evaluate the different roles of marketing and its cross-functional interaction within organisations • Marketing as an organisation function and orientation • Marketing as a co-ordinating force in the organisation • Marketing's interface with other organisational functions • Exchange, transactions and relationships • Markets, customers, competition and value creation • Marketers as planners, strategists and tacticians • Marketing in theory and in practice	1
1.2	Critically evaluate the synergistic planning process including the different components of the marketing plan and its links with delivering the organisation's corporate, business and marketing strategies • The purpose of marketing planning • Achieving a sustainable competitive advantage • The stages of the marketing planning process: analysis, planning, implementation and control • Sequential, cyclical, and iterative approaches to planning • The outcomes of planning and plans • Contents of a marketing plan • Documentation and reality	1
1.3	Critically evaluate the role of the marketing plan in relation to the organisation's philosophy and an organisation's strategy intent • The marketing plan as means of conveying organisational purpose and future vision • The marketing plan as vehicle for setting direction and focus • The marketing plan as an operational framework • The marketing plan as a method of resource and budget allocation • The marketing plan as a tool for performance measurement	1
1.4	Evaluate the relationship between corporate, business and marketing objectives at an operational level and describe how they impact upon the activities associated with the marketing plan • Identifying a hierarchy of objectives • Objectives at varying levels and time scales • Different types of objectives: organisational, innovation, financial, market, relationship-focused, societal, non-profit • Consistency of plans with objectives • Resource issues and constraints	2

1.5	Assess the external and internal influences on the formulation of objectives and specify the key environmental drivers of organisational change	2, 3
	• Recognition of environmentally driven marketing planning and the resource-based view of the firm	
	• Identify internal influences on objectives including objective setting process, corporate mission and strategy, culture, resources, capabilities	
	• Identify external influences on objectives including economic conditions, markets, competition, industry life cycle, technological development	
	• Identify drivers of organisational change including innovation, evolving consumer behaviours, globalisation, ethical consumption and corporate social responsibility, sustainability relationship managements, stakeholder relations	
1.6	Critically evaluate the wider impact of external and internal environmental forces on the setting of objectives at different levels and the process of planning marketing	2
	• Macro-environment: political, cultural, social, economic, technological, legal, ecological, ethical	
	• Micro-environment: market, customers, competitors, industry structure and dynamics, suppliers, intermediaries	
	• Internal environment: capabilities in functional areas, assets and core competences, product and service portfolio, innovation, business relationships and strategic partnerships, current market position and past performance, dynamic capabilities, competitive advantage	

SECTION 2 – The marketing audit and strategic outcomes (weighting 30%)

		Covered in chapter(s)
2.1	Critically evaluate the practicalities of undertaking a marketing audit including resource limitations and implications within the organisational context	4
	• Conducting a marketing audit in practice	
	• Scope, timing and frequency	
	• Responsibilities and objectivity	
	• Constraints and issues	
2.2	Assess the concept of the organisation as an open system faced with changing environmental conditions and internal capabilities	4
	• Complex and dynamic external environment	
	• Variability in organisational resource, asset and competence base	
	• Controllable and uncontrollable influences	
	• Responding to external and internal change	
	• Shaping strategy and plans proactively	
2.3	Appraise the process of auditing the marketing environment and make recommendations for the utilisation of various approaches in a range of different organisational contexts and sectors	4
	• Past, current, and future oriented perspectives	
	• Organising information for planning	
	• Marketing audit structures eg environment, strategy, organisation, systems, productivity and function audits	
	• External and internal sources of information	
	• Organisational and sectoral constraints	
	• Using models and frameworks to facilitate understanding	

		Covered in chapter(s)
2.4	Evaluate the external marketing environment through detailed analysis using a variety of marketing audit tools and techniques • The evolving nature and extent of external environmental change • Marketing intelligence and environmental scanning • Marco- and micro-environmental analysis frameworks • Gauging the impacts of external forces on marketing planning • Identifying key external issues and assumptions • External audit tools eg PESTEL, Porter's Five Forces, and strategic group mapping	5
2.5	Assess the internal marketing environment of an organisation through an audit process using a range of evaluation processes and approaches • The evolving nature and extent of internal organisational change • Developing resource-based planning and strategy • Internal environmental analysis frameworks • Establishing the effects of organisational resources and capabilities on marketing planning • Identifying key internal issues and assumptions • Internal audit tools eg product life cycle, portfolio models, and the value chain	6
2.6	Utilise the planning gap as a means to identifying and assessing key marketing planning requirements to fulfil the organisation's marketing strategy • Establishing objectives and the planning gap • Generating alternative strategic options • Filling the planning gap with new and existing strategies • Evaluation of marketing opportunities and the achievement of competitive advantage	4
2.7	Assess the issues and constraints arising from the marketing audit and consider the consequences for the organisation in order to develop its marketing plan • Prioritising issues and executing SWOT analysis • Specifying marketing objectives, strategies and plans • Consideration of timescales for implementation	4

SECTION 3 – Creating marketing strategies through segmentation, targeting and positioning (weighting 25%)

		Covered in chapter(s)
3.1	Critically evaluate the role of marketing strategies and demonstrates how they can be used to develop competitive advantage, market share and growth • Marketing strategies for meeting marketing objectives through satisfying customer requirements • Marketing strategies as product 'offers' providing benefit to customer segments • Identifying customers and offers for future development	7
3.2	Assess the importance of market segmentation as a basis of selecting markets to achieve the organisation's business and marketing objectives via customer satisfaction • Defining local, national, international and global markets and the parameters • Principle of market segmentation, targeting, and positioning • Benefits and costs of market segmentation • Conditions for successful segmentation	7

		Covered in chapter(s)
3.3	Critically evaluate the different segmentation approaches available to organisations in difference organisational contexts and sectors and make recommendations for their use • Segmentation variables for consumer markets • Segmentation variables for business markets • Profiling segments and defining customer types • Critical evaluation of segmentation techniques • Contemporary methods of segmentation such as relationship-based approaches and online behaviours	7
3.4	Assess the value of 'targeting' markets as an approach to achieving customer satisfaction, competitive advantage and retention • Focused effort and resource efficiency • Potential for achieving short-, medium-, and long-term objectives • Potential for achieving competitive advantage • Scope for competitive advantage through distinctive positioning	8
3.5	Critically evaluate a range of targeting coverage strategies for different organisational contexts and sectors • Undifferentiated marketing • Differentiated marketing • Concentrated marketing • Customised marketing	8
3.6	Assess the attractiveness and value of selected market segments • External and internal criteria for evaluation: size, growth, profitability, relationship potential, competition, capabilities • Segment evaluation process: factor weighting and ranking of alternatives • Fit between potential and internal considerations	8
3.7	Examine the concept of marketing positioning strategy and how it can be used to convey the organisation's value proposition • Differential advantage, customer value, and organisational benefits • Consideration of alternative positioning strategies • Relationship positioning strategies • Competitive positioning strategies • Selection of target markets and point of differentiation • Positioning and perceptual maps	9
3.8	Critically evaluate positioning options and their implementation within the context of the organisation and its markets • Criteria for effective positioning and competitive advantages • Positioning and the market mix • Positioning and repositioning in practice	9

SECTION 4 – Undertaking marketing planning in different contexts (weighting 20%)

		Covered in chapter(s)
4.1	Assess the significance of the key dimensions of implementing marketing planning in practice • Organisational structures, systems, and processes • Forecasting and budgeting • Time-scales and responsibilities	10
4.2	Critically evaluate the barriers and constraints to implementing marketing planning, and consider how they may be addressed by organisations • Managerial, organisational, and cultural shortcomings • Planning inadequacies • Poor and inadequate organisational resource • Lack of innovation • Failure to integrate into corporate planning systems • Monitoring performance metrics and control mechanisms • Contingency planning • Internal marketing	10
4.3	Propose and justify approaches to implementing the process of marketing planning in different contextual settings • Marketing planning for different stakeholder groups • Planning in consumer and business-to-business markets • Services marketing planning • Issues of marketing planning to large and small organisations • Internal marketing segmentation • Marketing planning in non-profit organisations • The international and global dimension of marketing planning • Marketing planning in highly competitive markets • Facilitating relationship-based marketing planning and customer retention • Planning marketing in the virtual marketplace	11

4 The CIM's Magic Formula

The Magic Formula is a tool used by the CIM to help both examiners write exam and assignment questions and you to more easily interpret what you are being asked to write about. It is useful for helping you to check that you are using an appropriate balance between theory and practice for your particular level of qualification.

Contrary to the title, there is nothing mystical about the Magic Formula and simply by knowing it (or even mentioning it in an assessment) will not automatically secure a pass. What it does do, however, is help you to check that you are presenting your answers in an appropriate format, including enough marketing theory and applying it to a real marketing context or issue. Students working through the range of CIM qualifications, are expected to evaluate to a greater extent and apply a more demanding range of marketing decisions as they progress from the lower to the higher levels. At the Chartered Postgraduate Diploma level, there will be an emphasis on evaluation while at the Introductory Certificate level the emphasis is on developing concepts.

Graphically, the Magic Formula for the Professional Diploma in Marketing is shown below:

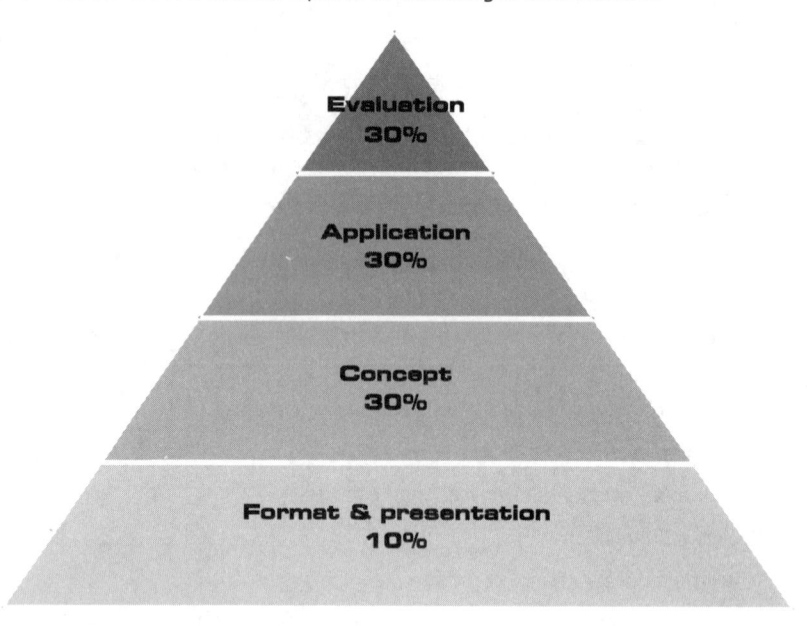

The Magic Formula for the Professional Diploma in Marketing

You can see from pyramid that for the Professional Diploma marks are awarded in the following proportions:

- **Presentation and format – 10%**

    Remember, you are expected to present your work professionally which means that it should ALWAYS be typed and attention should be paid to making it look as visually appealing as possible even in an exam situation. It also means that the CIM will stipulate the format that you should present your work in. The assessment formats you will be given will be varied and can include things like reports to write, slides to prepare, e-mails, memos, formal letters, press releases, discussion documents, briefing papers, agendas, and newsletters.

- **Concept – 30%**

    Concept refers to your ability to state, recall and describe marketing theory. The definition of marketing is a core CIM syllabus topic. If we take this as an example, you would be expected to recognise, recall, and write this definition to a word perfect standard to gain the full marks for concept. Understanding marketing concepts is clearly the main area where marks will be given within your assessment.

- **Application – 30%**

    Application-based marks are given for your ability to apply marketing theories to real life marketing situations. For example, you may be asked to discuss the definition of marketing, and how it is applied within your own organisation. Within this sort of question 30% of the marks would have been awarded within the 'concept' aspect of the Magic Formula. You will gain the rest of the marks through your ability to evaluate to what extent the concept is applied within your own organisation. Here you are not only using the definition but are applying it in order to consider the market orientation of the company.

- **Evaluation – 30%**

    Evaluation is the ability to asses the value or worth of something sometimes through careful consideration or related advantages and disadvantages or weighing-up of alternatives. Results from your evaluation should enable you to discuss the importance of an issue using evidence to support your opinions.

    Using the example of you being asked whether or not your organisation adopts a marketing approach, if you were asked to 'evaluate' this, it would be expected that you would provide reasons and specific examples why you thought they might take this approach but to also consider issues why they may not be marketing-oriented before coming to a final conclusion.

    You should have noticed that for the Professional Diploma, you are expected to consider the equal weightings of concept, application and evaluation in order to gain maximum marks in assessments.

5 A guide to the features of the Study Text

Each of the chapter features (see below) will help you to break down the content into manageable chunks and ensure that you are developing the skills required for a professional qualification.

Chapter feature	Relevance and how you should use it	Corresponding icon
Chapter topic list	Study the list. Each numbered topic denotes a numbered section in the chapter. Identified as a key concept within the syllabus.	–
Introduction	Shows why topics need to be studied and is a route guide through the chapter.	–
Syllabus-linked Learning Objectives	Outlines what you should learn within the chapter based on what is required within the syllabus.	–
Format & Presentation	Outlines a key marketing presentation format with reference to the Magic Formula.	(10% icon)
Concept	Key concept to learn with reference to the Magic Formula.	(30% icon)
Application	An example of applied marketing with reference to the Magic Formula.	(30% icon)
Evaluation	An example of evaluation with reference to the Magic Formula.	(30% icon)
Activity	An application-based activity for you to complete.	(pencil icon)
Key text links	Emphasises key parts to read in a range of other texts and other learning resources.	(books icon)
Marketing at work	A short case study to illustrate marketing practice.	(news icon)
Exam/ Assessment tip	Key advice based on the assessment.	(checkbox icon)
Quick quiz	Use this to check your learning.	
Objective check	Review what you have learnt.	

6 A note on pronouns

On occasions in this Study Text, 'he' is used for 'he or she', 'him' for 'him or her' and so forth. While we try to avoid this practice it is sometimes necessary for reasons of style. No prejudice or stereotyping accounting to sex is intended or assumed.

7 Additional resources

7.1 The CIM's supplementary reading list

We have already mentioned that the CIM requires you to demonstrate your ability to 'read widely'. The CIM issue an extensive reading list for each unit. For this unit they recommend supplementary reading. Within the Study Text we have highlighted within the wider reading links specific topics where these resources would help. The CIM's supplementary reading list for this unit is:

Dibb, S. and Simkin, L. (2008) Marketing Planning. London, Cengage. [ISBN 978-1844807827, £34.99]

Drummond G, Ensor J, and Ashford, R. (2007) Strategic marketing: planning and control. 3rd edition. Oxford, Butterworth, Heinemann. [ISBN 978-0750682718, £19.99]

Mcdonald, M. (2007) Marketing plans: how to prepare them, how to use them. 6th edition. Oxford, Butterworth, Heinemann. [ISBN 978-0750683869, £29.99]

Burk Wood, M. (2007) Essential guide to marketing planning. Harlow, FT Prentice Hall

Burk Wood, M. (2004) Marketing planning: principles into practice. Harlow, FT Prentice Hall

Dibb, S. and Simkin, L. (2007) Marking segmentation success: making it happen. Abingdon, Routledge. [ISBN 978-0790789129188, [£27.50]

Mcdonald, M. and Dunbar, I, (2004) Marking segmentation: how to do it, how to profit from it. Oxford, Butterworth, Heinemann.

Weinstein, A. (2004) Handbook of marketing segmentation. USA, Routledge.

7.2 Assessment preparation materials from BPP Learning Media

To help you pass the entire Professional Diploma in Marketing we have created a complete study package. **The Professional Diploma Assessment Workbook** covers all four units for the Professional Diploma level. Practice question and answers, tips on tackling assignments and work-based projects are written to help you succeed in your assessments. This unit is assessed by an assignment.

Our A6 set of spiral bound **Passcards** are handy revision cards and are ideal to reinforce key topics for the Delivering Customer Value through Marketing pre-seen case study exam.

7.3 BPP Learning Media's Online Material

To complement this Study Text, our Assessment Workbook and Passcards we have also produced some online materials for both students and tutors. These materials have not been designed to remain static but we will be developing more and adding to the content over time. If you have purchased a product within our CIM range then you will be able to access the online materials for free at:

www.bpp.com/lm/cim

Typical content will include:

- Links to the most useful web sites for marketers
- Syllabus links to key marketing developments and 'big news' stories
- Suggested exam answers to the most recent exams (available to those who purchase the Assessment Workbook)
- Pro forma's for key marketing documents such as Marketing Plans, Research Proposals etc
- Tutor only content including slides and case studies

We are also pleased to announce an exciting partnerships with Superbrands and The Centre for Brand Analysis to bring you a new online feature titled 'A Word From . . .'. This feature is covered online and from time-to-time will include more material gathered from the Superbrand Marketers.

8 Your personal study plan

Preparing a study plan (and sticking to it) is one of the key elements to learning success.

The CIM has stipulated that there should be a minimum of 50 guided learning hours spent on each Unit. Guided learning hours will include time spent in lesson, working on fully prepared distance learning materials, formal workshops and work set by your tutor. We also know that to be successful, students should spend *at least* an additional 50 hours conducting self-study. This means that for the entire qualification with four units you should spend 200 hours working in a tutor guided manner and at least an additional 200 hours completing recommended reading, working on assignments, and revising for exams. This Study Text will help you to organise this 50-hour portion of self-study time.

Now think about the exact amount of time you have (don't forget you will still need some leisure time!) and complete the following tables to help you keep to a schedule.

	Date	Duration in weeks
Course start		
Course finish		Total weeks of course:

Content chapter coverage plan

Chapter	To be completed by	Assignment prep work
1 Marketing the planning process		
2 External and internal influences on objectives		
3 Environmental drivers of organisational change		
4 The marketing audit process		
5 Appraising the external marketing environment		
6 Appraising the internal marketing environment		
7 Market segmentation		
8 Targeting		
9 Positioning		
10 Implementing marketing planning		
11 Marketing planning in different contexts		

Chapter 1
Marketing the planning process

Topic list

1. The roles of marketing
2. The planning process
3. The marketing plan

Introduction

This first chapter sets marketing in its wider organisational context considering the different roles marketing has to play and how the discipline interacts with other management processes. We examine the value that marketing can bring to organisations as they seek to build mutually beneficial long-term relationships with customers and look at the role of marketing staff, whom must successfully co-ordinate a wide variety of activities across the organisation, acting as planners, strategists and tacticians.

In Section 2, we look at the components of the marketing plan and how this can help deliver organisational strategies. The stages of the marketing planning process are examined with a detailed look at the contents of a typical marketing plan.

In Section 3, the role of the marketing plan is reviewed in relation to the organisation's philosophy, strategic intent and objectives.

Syllabus-linked learning objectives

By the end of the chapter you will be able to:

Learning objectives	Syllabus link
1. Understand the role of marketing within an organisation and how marketers work with other departments.	1.1
2. Understand the purpose and stages of marketing planning and how it fits within the strategic marketing process.	1.2; 1.3
3. Write your own marketing plan and evaluate barriers to its implementation.	1.2; 1.3

1 The roles of marketing

KEY CONCEPT

Marketing is the management process responsible for identifying, anticipating and satisfying customer requirements profitably. (CIM)

The Chartered Institute of Marketing developed the above definition in 1976 and it has remained as a benchmark ever since. In a 'Shape the Agenda' paper in 2007, the CIM called for a change in definition to:

'The strategic business function that creates value by stimulating, facilitating and fulfilling customer demand. It does this by building brands, nurturing innovation, developing relationships, creating good customer service and communicating benefits.

By operating customer-centrically, marketing brings positive returns on investment, satisfies shareholders and stakeholders from business and the community, and contributes to positive behavioural change and a sustainable business future.'

(CIM, 2007)

This proposed change recognises the strategic importance of marketing and its place as an essential business function that the whole organisation should participate in. It also highlights the move towards building and maintaining relationships with customers and satisfying a range of shareholders and stakeholders as well as the wider global community, with issues such as sustainability and corporate social responsibility firmly in mind. Sectors such as the not-for-profit and pubic sector have also more recently recognised the relevance of a marketing orientation.

1.1 Marketing as an organisational function and orientation

Marketing helps organisations to respond to the needs and wants of customers and compete effectively. This is particularly important in today's challenging economic climate. CIM define marketing as a business function (CIM, 2007) but Drummond, et al. (2008) describe marketing as *'more than a functional activity'* saying that it can be adopted as a business philosophy. An organisation will be more successful through understanding and meeting customers' needs. This approach demonstrates their adoption of a **marketing orientation**.

Not all organisations adopt a marketing orientation. Other orientations, (as described below), are still common and many companies may move through these prior stages before finally applying a marketing concept.

Production orientation: The concept that products will find their own markets if they are produced cheaply and to a good standard. Mass production, economies of scale and cost control are central to this concept, with a focus on achieving distribution efficiencies and using the sales-force to communicate the superior benefits of the product. This orientation can lead to *'marketing myopia'* where organisations concentrate on producing products that may be well-produced, but do not consider customer requirements. This business approach originated during the Industrial Revolution when firms were able to increase production due to new manufacturing processes. It can only work now when a sellers' market exists for the product in question. The most notorious example of this approach is Ford's Model T car. Henry Ford is frequently quoted telling customers *'You can have any colour you like as long as it is black'*. Regardless of the colour of car customers wanted, black was the most economical to produce and therefore matched the production possibilities. Over time as more car producers emerged, if Ford had continued with this strategy they would have been in dire trouble as customers switched to alternative producers who would meet their needs for colourful vehicles.

Product orientation: With this concept, product innovation is the most important issue to management. It assumes that customers will always buy the products that offer the most in terms of quality, performance and innovative features – often for their own sake. Customer needs, again, are not at the heart of this orientation (marketing myopia). By making continuous product improvements, organisations can become obsessed with technology. Examples include new versions of Microsoft Windows and many of the products that are rejected by the entrepreneurial panel on the BBC television programme, Dragon's Den.

Sales orientation: Success here is reliant on advertising, sales promotion, and often aggressive sales techniques to convince customers to part with their cash. Clear differentiation between the product and its competitors may not be apparent. This level of persuasion can lead to short-term gains as salespeople hit their targets, but fail to build long-term relationships, relying purely on a transactional approach. The concept may follow on from a production orientation as management attempts to create a demand for unwanted products. Examples include aggressive selling techniques for windows and conservatories.

Market orientation: With this ideal concept, customer needs and requirements are identified in every aspect of the organisation's activity. Products and services are designed according to market demand. A strong focus is placed on building long-term relationships with customers and providing sales and after-sales support. Organisations attempt to build loyalty and offer superior value consistently, by understanding their competitors' strategies and strengths. Examples include IKEA and Tesco who pay attention to the changing marketing environment and research their customers and stakeholders needs in order to adapt where necessary.

Kotler, et al. (2008) extends the marketing orientation and discuss the **Societal Marketing orientation**. This approach, considers the balance between company profits, consumer wants and society's interests.

KEY CONCEPT

*'The **societal marketing** concept holds that marketing strategy should deliver value to customers in a way that maintains or improves both the consumer and the society's well being.'*

(Kotler, et al, 2008)

The **Sustainable Marketing orientation** takes this even further, recognising the future of tomorrow's organisations and weighing-up today's consumption against that of future consumers and future society as a whole.

Organisations who adopt and successfully implement a marketing orientation would expect to see a sustainable competitive advantage. Blythe (2006) highlighted three components to determine the degree to which a company is marketing-oriented:

- **Competitor orientation**: the degree to which the organisation understands what its competitors are offering and customers' perceptions of those products or services.

- **Customer orientation**: the degree to which the organisation understands its customers. By understanding customers well (eg through market research), organisations are better able to create value for them.

- **Inter-functional orientation**: the degree to which the internal structure of the organisation and attitudes of members combine to deliver a marketing orientation, eg training staff to put customers first at all times.

ACTIVITY 1
application

Consider to what degree your own organisation has adopted a marketing orientation.

Achieving a marketing orientation can only be done by understanding customers, seeking to respond to their needs and wants, and incorporating marketing into the heart of the business. Successful organisations recognise the lifetime value of their customers and seek to build mutually beneficial long-term relationships. Acquiring new customers is estimated to cost four to six times more than selling to existing ones (Ronen, 2005). Conducting a regular programme of market research, can help companies define their markets, target customers appropriately and assess their levels of satisfaction, as well as being aware of the competition and the quality of their products and marketing activity.

1.2 Marketing as a co-ordinating force in the organisation

Bringing marketing to the forefront of an organisation requires structural changes, to ensure all departments can contribute to integrated and co-ordinated marketing. This can lead to the marketing department being perceived to have gained more can influence and authority within the company which may result in internal conflicts and politics. (Lancaster and Massingham, 2002)

The table below highlights where differences arise.

Department	Emphasis	Marketing's emphasis
Sales	Short-term sales	Long-term profits
	Sales most important	Customer satisfaction most important
	One department	Whole organisation
Purchasing	Narrow product line	Broad product line
	Standard parts	Non-standard parts
Finance	Hard and fast budgets	Flexible budgets
	Price to cover costs	Market-oriented pricing
Accounting	Standard transactions	Special terms and discounts
Manufacturing	Long runs	Short runs
	Few models	Many models
	Standard orders	Custom orders
	Long production lead times	Short production lead times

Effective co-ordination between the different functional groups can be achieved when conflict is managed. Handy (1976 cited in Lancaster, et al. 2002, p 27) proposed a number of methods to assist organisations:

- The **agreement of common**, overriding and realistic goals or objectives upon which departments are measured, eg customer satisfaction.

- The **establishment of information and control systems** that can be accessed by the different departments to see how their work has contributed to improving customer satisfaction.

- Regular **contact and communication** between marketing and other managers to build trust.
- The establishment of clear and agreed terms of reference for marketing and other departments in relation to duties, authority, etc.
- Clear and explicit **company policies** explaining the role and boundaries of functional departments.

In some industries, such as engineering, the marketing concept and a marketing culture has been slow to permeate as directors, without a marketing background, fail to find a reason to change the way they have always conducted their business or may feel threatened by 'new' ideas and theory suggested by junior managers.

MARKETING AT WORK application

An environmental consultancy, part of a multi-disciplinary engineering group, has been run since its inception by qualified engineers without a business or marketing background. Marketing has only been introduced in the company and at group level for the past five years but staff have been appointed at a middle management level with no direct board influence. The marketing manager has struggled to fully introduce marketing planning due to a lack of buy-in from the directors. She feels this is down to their ingrained perception that marketing is only about writing press releases and producing a corporate brochure.

The consultancy which provides services such as assessing contaminated land and flood risk sites, has a production orientation, believing it produces a range of good services which housing developers and other clients will want to buy. The directors have taken little account of changing needs and wants in the marketplace and consequently have had little success in winning tenders. The marketing manager has pointed out that there is no real brand identity or professional web site promoting the benefits of the consultancy's services. The customer database is out-of-date with customers opting out of communications with the company and repeat customers form an ageing population of 'old friends' nearing retirement.

A merger with a small specialist provider of environmental reports proves insightful. The company has been run by two directors with a business and marketing background and customers are their primary focus. All their services are designed around the needs of the marketplace and attention is paid to researching customer satisfaction and providing exemplary after-sales support. Repeat business is high and new relationships are being forged due to recommendations from existing clients. By working closely with the consultancy's marketing manager, marketing plans are being executed successfully despite very limited resources. The board finally realise they have to change and appoint a director with experience in marketing. The customer becomes the focus of the business rather than the services that were offered. Consultants are encouraged to adapt standard services to suit the needs of the client and local circumstances, and to consider the difference between cost and value. Directors start to consider the issues affecting their clients and design services appropriate to their needs and the changing economic climate affecting house-builders. Most importantly, the consultants shift their focus from pure transactions to being part of the project life cycle and start to build more effective long-term relationships with clients, which will help them develop a sustainable competitive advantage in a tougher economic climate.

The following diagram shows a typical marketing-oriented structure.

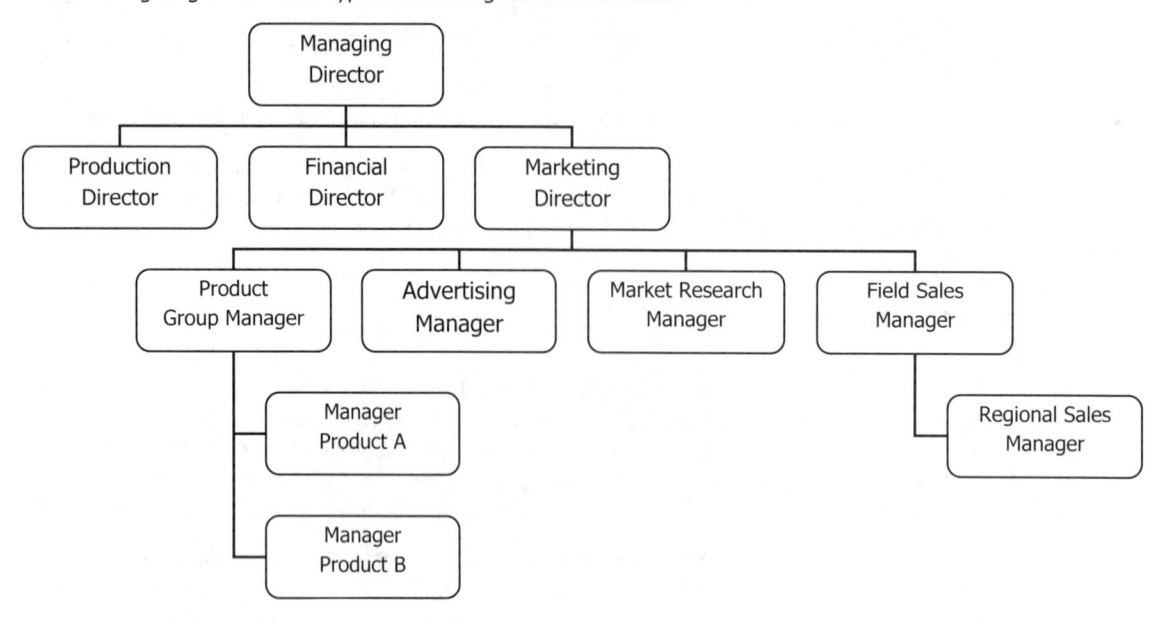

```
                        Managing
                        Director
         ┌─────────────────┼─────────────────┐
    Production         Financial         Marketing
    Director           Director          Director
                            ┌────────────┬────────────┬────────────┐
                       Product      Advertising   Market Research  Field Sales
                    Group Manager     Manager        Manager        Manager
                       ├──── Manager                                    │
                       │    Product A                              Regional Sales
                       │                                              Manager
                       └──── Manager
                            Product B
```

Source: Lancaster, et al. (2002)

The organisation chart shown shows an idealistic view of the marketing team consisting of experts in their own disciplines. Often (especially in times of stretched budgets) for small- to medium-sized enterprises, the team consists of only one busy marketing manager, with access to limited financial and human resources.

There is no single best way to organise a department. The format chosen will depend on the nature of the existing organisational structure, patterns of management and the spread of the firm's product and geographical interests. However it is organised, every marketing department must take responsibility for four key areas and can be organised along such bases:

- **Functions** (promotion, pricing)
- **Geographical** areas (domestic, EU, international)
- **Products** (research, development, support, innovations)
- **Markets** (personal, corporate)

1.2.1 Functional organisational structure

The department organised by function is typically headed by a marketing director who is responsible for the overall co-ordination of the marketing effort. A number of functional specialists such as a market research manager and a sales manager will be found in the second tier of management and they take responsibility for all activities in their functional specialism across all products and markets. This is a very simple format and is relatively straightforward in administrative terms. It also allows individuals to develop their particular specialisms, at the same time imposing a burden on the marketing director who will be required to co-ordinate activities to ensure the development of a coherent marketing mix.

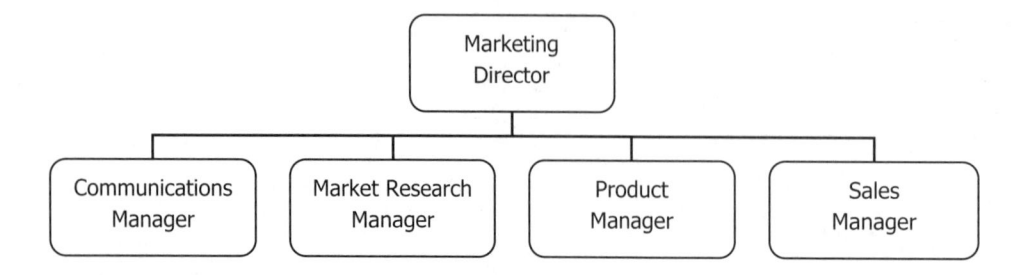

```
                        Marketing
                        Director
         ┌──────────────┬─────────────┬──────────────┐
   Communications  Market Research   Product        Sales
     Manager          Manager        Manager       Manager
```

With a limited range of products, a functional structure is unlikely to excessively burden the marketing director. As the organisation's range of products and markets expands, however, this form of structure will tend to be less efficient. There is always the danger that a particular product or market may be neglected because it is only one of several being handled by a specific functional manager.

1.2.2 Geographical organisational structure

A simple geographical structure for a marketing department is an extension of the functional organisation. Responsibility for some or all functional activities is devolved to a multi-functional office at regional level, through a national manager. This structure would probably be more common in firms operating internationally where the various functional activities would be required for each national market.

An FMCG manufacturing company, for example, may supply multiple grocery chains that are organised regionally, and therefore develop regional sales managers to link up with customers such as regional store managers. Where sales promotion activities are needed quickly in response to competition, there may be a case for regional promotions managers to decide and implement these in conjunction with regional sales managers.

```
                         Marketing
                         Director
           ┌─────────────┬────┴────┬──────────────┐
    Communications   Market Research   Product       Sales
       Manager          Manager        Manager      Manager
           │                                           │
       Regional                                     Regional
      Promotions                                  Sales Managers
       Managers                                      │
                                                  District
                                               Sales Managers
```

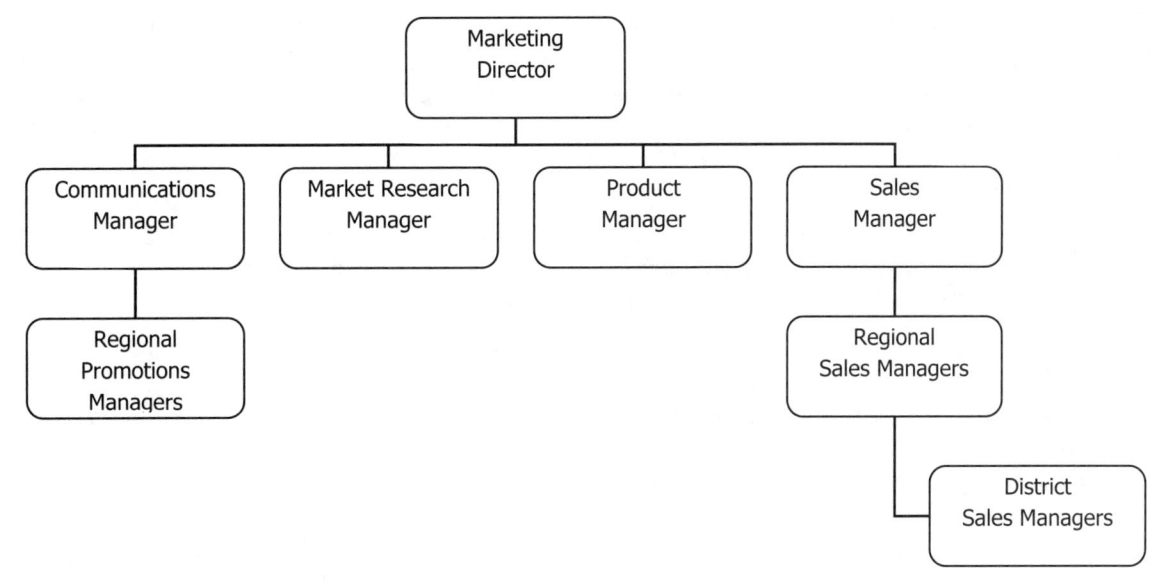

1.2.3 Product-based organisational structure

Product-based structures involve adding an additional tier of management to supplement the activities of functional managers. Product managers take responsibility for specific products or groups of products. This type of approach is likely to be particularly appropriate for organisations with either very diverse products or with a large range of products.

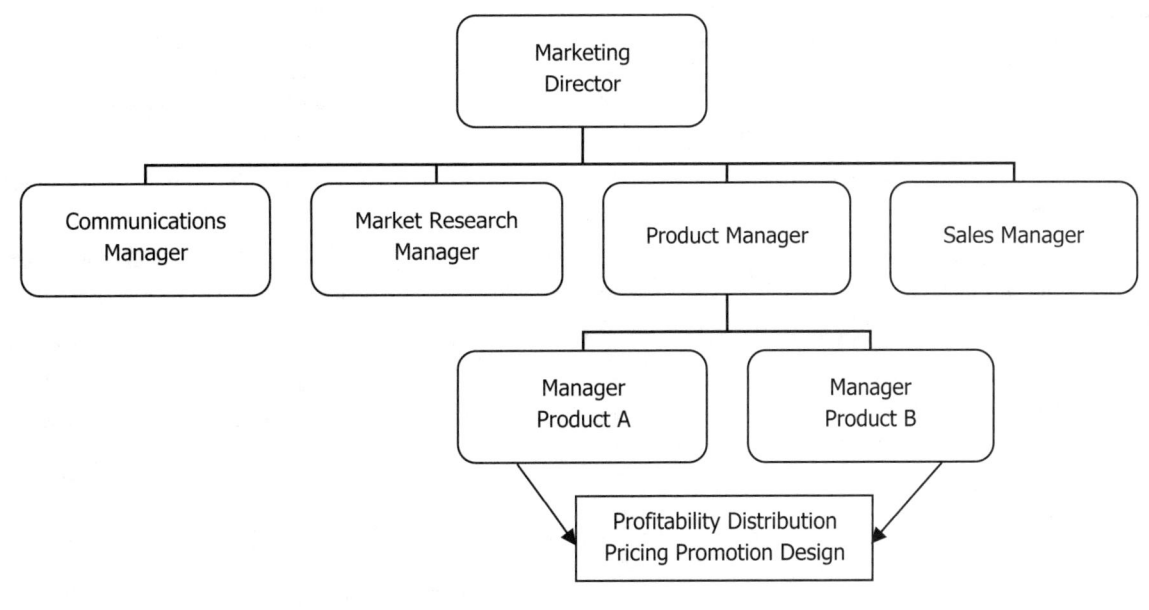

```
                              Marketing
                              Director
        ┌──────────────┬──────────┼──────────────┬──────────────┐
   Communications  Market Research  Product Manager        Sales Manager
      Manager         Manager            │
                                  ┌──────┴──────┐
                               Manager        Manager
                              Product A      Product B
                                   │             │
                                   └──────┬──────┘
                                 Profitability Distribution
                                  Pricing Promotion Design
```

1: Marketing the Planning Process

The individual product manager is responsible for developing plans to suit specific products, and ensuring that products remain competitive, drawing on the experience and guidance of functional managers. This allows the individual product managers to build up considerable experience and understanding of particular product groups, which is invaluable within a rapidly changing competitive environment. Very often, the title **brand manager** rather than **product manager** will be used. The product-based approach is becoming increasingly important, because the benefits of having managers with particular responsibility for specific product groups outweigh the costs associated with any loss of functional specialisation. Where the product group is large enough, the product manager may draw on the assistance provided by a product team, with individuals in that team concentrating on relevant functional specialism.

1.2.4 Organisation by customer type (market management)

In a variant on the product management structure, instead of individual managers taking responsibility for particular products they take responsibility for particular markets. The advantage of this approach lies in an organisation offering a variety of products into particular markets. The understanding of the product here is perceived to be slightly less important than the understanding of the market.

In the case of services, market management would be consistent with the need to develop relationships with customers, since the individual marketing manager would be in a position to understand the requirements of particular groups, and to draw on the organisation's product range to meet those needs. Individual market managers would also be able to draw on the skills and experiences of functional specialists as and when required. In contrast to the product management approach, market managers are likely to be well versed in the needs of their specific markets, but may be lacking in knowledge of a large and varied product range.

Where the buying motives and the buying behaviour of groups of customers differ radically from those of other groups, there is a case for organising marketing by customer type – often to the extent that each type will have its own dedicated marketing mix, its own dedicated marketing team and sometimes even a dedicated sales force.

1.2.5 Cross-functional teams

This is one of the more modern ways of working. According to Robbins and Coutler (2002), a cross-functional work team is a 'type of work team that is a hybrid grouping of individuals who are experts in various specialties and who work together on various tasks'. People work together on a flexible and interdisciplinary basis.

1.3 Marketing's interface with other organisational functions

The role and relationships of the marketing function within any business depends on a variety of practical factors particular to that business. These factors may include the corporate culture, the size of the business, the nature of the industry (manufacturing, service, agriculture, mining, public service etc), the position of its products and services in relation to the product or service life cycle, the nature of the product or service and the expectations of its customers and potential customers.

Some businesses are fragmented, and the functions operate independently. Other businesses are more integrated and operations have a high degree of co-ordination. Generally the marketing function must work closely with other departments to implement the marketing concept. However, marketers should be aware that other functions also have valid and valuable roles to fulfil in delivering customer satisfaction and implementing the corporate strategy. Here are some examples.

(a) The finance department is responsible for raising the working capital that permits the granting of favourable credit terms to customers.

(b) The HR department is responsible for recruiting and training the customer service personnel, delivery staff and service engineers who operate at the customer interface and help to build the organisation's image and reputation.

(c) Purchasing managers control much of the process by which a given level of quality and reliability is incorporated into products.

Customers are not interested in how a business is structured into different functions. Hence marketers should work together with other operations in the business to provide customers with a seamless service.

MARKETING AT WORK

application

The Priory Hospital Roehampton is a 107-bed acute psychiatric hospital offering a wide range of inpatient, outpatient, day patient and therapy services. The hospital cares for patients with a broad range of psychiatric disorders and offers a wide range of specialist services, including: child and adolescent mental health services, eating disorders, addictions and psychosis. The hospital, part of The Priory Group, targets public and private healthcare purchasers such as the NHS and BUPA as well as private individuals; the hospital is widely known for treating high profile patients with addictions.

The hospital is focused on delivering appropriate, high quality services to its customers and keeping abreast of trends in treatment and patient care. The marketing team must ensure it co-ordinates its efforts with all the key functions within the hospital: the clinical teams, nursing, finance and hospitality – responsible for hotel management and catering. Department managers are consulted on the construction of patient satisfaction surveys and debriefed on the results. All functions provide regular news articles for newsletters and contribute to seminars and events organised by the marketing team to promote the services delivered by the hospital to healthcare providers.

Each of the functions has a specific role to play in delivering the company's corporate strategy:

The finance department is responsible for managing the price and profitability of clinical services and negotiating with private and public healthcare providers to provide appropriate care programmes for patients, particularly those with eating disorders.

The hospitality team is charged with maintaining the quality of food and hotel services for patients while meeting financial targets.

The clinical teams must deliver patient services, nurture relationships with individual GPs who will refer new patients to their particular specialism, contribute to marketing seminars to promote all hospital services, and constantly review service delivery and new trends within psychiatry.

(The Priory Group, 2009)

1.3.1 Inter-departmental relationships

The harmony and effectiveness of inter-departmental working is likely to vary from one organisation to the next. It usually depends on a variety of factors such as corporate culture, structure and work practices. Some businesses have achieved a high degree of integration, whereas others are highly fragmented and the departments operate independently. In practice, customers have very little interest on how a company is organised internally, provided the service is satisfactory. The overall criterion of whether an organisation is structured appropriately depends on whether it maximises customer satisfaction.

1.4 Exchange, transactions and relationships

KEY CONCEPT

concept

An organised **system of exchange**, based on formalised procedures and an explicit legal framework, is fundamental to the working of any modern industrial economy.

Lancaster, et al. (2002)

The concept of exchange exists where something of value ie a product or service, is obtained from another party, by offering something else of value – this could be money or another product or service in a barter agreement (often referred to as a contra deal).

MARKETING AT WORK — application

An exhibition stand builder approaches a corporate hospitality trade magazine to buy advertising; the two parties agree to a contra deal where advertising pages are exchanged for stand design and build services for the next 12 months.

For exchange in society to be possible, at least two parties must have something of value to offer each other and they must be willing and able to participate in the deal. If they come to an agreement, each party should be better off, or at least equally compensated. The economic act of exchange therefore creates value (like production). This process is important to marketing as we are focused on how, why and when consumers choose to satisfy their needs and wants through exchange.

KEY CONCEPT — concept

A **transaction** is marketing's key unit of measurement. It is a trade between two parties that involves at least two things of value, agreed-upon conditions, a time of agreement and a place of agreement.
Kotler, et al. (2008)

A transaction is a trading of values between two parties, which can be a monetary or barter transaction. A symbolic transaction could even take place between a political party canvassing votes from a member of the public who then ticks the appropriate box in the polling booth. The political party has set out its beliefs and objectives and achieved its desired response amongst its electorate.

The concept behind the exchange process is that both parties are mutually satisfied by the transaction, and the buyer may wish to enter into another transaction in the future. Understanding more about the buyer, from basic details to their motivations, beliefs and attitudes, would give an organisation a greater chance of repeating the transaction, and leaving the customer with a sense of satisfaction in the purchasing process. This leads us onto the theory of relationship marketing.

KEY CONCEPT — concept

Relationship marketing is the process of creating, maintaining and enhancing strong, value-laden relationships with customers and other stakeholders.
Kotler, et al. (2008)

Relationship marketing recognises the value of developing long-term and mutually beneficial relationships with customers. The aim is to target new customers and move beyond one-off or short-term transactions by building relationships and delivering value – success should lead to customer retention and satisfaction. Successful relationship marketing can lead to loyal customers becoming advocates of a business which may lead to the acquisition of new customers and the start of another positive connection.

Marketers taking this approach should have a better understanding of customer needs, be able to provide more effective solutions to their problems, may deliver customer loyalty schemes and can bring a greater customer focus and ability to respond quickly to customers to the whole organisation.

1.5 Markets, customers, competition and value creation

KEY CONCEPT — concept

A **market** offering is a combination of products, services, information or experiences offered to a market to satisfy a need or want.
Kotler, et al. (2008)

A value proposition is a set of benefits promised to consumers to satisfy their needs which is fulfilled through a market offering. A market offering does not have to be a physical product; it can be a service, activity or other intangible benefit. It is important to remember that marketers are not selling a product, they are selling a solution to a need, and competitors may invent a new solution that can solve the problem better or at a lower cost. BBC's Dragon's Den covers many examples of entrepreneurs who spend a considerable amount of time and money inventing a solution to a need that does not exist, or can be solved by the consumer without the need to resort to buying a solution.

To deliver greater value, marketers examine the brand meaning behind the attributes of the products and services they represent and create brand experiences for consumers.

Consumers often have to make a choice between products or services that are offered in the market and will have expectations about the value of the goods and the level of satisfaction that they will receive. If their expectations are met or exceeded, they are likely to be satisfied, buy again, and recommend the product or service to others. If their expectations are not met, then the reverse is true. It is estimated that a dissatisfied customer will tell 10 to 20 people about their experience (Brown, 2000 cited by Gallagher Ardis, 2009). In 2007, eight million people in the UK switched their banks due to dissatisfaction with staff and services according to a nationwide survey by Pitney Bowes Group 1 Software (O'Sullivan, 2007).

Research by Anderson, et al. (2004 cited in Blythe, 2006, p. 6) showed a positive association between customer satisfaction and shareholder value which was argued to be a clear vindication of the marketing concept. Marketers must therefore manage the level of customer expectations to ensure satisfaction is met and buyers are attracted by the market offering.

KEY CONCEPT

Customer value is the consumer's assessment of the product's overall capacity to satisfy his or her needs. Smart companies aim to delight customers by promising only what they can deliver, then delivering more than they promise.

Kotler, et al. (2008)

A market is the actual and potential buyers of a market offering. These buyers will have certain characteristics in common, namely they have the same need or want that can be satisfied through an exchange.

Christopher, et al. (1994 cited in Drummond, et al. 2008, p. 236) developed a six-customer markets model which recognises the importance of retaining customers and generating repeat business. This model addresses the role of markets in developing customer alliances where customers view the organisation as their preferred provider and recommend it to others too.

The six-market model relating to an organisation's relationships:

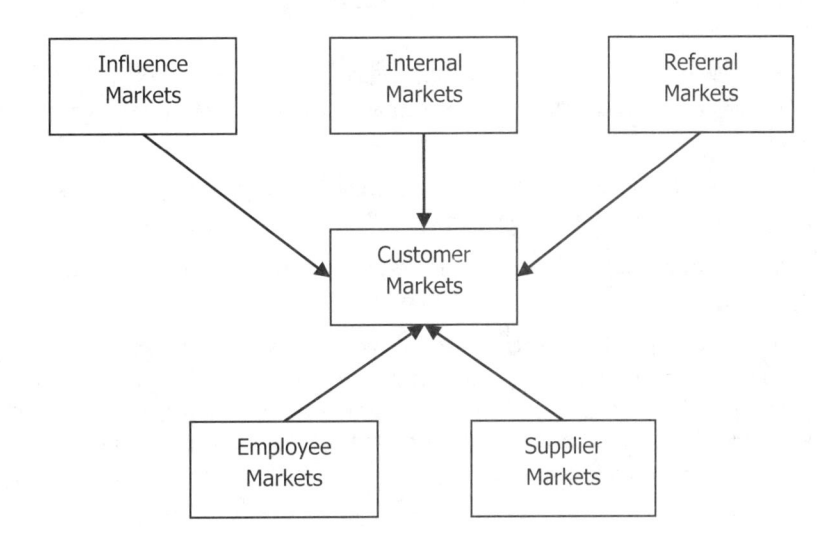

(a) **Supplier markets**: strong supplier links and joint innovation enable the supply chain to be optimised, leading to reduced costs and an improved customer experience.

(b) **Employee markets**: recruiting and retaining the right staff is important. Staff, directly or indirectly, deliver the desired levels of customer satisfaction.

(c) **Internal markets**: employees, departments and functions are also customers, and by treating them as such, we can deliver internal services and supports more effectively. This has the additional benefit of motivating staff, improving effectiveness and enhancing the external customer experience.

(d) **Influence markets**: external groups may have a significant influence on the organisation and its customer base, eg financial analysts, the media, local communities and campaign groups.

(e) **Referral markets**: these markets lead to new business. Referrals may come through existing customers, trade groups, distributors, etc.

To manage a market, we can introduce marketing activities such as product development, research, communication, distribution, pricing and service. This will help us identify and search for potential buyers, design good market offerings, examine the competition, set appropriate prices, undertake promotion and complete a transaction. Each level of a distribution chain can add value for the next level, for example, suppliers provide merchandise at low cost for a retailer to be able to pass on the low prices.

Marketers must be able to establish what customers they will serve (identify the target market) and how these customers can be served best (identify the value proposition) to design appropriate market strategies.

Deciding which customers to serve can be done through dividing the market into segments and selecting which segments to address (both topics are addressed later in this book). In brief, the company must select the customers it can serve well, profitably.

Companies must design value propositions that differentiate one brand from another and give them the greatest advantage in their target markets. This differentiation and positioning should help customers decide why to buy the organisation's brand over competitors.

1.6 Marketers as planners, strategists and tacticians

There are three key roles for the marketing function in an organisation:

(a) To act as an intermediary between the company and its customers' needs.

(b) To create company and marketing plans based on market data.

(c) To ensure company wide decision-making reflects company and marketing plans and the assessment of market and customer needs.

All companies are different so there are no definitive guidelines on how to share these responsibilities across the marketing function. There may also be hierarchies within the organisation which leads to different responsibilities being awarded to a management tier.

The four models of marketing, which follow, show different ways of allocating responsibilities across the planning, strategic and tactical roles for the marketing function.

- The **sales support** model of marketing is essentially reactive and includes such activities as telesales and organising exhibitions.

    The emphasis in this role is primarily reactive: marketing supports the direct sales force. It may include activities such as telesales or telemarketing, responding to enquiries, co-ordinating diaries, customer database management, organising exhibitions or other sales promotions, and administering agents. These activities usually come under a sales and marketing director or manager. This form of marketing is common in SMEs and some organisations operating in a B2B context.

- The **marketing communications** model of marketing is more proactive, promoting organisations, products and services at a tactical level.

  The emphasis in this role is more proactive: marketing promotes the organisation and its product or service at a tactical level, either to customers (pull) or to channel members (push). It typically includes activities such as providing brochures and catalogues to support the sales force. Some B2C organisations may use marketing to perform the selling role using direct marketing techniques, and to manage campaigns based on a mix of media to raise awareness, generate leads and even take orders. In B2B markets, larger organisations may have marketing communications departments and specialists to make efficient use of marketing expenditures and to co-ordinate communications between business units.

- The **operational marketing** model of marketing includes a co-ordinated range of marketing activities, from marketing research, through brand management and corporate communications to customer relationship management.

  The emphasis in this role is for marketing to support the organisation with a co-ordinated range of marketing activities including marketing research, brand management, product development and management, corporate and marketing communications and customer relationship management. Planning is also usually performed in this role.

- The **strategic marketing** model requires marketing to contribute to corporate strategy.

  The emphasis in this role is on marketing to contribute to the creation of competitive strategy. As such, it is practiced in customer-focused and larger organisations. In a large or diversified organisation, it may also be responsible for the co-ordination of several marketing departments.

  The strategic marketing model, and sometimes even the operational marketing model, is likely to be found in organisations with a strong market or customer orientation, or with separate marketing departments in business units that require central co-ordination.

In organisations with a weak customer orientation (typically a production, sales, product or technology orientation), the role of marketing is likely to be manifested in terms of sales support or marketing communications.

Operational marketing activities: This includes a variety of activities as illustrated in the CIM's Statement of Marketing Practice. It includes:

- Research and analysis
- Contributing to strategy and marketing planning
- Managing brands
- Implementing marketing programmes
- Measuring effectiveness
- Managing marketing teams

The CIM's Statement of Marketing Practice can be found at www.cim.co.uk

1.6.1 The role of operational marketing

(a) The primary role of operational marketing is to support the organisation's business or corporate objectives and strategies. Marketers at this level may also have an input to business strategy and influence the culture of the organisation to ensure that both have a strong customer focus. The role usually entails the planning and implementation of marketing strategies. These activities are usually carried out by a marketing manager and staff, often within a department called 'marketing'.

(b) In terms of planning, operational marketing involves making decisions about marketing resource utilisation, as well as the selection of the most appropriate marketing tools. Available tools include brands, innovation, customer relationships and service, alliances, channels and communications, and, increasingly, price.

(c) Marketing works not in isolation but closely with other functions in the business, including management, sales, product development engineers and HR. This has important consequences for the levels of business skill and knowledge that marketers are expected to use, as well as their basic technical marketing skills.

(d) Operational marketing supports the organisation's specific competitive position, which has been developed at the strategic planning stage.

A CIM and Accenture cross-industry research survey in the UK, published in 2009, revealed that 82% of marketing leaders are dissatisfied with the role and positioning of marketing within their organisation. The findings also revealed many top marketers felt they were divorced from a strategic role within their organisation (Charles, 2009). CIM Research Director, David Thorp, said, '*All too often marketing is viewed tactically – purely as adverts, brochures and promotions – even in the largest organisations. Yet in these difficult times, it has never been more important to ensure a wider marketing input to organisational strategy.*'

1.7 Marketing in theory and in practice

Marketing theory has been challenged by new issues affecting companies such as corporate social responsibility, internal marketing and relationship marketing, as well as its widening applicability to a variety of organisations such as business-to-business, services, small- and medium-sized businesses, international and global markets, and not-for-profit/non-business marketing – even churches have engaged in high profile contentious advertising campaigns and conducted mystery shopping research to ensure they remain relevant to their members in changing societies.

Traditionally, marketing has been centred on generating and sustaining profits but many organisations these days are utilising the same skills, tools and techniques to achieve objectives other than monetary gain.

Marketers are also facing criticisms over some practices and the misuse of marketing which often gains media attention. Having received acres of press coverage recently, impacts upon society and the environment are a constant concern, from the overuse of certain resources such as packaging to products that contain chemicals that harm health. The ethical production of goods is also constantly reviewed, both by marketers, industry watchdogs and the media. Taking these issues a step further, there are also deeper debates over the economic and ethical roles of marketing in the satisfaction of needs and the allocation of global resources.

MARKETING AT WORK   application

In 2009, global drug company, GlaxoSmithKline displayed a major change of strategy by cutting prices on medicines targeted at the poorest countries, returning profits to be spent on hospitals and clinics and sharing knowledge about potential drugs currently protected by patents to help find cures for neglected life-threatening illnesses.

Chief Executive, Andrew Witty, said in The Guardian, '*[I'm] trying to make sure we are even-handed in terms of our efforts to find solutions not just for developed but for developing countries.*

I think the shareholders understand this and it's my job to make sure I can explain it. I think it's absolutely the kind of thing large global companies need to be demonstrating, that they've got a more balanced view of the world than short-term returns.'

(Boveley, 2009)

2 The planning process

To understand marketing planning, we must first understand its strong links with the strategic planning process. Strategic planning forms the foundations for marketing planning, setting the objectives that the marketing department, together with other departmental functions, will seek to achieve. The marketing department will also contribute information that will guide the creation of the strategic plan.

According to Kotler et al. (2008) 'Failing to plan means planning to fail'.

The strategic plan will define the purpose and mission of the organisation which will develop into measurable corporate objectives. The next stage is a corporate audit, reviewing information on the company, its competitors, the market in which it operates and the competitive environment. The company will decide which products or services to promote to consumers and will develop strategic objectives for them. These will then be used by the various departments to develop marketing and other functional plans. For large FMCG organisations, there could be a number of marketing plans filtering down from product categories to individual brands, that ultimately feed into the overall strategic plan.

The framework of corporate strategic planning:

(a) Development of the organisation's mission statement
(b) Statement of objectives
(c) Situation analysis
(d) Strategy development
(e) Specific plans
(f) Implementation.

The corporate plan, therefore, has to consider **all aspects** of the organisation's business, its long-term direction and opportunities to attain competitive advantage, while a marketing plan is principally about **marketing activities**. The marketing plan is aligned with the corporate plan and **supports** it.

Specific marketing strategies will be determined within the overall corporate strategy. To be effective, these plans will be interdependent with those for other functions of the organisation.

(a) The **strategic** component of marketing planning focuses on the direction which an organisation will take in relation to a specific market, or set of markets, in order to achieve a specified set of objectives.

(b) Marketing planning also requires an **operational** component that defines tasks and activities to be undertaken in order to implement the desired strategy. The **marketing plan** is concerned uniquely with **products** and **markets**.

2.1 The synergistic planning process

The syllabus looks for an understanding of the synergistic planning process, but what does this term actually mean? A dictionary definition of synergy is 'the combined effort of two or more people, organisations, or things, especially when the result is greater than the sum of their individual effects or capabilities.' The concept of synergistic planning is also referred to as '2+2=5' which is said to originate from the Communist slogan in the USSR referring to the five-year plan to increase production. By coming together in a combined effort, the goals of the five-year plan could be achieved in four years. Hence, **synergistic planning** is a rational process of determining future action, based upon consideration of the current situation, the desired future position and possible routes from one to the other and can be achieved through the combined efforts of the functional departments in an organisation.

Synergistic planning can be examined under four main headings:

(a) Determining the **desired future position**

Any process of planning must start with a clear statement of what is to be achieved. This process of objective setting is frequently undertaken in a very superficial manner in the real world and sometimes hardly performed at all. There may be an assumption that everybody knows what is required, or reference to long-established objectives that have lost some or all of their relevance. Only when objectives are clearly defined can courses of action be assessed, and eventual success or failure be measured.

(b) Analysing the **current situation**

Any plan must take into account the circumstances that will affect attainment of the objective. The first step is to establish just where the individual or organisation stands. Current circumstances will include a vast array of factors. An important aspect of the current situation is the potential that exists for future developments. Strengths and weaknesses exist now; opportunities and threats have potential for the future.

(c) Designing **possible routes** to a solution

Simple problems, when analysed, often suggest a single route to a satisfactory solution. The analysis of more complex problems will tend to suggest a range of possible courses of action. One approach is to adopt solutions that have worked in the past. Another is to seek and evaluate more innovative solutions.

(d) Deciding **what** to do and **how** to do it

The identification of alternative plans is usually followed by an evaluation process to determine the one which is likely to maximise the achievement of the planning objectives. This involves consideration of various factors.

(i) Probability of success
(ii) Resources required
(iii) Acceptability of the proposed action and its implications
(iv) Potential barriers to success

After the optimal route has been selected, detailed plans need to be prepared and communicated to all the groups and individuals involved. These must be properly **integrated** to ensure that all action undertaken supports the attainment of the overall objective. **Performance measures** and **control mechanisms** must also be established.

2.2 The purpose of marketing planning

KEY CONCEPT

Marketing planning is a systematic process involving assessing marketing opportunities and capabilities, determining marketing objectives, agreeing target market and brand positioning strategies, seeking competitive advantage, creating marketing programmes, allocating resources and developing a plan for implementation and control.

(Dibb and Simkin, 2008)

Many companies these days adopt formal marketing planning processes. Marketing planning ensures companies understand their marketplace and any potential threats from competitors; keeps them in the loop with new trends and thinking; ensures they are meeting customer needs; helps plan company resources appropriately; ensures everyone is working to the same set of objectives and ideally, highlights the onset of major issues. Doyle (1994, cited by Drummond, et al, 2008 p. 247) says that planning can help companies deploy their resources to meet strategic '*windows of opportunity*' which are major changes in the market such as: new technology; new market segments, new channels of distribution, market redefinition where the nature of demand changes; legislative changes and sudden unexpected economic or political change.

Marketing planning is clearly a useful and very important process, albeit incredibly time consuming and difficult to pull together. The reason for this difficulty is the vast amount of information to process and compile into a coherent marketing plan with co-ordination, input and expertise coming from all parts of the organisation.

Dibb & Simkin, (2008) provide the following summary to define the goals of marketing planning:

- Hitting the best customer targets
- Winning new customers
- Expanding markets
- Beating the competition
- Keeping abreast of market developments
- Maximising returns
- Using resources to best advantage
- Minimising threats
- Identifying company strengths or weaknesses
- Aligning an organisation around shared objectives and planned actions
- Enhancing performance

The process can also add greater insight to the numbers that appear on sales forecasting and budgeting systems. Companies generally want to focus on maximising revenue, profits and return on investment and minimising costs. By considering these objectives in isolation from what is really happening in the market, targets certainly be set but they can be purely theoretical in nature. An awareness of the market conditions and the competitive environment can allow the company to set more concrete objectives and accurate targets based on real market data.

The marketing plan can also highlight the contribution to profits from the blend of products and services delivered by the company over the specified time period. Porter (1980, quoted by McDonald (2007), p. 35) describes companies as having a mix of different types of market that can be classified as: disaster products; lowest cost products; niche products and outstanding success products. Equally, products and services can produce different levels of sales and profit margins and it is equally important to consider the optimum combination of turnover and profit occurring from these lines, eg one product line may deliver a low profit margin but high turnover, while another may have a high margin but low turnover.

An additional benefit to the planning process is the opportunity to engage staff in the organisation's plans and vision for the future. Many companies 'present' the finalised marketing plan to staff to communicate shared values and goals and to motivate them to achieve the set objectives. This can help achieve commitment from the teams that will be implementing the plan over the next three-year period (or longer in some cases).

Dibb & Simkin (2008) Chapter 1 has useful tasks for you to complete in their workbook for marketing managers.

2.3 Achieving a sustainable competitive advantage

The aim of strategic marketing planning is to attain a sustainable competitive advantage combined with healthy profits. A strategic plan will review the company's resources and opportunities and assess how the organisation may have to adapt to survive and / or thrive in what can often be a rapidly changing competitive environment.

MARKETING AT WORK — application

The business of selling advertising in international business and news magazines, such as The Economist, changed over the course of a few hours on September 11th, 2001. The shock and devastation of the terrorist attack in New York led to advertising campaigns, booked many months before, being pulled for fear of appearing to be insensitive.

Marketing plans for airlines and investment banks were torn up as the world wondered if and where the terrorists would strike next. The concept of advertising was questioned. Was advertising appropriate and effective in the new climate? The context and content of advertising creative was examined and analysed in detail for its appropriateness and any alternative meanings. Regular advertisements facing gruesome photography provoked huge comment. Time and Newsweek publications went as far as cancelling all advertising in their special editions on the attacks.

Advertising in previously buoyant categories remained on hold for months afterwards. No amount of contingency planning, on the part of the international magazines or advertisers, could have considered the speed or impact of change upon the competitive environment. Competitive advantage shifted from profits to 'doing the right thing'.

Companies have to work hard to achieve and maintain competitive advantage, namely a profitable position in the market(s) of their choice. Competitive advantage is about finding a means of differentiation on which to compete and delivering this advantage to the marketplace in the form of a marketing strategy. Davidson (1997 quoted by Drummond, p. 157) says that competitive advantage is achieved '*whenever you do something better than competitors. If that something is important to consumers, or if a number of small advantages can be combined, you have an exploitable competitive advantage*.'

Perceptions of products, based on successful image campaigns and desirability can be quite different to its actual performance. This is particularly useful to consider for professional services where it might be harder to find points of differentiation amongst companies delivering fairly generic services. Accountants, engineers and estate agents perform the same types of work and through the nature of their businesses, should perform to the appropriate legal standards. Selection of a service provider could be made on price, skill, knowledge, reputation or ethics but it still may be difficult to identify differences between competitors. Finding a source of competitive advantage in this instance could be through superior knowledge in a new area, negotiation skills, networking or increasingly for professional services, brand image.

Davidson (1997) cited in Drummond et al. (2008) identified sources of competitive advantage as shown in the following table.

Sources of competitive advantage: Adapted from Davidson (1997) by Drummond, et al. (2008)

Sources of competitive advantage	Examples
Actual product performance	Robust, economic, easy to use
Perception of product	Brand image, product positioning
Low cost operations	Location, buying power
Legal advantage	Patents, contracts and copyright
Alliances and relationships	Networking, procurement
Superior skills	Database management, design skills
Flexibility	Developing customised solutions
Attitude	Aggressive selling, tough negotiation

Porter (1980, quoted by Drummond, p. 152) has spent his academic career discussing competitive advantage and strategy and identified three generic strategies (cost leadership, differential and focus) for competitive advantage.

For a list of Michael Porter's key works on competitive advantage, refer to 'http://en.wikipedia.org/wiki/Michael_Porter'

The diagram below outlines the generic strategies.

Strategic advantage

	Uniqueness perceived	Low cost position
Broad Industry wide Strategic target	Differentiation	Overall cost leadership
Narrow Specific segment	Focused differentiation	Focused cost leadership

(Porter, 1980)

Cost leadership – Those seeking this position within an industry or sector, will need to pursue a low cost structure by controlling overheads, economies of scale, minimal costs in marketing and R&D, global sourcing of materials and the use of new technology. Difficulties that may occur is that this strategy can be hard to maintain, particularly if the market share falls, making it hard to achieve economies of scale. Fixed costs, eg overheads, can be hard to reduce in the short to medium term. Larger, better resourced competitors may enter the market and this can lead to strategies such as price discounting and price wars – which can be damaging to a brand's perceived value by customers in the future, eg newspaper cover price wars.

Drivers of cost leadership identified by Porter are:

- **Economy of scale** – volume can drive efficiency and enhance purchasing leverage
- **Linkages and relationships** – just-in-time manufacturing systems can reduce stockholding costs and enhance product quality
- Forge **relationships** with other industry specialists or partners to share development and distribution costs
- **Infrastructure, location, availability of skills** and **government support** can also all affect the cost base. Some companies may choose to have a worldwide infrastructure and place some activities in low cost areas, eg call centres.

Differentiation – Companies taking this route will deliver a product that is distinct and differentiated from competitors. As Davidson was cited earlier in this section, this is done on the basis of value to a customer. A point of differentiation should be unique, command a price premium and create a reason for purchase. This strategy can be expensive with costs outweighing the benefits. Some points of differentiation may be easy to replicate for competitors. It is also important to keep abreast of customers' changing needs and their views towards the point of differentiation versus other product attributes.

Sources of differentiation identified by Porter are:

- Product performance – does this enhance value to the customer?
- Product perception – enduring emotional appeal can lead to brand loyalty (achieved through communications, etc).
- Product augmentation – differentiating by augmenting the product in a way that adds value such as high service levels, after-sales support, competitive pricing, etc. Distributors can also provide added value augmentation too.

Focus – Pursuing this strategy means the organisation should focus their efforts on narrower activities, eg a specific market segment. This should lead to better knowledge and understanding of customers. It can generate the benefits of cost leadership or differentiation within a market segment. However, competitors may also be attracted to the same segment and this strategy can leave the company more open to downturns in the behaviour of key customer groups.

A focus strategy can be based on factors such as:

- Geographic area – a geographic segmentation can focus on producing regional goods or tailoring the offering to local needs or a small market.
- End-user focus – this is a focus on the type of user of the product and allows the company to offer types of service or economies of scale not available to broader based competitors. The company should focus on a price / quality point within the market.
- Product / product line specialist – a focus on a single product type or line with value derived from specialisation of skills, volume and range.

ACTIVITY 2   application

Try to identify which of the generic strategies is used within your own organisation.

In the reality of modern marketing, cost is important to all management teams. Hybrid strategies can be followed that offer added value and lower costs. Some theorists say that cost leadership and differentiation are not mutually exclusive – that we cannot view them separately with no overlap – and that total quality programmes are one solution where superior quality and cost reductions can be achieved. Not every company manages to achieve competitive advantage and may be lost in the middle of the competitive environment in which they operate.

2.3.1 Tactical and strategic marketing plans

As we talk about competitive advantage, it is worth mentioning the difference between a tactical and a strategic marketing plan. A strategic marketing plan takes a longer time frame. It defines the changing and competitive business environment and looks at the segmentation of markets and the positioning of products. It also examines all of the company's marketing activities and strategies for the marketing mix. The tactical marketing plan takes a shorter time frame and looks at day-to-day activities. It is an operational plan and looks at the individual parts of the marketing mix.

The difference between the two and their use, can certainly make the difference to a company's success. In times of growth, when it is easy to market products and services, a tactical marketing plan (taking a short-term view) may reap rewards. In difficult markets and economic circumstances, writing the detailed one-year plan first, and then trying to fit this to a three-year plan, can be a recipe for disaster. The strategic marketing plan should be developed first with its emphasis on the external environment, and covering a period of three to five years. This can be followed by the one-year operational plan.

To maintain the competitive advantage that has been won, the advantage must be relevant to the market's needs and keep that relevance over time. It should be achievable with current resources and the point of advantage must be defensible, eg it should not be easy for other competitors to come up with their own version of the product and sell it immediately for a lower price. A defensible competitive advantage might be a patent on the product design. Other examples of defensible competitive advantage are: asset-based (location, plant and machinery, etc) and skills-based (product design, IT, etc).

2.4 The stages of the marketing planning process

The process of planning takes the same form, whether it is for strategic marketing or marketing planning. We call this the planning cycle and it is made up of four stages: analysis, planning, implementation and control. Information from these stages is fed back to ensure objectives and the marketing strategy are reviewed and amended if required.

Stages of the marketing planning process: (Kotler, et al. 2008)

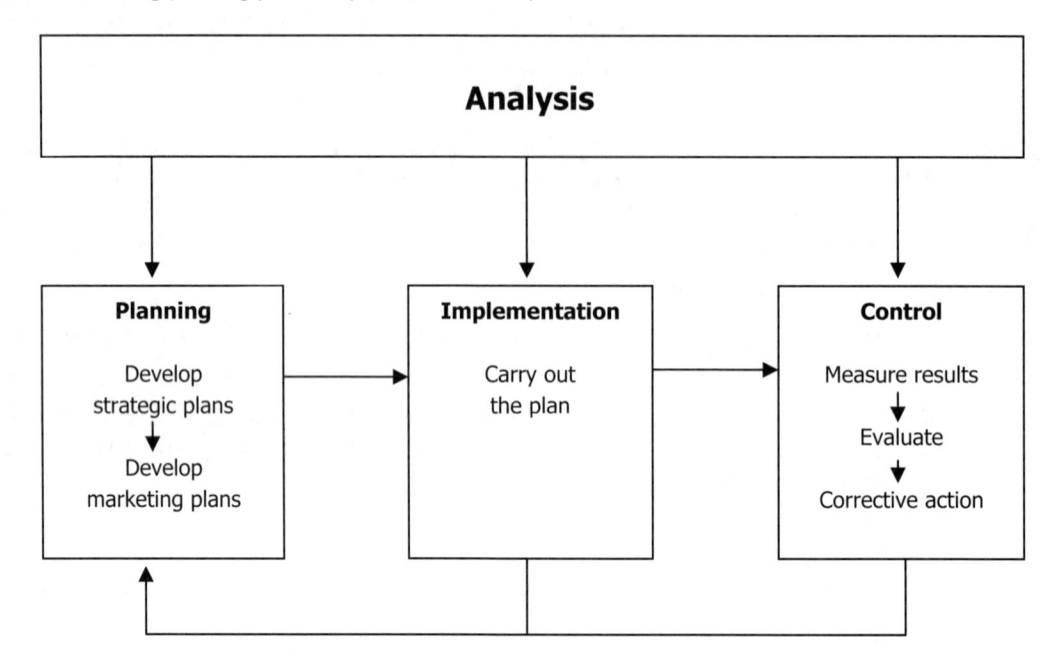

```
                        ┌─────────────────────┐
                        │      Analysis       │
                        └─────────────────────┘
                           │       │       │
                           ▼       ▼       ▼
         ┌──────────────┐  ┌──────────────┐  ┌──────────────┐
         │   Planning   │  │Implementation│  │   Control    │
         │              │  │              │  │              │
         │   Develop    │→ │  Carry out   │→ │Measure results│
         │strategic plans│  │   the plan   │  │      ↓       │
         │      ↓       │  │              │  │   Evaluate   │
         │   Develop    │  │              │  │      ↓       │
         │marketing plans│  │              │  │Corrective action│
         └──────────────┘  └──────────────┘  └──────────────┘
                ▲                                    │
                └────────────────────────────────────┘
```

We will now examine each of those phases.

Analysis

The first task for a company is to answer the question, 'Where are we?' The organisation must assess its environment to analyse its strengths and weaknesses, find new opportunities and identify (and ideally avoid) environmental threats. This SWOT analysis (strengths, weaknesses, opportunities and threats) will help the company decide its direction going forward. Analysis from research and forecasting in this section is fed into the other stages of the process.

Planning

At the strategic marketing stage, the company will have established the direction for each business unit. Here, marketing planning helps the company decide upon the marketing strategies that will help it achieve its overall strategic objectives, position products correctly and achieve competitive advantage. Marketing, product and brand plans will be written.

Implementation

Strategic plans are now turned into actions to achieve the company's objectives. Marketing plans are implemented by focusing on elements of the marketing mix (product, price, place and promotion). Organisational structures and systems must be put into place to ensure the plans can be implemented. Companies must consider budgets, resources, staff, the allocation of responsibilities and timings.

Control

All plans and activities will be measured and evaluated for their levels of success. Any corrective action will be taken to ensure objectives are still being achieved. A control system should ensure that standards are set for performance, that performance can be evaluated against these benchmark standards and action can be taken if performance differs from these standards.

Drummond, et al. (2008) breakdown the planning stages in more detail as follows:

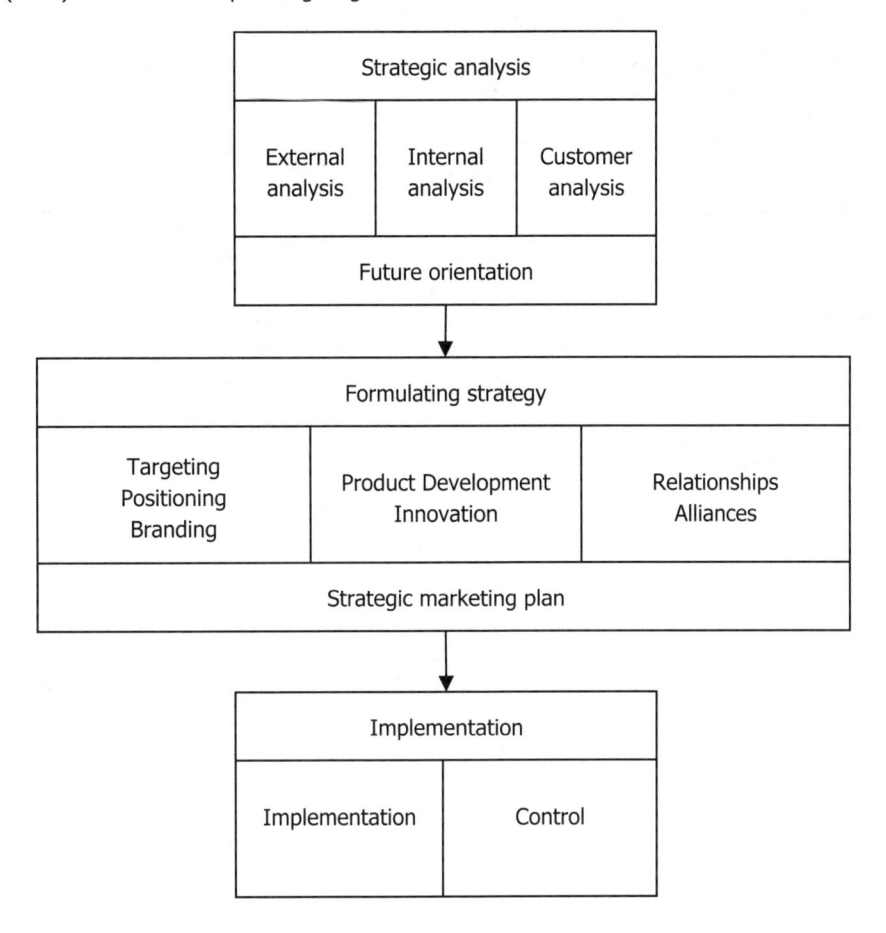

```
┌─────────────────────────────────────────────┐
│            Strategic analysis               │
├──────────────┬──────────────┬───────────────┤
│   External   │   Internal   │   Customer    │
│   analysis   │   analysis   │   analysis    │
├──────────────┴──────────────┴───────────────┤
│            Future orientation               │
└─────────────────────┬───────────────────────┘
                      ▼
┌─────────────────────────────────────────────┐
│            Formulating strategy             │
├──────────────┬──────────────┬───────────────┤
│  Targeting   │   Product    │ Relationships │
│ Positioning  │ Development  │   Alliances   │
│  Branding    │  Innovation  │               │
├──────────────┴──────────────┴───────────────┤
│          Strategic marketing plan           │
└─────────────────────┬───────────────────────┘
                      ▼
┌─────────────────────────────────────────────┐
│              Implementation                 │
├──────────────────────┬──────────────────────┤
│    Implementation    │       Control        │
└──────────────────────┴──────────────────────┘
```

2.4.1 Control systems

Drummond, et al. (2008), state that an effective control system needs to be designed carefully with a degree of flexibility and commonsense. Employees should be involved in the process and encouraged to set their own targets; this has the benefit of promoting ownership and developing staff. Targets should be set that are objective, measurable, achievable but challenging. Management attention should be focused on areas of need which can be done by identifying what constitutes an exception to the norm through benchmarking and tolerances. Measurements should be accurate, valid and consistent targeted at measuring what is important, not just what is easy to quantify. Finally, control systems should stimulate action to solve problems.

Drummond, et al. (2008) Chapter 14 Control will add significantly more detail if you would like to read further.

2.4.2 Achieving control

Kotler (quoted by Lancaster, et al. 2002) identified four types of marketing control with control of the marketing plan and strategic control of most interest to marketing management.

(a) Control of the annual marketing plan
(b) Control of profitability
(c) Control of efficiency
(d) Strategic control

Marketing plan control can identify how successful marketing activities have been in the last year. Useful control techniques are sales analysis and market share analysis.

- Sales analysis: budgeted sales revenue can be compared to actual sales revenue with detailed analyses on product lines, territories, customers, etc.
- Market share analysis: with this type of analysis, comparisons can be made with competitors. This can be more useful than looking at sales analysis in isolation as it could show that the company has performed well in a declining market. Many marketing objectives will be expressed in terms of market share growth.

Contingency plans should be part of the control process for when there are major differences between planned and actual performance. Issues that lead to this development could be changes in the environment, competitive forces or factors, eg an unexpected political event, economic changes or a terrorist attack. Marketing management should make assumptions during the planning process based on information such as likely trends to plan for any untoward circumstances.

Annual plan control can lead to objectives, strategies and tactics being re-evaluated and will guide the next year's operations plan. Sometimes, a greater review of these areas is required based on a detailed analysis of the company's marketing operation, performance and environment. The full marketing audit will be covered in a later chapter.

2.5 Scheduling of plans

Companies conduct planning in cycles. A marketing plan will cover the marketing programmes, costs, control measures, the allocation of staff and resources, and a schedule for marketing activities for a specified time period. This time period can vary from organisation to organisation. Short-range plans cover a period of one year or less and would be operational in scope. Medium-range plans are for two to five years and long-range plans cover a period of more than five years but are less common. Marketing management may have plans running concurrently for all of these time periods.

ACTIVITY 3
application

Think about the planning cycle within your own organisation:

(a) When are plans constructed?
(b) How effective is the planning process?

It is usual to update marketing plans in detail for the next twelve months with an overview for the subsequent two years, thus creating a three-year plan. Any changes in the company's structure or strategy, or the marketing environment, will affect a change in the marketing plan. This cycle then repeats to ensure plans evolve and adapt to the changing market. On average, companies start the planning process between six to nine months before the start of the next fiscal year to allow for analysis and research to take place.

3 The marketing plan

KEY CONCEPT
concept

A **marketing plan** is a specification of all aspects of an organisation's marketing intentions and activities. It is a summary document, providing a framework that permits managers and specialists to undertake the detailed work of marketing in a co-ordinated and effective fashion. The creation of a good marketing plan is likely to be a time-consuming exercise, since it should deal with both current circumstances and plans for the future.

(a) It should be based on **detailed knowledge** of both the **target market** and the company involved.
(b) It should give sufficient detail of intentions to support the design and operation of all **marketing-related activities**.

3.1 What goes into the marketing plan?

There is no standard template or list of contents for a marketing plan. Different organisations will find it appropriate to consider different things at different times in their development. First, we will look in general terms at what is likely to appear in most marketing plans.

3.1.1 The marketing plan – an outline

(a) **Situation analysis**

PESTEL – SWOT – Market analysis and marketing objectives

(b) **Marketing strategy**

Objectives – tactics – marketing mix

(c) **Numerical forecasts**

Sales – expenses

(d) **Controls**

Marketing organisation – performance measures

These four basic elements constitute a logical sequence of development for the basic building blocks of the marketing plan.

(a) **Situation analysis** – Any planning process should start with the collection and analysis of basic data. In the marketing context this is often called situation analysis. It may be appropriate for situation analysis to consider the items listed below:

    (i) The wider environmental factors of the PESTEL model
    (ii) Strengths, weaknesses, opportunities and threats
    (iii) Marketing research data, including demographics data, trends, needs and growth
    (iv) Current and planned products and services
    (v) Critical issues

(b) **Marketing strategy** – The statement of marketing strategy will describe in detail all the marketing concepts, practices, activities and aids that will be used. It will reiterate the marketing objectives in some form, and will probably give a detailed account of how the chosen marketing mix will be applied. This section is likely to be of considerable size.

(c) **Numerical forecasts** – The marketing plan must include quantitative data about required resources and forecast results. Costs must be given in detail and realistic sales estimates must be provided. In particular, the cost of marketing activities must be specified.

(d) **Controls** – Planning is worthless unless control mechanisms are established to ensure that the plan is properly executed. These may include intermediate organisational and sales milestones, the design of routine performance measures, the establishment of an appropriate marketing organisation, and the development of contingency plans.

3.2 The marketing plan in detail

3.2.1 Executive summary

It is common practice to place an executive summary at the beginning of the marketing plan. Executive summaries are provided, as their name implies, for the convenience of senior executives who require a fast overview in order to avoid the time involved in detailed study. As a general rule, such summaries should be confined to a brief exposition of important material.

(a) Background information that helps explain why particular proposals have been made or decisions taken.
(b) A description of proposed action with an indication of timescale
(c) A summary of the aims or targets that are intended to be achieved
(d) An assessment of any wider implications of the proposed action
(e) A statement of the required investment, where appropriate

The executive summary for a marketing plan is likely to include material on the following specific matters.

- Marketing research
- Target markets and segments
- The proposed marketing mix
- Sales forecasts
- Situation analysis

Situation analysis involves consideration of both the environment and internal factors. The environment can be divided into the macro-environment, consisting of the six PESTEL elements, and the micro- or market environment. Internal and environmental factors are summarised in a SWOT analysis.

(a) **The business environment**. The operation of any business implies interaction with its environment and the first stage of the detailed planning process is likely to be the collection and analysis of environmental information. For this purpose, the business environment is often split into two parts.

  (i) The macro-environment may be analysed into six elements.

   - Political – Technological
   - Economic – Ecological or 'green'
   - Social – Legal

   The acronym PESTEL may be used. PEST and STEP are also common, when the legal environment is included under politics and so-called 'green' issues are included under the social heading. A marketing plan need not include a detailed PESTEL analysis, but it should explain those aspects of it that have affected its development.

  (ii) The **micro-environment** consists of the markets in which the business operates or plans to operate. It includes current and prospective customers and existing and potential competitors. The micro-environment also includes any distribution systems used by the business. Headings such as those below may be appropriate.

   - Target markets – products and services
   - Market needs – competition
   - Market geography – costs
   - Market demographics – suppliers
   - Market trends – critical issues
   - Market forecasts
   - Market growth

(b) **Internal analysis**. Like the overall strategic plan it is derived from, a marketing plan should reflect the characteristics of the business concerned. It will inevitably refer to current and planned products and capabilities and be designed to exploit the organisation's resources to the full. An important aspect of the internal analysis is product-market background, which sets the scene for those less familiar with the products and markets involved.

The environmental and internal analyses are traditionally summarised and entered into the plan under the headings of strengths, weaknesses, opportunities and threats. This SWOT analysis highlights aspects of the overall situation that need action by the business. The aim is to exploit strengths and opportunities, remedy areas of weakness and develop actions which minimise threats. The analysis of SWOT must be prepared honestly and objectively as it is a key foundation on which the marketing strategy is built.

3.2.2 Marketing strategy

Marketing strategy includes objectives and methods and may deal with such matters as gap analysis, target markets, the marketing mix and marketing research. The marketing strategy section of the marketing plan should describe in detail the organisation's marketing objectives and methods.

(a) **Marketing objectives**. The objectives of the marketing plan are derived from the corporate plan, which is designed to support the overall corporate mission. A clear statement of marketing objectives serves a number of purposes.

  (i) It provides a focus for activity and a sense of purpose. This should stimulate activity, particularly when overall objectives are broken down into personal targets.

(ii) It provides a framework for co-ordination of activity across the organisation.

(iii) IT is fundamental to the control process, since it defines success. Actual performance is compared with what was intended, and control action taken to correct any discrepancy. When objectives have been considered in detail, it is possible to use them to refine a plan by means of gap analysis. This is discussed in detail later in this Study Text.

Objectives will relate to both market dynamics and financial results, and should be expressed in concrete form. Objectives may be set for such business parameters as those below.

- Revenue growth
- Market share
- Profitability
- Number of outlets
- Customer retention
- Brand recognition
- Marketing expenses
- Staff levels and training

(b) **Target markets**. It will be appropriate to define clearly just what the target market is. The nature of this definition will depend partly on the scale of the marketing operation envisaged. For example, a company operating nationally in a lifestyle segment might target prosperous retired people nationwide, while a locally based professional service business might target start-ups and small traders within a 20-mile radius of its base.

(c) **Products and their positioning**. Product positioning is a continuation of the process of determining the target market. Product positioning is about the way the target market perceives the product's characteristics, in relation to those of competing products.

There are two basic product positioning strategies.

(i) 'Me too': the product is positioned to meet the competition head-on.
(ii) Gap-filling: the product is positioned to exploit gaps in the market.

(d) **The marketing mix**. A marketing plan will not necessarily give complete details of every component of the marketing mix. Instead, it will concentrate on those parts that are new or crucial to success. For example, a plan built around a new or enhanced product that will be distributed through established channels is likely to give significant product detail, and explain the aim of the new features in market terms. Place, on the other hand, is unlikely to receive more than a brief mention.

(e) **Marketing research**. Early marketing research should have played its part in supporting the design of the marketing plan. However, it is not confined to this phase of operations. Marketing research activities should form part of the marketing plan, so that continuing feedback may be obtained upon the degree of success achieved.

3.2.3 Numerical forecasts

Numerical forecasts tie down what is to be achieved and form the basis of the control process. This section of the marketing plan could also be called a budget.

Typical forecast quantities:

- Turnover
- Market share
- Marketing spend
- Units of sales
- Costs
- Breakeven analysis

It will be appropriate to present numerical forecasts broken down in two ways.

(a) **Phased by time period**. A year's total may be broken down into monthly or quarterly increments.

(b) **Analysed by marketing characteristic**. For example, sales and expenses might be analysed by product type or by market segment.

3.2.4 Breakeven analysis

Breakeven analysis is a management accounting technique that should be of interest to marketing managers. The cumulative sales of a product reach their breakeven point when the total revenue is high enough to cover both the variable and fixed costs of producing and selling that quantity of product. The breakeven point is a vital hurdle that must be cleared if the marketing plan is to be considered successful, and a profit made on the sale of the product.

3.2.5 Controls

Control is vital if management is to ensure that planning targets are achieved. The control process involves three underlying components.

- Setting standards or targets
- Measuring and evaluating actual performance
- Taking corrective action

(a) **Performance measures**. The data contained within the numerical forecasts section of the plan provides the raw material for performance measures. Mechanisms must be put in place for collecting information on actual results, so that comparisons can be made and control action taken. Overall performance is often judged by analysing two main indicators: sales and market share.

   (i) **Sales analysis** is based on the comparison of actual with budgeted turnover, but this is only the first stage. It is appropriate to delve deeper and consider the effects of differences in unit sales and selling price. Further analysis by product, region, customer and so on may be required.

   (ii) **Market share analysis**. Market share is important to overall profitability, and the attainment of a given market share is likely to be an important marketing objective. Market share should always be analysed together with turnover, since the growth or decline of the market as a whole has implications for the achievement of both types of objective.

(b) **Marketing organisation**. Individual responsibilities within the overall marketing plan should be given and the persons responsible named. One example of a specific responsibility is the preparation of performance reports. Other roles will include that of overall responsibility (probably discharged by the marketing manager or brand manager), management of promotional effort and management of marketing research effort.

(c) **Implementation milestones**. Progress in implementing a programme can be monitored by the establishment of milestones and the dates by which they should be achieved.

(d) **Contingency planning**. Events in the real world very rarely go according to plan. It is necessary for planners to consider problems that might arise and make appropriate preparations to deal with them. There are several requirements.

   (i) The organisation must have the capability to adapt to new circumstances. This will almost certainly imply financial reserves, but may require more specific resources, such as management and productive capacity.

   (ii) There is a range of possible responses to any given contingency. The organisation should consider its options in advance of needing to put them into action.

   (iii) A prompt response will normally be appropriate. Achieving this depends to some extent on having the resources and having done the planning mentioned above, but it will also depend on a kind of organisational agility. In particular, decision-making processes need to be rapid and effective.

3.3 Documentation and reality

The difference between documentation and reality is principally that of implementation. It is easy to promise a lot on paper but more difficult to successfully implement a marketing strategy. Effective implementation was defined by Drummond, et al. (2008) as, '*Understanding the fundamental principles of implementation; assessing the ease of implementing individual projects; and applying project management techniques*'.

Implementation can also be hindered by people, power and politics. Some staff members may be unwilling to support a particular marketing strategy and this failure to buy-in to the concept can lead to disharmony and internal politics. This is particularly difficult when the staff member has influence at a decision-making level. Tactics to improve relations include converting or isolating the opposition, seeking back-up from influential supporters, negotiation and trade-offs.

Companies may also underestimate the amount of resources required to implement the marketing plan. This may be because of a lack of understanding of the planning process, inexperience, or a lack of support from senior management. The quality or amount of data utilised in the analysis section of the plan may be insufficient, eg a lack of competitor intelligence. There may also be poor co-ordination between the departmental functions therefore reducing the amount of good quality data submitted for analysis and slowing down and reducing the effectiveness of the planning process.

Finally, marketing plans may have been written in a more favourable economic climate. Marketers can introduce control measures and contingency plans but many industries are experiencing static or rapidly declining demand, leaving the organisation falling far short of previously planned performance measures. Markets can become volatile, with over capacity, price discounting, reduced profit margins and downsizing. This can lead to the marketing plan and the control systems becoming irrelevant for the current environment, and leaving marketing management to return to the drawing board.

Aaker (1995 quoted by Drummond p. 173) provides a number of strategic options for declining and/or hostile markets:

- **Generate growth** – can the industry be revitalised by finding growth? It may be possible to encourage existing users to increase their usage, create new markets for products, and find new applications for existing products or technologies. The Ansoff Matrix can be applied here.

- **Survival** – this strategy is focused on staying afloat during difficult times by managing costs and signalling commitment to the industry and customers. Economies of scale must be managed as best as possible and experience effects (becoming more efficient through learning) become vital. The company may have to rationale the product portfolio and focus on larger, more profitable customers or may expand its range to cover the maximum number of customers at a wide range of price points. Takeovers, mergers and acquisitions become common. A portfolio approach can be taken with cash cows supporting operations and products which are struggling but have long-term potential.

- **Exit strategy** – the company may withdraw from the industry. This does overcome exit barriers such as costs with downsizing – redundancy, legal costs of breaking contracts, handling commitments from existing customers. It can be rapid or slowly run down. This strategy can affect goodwill and customer confidence if the company is just exiting a market not all its operations.

MARKETING AT WORK

application

Established in the 1980s, a services contractor, which installs multi-discipline building and engineering services, has gained competitive advantage by becoming one of the leading players in its field. Year-on-year, the privately owned company has grown in turnover and geographical spread with no financial borrowings by recognising the importance of meeting the demands and requirements of its clients. The majority of the company's work comes from repeat business.

The company has followed a strategy of overall cost leadership by providing services to a wide sector of industry from banks, retail, hospitals and transportation to the more complex restoration of heritage buildings. Overhead costs are aggressively kept down by employing strong negotiation skills with suppliers and the set-up of a buying department to achieve economies of scale. Strong project management skills by the engineers working on client sites means that equipment and parts are delivered at the point they are to be installed, eliminating the need for storage costs or wastage.

After a number of years of strong growth and profits, the downturn in the economy has brought the building industry to a halt. As existing projects run their course, no new work is materialising and many previously won projects have suddenly been reduced in scope, eg one landmark London tall building that has been granted planning permission has lost investors and has decided to build the first floor only as a show office until the economy recovers.

In a bid to survive, the company's directors have cancelled the use of freelancers, closed a main office, and cut the workforce by half. Projects continue to be delivered under budget, on time, safely and to a high quality. The management team hopes that by continuing to signal their commitment to their loyal customers, they will continue to win projects and remain competitive in the industry.

3.4 The role of the marketing plan

In summary, the marketing plan is an important document that is developed through the marketing planning process and sets a blueprint for the company's marketing strategy for the next three years, focusing in detail on the year ahead. It covers all of the company's marketing activities, control measures including contingency plans, schedules and costs of activities, the allocation of resources and key responsibilities.

Dibb & Simkin (2008) looked at the purposes of a marketing plan:

- It updates the organisation's marketing strategy and determines marketing objectives
- It offers a road map for implementing strategy and achieving its objectives
- It assists in management control and monitoring of strategy implementation
- It informs new participants in the plan of their role and function
- It specifies how resources should be allocated and prioritised
- It stimulates thinking and makes better use of resources
- It assigns responsibilities, tasks and timing
- It makes participants aware of problems, opportunities and threats to address
- It assists in ensuring organisations are customer-focused, aware of their market and competitors, realistic in their expectations and use resources appropriately
- And finally, it aligns senior management to market conditions and agreed priorities

Learning objective review

Learning objectives	Covered
1. Understand the role of marketing within an organisation and how marketers work with other departments.	☑ Marketing definition ☑ Marketing orientation ☑ Interface with other departments ☑ Transactions, exchange and relationships ☑ Marketing in practice
2. Understand the purpose and stages of marketing planning and how it fits within the strategic marketing process.	☑ Planning process ☑ Purpose of planning ☑ Sustainable competitive advantage ☑ Porter's generic strategy ☑ Tactical and strategic plans ☑ Stages of marketing planning
3. Write your own marketing plan and evaluate barriers to its implementation.	☑ Elements within a marketing plan ☑ Documentation and reality ☑ Role of a networking plan

Quick quiz

1. Product orientation means that success will be determined by the level of advertising. True or False?
2. What is the sustainable marketing option?
3. Match the correct terms with the appropriate quadrant.

    (i) Focused cost leadership
    (ii) Differentiation
    (iii) Focused differentiation
    (iv) Overall cost leadership

Strategic advantage

	Uniqueness perceived	Low cost position
Broad Industry wide Strategic target	A	B
Narrow Specific segment	C	D

(Porter, 1980)

4. What does the term 'synergistic planning process' mean?
5. What is the correct order according to Kotler to plan marketing as a process?

    (a) control
    (b) planning
    (c) implementation
    (d) analysis

6. What numerical measures can be applied to forecast demand?

Activity debriefs

1. This will depend on your own organisation. If you were having trouble identifying the orientation, talk to colleagues about where they see the focus.

2. This will depend on your own research.

3. Many organisations find that planning cycles (no matter how good original intentions are) are often squeezed into the last possible moment. Try to also consider the actual process of planning and how this might be improved.

Quiz answers

1. False: Advertising will impact a sales orientation.

2. Recognising that sustainable competitive advantage will be achieved by considering the needs of future consumers and society as a whole.

3.
   - (i) Focused cost leadership = D
   - (ii) Differentiation = A
   - (iii) Focused differentiation = C
   - (iv) Overall cost leadership = B

4. A rational process determining future action based upon the current situation. Often thought to mean 2+ 2 = 5. There are four stages:

    1. Determine the desired future position
    2. Analyse the current situation
    3. Design possible routes to a solution
    4. Plan what to do and how to do it

5. (d), (b), (c), (a).

6. Turnover, market share, marketing spend, units of sales, costs, breakeven analysis.

References

Blythe, J., (2006) Principles & Practice of Marketing. Cengage Learning, London.

Bogle, N. (2001) '*The day the advertising had to change*'. [Online] (Copyright 2008) Available at: http://www.independent.co.uk/news/media/the-day-the-advertising-had-to-change-670616.html [Accessed 24 March 2009].

Boseley, S.,(2009) '*Drug giant GlaxoSmithKline pledges cheap medicine for world's poor*'. The Guardian, [Online] 13 Feb 2009. Available at: http://www.guardian.co.uk/business/2009/feb/13/glaxo-smith-kline-cheap-medicine [Accessed 19 March 2009].

Charles, G.,(2009) 'Marketers feel divorced from strategic role in workplace'. Marketing Magazine, [Online] 03 Mar 2009. Available at: http://www.marketingmagazine.co.uk/news/rss/886793/Marketers-feel-divorced-strategic-role-workplace/ [Accessed 19 March 2009].

CIM,(2007) '*Shape the Agenda Tomorrow's Word: Re-evaluating the role of marketing*'. [Online] CIM, Maidenhead, Available at: http://www.cim.co.uk/ShapeTheAgenda/RoleOfMarketing/AgendaPapers.aspx [Accessed 13 March 2009].

CIM, (2007) 'Leading body calls for a new definition of marketing'. [Online] (Updated 21 Sep 2007) Available at: http://www.cim.co.uk/NewsAndEvents/MediaCentre/NewsRelease/Leading%20body%20calls%20for%20a%20new%20definition%20.aspx [Accessed 09 March 2009].

Drummond, G., Ensor, J. & Ashford, R.,(2008) Strategic Marketing Planning & Control. (3rd ed.), Butterworth-Heinemann, Oxford.

Dibb, S. & Simkin, L., (2008) Marketing Planning – A Workbook for Marketing Managers. Cengage Learning, London.

McDonald, M., (2007) Marketing Plans – How to Prepare Them, How to Use Them. (6th ed.), Butterworth-Heinemann, Oxford.

Friend, G. & Zehle, S.,(2004) The Economist Guide to Business Planning. The Economist in assoc. with Profile Books, London.

Gallagher Ardis, M. (2009) 'Turning dissatisfied customers into repeat customers'. [Online] (Copyright 2009) Available at: http://www.staples.com/sbd/content/article/c-d/dissatisfiedcustomers.html [Accessed 19 March 2009].

Kotler, P. Armstrong, G. Wong, V. & Saunders, J.,(2008) Principles of Marketing. (5th European ed.), Pearson Education, Harlow.

Lancaster, G. Massingham, L. & Ashford, R.,(2002) Essentials of Marketing. (4th ed.), McGraw-Hill Education, Maidenhead.

Needham, D. & Dransfield, R., (1994) Business Studies. (2nd ed. revised). Nelson Thornes. London.

O'Sullivan, A.,(2007) '*8m dissatisfied customers change bank*'. This is Money, [Online] 06 Dec 2007. Available at: http://www.thisismoney.co.uk/saving-and-banking/article.html?in_article_id=427312&in_page_id=7 [Accessed 19 March 2009].

Robbins, S. P., & Coutler, M., (2002) ActiveBook, Management. (7th ed.), Pearson Oxford.

Ronen, D.,(2005) '*Calculating the cost of new custom*'. Times Online, [Online] 20 Oct 2005. Available at: http://business.timesonline.co.uk/tol/business/entrepreneur/article580767.ece [Accessed 15 March 2009].

The Priory Group, (2009). '*The Priory Hospital Roehampton*'. [Online] Updated 2009. Available at: http://www.priorygroup.com/facilitySearch/viewFacility.asp?facname=The%20Priory%20Hospital%20Roehampton [Accessed 17 March 2009].

Wikipedia, (2009). '2+2=5'. [Online] 21 Mar 2009. Available at: http://en.wikipedia.org/wiki/2_%2B_2_%3D_5 [Accessed 26 March 2009].

Wilmshurst, J. & Mackay, A.,(2002) The Fundamentals & Practice of Marketing. (4th illustrated ed.), Butterworth-Heinemann, Oxford.

Chapter 2
External and internal influences on objectives

Topic list

1. Corporate, business and marketing objectives
2. Influences on the formulation of objectives
3. The impact of environmental forces

Introduction

Marketing management's role in planning is to set objectives to determine the direction of the organisation. The marketing function must then formulate strategies and tactics to achieve these objectives, and set timescales for the implementation of these activities, incorporating control measures. Objectives are undoubtedly at the heart of the planning process. This chapter focuses on objectives and examines the relationship between the different levels of objectives and their impact upon the marketing plan. We identify and examine the internal and external influences that affect the formulation of objectives and finally, look at environmental factors and their bearing on objective setting.

Syllabus-linked learning objectives

By the end of the chapter you will be able to:

Learning objectives	Syllabus link
1. Understand the different types and levels of objectives set by organisations.	1.4
2. Understand and identify the internal and external influences on objectives.	1.5
3. Evaluate the impact of internal and external environmental forces on objectives.	1.6

1 Corporate, business and marketing objectives

Objectives are important to an organisation for a number of reasons:

- They give a sense of **purpose and direction** to all functional departments and provide focus for management
- They help departments direct their activities towards the same **goals** in a consistent way
- They **motivate staff** to achieve them particularly if they are tied in to **performance measures**
- They give a **benchmark for control** so organisations can assess whether they are meeting the set objectives

These objectives should be both acceptable and understandable to internal managers and external stakeholders, so they are clear about what needs to be achieved. Objectives should also be flexible to adapt to changing environments. Objectives should also be appropriately designed to suit the conditions of the marketing environment in which the organisation operates. Consistency of objectives is essential because a number of goals may be set by the company at any one time at different levels. Finally, objectives should be quantifiable in terms of performance and timings.

Many theorists talk about the importance of **SMART objectives**, but this is one acronym with more definitions than initials! Here are the principle definitions you may come across:

Specific – should define precisely what needs to be achieved to ensure clarity within the organisation.

Measurable – should be stated clearly with targets which can be measured over time.

Achievable – within stated time frame. **A**ccurate – in its definition. **A**spirational – challenging for individuals but not demoralising.

Relevant – in the context of the company's vision. **R**ealistic – achievable and reflecting the company's current position and how this can be improved. **R**esults-oriented – stated in terms of outcomes.

Time bound – to enable the organisation to measure performance against a set deadline.

MARKETING AT WORK

application

The University of Surrey provided staff with examples of SMART objectives to help with the planning process and become more marketing-oriented. Here are a few to illustrate the concept:

- To improve the percentage of undergraduates achieving 2:1 classification and above by 5% year-on-year.
- To improve overall student satisfaction from x in 20XX to y in 20XX.
- To grow the alumni register from x in 20XX to y in 20XX.
- To plan and conduct three skills building workshops each for 30 members of staff by 1 March 20XX.
- To achieve a 25% return on investment by 31 December 20XX.

Companies will have a range of objectives which may cover all or some of the following areas:

- **Profitability** – targets can be established for financial returns including earnings per share or return on equity.
- **Sales/market share/growth** – objectives relating to the company's success and market standing can be set.
- **Technical/innovation/productivity** – this could cover areas such as product and service development, cost reduction, financing, operational performance, human resources and management information.
- **Physical and financial resources** – relating to the acquisition and use of resources.
- **Manager or employee performance**, **development and attitude** – objectives can be used to set performance standards and to measure achievement and positive contributions.
- **Social responsibility** – could relate to responsibility in production of goods or contributions to charity.
- **Survival** – could relate to the reduction in production or service delivery costs, or human resources.

1.1 The vision, mission and corporate objectives

KEY CONCEPT

concept

Vision: Sets out the purpose of the organisation (what business it is in) and the direction (where it is trying to go).

Mission: Outlines how the vision can be translated into reality (what should be done to achieve it).

Objectives: Sets specific quantified targets against which the corporate strategy's success can be measured.

The Economist (2004)

The strategic planning process starts with a definition of the overall purpose of the company and the creation of a **mission statement**. Next, a company will develop measurable **corporate objectives**. This key stage is followed by the **corporate audit** where information is collated and analysed on the company, its competitors, the market and environment in which it operates. A SWOT analysis will be used to summarise this information. It is at this point that the company must decide which products and services to support and consider how this might be done. **Strategic objectives** will be written which should guide the company's activities. These activities will be included in detailed functional and marketing plans.

Once plans are implemented marketers should ensure that they monitor outcomes so that corrective action can be taken if required.

This process, the timings and development of the different levels of objectives can be seen in the following diagram of the marketing planning process.

```
┌─────────────────────────────┐
│ Corporate objectives /      │
│ business mission            │
└─────────────────────────────┘
┌─────────────────────────────┐
│ Marketing audit             │
└─────────────────────────────┘
┌─────────────────────────────┐
│ SWOT analysis               │
└─────────────────────────────┘
┌─────────────────────────────┐
│ Business objectives         │
└─────────────────────────────┘
┌─────────────────────────────┐
│ Marketing objectives        │
└─────────────────────────────┘
┌─────────────────────────────┐
│ Marketing strategies        │
└─────────────────────────────┘
┌─────────────────────────────┐
│ Marketing tactics /         │
│ marketing mix decisions     │
└─────────────────────────────┘
┌─────────────────────────────┐
│ Implementation              │
└─────────────────────────────┘
┌─────────────────────────────┐
│ Monitoring and control      │
└─────────────────────────────┘
```

(Adapted from Lancaster, et al. (2002))

1.1.1 The vision and mission of an organisation

Many theorists see the vision and mission as separate but complementary **statements of intent** from the organisation. Many marketing planning texts combine these two concepts into one (the mission statement which includes corporate vision). Many companies do try to include both mission and vision with one statement.

Entrepreneurs such as Richard Branson, are said to be converts to big and bold vision statements. Since the 1970s he has had the same vision for his portfolio of companies: 'to be the consumer champion by delivering to their brand values which are *Value for Money, Good Quality, Brilliant Customer Service, Innovative, Competitively Challenging and Fun*'. This is why he has been able to create businesses in such diverse categories under the Virgin umbrella. Lindstrom (2007) says a vision statement *'needs to be so distinct that you can remove any references to the brand name and still instantly recognise who's behind it.'*

MARKETING AT WORK

application

The following example from the United States Secret Service shows an organisation that has defined both its vision and mission separately. As you can see from The Economist definition we covered earlier, the vision statement sets out the purpose of the organisation and its direction, whereas the mission states how it will achieve this.

Vision statement

The vision of the United States Secret Service is to uphold the tradition of excellence in its investigative and protective mission through a dedicated, highly-trained, diverse, partner-oriented workforce that employs progressive technology and promotes professionalism.

Mission statement

The mission of the United States Secret Service is to safeguard the nation's financial infrastructure and payment systems to preserve the integrity of the economy, and to protect national leaders, visiting heads of state and government, designated sites and National Special Security Events.

Sainsbury's supermarket sets out its statement of intent differently but the concept is the same: a corporate vision and values which set out its mission.

Our goal

At Sainsbury's we will deliver an ever-improving quality shopping experience for our customers with great products at fair prices. We aim to exceed customer expectations for healthy, safe, fresh and tasty food, making their lives easier everyday.

Our values

The values of the Sainsbury's brand – passion for healthy, safe, fresh and tasty food, our focus on delivering great products at fair prices, a history of innovation and leadership and a strong regard for the social, ethical and environmental effects of our operation – have continued to stand the test of time.

Five principles are at the core of our business:

- The best for food and health
- Sourcing with integrity
- Respect for our environment
- Making a positive difference to our community
- A great place to work.

These principles provide differentiation from our major competitors and define and direct all our activities.

Sources: www.sainsburys.co.uk, www.secretservice.gov

For the rest of this section, the mission and vision will be discussed as an all-encompassing concept. A mission tells us the organisation's purpose. It is most important to define when the company is being set-up. For any long-running firm, the mission can change or dilute over time so it is important to review the purpose or the organisation and remind staff what business they are in. Research studies claim that mission statements can have a positive impact on profitability and can increase shareholder equity. Almost 40% of employees however do not know or understand their company's mission (McMillan, 2009). Avoiding jargon and meaningless buzzwords can certainly help communicate ideas more effectively!

As Kotler (2008) states that, asking basic questions about the company's core business proposition like *'what sort of business are we?'*, *'what makes us special?'* and *'what do consumers value?'* is a sign of strength, not uncertainty. These questions should be carefully considered to design a meaningful mission statement which is market-oriented and will guide staff to achieving the corporate goals.

1.1.2 What business are we in?

Kotler (2008) recommends market definitions of a business are more useful than product or technological definitions. This is good logic particularly as technological markets move so quickly. If you consider a company like BT, it used to be known only for supplying telephone connections, now you might consider it to be a global communications company. BT's current vision is, in fact, to help customers *'thrive in a changing world'* in the business of voice and data services. The market is changing so rapidly that the definition of the business they are in is not even clearly stated on the strategic vision and values page of their corporate web site! Business definitions can also come from stating the benefits provided or needs satisfied, rather than saying what products are manufactured.

1.1.3 Who are our customers?

This can be less straightforward than you might expect. In the example below, the NHS Trust perceives its customers as patients, their carers and their families. These three audiences would have very different experiences of dealing directly with the Trust but are all important to the overall public perception.

The mission can also highlight distinctive competences and ideas of the company's future direction – what they **will** do, **may** do, or will **never** do. It should be specific to the company, and no other.

Lancaster, et al. (2002) set out a number of criteria to help define a business which reflects and supports overall corporate objectives:

(a) The definition should be neither too broad nor too narrow.

(b) The definition should specify the customer groups to be served; the customer needs to be served; and the technologies to be utilised.

(c) The definition should help motivate and inspire members of the organisation to look to the future, being both forward looking and aspirational in nature.

Contemporary mission statements may also cover areas such as the proper treatment of staff, customer service and satisfaction, environmental consciousness and social responsibility, product quality and innovation, profitability and shareholder value.

Some stakeholders may not support the adoption of a mission statement. The following diagram was adapted from Johnson and Scholes (1999) by Drummond, et al. (2008), p. 139, showing the nature of this support and stakeholder influence:

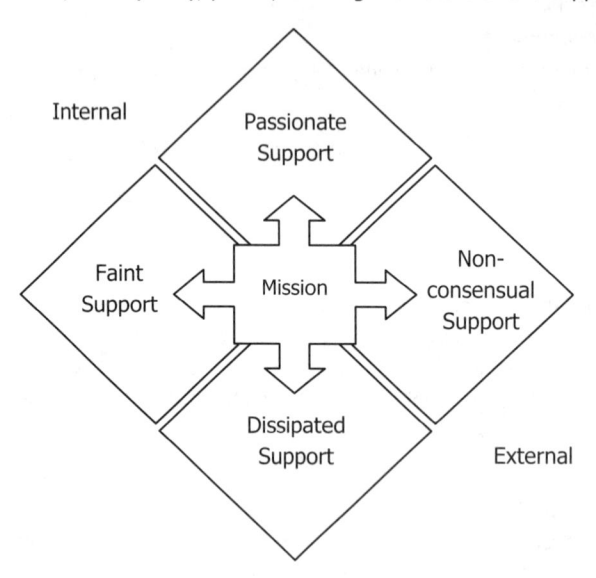

- **Faint support**

    Mission statements will have little influence on the organisation's strategic development if internal managers don't support it and identify with stakeholder needs.

- **Passionate support**

    Internal managers who identify with the values and philosophy of the organisation, and keep the mission statement central to their activities.

- **Dissipated support**

    Where strategic decisions are the realm of external stakeholders, then regulation and processes will dominate the enterprise. The original mission will be lost in a sea of paperwork and regulations.

- **Non-consensual support**

    Where external stakeholders hold passionate ideological views and dominate the strategic processes. It may become difficult to introduce a mission acceptable to all stakeholder groups without becoming political. This could occur, for example, where the government is a stakeholder in state-owned industries which are not performing well. Closure of state-owned industries however would lead to mass redundancies and a rise in unemployment.

    The mission statement will lead to a hierarchy of objectives beginning with corporate level objectives and leading down to business and marketing objectives. The mission presents the company's philosophy and direction while the strategic objectives are measurable goals.

1.1.4 Corporate objectives

The marketing planning process begins with the formulation of corporate objectives. Marketing has a role to play in providing analysis that will guide objective setting and later, will help achieve these corporate goals through its own activities. Corporate objectives relate to what the business wants to achieve and tend to cover measurable outcomes such as:

- growth
- financial performance
- innovation
- corporate reputation

The corporate strategy should be employed to meet these objectives. Corporate strategies should in turn direct operational, functional division objectives and their subsequent strategies and tactical plans.

This diagram illustrates the cascading hierarchy of objectives, strategies and tactics.

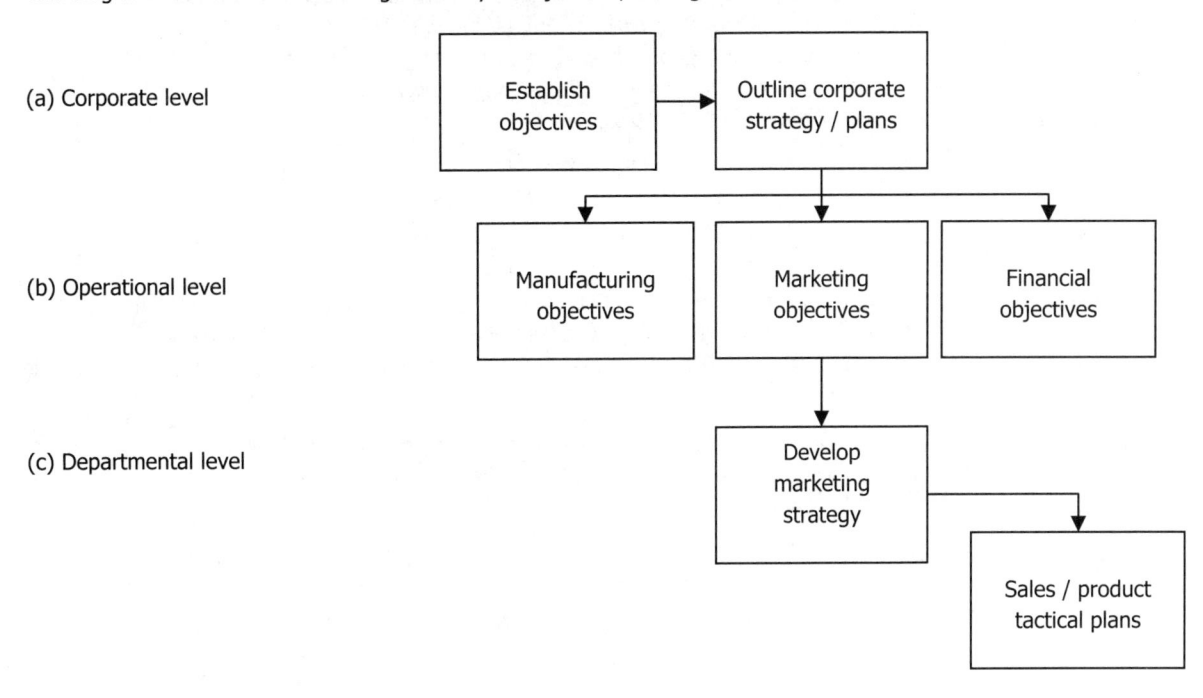

(a) Corporate level: Establish objectives → Outline corporate strategy / plans

(b) Operational level: Manufacturing objectives | Marketing objectives | Financial objectives

(c) Departmental level: Develop marketing strategy → Sales / product tactical plans

MARKETING AT WORK — application

In the earlier example in this chapter, we looked at the mission and visionary values of Sainsbury's. The supermarket specified how customer needs will be met through a quality shopping experience, with healthy and good quality food at reasonable prices. Staff would be inspired to see their company has a vision to grow and improve their offering to customers. Now we can see an example of recent corporate objectives which accompanied that statement:

'Our business priorities

We have identified five areas of focus to take Sainsbury's from recovery to growth:

Great food at fair prices: To build on and stretch the lead in food. By sharing our customers' passion for healthy, safe, fresh and tasty food, Sainsbury's will continue to innovate and provide leadership in delivering quality products at fair prices, sourced with integrity.

Accelerating the growth of complementary non-food ranges: To continue to develop and accelerate the development of non-food ranges following the same principles of quality, value and innovation and to provide a broader shopping experience for customers.

Reaching more customers through additional channels: *To extend the reach of the Sainsbury's brand by opening new convenience stores, developing the on-line home delivery operation and growing Sainsbury's Bank.*

Growing supermarket space: *To expand the company's store estate, actively seeking and developing a pipeline of new stores and extending the largely underdeveloped store portfolio to provide an even better food offer while also growing space for non-food ranges.*

Active property management: *The ownership of property assets provides operational flexibility and the exploitation of potential development opportunities will maximise value.'*

A contrasting organisation, The Cornwall Partnership NHS Trust, defined its corporate objectives to reflect the overall objectives of the NHS going forward. Customer groups have been defined as patients, carers and families and the importance of staff and their development is firmly stated.

'The 2008 / 2009 objectives for the Cornwall Partnership NHS Trust are:

- *To deliver fair, personalised, effective and safe services for service users, their carers and families.*
- *To engage, involve and value our staff and in so doing get the best from them.*
- *To deliver the financial and business targets building sustainability for future years.*
- *To operate robust internal control that demonstrates effective governance.*
- *To work maturely and effectively with our key partners.'*

1.1.5 Business and marketing objectives

Although companies adopting a marketing concept may see their success as based on satisfying consumer needs at a profit, this does not mean that corporate and marketing objectives are one and the same thing. Corporate strategies should cover the whole organisation and not just the marketing function, although marketing does have a significant role to play in aiding their formulation.

The strategic (corporate) objectives will provide an overall guide for managers of each business unit and function. Each functional manager will then have their own objectives with responsibility for meeting them. There must be strong co-ordination between functional departments to ensure goals do not conflict.

Marketing objectives are set in order to guide the marketing strategy. They should refer to the mission statement and corporate goals and objectives and will only be about products and markets. They should be clear statements of where the organisation wants to be in marketing terms, and what it expects to achieve as a result of its planned marketing actions.

Remembering the SMART criteria, examples of marketing objectives might look like this:

'To increase market share from the current X% to Y% by 20XX.'

'To achieve a sales revenue of £X million at a cost of sales not exceeding 80% in 20X1.'

'To increase product awareness in the target market from V% to W% in 20X1.'

Marketing objectives may start with at a broader level and develop into specific objectives for particular markets. They should cover new and existing products or services, and new or existing target markets.

These markets can be defined as following using Ansoff's Matrix:

- Selling existing products to existing markets
- Extending existing products to new markets
- Developing new products for existing markets
- Developing new products for new markets

```
                PRESENT      NEW
                      Products
              ┌─────────────┬─────────────┐
              │   Market    │   Product   │
   PRESENT    │ Penetration │ Development │
              │             │             │
   Markets    ├─────────────┼─────────────┤
              │   Market    │             │
     NEW      │  Extension  │Diversification│
              │             │             │
              └─────────────┴─────────────┘
```

The marketing strategies to achieve the marketing objectives can lead to advertising objectives and advertising strategies, (and objectives relating to other elements of the marketing mix) which form the lowest level of the hierarchy of objectives.

ACTIVITY 2.1 evaluation

Evaluate how your organisation develops objectives.

- Who is responsible for devising objectives?
- What process is used to refine objectives?
- How effective is this?
- Are members of staff aware of the corporate mission and objectives?

2 Influences on the formulation of objectives

Once management has written the mission and vision for the company, they can turn their attention to objectives and strategy. There are many influences, both internal and external, that affect an individual organisation and this becomes very clear when trying to set objectives. Johnson and Scholes (1998-9) have written extensively on this topic and are quoted by Drummond, et al. (2008) and Wilson and Gilligan (2005).

2.1 Four areas of influence

The influences on objectives can be seen in the following diagram.

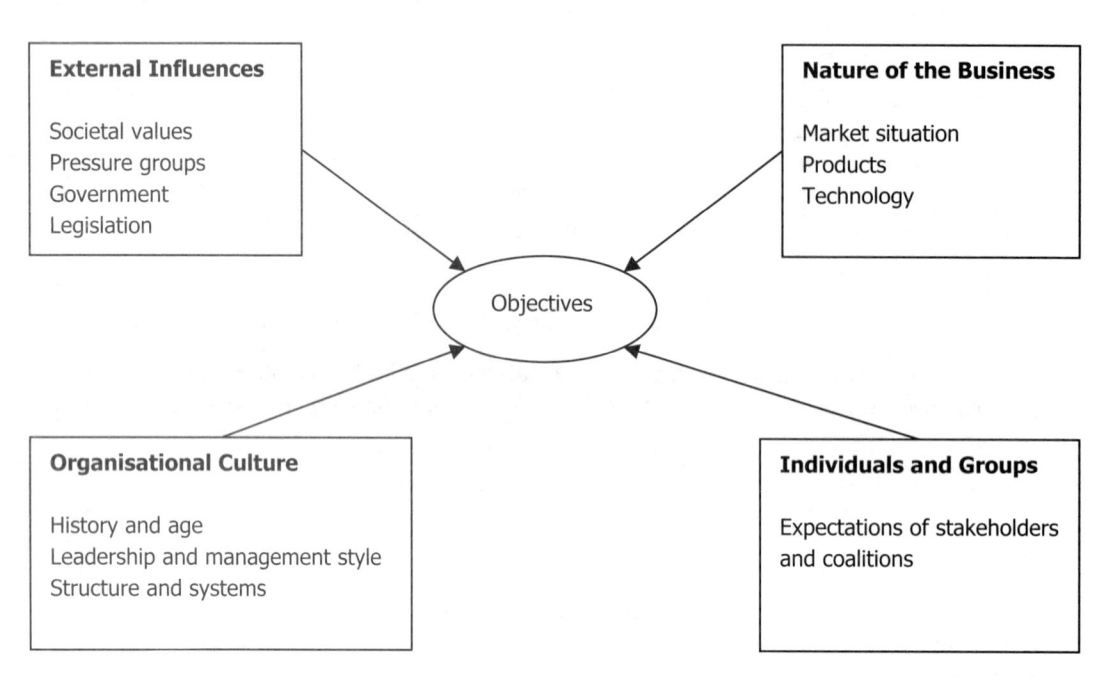

External Influences
- Societal values
- Pressure groups
- Government
- Legislation

Nature of the Business
- Market situation
- Products
- Technology

Organisational Culture
- History and age
- Leadership and management style
- Structure and systems

Individuals and Groups
- Expectations of stakeholders and coalitions

→ Objectives

(Adapted by Wilson and Gilligan (2005) from Johnson and Scholes (1998))

- **Internal influences**

    Cultural values are likely to influence the internal situation of an organisation. It is equally important to understand the broader values of society and the influence of organised groups.

    Individuals influence an organisation. Individuals may share expectations of how the objectives and strategies will be interpreted with their departmental colleagues but there may be alternative individual views or other alliances that develop across the organisational structure. Internal groups and individuals may be influenced by contacts with external stakeholders who have an interest in the company's operation. These could be customers, shareholders, suppliers or unions. However, it is important to note that individuals or groups (internal or external) cannot influence company strategies unless they have an influencing mechanism, eg all of the 69,000 John Lewis staff are partners in the organisation and have a say in the way the company is run through official councils and committees.

    Organisational objectives have a central role in influencing strategy which may be viewed as preordained and unchangeable. Johnson and Scholes (1998) believe objectives should be part of the strategic equation and open to amendment and change as strategies develop.

    Objectives are likely to be the *'wishes of the most dominant coalition'*, probably to be the management team. The dominant group is strongly influenced by their reading of the political situation and may set aside some of their expectations in order to improve the chance of achieving others.

- **External influences**

    The values of society in which the organisation is operating and the behaviour of organised groups are very important factors for a company to consider. This could be in terms of what society will or will not tolerate in terms of business behaviour. Society's concerns over pollution and animal testing certainly led to major changes in the way companies managed their strategies. These days, ethical production of mass-produced clothing and the actions of bankers are topical concerns for society at large. You will already be aware of the massive increase in corporate social responsibility as a marketing topic.

    Objectives and strategy are also affected by the behaviour of organised groups within the organisation. These could be trade unions or trade associations who seek to influence members formally and informally through codes of conduct and norms of behaviour.

- **Nature of the business**: The nature of the business, the market situation faced by the company, the life-cycle stages of products in its portfolio and the types of technology used are also strong influences.
- **Organisational culture**: this relates to the core beliefs held by the company and determines how people within the company behave and respond.

Further work in 1999 by Johnson and Scholes identifies some additional elements of influence on a company's mission and objectives.

- Corporate governance and who the organisation is accountable to (eg regulatory frameworks) can influence overall direction. A regulatory framework can protect the rights of stakeholders and limit management freedom.
- Stakeholders (such as customers, suppliers, shareholders, employees, financiers and the wider social community) may have varying degrees of influence depending on the power they wield. Management could be inclined to further the interests of a group depending on the power they hold.
- Business ethics affects the mission and the objectives for a company. This may relate to corporate social responsibility towards a certain stakeholder group.
- Cultural context – the parts of the mission that are prioritised may relate to the cultural environment surrounding the company. There could be many layers of cultural influence at different levels of the organisation from national cultures down to professional reference groups.

A mission statement and the company's objectives are therefore influenced by a range of internal and external factors, and management must address these interests and demands with careful consideration.

2.2 The resource-based view of the firm

Organisations are only able to operate within the boundaries of the resources that they have available to them (eg human resources, materials, finance, time etc). Objectives are therefore naturally restrained because it is unlikely that the firm will have finite resources. Theoretical arguments surround the concept of the resource-based view of the firm which clearly states that to gain competitive advantage, the organisation must utilise resources which cannot be imitated. If you imagine for a moment that two brand new start-up organisations specialise in manufacturing a new range of flying bicycles. One (Birdiecycle) may have excellent knowledge in terms of expert staff who have devised the most effective product specification. The other firm (ETbikes) may have significantly higher financial support. When devising their objectives, Birdiecycle should focus on their core competence related to their high levels of expertise and technically superior product. ETbikes, on the other hand, would be developing objectives with the knowledge that they may be able to prop up their product and sustain a short-term loss as a result of their large financial resources.

3 The impact of environmental forces

In order to operate effectively, the organisation must understand the impact of the world it operates within. The stages of conducting internal and external analysis have a major effect upon the creation of the organisation's mission and the hierarchy of objectives. The first stage of the auditing process gathers the information and analysis needed for the organisation to identify the key issues that will input into the design of a successful strategy – this is the external analysis. The internal analysis helps the organisation identify the key assets and competences on which the company can build a strategic position. At the Professional Certificate level you will have developed an understanding of what is meant by the marketing environment. Within this section we provide a quick re-cap.

3.1 The macro-environment

The wider **macro**-environment may be analysed using the **PESTEL** mnemonic. The **business environment** comprises all the economic, political, social, cultural, legal, technological and demographic influences acting on the markets within which the organisation operates. It encompasses influences on customers and the behaviour of competitors and suppliers in these markets. All these factors have an impact on the performance of the organisation, but cannot be controlled by management.

'The essence of formulating competitive strategy is relating a company to its environment... Every industry has an underlying structure or set of fundamental economic and technical characteristics... The strategist must learn what makes the environment tick.'

Porter (1996)

The macro-environment may be analysed under the following headings: Political, Technological, Economic, Environmental, Social and Legal (**PESTEL**).

3.1.1 The political environment

An organisation's freedom of action is constrained by what is politically acceptable. **Note** that this is not the same thing as 'legal'.

Changes in society are reflected in the priorities of politicians and governments have many ways of bringing pressure to bear on business. They frequently use such levers as economic power, codes of conduct and statements of policy to set the ground rules for organisational life. The government **controls** much of the economy, being the nation's largest supplier, employer, customer and investor. It also influences the **money supply**, controls the level of **interest rates** and sets **exchange rate** policy.

3.1.2 Political factors

- The possible impact of political change on the organisation
- The likelihood of change taking place and the possible need for contingency plans
- What needs to be done to cope with the change ('scenario planning')

3.1.3 The economic environment

The general state of the economy influences prospects for all businesses. Generally, economic growth produces a benign environment with healthy demand for most goods and services.

Some **economic influences**:

- The rate of inflation
- Unemployment and the availability of manpower
- Interest rates
- The level and type of taxation
- The availability of credit
- Exchange rates

3.1.4 Economic trends – regional, national and international

The **local** economic environment affects wage rates, availability of labour, disposable income of local consumers and the provision of business infrastructure and services.

National economic trends will affect prospects for growth, inflation, unemployment and taxation levels.

World trends have an important influence on the future of any company with plans to trade abroad, whether buying imports or selling as exporters.

During the global recession, from 2009 market speculators regularly plotted signs of decline or recovery on a country by country basis in order to predict the effects on a global scale.

3.1.5 The social environment

Social change involves changes in the nature, attitudes and habits of society.

(a) **Rising standards of living** may result in wider ownership of items such as DVD players, computers, dishwashers, mobile phones, microwave ovens, compact disc players and sailing boats.

(b) **Society's changing attitude to business** tends to increase companies' obligations and responsibilities with respect to environmental protection and ethical conduct.

(c) An increasing proportion of people are employed in clerical, supervisory or management jobs.

3.1.6 Cultural changes

Cultural variables are particularly significant for overseas marketing. **Language differences** have clear marketing implications. For example, brand names have to be translated, often leading to entirely different (and sometimes embarrassing) meanings in the new language.

Cultural differences may affect business in a variety of ways.

- Design of goods
- Trading hours
- Distribution methods
- Business relationships and communication
- Marketing messages
- Product usage or need
- Social responsibilities

3.1.7 Socio-economic groups

Marketing interest stems from the observable fact that members of particular groups have similar lifestyles, beliefs and values which affect their purchasing behaviour. Socio-economic classification involves taking factors such as occupation, education and income into account.

3.1.8 Family

Family background is a very strong influence on purchasing behaviour. Family structure is changing in most of the developed world. There are more single person and single parent households due to the increased divorce rate and population ages. The traditional nuclear family represents a relatively small proportion of all families.

The technological environment

(a) **Types of products and services.** Within consumer markets we have seen the emergence of home computers and internet services.

(b) **The way in which products are made.** Modern automated systems of design and manufacture have revolutionised manufacturing.

(c) **The way in which services are provided.** Call centres and internet trading have expanded widely.

(d) **The way in which markets are identified.** Database systems make it easier to analyse the marketplace. New types of marketing strategy, and new organisational structures, have been developed.

The effects of technological change are wide-ranging.

- Cuts in costs may afford the opportunity to reduce prices.
- The development of better quality products and services provides greater satisfaction.
- Products and services exist that did not exist before.

3.1.9 The ecological (green) environment

Public awareness of the connections between industrial production, mass consumption and environmental damage is higher than it has ever been, with information flooding out through the mass media and sometimes generating profound public reaction. Modern marketing practice needs to reflect awareness of these concerns, and is itself being changed by the issues that they raise.

3.1.10 Green concerns

The modern green movement is animated by concerns over pollution, overpopulation and the effects of massive growth on the finite resources of the earth. Green economists have tried to put together an economics based on alternative ideas.

- Monetary valuation of economic resources
- Promoting the quality of life
- Self-reliance
- Mutual aid
- Personal growth
- Human rights

3.1.11 The impact of green issues on marketing practices

Environmental impacts on business can be direct or indirect:

(a) **Direct**

   (i) Changes affecting costs or resource availability
   (ii) Impact on demand
   (iii) Effect on power balances between competitors in a market

(b) **Indirect**

   Examples are pressure from concerned customers or staff and legislation affecting the business environment.

Sustainability requires that the company only uses resources at a rate which allows them to be replenished, and confines emissions of waste to levels which do not exceed the capacity of the environment to absorb them. **Policies based on sustainability have three aims**.

- To pursue equity in the **distribution** of resources
- To maintain the integrity of the world's **ecosystems**
- To increase the capacity of human populations for **self-reliance**

3.1.12 Green marketing

There are strong reasons for bringing the environment into the business equation. The green consumer is a driving force behind changes in marketing and business practices. Green consumption can be defined as the decisions related to consumer choice which involve environmentally-related beliefs, values and behaviour. There is extensive evidence that this is of growing importance to business, provided by:

- Surveys which indicate increased levels of environmental awareness and concern
- Increasing demand for, and availability of, information on environmental issues
- Value shifts from consumption to conservation
- Effective PR and marketing campaigns by environmental charities and causes

3.1.13 Segmenting the green market

Profiles of green consumers show that the force of green concern varies. Many consumers have not resolved the complex, confusing and often contradictory messages which are being sent out by various interest groups in this area. Broadly, females are more environmentally-aware than males, and families with children are more likely to be concerned about making green consumption choices. The evidence also shows that consumers are becoming both more aware and more sophisticated in their approach.

Marketing diagnostics has developed a typology of green consumers which identifies four main groups.

(a) **Green activists** (5 – 15% of the population) are members or supporters of environmental organisations.

(b) **Green thinkers** (30%, including the activists) seek out green products and services, and look for new ways to care for the environment.

(c) **Green consumer base** (45 – 60%) includes anyone who has changed behaviour in response to green concerns.

(d) **Generally concerned** (90%) claim to be concerned about green issues.

Studies show that consumer behaviour varies in greenness according to the information which is available about the product, the regularity of purchase, the price-sensitivity of the purchase involved, their degree of brand loyalty to existing brands, the availability of substitutes and the credibility of green products.

3.1.14 The legal environment

The legal system may be thought of as part of the political environment. It lays down the framework for business, with rules about business structure and ownership such as the Companies Act. It regulates business relationships with contract law and guarantees individual rights with employment law. There is a wide range of regulations dealing with general business activities such as health and safety regulations, rules about emissions into the environment and planning regulations.

3.2 The micro-environment

An analysis of the **micro**-environment concentrates on **customers** and **competitors**. The micro-environment is also known as the **task** environment. The nature of **competition** is a key element in the environment of commercial organisations.

There are four main issues: identifying the competitors, the strength of the competition, characteristics of the market and the likely strategies and responses of competitors to the organisation's strategies.

3.2.1 Porter's five competitive forces

Porter's five competitive forces influence the state of competition in an industry and its profit potential. In discussing competition, Porter (1996) distinguishes between factors characterising the nature of competition.

(a) **In one industry compared with another** (eg in the chemicals industry compared with the clothing retail industry). Which factors make one industry as a whole potentially more profitable than another?

(b) **Within a particular industry**. These relate to the competitive strategies that individual firms might select.

Five **competitive forces** influence the state of competition in an industry, which collectively determines the profit potential of the industry as a whole.

(a) **The threat of new entrants**

   A new entrant into an industry will bring extra capacity and more competition. The strength of this threat is likely to vary from industry to industry, depending on: the strength of the **barriers to entry** which discourage new entrants, and the likely **response of existing competitors** to the new entrant.

(b) **The threat from substitute products**

   A **substitute product** is a good/service produced by **another industry** which satisfies the **same customer needs**. Substitutes put a lid on what firms in an industry can charge.

(c) **The bargaining power of customers**

   Customers want better quality products and services at a lower price. Satisfying this want might force down the profitability of suppliers in the industry. Customer strength depends upon such factors as how much the customer buys, or how price sensitive he or she happens to be.

(d) **The bargaining power of suppliers**

   Suppliers can exert pressure for higher prices, depending upon such factors as whether there are just **one or two dominant suppliers** to the industry, able to charge monopoly or oligopoly prices. It will also depend on whether the suppliers have **other customers** outside the industry, and do not rely on the industry for the majority of their sales.

(e) **Rivalry amongst current competitors in the industry**

   The **intensity of competitive rivalry** within an industry will affect the profitability of the industry as a whole. Competitive actions might take the form of price competition, advertising battles, sales promotion campaigns, introducing new products for the market, improving after-sales service or providing guarantees or warranties. Intensity of competition is related to three main factors.

   (a) **Whether there are many equally balanced competitors**. Markets involving a large number of firms are likely to be very competitive, but when the industry is dominated by a small number of larger firms, competition is likely to be less intense.

   (b) **The rate of growth in the industry**. Fast growth is likely to benefit a larger number of firms, and so their rivalry will be less intense. Rivalry is intensified where growth is slow or stagnant.

   (c) **Whether fixed costs are high**. If fixed costs are high, and variable costs are a relatively small proportion of the selling price, high volumes are necessary. It is tempting for firms to compete on price, even though this may mean a failure to cover fixed costs and make an adequate return in the longer run.

   Competition may **help the industry to expand**, stimulating demand for new products. On the other hand, demand may be left unchanged, so that individual competitors will simply be spending more money, charging lower prices and making lower profits. The only benefits involve maintaining market share.

3.2.2 Schemes for assessing competitors

Here are five key questions for the assessment of competitors.

1. **Who** are we competing against?
2. What are their **objectives**?
3. What **strategies** are they pursuing, with what success?
4. What **strengths and weaknesses** do they possess?
5. How are they likely to react?

3.2.3 Factors affecting customer behaviour

Consumer behaviour can be defined as the behaviour that consumers display in searching for, purchasing, using, evaluating and disposing of products. It provides the foundation knowledge which guides subsequent marketing strategy.

A number of factors influence the consumer buying process.

- **Cultural factors** – Culture/sub-culture/social class
- **Social factors** – Reference groups/family/roles and status
- **Personal factors** – Age and life-cycle stage/occupation/economic circumstances/lifestyle and personality
- **Psychological factors** – Motivation/learning/perception/beliefs and attitudes

3.2.4 The Buyer

(a) **Cultural factors** exert the broadest and deepest influence on consumer behaviour. The culture in which we live determines our **values**, **beliefs and perceptions**. **Buying behaviour** is also affected by **subculture** and **social class**. Different social classes also display distinct brand preferences in areas such as clothing, decorative products and cars.

(b) A consumer's behaviour is also influenced by **social factors**. People are influenced in their buying by the groups they are members of, called **associate groups**, and by the groups whose behaviour they reject, called **disassociate groups**. Marketers, in planning their target market strategy, should try to identify the groups and the key individuals whose behaviours and lifestyles are followed. For example, football stars are used in advertising to appeal to the male youth market.

(c) A buyer's decisions are also influenced by **personal factors**.

   (i) The **family life cycle model** proposes that as we move through different phases of our lives, we buy different products and services and change our priorities.

   (ii) **Occupation** also influences consumption patterns.

   (iii) A person's **lifestyle** also influences what is deemed important to purchase, where they search for information on those goods and how they make the purchase decision.

(d) Finally **psychological factors** such as motivation, learning, perception, beliefs and attitudes influence the consumer buying process.

Learning objective review

Learning objectives	Covered
1. Understand the different types and levels of objectives set by organisations.	☑ Corporate business and money ☑ Vision and mission ☑ Objectives as part of the planning process
2. Understand and identify the internal and external influences on objectives.	☑ External influences (social groups, pressure groups, government, legislation) ☑ Nature of the business ☑ Organisational culture ☑ Individuals and groups
3. Evaluate the impact of internal and external environmental forces on objectives.	☑ Macro-environment ☑ Micro-environment

Quick quiz

1. Which of the following is not a term used to describe the level of support for a mission statement.

    (a) Faint support
    (b) Competent support
    (c) Dissipated support

2. Put the following stages of the marketing planning process into the correct order.

    (a) SWOT analysis
    (b) Monitoring and control
    (c) Marketing objectives
    (d) Marketing audit
    (e) Business objectives
    (f) Corporate objectives
    (g) Marketing strategies
    (h) Implementation
    (i) Marketing tactics

3. How does the political environment impact marketing strategy?

4. What is the resource-based view and how does this impact marketing planning?

5. What key questions might you ask when assessing competitors?

Activity debrief

Worksheet activity 2.1

You will find that culturally organisations differ considerably in their objective setting behaviour. Top level directors may set required performance levels and objectives. Financial departments may then devise departmental objectives.

Some handle them in a highly autocratic manner while others use a more collaborative approach.

Identifying whether the objectives were effective involves more than simply stating whether or not they were achieved in many cases. How effectively individual teams and departments worked together in order to achieve objectives is just as important to the long-term success of the organisation.

Quiz answers

1. (b). Competent support is not a term. See section 1.1.3.
2. (f), (d), (a), (e), (c), (g), (i), (h), (b).
3. Issues such as what is politically acceptable will determine strategies, codes of conduct at government and industry levels may change. The political impact on the economy will also require considering during marketing planning.
4. Organisations compete according to the resources at their disposal. Resources require considering when planning what is a possible marketing strategy.
5.
   - (i) Who are we competing against?
   - (ii) What are their objectives?
   - (iii) What strategies are they pursuing, with what success?
   - (iv) Success?
   - (v) How are they likely to react?

References

BT, (2009). *'Our Values'*. [Online] Copyright 2009. Available at: http://www.btplc.com/Thegroup/Ourcompany/Companyprofile/Ourvalues/index.htm [Accessed 01 April 2009].

Cornwall NHS Trust, (2009). *'Corporate Objectives'*. [Online] Copyright 2008. Available at: http://www.cornwall.nhs.uk/CornwallPartnershipTrust/TheTrust/CorporateObjectives.aspx [Accessed 03 April 2009].

Dibb, S. & Simkin, L., (2008) Marketing Planning – A Workbook for Marketing Managers. Cengage Learning, London.

Drummond, G., Ensor, J. & Ashford, R.,(2008) Strategic Marketing Planning & Control. (3rd ed.), Butterworth-Heinemann, Oxford.

Friend, G. & Zehle, S.,(2004) The Economist Guide to Business Planning. The Economist in assoc. with Profile Books, London.

John Lewis, (2009). *'About Us'*. [Online] Copyright 2009. Available at: http://www.johnlewispartnership.co.uk/ [Accessed 02 April 2009].

Kotler, P. Armstrong, G. Wong, V. & Saunders, J.,(2008) Principles of Marketing. (5th European ed.), Pearson Education, Harlow.

Lancaster, G. Massingham, L. & Ashford, R.,(2002) Essentials of Marketing. (4th ed.), McGraw-Hill Education, Maidenhead.

Lindstrom, M., (2007). *'Vision statements must be more than just words'*. [Online] Copyright 2007. Available at: http://www.brandrepublic.asia/Media/Opinionarticle/2008_08/Vision-statements-must-be-more-than-just-words/7094 [Accessed 02 April 2009].

McDonald, M., (2007) *'Marketing Plans – How to Prepare Them, How to Use Them'*. (6th ed.), Butterworth-Heinemann, Oxford.

McMillan, A., (2009). *'Mission-Vision Statements'*. [Online] Copyright 2009. Available at: http://www.enotes.com/management-encyclopedia/mission-vision-statements [Accessed 02 April 2009].

Sainsbury's, (2009). *'Company Overview'*. [Online] Copyright 2009. Available at: http://www.j-sainsbury.co.uk/index.asp?pageid=12 [Accessed 03 April 2009].

The Times, (1995-2009). *'Long Term Maintenance of a Classic Brand Name Nestle'*. [Online] Copyright 1995-2009. Available at: http://www.thetimes100.co.uk/case-study--long-term-maintenance-classic-brand-name--7-92-4.php [Accessed 03 April 2009].

University of Surrey, (2009). *'SMART Examples'*. [Online] Copyright 2009. Available at: http://portal.surrey.ac.uk/pls/portal/docs/PAGE/HUMANRESOURCES/STRUCTURE/STAFFDEVELOPMENT/SDR/SMART%20EXAMPLES.DOC [Accessed 02 April 2009].

USSS, (2008). *'Mission Statement'*. [Online] Copyright 2008. Available at: http://www.ustreas.gov/usss/mission.shtml [Accessed 02 April 2009].

Wilson, R. M. S. & Gilligan, C, (2005) *'Strategic Marketing Management: Planning, Implementation & Control'*. (3rd ed.), Butterworth-Heinemann, Oxford.

Winnett, R. & Johnson, S. (2009). *'Jobs for British protestors threaten strike against power supplies'*. [Online] Updated 02 Feb 2009. Available at http://www.telegraph.co.uk/news/newstopics/politics/4424912/Protesters-threaten-co-ordinated-national-strike-as-industrial-action-escalates.html [Accessed 04 April 2009].

Chapter 3
Environmental drivers of organisational change

Topic list

1. Innovation
2. Evolving consumer behaviour
3. Globalisation
4. Ethical consumption and corporate social responsibility
5. Stakeholder relations
6. Sustainable relationship management

Introduction

The planning process provides us with clear objectives at different levels of the organisation, for both short-term goals and longer-term aims to build relationships with our target customers. The marketing environment is a constantly changing element and it is important to understand the external drivers of change that will affect our organisations' internal and external environment. These drivers impact upon the development of marketing strategy in the planning process.

This chapter considers a range of environmental drivers and shows how they impact the planning process.

Syllabus-linked learning objective

By the end of the chapter you will be able to:

Learning objectives	Syllabus link
1. Appreciate and understand the key environmental drivers of organisational change: innovation; evolving consumer behaviour; globalisation; ethical consumption and corporate social responsibility; sustainability relationship management; and stakeholder relations.	1.5

1 Innovation

Marketers naturally need to keep abreast of trends in their marketplace. Appropriate marketing strategies can only be planned if the reality of the marketing environment is well understood. To misunderstand the new developments occurring in industries would lead to ineffective future strategies. In this scenario it would be impossible to correctly segment and target appropriate groups of consumers with appropriate offerings. Environmental drivers are likely to have an impact on customers and their behaviour and so companies should be aware of potential market forces and plan accordingly. Many of these factors cannot be controlled by companies, but they can control how they handle them and react to these issues.

So, how do we know what is driving organisational change? There are many factors which may cause change, including the challenges of growth particularly globally, changes in strategy, technological changes, competitive pressures, customer pressure including shifts in their make-up and behaviour, and government legislation and initiatives. Marketers must monitor current and predicted trends and conduct regular environmental scanning. This should be conducted using a wide range of secondary sources, databases and primary research, as well as consulting other functional departments. Environmental scanning can be focused along the lines of the PEST model (or its extended variations ie SLEPT, PESTLE and STEEPLE) looking at Political, Economic, Social and Technological factors. The analysis of these trends can show marketers what the future environment may look like and what future conditions may be like. Companies that do not assess their environment regularly or effectively, and indeed do not react quickly, could find themselves becoming market followers rather than market leaders.

The Professional Certificate unit Assessing the Marketing Environment covers this aspect in detail.

MARKETING AT WORK

application

The Futures Company (incorporating The Henley Centre) is a consultancy that specialises in identifying global trends and futures across a wide range of industries. A recent major study focused on the 'New Green Consumer' and created new segmentation criteria on the UK population to help companies understand the impact of rapidly changing consumer behaviour.

The consultancy identified the impact of climate change would be the biggest challenge facing governments and businesses for decades. Analysts also realised that the attitudes and expectations of consumers was moving at a faster pace than businesses and other organisations could adapt to. The research showed that more than three-quarters of the British population had changed their behaviour as a result of environmental issues.

Research indicates (CIPD, 2007) that organisations are undergoing major change around once every three years, with smaller changes happening continuously. CIPD (2007) research found that this pace of change will not slow down, and clearly economic factors have had a major impact on businesses since this time.

1.1 The Importance of innovation

KEY CONCEPT — concept 30%

Innovation can be described as the successful exploitation of new ideas and is recognised as a way for companies to achieve market leadership and sustained competitive advantage. Innovation can be incremental when an idea is adapted or modified, or radical when a completely new idea is coined.

So why is innovation so important? Companies are facing a faster change of pace in their environments. Technological processes are constantly adapting, leading to new product variations coming to market, eg Apple. Globalisation and climate change are other factors that can force companies to consider the need to innovate. Economic factors can lead governments to encourage innovation in their workforce in order to compete globally and survive against lower-cost manufacturing and service bases. Innovation can also be found in the way we understand consumers. Research and data collection methods have been transformed by developments in technology. The growth and use of the internet, particularly broadband, as well as advancements in customer databases and neurological techniques has led to innovation in research methods and data analysis that has transformed the level of understanding marketers have about their target markets. This helps them to respond to changing customer needs faster and ahead of the competition. Superior databases help us keep track of customer issues, maintain connections, improve service and loyalty, and ultimately raise retention levels. Intranets have transformed the way we hold and share data across global organisations thereby harnessing tacit knowledge and improving internal marketing and communications.

Innovation in product development can break down into three categories:

- **New products** – These are innovative products that are new to the customer and provide alternatives to existing products which serve existing markets.
- **Replacement products** – These are not totally innovative but provide different attributes to those currently on offer.
- **Imitative products** – These are new to a company but established in the marketplace. They are also known as 'me too' products. If a company has good financial resources and marketing expertise, being the innovator in the market can reap rewards. Other companies may prefer to benefit when the market is established and can promote different benefits to the consumer which may lead them to perceive the imitator as a new product.

As product life cycles shorten, global competition increases and the pace of technological change shows no sign of slowing down, innovation becomes more important as a strategy.

We will return to consider innovation in more detail in Chapter 6.

2 Evolving consumer behaviour

Consumer behaviour is affected by a broad range of demographic factors as well as our individual experiences, motivations, beliefs and attitudes which impact upon the way we react to organisations' marketing activities. Some factors are shifting over time, such as the ageing population of many Western countries, and others may be much more immediate, eg consumers' perceptions of affordability.

2.1 Demographics

The age of consumers is considered to be a strong indicator of behaviour. Life expectancy has increased in many countries and older people can now expect to be more active and healthier due to advances in medical care and provision. The important target segment of Baby Boomers (within Western markets), those born between 1946 and 1964, are now retiring and creating a new lucrative market. They are likely to be active in the housing market, remodelling their homes, and even setting up new homes as divorce rates amongst older people climb. Financial services may be important as they plan their savings and investments. Enjoying life is also key and they are big spenders on travel, entertainment, eating out, health and fitness.

The younger segment known as Generation X (born between 1965 and 1976) have a more cautious attitude to life than their parents born in the sexual revolution! They have grown up in times of recession, facing the threat of AIDS, and are likely to have had parents who divorced or seen their mothers working away from the home, leaving them to become the first generation of 'latchkey' children. Generation X cares about the environment and are more likely to respond to socially responsible companies. Although they want to succeed in life, family comes first and a work/life balance is eagerly sought.

Generation Y, born between 1977 and 1994, are likely to be viewed as the digital revolution generation. They have grown up with computers, digital and internet technology and cannot remember a time without the internet and mobile phones!

Consumers are also affected by personal and psychological influences. These are perceptions, motivations, attitudes, social influences, roles, family, culture, the economic situation, marketing efforts and social class. Social class, particularly in the UK, was once a key denominator of consumer behaviour and used religiously in segmentations by marketers. It is no longer seen as such an accurate predictor of behaviour. These days, aspirations and lifestyles are viewed as more important factors. Marketers still use newspaper readership to break down consumer segments but even this can be misleading.

MARKETING AT WORK — application

BBC News (2007) were interested to assess UK consumers' views on what social class they perceived themselves to be. Interestingly, in the British Social Attitudes Survey conducted by the National Centre for Social Research, 57% of Britons considered themselves to be working class. Based on social classification data from the same time period, only 31% of Britons could be considered to have 'blue collar' jobs and be classified as working class.

During the broadcast, sociologist, Wendy Bottero, said, *"It is not uncommon for people to put themselves in a class category that an official observer might not. This is because people define class by many things, like status and social origins, not just jobs and education. Socially and morally, it is a heavily-laden term."*

2.2 Culture

Culture is about beliefs and values that are passed on from generation to generation. These values, however, can change which will lead to a change in culture. Kotler (2008) says that culture is the most fundamental determinant of wants and behaviour.

Our social values are changing. Lancaster (2008) says that values of health, economic security and stable relationships are returning us to the values of the pre-1960s. We are also increasingly drawn to developing strong views towards ecological and environmental issues. Consumers may want to account for their carbon footprint and find ways to negate the effect of business and marketing practice. In recent years, consumers have displayed a cavalier approach to credit which may now begin to change. The importance of health, particularly because of increasing life expectancy and the prevalence of obesity, means consumers are concerned about taking care of themselves and their families. Lancaster (2008) highlights the changing cultural values in the young. They may question materialism and its values. They have little respect for authority and the law. They also believe in their right to be confrontational and have a desire for innovation and change.

Sub-cultures are also important to assess, eg the cultural differences of ethnic populations. Understanding these differences enables marketers to meet their specific needs, tastes, and language in the marketing mix.

2.3 'Demanding' consumers

There has been a shift in behaviour with consumers becoming much more demanding in terms of their expectations and perceptions of the 'bundle of benefits' provided by an organisation, whether for a business-to-business or business-to-consumer scenario. The marketing planning process is an opportunity to keep the plan relevant for consumers' evolving and demanding behaviour.

Dibb and Simkin (2008) highlight a number of factors that can be considered when reviewing customer needs:

- What benefits are they seeking from products or services?
- Are they looking for tangible or intangible benefits?
- Do they have any other related needs which may affect the purchasing decision?
- How important are issues like quality, delivery, service, price, product range, innovation, brand reputation and the influence of promotional activity?
- How do they search for information on the product or service?
- What is the impact of their previous experiences?
- How do they identify and select from the competitive set?
- Who else influences the decision-making process?
- What are their key customer values – the factors they expect and consider to be important?

Another impact on consumer behaviour is affordability. The credit crunch has altered what consumers buy, the price they consider appropriate and the impact of promotional offers. Some wealthy shoppers have been consuming 'inconspicuously' via internet shopping or using discreet packaging in boutiques. Second-hand purchasing may also increase.

The consumer voice has never been stronger with the accessibility of public forums to express post-purchase dissonance. Customer care must be an important focus for corporate objectives. Consumer rights have increased in recent years and are generally accepted to follow these principles: the right to safety, to be informed, to choose, to be heard, the right to privacy and the right to a clean, healthy environment. The consumer's ultimate right is not to buy the product which an organisation with the aim of increasing loyalty and retention would wish to avoid.

Dibb & Simkin (2008) Chapter 5 and Lancaster, et al. (2002) Chapter 3 cover customers and consumer behaviour in more detail."

3 Globalisation

The marketing environment is dynamic and constantly changing. Understanding the forces impacting upon our domestic markets is challenge enough, but with global markets, this is magnified. Organisations will face both **controllable** and **uncontrollable** elements. Controllable elements of the marketing mix may need to be adapted to different environments (and include things that the marketer is responsible for such as the marketing mix). Uncontrollable elements may vary on a country by country basis. These could include aspects such as the economic environment (unemployment or consumer confidence), new technologies or competitors, government regulations and changing consumer preferences. Natural and man-made disasters can also cause an enormous impact. All these aspects can impact on existing plans and strategies.

Countries are classified by the type of economic market they currently fall into. Over time, this classification may change. It may be difficult to classify a nation especially if development and change is rapid.

The types of economic market across the globe are broken down as follows:

- **Subsistence economies**: These are nations that are dependent on primitive agriculture with limited infrastructure and high dependence on foreign aid, eg most of Africa and parts of Asia.
- **Developing countries**: These countries have developing infrastructure and industrialisation. They are heavily reliant on raw material exports and often based on extractive industries, eg Nigeria, Mexico and parts of the Middle East.

- **Industrialising countries**: These countries are likely to be enjoying a more open-market economy. There may be capital investment from outside countries. Production may be switching from agricultural industries to more complex sectors. Examples include Brazil and some other South American countries, Poland and Greece.
- **Industrialised countries**: Examples include the major Western industrial countries of Europe, North America and Japan.

The marketing of goods and services across national borders is becoming easier. However, when organisations are looking for markets to enter, they should consider market accessibility and tariff and non-tariff barriers to trade. Tariffs are taxes on products crossing a frontier. These are set up to protect local industry from overseas competition. The World Trade Organisation provides a worldwide forum for discussion in an attempt to avoid tariffs. Non-tariff barriers are other forms of government action to restrict imports, eg quotas. These are specific limits, by volume or value, on the amount of goods exported to specific markets and may be applied to a nation or a group of nations. Other barriers may be exchange rate policies, customs procedures, administrative and technical regulations, geographic and climate barriers.

Additionally, organisations must appreciate the differences between countries in relation to social and marketing practices, political and commercial institutions and language. A product that succeeds in one country may fail in another even if they seem similar in shared customs, language and lifestyles. Even in one country, regional variations on marketing strategies may be required. Customs, tastes, likes and dislikes can be very different.

Once the market has been chosen, the method of entry has to be chosen from indirect export through to export houses, international trading companies, customers' UK buying offices or co-operative exporting. Direct export can be achieved through selling direct, trading companies, agents, distributors, branch offices or marketing subsidiaries.

3.1 Multinationals

Multinational organisations with bases in several countries have a global outlook. They may have their origins in a particular country but their operations span the globe. Manufacturing may be in a number of countries and goods are sold worldwide. There may be influence or control of the company's marketing activities from outside the country in which it is selling or producing.

Lancaster, et al. (2008) highlight a number of advantages for multinationals:

- **Programme transfers**: Multinationals can draw upon strategies, products, advertising campaigns, sales practices and promotional ideas that have been tested in comparable markets.
- **Systems transfer**: The successful implementation of systems can be rolled out to new markets, such as planning, budgeting, new product introduction and other processes and software packages.
- **People transfer**: Skilled members of staff can be deployed across national boundaries. Many multinationals introduce successor strategies (the future of senior management) and expect staff to work across functions, cultures and geographic borders during their apprenticeship.
- **Scale economies in manufacturing**: Components manufactured on scale-efficient plants in different countries can be brought together into the finalised product.
- **Economies of centralisation of functional activities**: Activities by functional teams can be concentrated on single locations in order to develop greater competence and reduce costs, eg marketing or the market research department. A disadvantage is that they may not appreciate the complexities of distant markets and may not design appropriate strategies or projects for them. This is particularly true as multinationals cut budgets for foreign travel.
- **Resource utilisation**: The globe can be scanned to identify sources of manpower, money and materials so the organisation can compete effectively in world markets.
- **Global strategy**: The world can be scanned for markets that provide opportunities to apply the company's skills, match markets with resources, exploit opportunities, and create and shift resources to tap identified opportunities.

3.2 Marketing products globally

Economies of scale may be possible if companies could market standard products globally. Unfortunately, in practice, markets often require legal, technical or climatic modifications. Local tastes and culture may also influence product changes.

Keegan developed a useful framework for international marketing strategies (1969, quoted by Lancaster, et al. 2008, p. 438):

- **Straight extension**: The product takes the same form and communications as in the domestic market. No additional manufacturing or marketing costs are required.
- **Communications adaptation**: The promotional theme is modified but the product remains unchanged. Major manufacturing costs are not incurred.
- **Product adaptation**: The product is modified but the communications theme is retained.
- **Dual adaptation**: Both the product and communications are modified to meet the needs of specific markets.

The following diagram summarises this framework.

		Products		
		No change	Adapted	New product
Marketing Communications	No change	Straight extension	Product adaptation	
	Adapt	Communication adaptation	Dual adaptation	Product invention

Once product decisions have been made, pricing strategies can be fixed. These will depend on the needs and requirements of the market. They could be similar to the price paid in the domestic market. Terms of payment on how the goods are sold to the export market could also help determine the price. Currency issues are also a factor.

Globalisation is set to continue as we see faster communications, and better transportation and financial flows. Competition is intense. Globalisation is important to governments and economies so measures are likely to be introduced to encourage more activity. The collapse of communism and the rise of Eastern Europe has also brought new opportunities. Countries like Singapore, Malaysia and South Korea are becoming industrialised and will see new competitors bringing technological capabilities as well as lower labour costs to global markets. Despite the rise of the anti-globalisation movement, bank loan problems and low-paid sweat shop workers, the process of globalisation is progressing at a rapid pace.

Lancaster, et al. Chapter 14 covers globalisation in detail.

4 Ethical consumption and corporate social responsibility

Marketers must strike a balance between satisfying customer needs and wants profitably and societal welfare. Not all products marketed to consumers are beneficial to society or good for us (eg tobacco, alcohol, high fat and sugar foods). Food manufacturers and supermarkets are encouraged by the Food Standards Agency in the UK to sign up to traffic light labelling to highlight foods that are high in saturated fats, salts or sugars. This initiative aims to halt the rise in obesity, particularly amongst children, but marketers could stop manufacturing and promoting the unhealthy product to consumers in the first place. Smoking is now proven to be bad for our health and there are restrictions on advertising practice. However, there are many people who still want to smoke and cigarette companies want to be profitable.

It is clear that certain marketing practices are damaging to individual consumers, society as a whole, and other organisations. There is increasing interest from consumers and governments in the protection of the environment and consumers against marketing malpractice and dangerous goods.

MARKETING AT WORK

application

In 2009, news headlines revealed contamination in baby milk products which led to the death of six babies and severe sickness and organ failure in 300,000 others in China. Initially, the problem was thought to be down to a freak contamination at the manufacturing plant but the truth was more sinister.

A Beijing court pronounced a death sentence and a life sentence on the two siblings from the Sanlu Group who had produced and sold milk products containing the chemical melamine. They were convicted of endangering public safety.

Melamine is commonly used in coatings and laminates, wood adhesives, fabric coatings, ceiling tiles and flame retardants. Some Chinese dairy plants added the chemical to milk products so they would appear to have a higher protein level. Victims of tainted baby formula have been offered compensation by the 22 Chinese dairy producers that made the milk but this was little recompense when faced with the death or serious illness of their child.

Adapted from CNN (2009)

4.1 Societal marketing

As companies try to produce recyclable products, improve packaging and reduce pollution, there are many calls from theorists for a 'societal' based view of marketing. This moves from our traditional concept of providing products that satisfy consumer needs efficiently and profitably to one where marketing is considered as a force that reflects and influences social views. Marketers would therefore have to consider the wider social implications of their products and marketing activities. They should try to promote the welfare of society such as reducing poverty, improving education, providing access to appropriate drugs, improving levels of health and activity, etc. It is a difficult task to find a balance between social concerns and commercial enterprise but many marketers are now considering the social consequences and implications of their actions.

ACTIVITY 3.1

application

The CIM has looked at societal marketing as part of its 'Shape the Agenda' research programme. Look at the range of articles and reports available on the CIM web site within the 'Knowledge Hub' area.

An organisation can adopt one of four types of strategy for dealing with social responsibility issues:

(a) **Proactive strategy**: A proactive strategy implies taking action before there is any outside pressure to do so and without the need for government or other regulatory intervention. A company which discovers a fault in a product and recalls the product without being forced to, before any injury or damage is caused, acts in a proactive way.

(b) **Reactive strategy**: A reactive strategy involves allowing a situation to continue unresolved until the public, government or consumer groups find out about it. The company might already know about the problem. When challenged, it will deny responsibility, while at the same time attempting to resolve the problem. In this way, it seeks to minimise any detrimental impact.

(c) **Defensive strategy**: A defensive strategy involves minimising or attempting to avoid additional obligations arising from a particular problem. There are several defence tactics:

   (i) Legal manoeuvring
   (ii) Obtaining support from trade unions
   (iii) Lobbying government

(d) Adopting an **accommodation strategy**: An accommodation strategy involves acknowledging responsibility for actions, probably when one of the following circumstances pertain.

   (i) There is encouragement from special interest groups
   (ii) There is a perception that a failure to act will result in government intervention.

The essence of the strategy is action to forestall more harmful pressure. This approach sits somewhere between a proactive and a reactive strategy.

4.2 Marketing – as the 'big bad wolf'

Another criticism of marketing is that it creates materialism and that needs and wants are created in consumes that otherwise would not have existed. Advertising is often blamed for this factor. Theorists and commentators are divided on whether this is actually the case. Some believe our wants are about satisfying an inner psychological need and others that a rise in living standards leads to a rise in spending. Lancaster, et al. (2008) highlighted a trend towards more basic values and social commitment but there is still a marked infatuation with material things, especially in the young.

Marketing is also said to drive higher prices. This can be due to high costs of distribution perhaps through the number of intermediaries. They may be inefficient, or provide unnecessary or duplicated services (the value chain can help evaluate this). Intermediaries may also mark-up prices beyond the value of the services offered. Supermarkets have often been criticised for the cost of goods. They say they need to pay for the additional services required by customers, such as better opening hours, and that profit margins are not high. Some products are viewed as excessively marked-up. Critics cite cases such as the pharmaceutical or perfume industries but marketers say the costs must cover the lengthy production and research time to bring these to market and protect them from competition.

High advertising and promotion costs are also criticised for pushing up prices. Promotion and packaging can amount to 40% of the manufacturer's price to the retailer. Critics say this does not add functional value to the product. Marketers say that advertising adds value, informing the customer about the product and branding gives assurances of the quality. Consumers are also willing to pay more for products that provide additional psychological benefits, eg makes them feel wealthy, etc.

Unfortunately deceptive practices in marketing departments do exist. These include deceptive pricing, promotion and packaging. This could be if a company falsely advertises a discount from a retail price or misrepresents a product's features or performance. Another tactic is to 'bait and switch' where the customer is drawn into the store with a promotion that is then 'out of stock' and the customer is then sold a higher ticket item by the sales staff. Other problems can be exaggerating the package contents through pack design, not filling the package to the top, misleading labelling or describing the size in misleading terms. Legislation and consumer practice have been brought in to protect consumers but ultimately if the customer feels deceived, they will switch, leading to the company losing customers and probably receiving negative word-of-mouth communications.

High pressure selling happens in categories such as motors, insurance and double glazing. Salespeople working on commission are reluctant to leave the customer's home until a deal has been forced through. This can be particularly distressing for older people. This type of situation can only be used for one-time selling situations for short-term gain, eg replacing the windows in a house as the customer is unlikely to return. This author had to threaten to call the police before one double glazing representative agreed to leave the property after two hours of aggressive sales techniques.

Shoddy, harmful or unsafe products may demonstrate poor product quality or function. Services may not be performed well or products may deliver little benefit or be harmful as in the case above. Fast food is now included in this category as restaurants sell fat laden options (although McDonalds has been conducting a vigorous campaign to promote its healthier salad range).

Manufacturers are often accused of developing products with planned obsolescence, where they plan products to become obsolete before they need replacement. Consumers often feel modern washing machines are designed to have a shelf life that takes them just out of the guarantee period. Other manufacturers change styles or bring in new features to encourage purchase of the newer model, eg tent manufacturers change the colours of their stock each season even though the models are very similar; tent suppliers then have to buy in the new range and accessories and discount last year's stock. Companies should not want their products to break down early as customers will not repurchase, but they do want to encourage upgrading so products meet or exceed customer expectations.

Some companies are accused of providing a poor service to disadvantaged consumers, particularly major supermarkets. Community stores are shutting or being forced to charge higher prices to survive but large grocery stores are not necessarily setting-up shop in poorer neighbourhoods, in fact in the UK it is reported that some supermarkets will not deliver to certain housing estates (Grant, 2009b)! This makes it difficult for those without a car or good access to facilities to buy fresh food at cheaper prices. The use of geodemographic systems such as ACORN and MOSAIC also make it likely that poorer segments are not targeted, unless it is for products such as consolidation loans, etc.

4.3 Environmentalism

Environmentalism refers to consumers' concern with marketing's effects on the environment and the associated cost of serving consumer needs and wants. Environmentalists want people and organisations to care more for their surroundings and protect life quality. This movement has progressed from campaigning (eg Greenpeace) about the damage to the ecosystem and health problems, to the introduction of government legislation to protect the environment against industrial practices. Now companies are accepting responsibility for doing no harm to the environment.

Environmental sustainability is a management approach that involves developing strategies that sustain the environment and produce company profits. There is a difference between those companies that do what they have to do to stay within the confines of current legislation and those that do more because it's the right thing to do. Companies can also think through the whole product life cycle and consider their products' impacts in manufacturing and reuse / recycling afterwards. This is called **product stewardship**. Companies may also develop environmental strategies where they can develop new technologies that limit use of energy and plastics.

A sustainability vision serves as a guide for the future and shows how products, services, processes and policies must evolve and what new technologies must be developed to get there. The sustainable sourcing of materials is currently in the spotlight.

Grant (2009b) notes, 'The protests over palm oil, biofuels and water [consumption] is the new child labour'.

Globalisation has seen international trade barriers come down and global markets expand, so environmental issues will start to have more effect on international trade. More countries are developing environmental policies but it is still a difficult task for international companies to develop standard environmental practices as there are such varying standards at this point in time.

Consumers are yet to appreciate the cost of a sustainable vision. A survey in 2009 by Gyro International discovered that only 28% of UK consumers are willing to pay a premium for environmentally friendly products and services. Thirty per cent said they would pay a premium for 'green goods' given the current economic climate and 32% said they wouldn't. Grant (2009b) suggests an educative approach to change the market. When consumers see the benefits to the environment and their own health, the premium no longer feels like paying extra.

ACTIVITY 3.2 — application

Think about your own organisation. How much consideration of green marketing is evident within the marketing strategies employed?

4.4 Enlightened marketing

KEY CONCEPT — concept

Enlightened marketing

'Strategic marketers understand that it is changing behaviours and influencing customer choice that are the keys to successful marketing – not finding ways of persuading customers to consume more, as it is sometimes supposed, or trying to create a need or a want for a particular product or service.'

CIM Shape the Agenda 2009

Enlightened marketing consists of five principles and it is a marketing philosophy to support the best long-run performance of the marketing system:

(a) **Consumer-oriented marketing**: The company views and organises marketing activities from the consumer's point of view. It will satisfy the needs of defined group of customers.

(b) **Customer value marketing**: Marketers should put resources into value-building marketing investments. They should avoid those actions that only raise sales in the short-term but add less value. Consumers want to see real improvements in the product quality, features or convenience. The organisation seeks long-run consumer loyalty and relationships. By creating value, it is possible to capture value from consumers in return.

(c) **Innovative marketing**: Organisations seek real product and marketing improvements. Companies that ignore new or better ways to conduct their business will lose out to those that can harness new opportunities.

(d) **Sense-of-mission marketing**: The corporate mission is defined in broad social terms rather than narrow product terms. This gives employees a sense of direction and a feel good factor.

(e) **Societal marketing**: Marketing decisions are based on consumers' wants and long-run needs, the company's requirements and also society's long-run interests. Neglecting consumers and society's long-term interests provides a disservice to consumers and society. Marketers have to weigh-up the differences between what consumers want and what is good for them and society. They should be aware of these inconsistencies and try to establish best practice in the industry to avoid further government legislation and pressures.

Corporate responsibility is now becoming part of normal strategic planning within companies. By embracing ethical responsibilities and taking a long-term societal approach to business, firms can help raise the reputation of marketing and distance it from suspicions by certain segments that it is the 'big bad wolf'. Consumer understanding can also lead to positive social change and support companies to achieve economic success.

MARKETING AT WORK — application

Proctor & Gamble's launch of a new laundry detergent under the Ariel brand name, designed to wash clothes at 30°C, formed part of a 'Turn to 30' campaign. The advertising was designed to educate consumers about the need to reduce energy consumption as well as reassuring them that the product could still work effectively at this low temperature.

Before launch, the company ensured they understood the barriers to behavioural change and what motivators would encourage it. The campaign promoted the benefits of the new 'cool cleaning' technologies and shifts in green behaviour. The company proved to its customers that the campaign was sincere and based on facts.

Since this campaign began, more than 1m households in the UK started washing at the new lower temperature generating 40% in energy savings. Eighty-nine per cent of customers said in research that they would continue to buy the detergent and stick to 30°.

The key link between social and commercial marketing, according to CIM (2009), is the emphasis on relationship marketing. Change, brand building, competitive advantage and profitable growth cannot be achieved unless marketers build long-term, mutually trusting relationships with their customer base.

Kotler et al. (2008) Chapter 2 looks at the concepts of relationships and would be useful for you to read.

5 Stakeholder relations

Stakeholders are those who can affect (or be affected) by a business. External stakeholders could be lenders, customers, suppliers, the government and society at large. Internal stakeholders have a direct interest in the business as shareholders, owners, managers and employees. Stakeholders may have conflicting interests and a company may need to order their needs based on whose interests matter most.

The following diagram details the range of stakeholder relationships an organisation must manage and the type of power and influence they hold (Friend and Zehle, 2004).

Stakeholder	Expectation and objectives	Power and influence
Shareholders	Share price growth and dividends	Appoint board
Lenders	Interest to be repaid, maintain credit ratings, risk averse	Can enforce loan covenants
Directors and managers	Success on CV, salary, share options, pensions, job satisfaction	Make most decisions, have detailed information
Staff and unions	Salary, job security, job satisfaction, flexible working	Customer experience, strike, staff turnover
Suppliers	Long-term orders, payment	Pricing, quality
Customers	Reliable supply of goods / services	Source of revenue
Community	Environment, local impact, local jobs	Indirect, local planning, opinion leaders
Government	Operate legally, tax receipts, jobs	Regulation, subsidies, taxation, planning

Kotler, et al. (2008) examined stakeholders in terms of types of public. These are groups with an actual or potential interest in, or an impact upon, an organisation's ability to achieve its objectives.

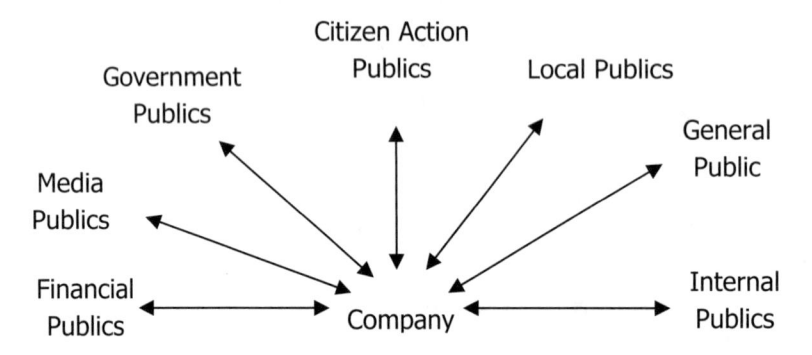

(a) **Financial publics** influence a company's ability to obtain funds. Examples include banks, investment houses and stockholders.

(b) **Media publics** can be newspapers, magazines, radio and television stations that carry news, features and editorial opinion.

(c) **Government publics** means taking government developments into account. Companies must consult their lawyers on issues of product safety, truth in advertising and other matters.

(d) **Citizen action publics** – marketing decisions may be questioned by consumer organisations, environmental groups, minority groups and other pressure groups. PR can help companies stay in touch and retain positive relations with consumer and citizen groups.

(e) **Local publics** – eg neighbourhood residents and community organisations. Companies may have a community relations officer to deal with the community, attend meetings, answer questions and contribute to worthwhile causes. Tesco is very involved in the community and regularly invite school children to its stores, eg a recent recycling initiative in Hertfordshire saw children 'open' a new hi-tech recycling centre. They spent the morning learning about recycling, got a tour behind the scenes of the store, and had their picture taken for the local newspaper.

(f) **General publics** – covering general attitudes to products and activities. The public's image of a company affects their purchasing behaviour.

(g) **Internal publics** – includes company's staff, managers, volunteers and board of directors. Organisations may use newsletters to inform and motivate their internal publics. Positive employees can lead to a positive attitude which spills over to the external publics.

ACTIVITY 3.3

application

Begin to understand your own organisation's stakeholders by identifying relevant stakeholders for each of the categories outlined above.

Marketing plans and strategies can be prepared for these individual groups if goodwill, word of mouth recommendations, or donations of time and money are required.

Supplier relations need to be managed very carefully. A company with too much dependence on particular suppliers can lead to failure. Music store, Zavvi went into administration partly due to an over-reliance on its music supplier, Woolworths, which had recently collapsed. Suppliers and retailers rely on each other for their well-being and seek security and long-term stability. Supermarkets often dictate prices to suppliers and force them to deliver unprofitably in some cases. Just-in-time systems can work very effectively but may lead to problems in the supply chain if new products cannot be delivered quickly.

5.1 Internal stakeholders

Internal stakeholders range from staff, to managers, owners and shareholders. Directors can be responsible for the delivery of corporate philosophies and their leadership can dictate the overall ethos of a company during their time at the helm. They can also be responsible for how far a marketing concept is adopted. Conflict can be created at different levels due to varying points of view on corporate strategy and the mission. Often, change in senior management can lead to a change in organisational structure and different priorities and policies being introduced. The management and relations between senior stakeholders is clearly very important.

Staff are also important. Unions are still a strong force in many industries which can lead to strained relations. Recent news coverage has seen stories on controversial CEO pension pots but no bonuses for lower tiers, redundancies, the outsourcing of work to foreign workers, and companies having to develop strategies and policies to deal with the growing number of staff seeking flexible working terms or support while having IVF treatment. Maintaining a positive and co-operative approach to internal relations and maintaining communications can reap dividends.

Internal marketing is any form of marketing in an organisation which focuses staff attention on the internal activities that need to be changed in order to enhance external marketplace performance (Lancaster, et al. 2008). The aim is to get employees to help achieve customer satisfaction using systems, procedures and plans to improve customer awareness throughout the organisation. Good internal marketing requires good internal communications, suitable organisational structures, adequate training and resources. There should be a strong commitment to improve customer service and satisfaction. Providing superior value to customers means companies can gain a competitive edge and secure retention and loyalty.

MARKETING AT WORK

application

Potters Leisure Resort, on the borders of Norfolk and Suffolk, is an independent and family-run business that puts its broad range of publics and stakeholders at the heart of everything it does.

The company employs 400 local people in its team who are dedicated to providing an informal but outstanding service to every guest. They have a ratio of 1 member of staff to 1.5 guests which is highly unusual in this sector. All staff members regardless of job role, have a positive attitude and spend time talking to guests. They speak very favourably of the Potters family who still split responsibility for different functions of the business between the family members.

Local publics are also able to use the extensive facilities such as the swimming pool, evening entertainment and beauty salon at reasonable rates. This is a positive approach to take as the resort borders onto a private beach and is a large site, thus allowing local residents to enjoy the scenery and maintain positive relations with a key employer.

6 Sustainable relationship management

Relationship marketing recognises the long-term value of customers. As a philosophy, it aims to move beyond the profitability of each transaction into developing long-term relationships with customers. By enjoying a good relationship with the customer base, organisations should expect to retain them and create an advantage which cannot easily be copied by competitors.

Kotler (2008) says relationship marketing is about building up long-term trusting relationships with valued customers to the benefit of the customer and organisation. Organisations should provide consistent good quality products backed-up by consistent service and fair prices. Relationship marketing helps them develop and maintain strong, economic, technical and social ties with valued customers.

Relationship marketing involves the use of a wide range of marketing, sales, communications and customer care techniques and processes to: identify named individual customers, create a relationship between the company and these customers, and manage that relationship to the benefit of both customers and company.

There is a good reason to keep your customers happy. Customer dissatisfaction will prevent repurchase and Stone and Young, (1992, quoted by Lancaster, et al. (2008), p. 409) says customers with bad experiences are twice as likely to tell other customers or potential customers as those with good experiences. Satisfied customers are more likely to return and become loyal thus moving them up the relationship ladder of loyalty, from prospect to partner. The cost of acquiring new customers is also a reason to keep the existing ones happy. Kotler (2008) says it can cost up to ten times more to acquire a new customer than to keep an existing one.

Customers expect greater levels of customer care and satisfaction these days and are more ready to challenge poor service or product quality. They are informed on the consumer rights and have ready access to the media and public forums. We are also seeing the litigation culture of the USA creep into Europe.

Customer care standards can be incorporated into mission statements. Consideration can be made during the marketing audit and SWOT analysis on the changing cultural and social values that might reflect on customers' expectations for customer care levels. Gap analysis can be used to identify and correct gaps in required versus achieved levels of customer care.

The following table is adapted from Kotler (1991) by Lancaster, et al. (2008), p. 419, and shows the differences between the one-off transaction marketing approach and relationship marketing:

Transaction marketing	Relationship marketing
Focus on single sale	Focus on customer retention
Orientation on product features	Orientation on product benefits
Short timescale	Long timescale
Little emphasis on customer service	High customer service emphasis
Limited commitment to customer	High commitment to customer
Moderate customer contact	Extensive customer contact
Quality is primarily concern of production	Quality concern of all functions

Kotler highlights the importance of customer retention which can be achieved through adding financial benefits, social benefits, learning about customers' individual needs and requirements, adding more personal service, specific marketing programmes or adding structural ties. However, it is important to retain the right types of customers who will be profitable and provide mutually beneficial relationships. Customers can be viewed as assets and managed accordingly.

Customers can be placed into four groups with each requiring a different relationship management strategy. The following diagram is adapted from Reinartz and Kumar, (2002) by Kotler, et al. (2008) p. 30.

	Short-term customers	Long-term customers
High Profitability	Butterflies – Good fit between company's offerings and customer's needs; high profit potential.	True Friends – Good fit between company's offerings and customer's needs; highest profit potential.
Low Profitability	Strangers – Little fit between company's offerings and customer's needs; lowest profit potential.	Barnacles – Limited fit between company's offerings and customer's needs; low profit potential.

(Vertical axis: Potential Profitability; Horizontal axis: Projected Loyalty)

Butterflies are profitable but not loyal. The can be enjoyed for a short while and then they are gone. Efforts to convert butterflies are rarely successful due to their flighty nature. Promotional blitzes may attract them, satisfying and profitable transactions can be created with them, then the company should cease investing in them until the next time around.

True Friends are profitable and loyal. Firms want to make continuous relationship investments to delight these customers and nurture, retain and grow them. This should turn them into true believers who return regularly and tell others about their positive experiences.

Strangers show little profitability and projected loyalty. There is no particular fit between their needs and the company's offerings. The strategy here is not to invest in them.

Barnacles have a limited fit between their needs and the company's offerings. They can create drag. The company could try to increase their profitability by selling them more or raising fees or reducing service levels, however, if they cannot be made profitable, then the relationship should cease

The overall goal of relationship marketing is to build the right relationships with the right customers!

Lancaster et al. (2002) Chapter 13 provides good coverage of relationship marketing.

Learning objective review

Learning objective	Covered
1. Appreciate and understand the key environmental drivers of organisational change: innovation; evolving consumer behaviour; globalisation; ethical consumption and corporate social responsibility; sustainability relationship management; and stakeholder relations.	☑ Innovation = new products, replacement products, imitative products ☑ Evolving consumer demographics, culture and customer demands ☑ Globalisation – types of market, multinationals, Keegan's framework ☑ Ethical consumption and CSR ☑ Stakeholder relations and relationship management

Quick quiz

1. Innovation in marketing always refers to a brand new product. True or False?

2. Identify at least three factors that could be considered when reviewing customer needs.

3. Which of the following is not a type of economic market.

    (a) Industrialising countries
    (b) Industrialised countries
    (c) Subsistence economies
    (d) Uncontrollable economies

4. Multinational organisations always originate in multiple countries. True or False?

5 According to Keegan, there are a number of global marketing strategies. Complete the following framework.

		Products		
		No change	Adapted	New product
Marketing Communications	No change			
	Adapt			

Activity debriefs

Worksheet activity 3.1

This will depend on your own research. As a main agenda topic in recent years it is unlikely that you will not find any articles on the topic of societal marketing and related areas such as:

- Green marketing
- Cause– related marketing
- Corporate social responsibility

Worksheet activity 3.2

This will depend on your own research. It is likely that you will have found evidence of some green marketing. It is also quite possible you can identify areas for future improvements.

Worksheet activity 3.3

This will depend on your own research. You should find it relatively easy to identify at least three stakeholders for each category.

Quiz answers

1. False. Replacement products and imitative products also exist.

2. Dibb and Simkin (2008) highlight a number of factors that can be considered when reviewing customer needs:

   - What benefits are they seeking from products or services?
   - Are they looking for tangible or intangible benefits?
   - Do they have any other related needs which may affect the purchasing decision?
   - How important are issues like quality, delivery, service, price, product range, innovation, brand reputation and the influence of promotional activity?
   - How do they search for information on the product or service?
   - What is the impact of their previous experiences?
   - How do they identify and select from the competitive set?
   - Who else influences the decision-making process?
   - What are their key customer values – the factors they expect and consider to be important?

3. (d). The three previous market types are discussed in section 3. Developing countries is the other market.

4. False. They often establish in one country.

5.

		Products		
		No change	Adapted	New product
Marketing Communications	No change	Straight extension	Product adaptation	
	Adapt	Communication adaptation	Dual adaptation	Product invention

References

BBC. (2007). *'What is working class?'* [Online] Updated 25 Jan 2007, 13:06. Available at http://news.bbc.co.uk/1/hi/magazine/6295743.stm [Accessed 17 April 2009].

CIM. (2009). *'Shape the Agenda: Less Smoke, More Fire: The Benefits and Impacts of Social Marketing'*. The Marketer, April 2009, p46-49.

CIPD. (2007). *'Corporate Strategy and Change Management'* [Online] Updated Nov 2007. Available at http://www.cipd.co.uk/subjects/corpstrtgy/changemmt/chngmgmt.htm [Accessed 23 April 2009].

CNN. (2009). *'Convictions Upheld in China Milk Scandal'* [Online] Updated 26 Mar 2009, 3:36am. Available at http://www.cnn.com/2009/CRIME/03/26/china.milk/ [Accessed 21 April 2009].

Dibb, S. & Simkin, L., (2008) Marketing Planning – A Workbook for Marketing Managers. Cengage Learning, London.

Drummond, G., Ensor, J. & Ashford, R.,(2008) Strategic Marketing Planning & Control. (3rd ed.), Butterworth-Heinemann, Oxford.

Friend, G. & Zehle, S., (2004) The Economist Guide to Business Planning. The Economist in assoc. with Profile Books, London.

Grant, J. (2009). *'The Heart of the Revolution?'* The Marketer, February 2009, p13.

Grant, J. (2009). *'Going Green for Groceries'*. The Marketer, April 2009, p13.

Henley Centre/Headlight Vision. (2007). *'The New Green Consumer'* [Online] Updated 19 Jun 2007. Available at http://www.headlightvision.com/Asp/uploadedFiles/File/New%20Green%20Consumer%2019%20June%202007.pdf [Accessed 22 April 2009].

Kotler, P. Armstrong, G. Wong, V. & Saunders, J.,(2008.) Principles of Marketing. (5th European ed.), Harlow: Pearson Education, Harlow.

Lancaster, G. Massingham, L. & Ashford, R., (2002). Essentials of Marketing. (4th ed.), Maidenhead:. McGraw-Hill Education, Maidenhead.

McDonald, M., (2007) Marketing Plans – How to Prepare Them, How to Use Them. (6th ed.), Butterworth-Heinemann, Oxford.

Potters. (2009). *'The Potters Team'* [Online] Updated 2009. Available at http://www.pottersholidays.com/Resort-Information/The-Potters-Team [Accessed 20 April 2009].

Chapter 4
The marketing audit process

Topic list

1. Marketing audits and marketing plans
2. Conducting a marketing audit
3. The marketing audit framework
4. The planning gap
5. SWOT analysis

Introduction

This chapter deals with the marketing audit, looking at the current and future position of the organisation. The process of conducting an audit will be reviewed, highlighting constraints and challenges organisations may face when pulling together information from a range of sources. The planning gap model and SWOT analysis are also covered in this section as additional tools to help the organisation understand, evaluate and prioritise marketing issues and strategies.

Syllabus-linked learning objectives

By the end of the chapter you will be able to:

Learning objectives	Syllabus link
1. Understand the purpose and practicalities of undertaking a marketing audit.	2.1; 2.2; 2.7
2. Conduct a marketing audit.	2.1; 2.3
3. Understand and utilise the planning gap model.	2.6
4. Conduct SWOT analysis.	2.7

1 Marketing audits and marketing plans

Corporate strategic plans guide the overall development of an organisation. Within each strategic plan, are marketing plans for each business unit, product or brand. Marketing planning is subordinate to corporate planning but makes a significant contribution to it and is concerned with many of the same issues. The corporate audit of product/market strengths and weaknesses, and much of its external environmental analysis is directly informed by the marketing audit.

The marketing audit is an important component of the marketing plan. It assesses the current marketing situation bringing together information from a range of sources on the market, product, competition and distribution channels, as seen in the following framework created by Kotler, et al. (2008). This important assessment of the company's situation can then be utilised to conduct SWOT analysis looking at the strengths and weaknesses of the organisation and relevant opportunities and threats in the marketing environment. The marketing audit and SWOT analysis are then used by the marketing department to create appropriate objectives and strategies, which will then be implemented and assessed using control systems.

This framework by Kotler, et al. (2008) illustrates the contents of the marketing plan.

Section	Purpose
Executive summary	Presents a quick overview of the plan for management review.
Current marketing situation	The marketing audit presenting background data on the market, product, competition and distribution.
SWOT analysis	Identifies the company's main strengths and weaknesses and the main opportunities and threats facing the product.
Objectives and issues	Defines the company's objectives in the areas of sales, market share and profits, and the issues that will affect these objectives.
Marketing strategy	Presents the broad marketing approach that will be used to achieve the plan's objectives.
Marketing implementation	Specifies what will be done, who will do it, when it will be done and what it will cost.
Budgets	A projected profit-and-loss statement that forecasts the expected financial outcomes from the plan.
Control	Indicates how the progress of the plan will be monitored.

ACTIVITY 4.1

evaluation

Obtain a copy of a marketing plan used within your own organisation Estimate how effective you think it is as a planning document.

KEY CONCEPT

concept

The **marketing audit** is a systematic and periodic examination of a company's environment, objectives, strategies and activities to determine problem areas and opportunities
Kotler, et al. (2008)

The audit section of the marketing plan should provide information about the market, product performance, competition and distribution. It should include a description of the market and its target segments, as well as total market size and segment sizes over time. Customer needs should be reviewed, as should factors in the marketing environment that may affect their purchasing behaviour. Products, competition and distribution should also be analysed, looking at areas such as sales, prices, competitor strategies, market shares, recent sales trends and developments in the key distribution channels.

The marketing audit includes external analysis, competitor and customer analysis, internal analysis and SWOT analysis. It should be comprehensive, objective and carried out on a regular basis. This review of a firm's marketing activities should cover: the marketing environment, the marketing organisation, marketing strategies, the marketing function, marketing systems and marketing productivity.

The diagram below shows how the marketing audit fits into the overall setting.

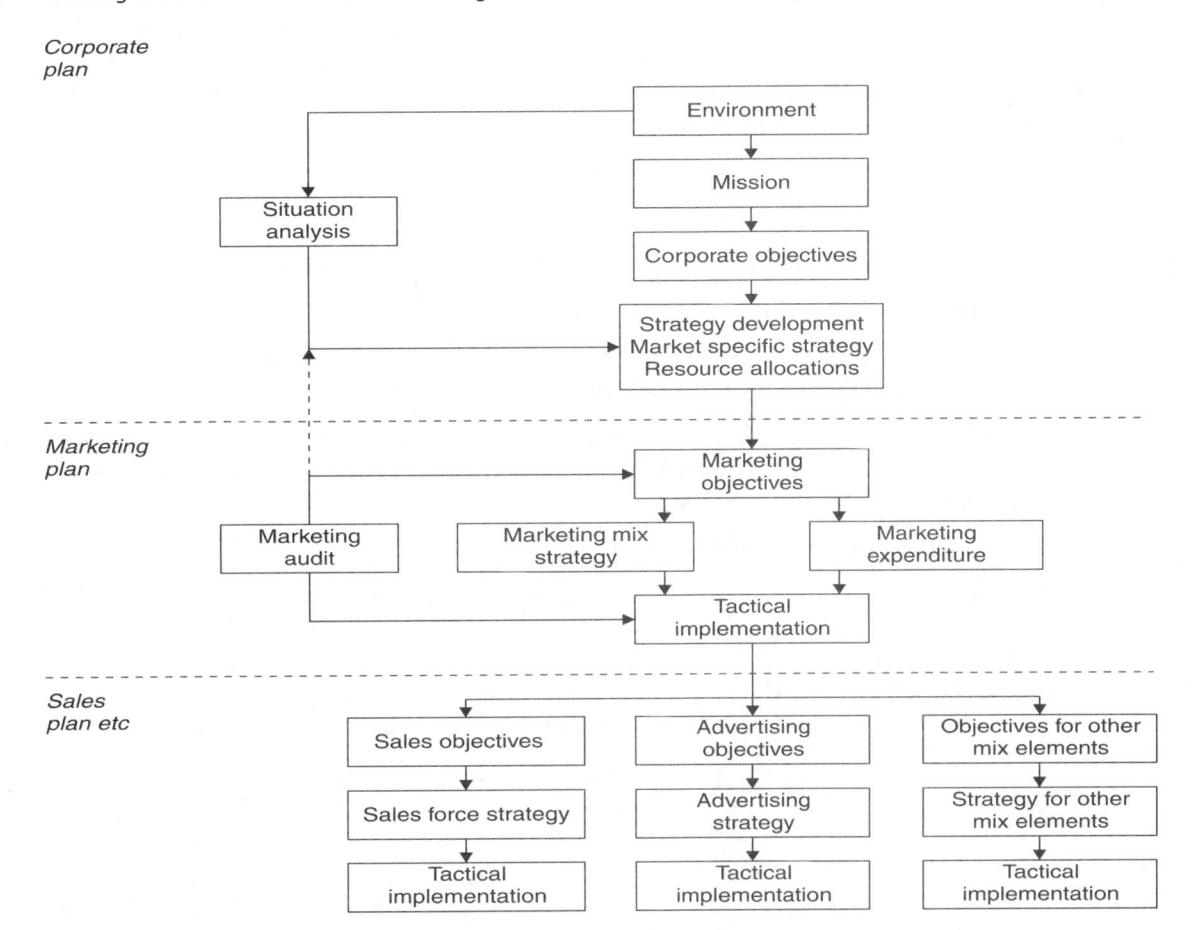

Corporate plan

- Environment
- Mission
- Corporate objectives
- Strategy development / Market specific strategy / Resource allocations
- Situation analysis

Marketing plan

- Marketing objectives
- Marketing audit
- Marketing mix strategy
- Marketing expenditure
- Tactical implementation

Sales plan etc

- Sales objectives → Sales force strategy → Tactical implementation
- Advertising objectives → Advertising strategy → Tactical implementation
- Objectives for other mix elements → Strategy for other mix elements → Tactical implementation

4: The marketing audit process

Companies exist within complex marketing environments and must manage the controllable marketing-mix variables but also face uncontrollable forces to which the company must adapt. The marketing environment includes forces close to the company that affect its ability to serve its customer such as other company departments, channel members, suppliers, competitors and other publics. It also includes broader demographic and economic forces, political and legal forces, technological and ecological forces and social and cultural forces. All of these forces must be taken into account when developing and positioning its offer to the target market. If the analysis has not been conducted effectively, the recommendations generated by the marketing team will be based on an inaccurate view of the market and the company's opportunities. More detail on the external and internal marketing environments can be found in Chapters 5 and 6.

2 Conducting a marketing audit

McDonald (2007) recommends conducting a marketing audit once a year, at an appropriate point in the planning cycle. For some organisations, the trigger to perform an audit may come simply because they are in crisis. Others are more proactive and start the financial year with a formal audit. McDonald states that an audit is, *'a way of defining problems, and hopefully preventing them from happening'*. An objective and critical approach must be taken to ensure full value is gained from this process.

In order to exercise proper strategic control, a marketing audit should satisfy four requirements:

(a) It should take a **comprehensive** look at every product, market, distribution channel and ingredient in the marketing mix.

(b) It should **not be restricted** to areas of apparent ineffectiveness such as an unprofitable product, a troublesome distribution channel, or low efficiency on direct selling.

(c) It should be carried out according to a set of **predetermined, specified procedures**.

(d) It should be conducted **regularly**. The auditors should be independent of particular job and organisational interests.

Each manager tasked with performing an audit on their area of responsibility should avoid making forecasts from previous performance and will need to use data from the marketing information system, sales data and other valid sources. Checklists can be issued to each manager who needs to contribute to the process. A hierarchy of audits may be created by various managers with detail varying from level to level, business unit to business unit within the organisation group. The top level audit would look at issues globally from a strategic level.

McDonald breaks down the key information required into the external and internal audit.

The external audit should cover:

- **Business and economic environment** – economic, political, fiscal, legal, social, cultural, technological.
- **The market** – total market, size, growth and trends.
- **Market characteristics** – developments and trends: products, prices, physical distribution, channels, customers, consumers, communication and industry practices.
- **Competition** – major competitors, size, market share / coverage, market standing and reputation, production capabilities, distribution policies, marketing methods, extent of diversification, personnel issues, international links, profitability, key strengths and weaknesses.

The internal audit should cover the organisation and look at:

- Sales – total, by geographical location, by industrial type, by customer, by product.
- Market shares.
- Profit margins and costs.
- Marketing information / research.
- Marketing mix variables: product management, price, distribution, promotion, operations and resources.

3 The marketing audit framework

The following areas should be considered in the marketing audit:

- **The marketing environment**

    Micro: What are the organisation's major markets, and what is the segmentation of these markets? What are the future prospects of each market segment?

    – Who are the customers, what is known about customer needs, intentions and behaviour? How do they rate the company on product quality, service and price?

    – Who are the competitors, and what is their standing in the market? What are their strategies, strengths and weaknesses?

    Other aspects to consider are the channels of distribution used and how they are performing; trends affecting suppliers; the availability of key production resources; what key publics provide problems or opportunities and how should the company deal with them?

    Macro: Have there been any significant developments in the broader environment, for example, economic (income, prices, savings, credit) or political changes, population or social changes, etc? What is the cost and availability of natural resources and energy? Is the company environmentally responsible? Have there been any technological or cultural changes?

- **Marketing strategies**

    What are the organisation's marketing objectives and how do they relate to overall objectives? Are they reasonable? Is the mission clearly defined and market-oriented?

    Are appropriate resources being committed to marketing to enable the objectives to be achieved? Is the division of costs between products and geographic areas satisfactory?

- **Marketing systems**

    What are the procedures for formulating marketing plans and management control of these plans? Are they satisfactory? Is marketing intelligence providing accurate and timely information on developments? Are decision-makers using research properly? Does the company prepare annual, long-term and strategic plans? Are they used? Are annual plan objectives being reached? NPD – do they gather, generate and screen new product ideas?

- **Marketing organisation**

    Does the organisation have the structural capability to implement the plan? Is there co-ordination across functions on the marketing effort?

- **Marketing function**

    A review of the effectiveness of each element of the mix (eg advertising and sales promotion activities) should be carried out. A review of sales and price levels should be made (for example supply and demand, customer attitudes, the use of temporary price reductions, etc). A review of the state of each individual product (ie its market 'health') and of the product mix as a whole should be made. A critical analysis of the distribution system should be made, with a view to finding improvements.

- **Marketing productivity**

    How profitable are the company's products, markets and channels of distribution? How cost-effective is the marketing programme?

    A well-executed marketing audit should reduce the need for crisis management, identify information needs and force executives to think carefully about the next steps ahead for the organisation.

The auditing process can also be used as a control mechanism, to check where we are now, where we want to be, how we can get there, and ensure the best methods for achieving this and evaluating success. This supports the view that marketing planning is a cyclical process.

ACTIVITY 4.2

application

Think about the marketing processes in operation within your own organisation. Conduct a mini marketing audit using the questions detailed above.

4 The planning gap

Gap analysis is a tool to help organisations achieve their strategic goals. Recent and current turnover, or volume achievements should be plotted onto a gap analysis graph. Forecast turnover or volume should then be plotted on the graph, assuming no changes to the current strategy. The space between the two lines which represent the actual and predicted figures represent the gap which the marketing plan's proposed marketing programmes should fill if new strategies are introduced.

This model quantifies the size of the gap between the objective/targets for the planning period, and the forecast based on the extrapolation of the current situation. The organisation must then identify different strategies to fill the gap. Gap analysis is a planning technique which identifies likely shortfalls in future performance and considers how best they can be filled. It starts with a comparison of what the organisation wishes to achieve and what it is likely to achieve if nothing changes.

The Fo forecast is a forecast of future results assuming that the company continues to operate as at present. It is prepared in stages:

(a) The analysis of revenues by units of sale and price, and the analysis of costs into variable, fixed, and semi-variable.

(b) Projections into the future, based on past trends, to the end of the planning period.

(c) Consideration of other factors affecting profits and return, such as the likelihood of deterioration in labour relations or machine serviceability and the possibility of scarcity of raw materials.

(d) Combination of these items into a single forecast.

When complete, the Fo forecast may be compared with the organisation's objectives. Differences constitute the gap which has to be filled. The gap may have several elements such as a **profits gap** or a **sales gap**.

The **profit gap** is the difference between the target profits and the profits on the F_o forecast. The options for bridging the gap need to be identified. The same basic technique can serve as the basis for formulating any particular strategy. In planning for human resources, gap analysis would be used to assess the difference over time between two quantities.

(a) What the organisation **needs to have** in terms of staff of differing skills and seniority

(b) What the organisation is **likely to have**, allowing for natural wastage of staff.

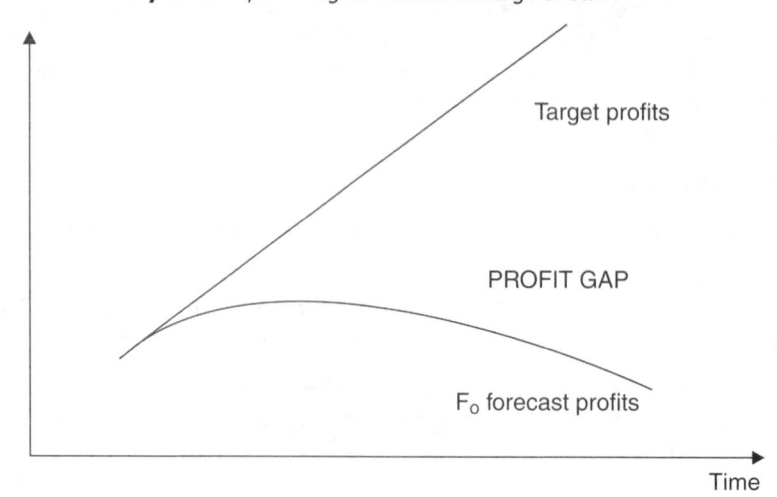

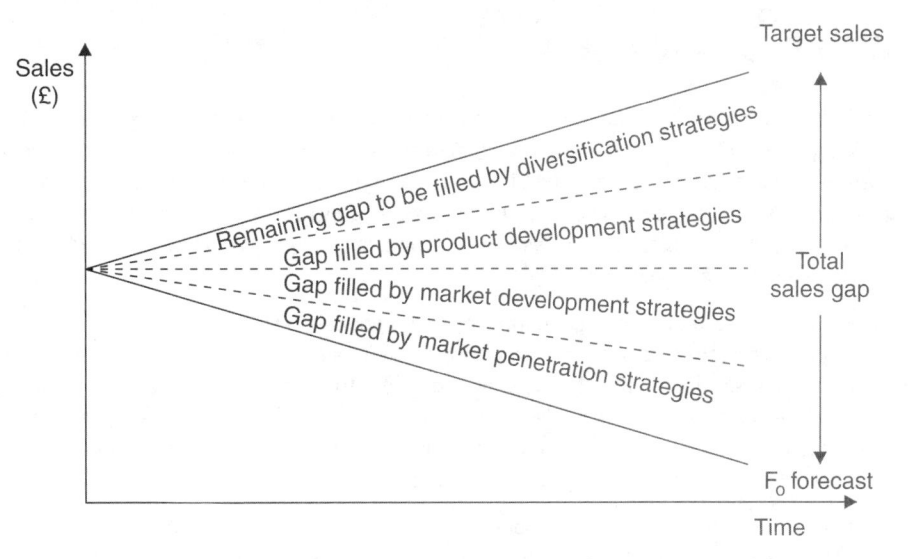

```
                                           Target sales
Sales                              _____
 (£)                      _____
              _____         Remaining gap to be filled by diversification strategies
             ----------
                         Gap filled by product development strategies    Total
                                                                         sales gap
                      Gap filled by market development strategies
                  Gap filled by market penetration strategies
                                                              F₀ forecast
                                                              Time
```

A strategy would then be needed to fill the gap between target and current forecasts.

The gap can be filled with four strategic options:

- **Market penetration** – increased market penetration and productivity through, for example, more sales calls, cost reduction, decreased prices, better product or customer mix, etc.
- **Market development or extension** – find new markets for existing products.
- **New product development** – the development of new or improved products for existing markets.
- **Diversification** – the development of new products for new markets through, for example, changing the asset base, investment or acquisition.

Marketers need to consider the current product life cycle stage and competitors' positions to ensure their recommendations are realistic in terms of competitor actions and strengths. From the gap analysis, it should be feasible to work out how the gap can be most effectively filled.

Sometimes a range of strategies will be required while on other occasions one successful strategy will suffice.

MARKETING AT WORK   application

We have previously mentioned Virgin in earlier chapters. Virgin is a great example of how diversification strategies are employed in order to fill the gaps at a corporate level between their corporate group forecast and actual sales within their specified planning period. At an individual company and brand level, Virgin has a plethora of examples of gap filling strategies. If we take as an example Virgin Drinks (which launched in 1994 as Virgin Cola), we can see how the organisation has used a variety of strategies in order to grow over their lifespan.

Virgin Drinks in recent years has been seen to use the following strategies:

1. Market penetration – price promotions and increasing sales efforts to gain distribution outlets for Virgin Cola
2. Market development or extension – Virgin Colours (a range of flavoured soft drinks available in selected countries where Virgin was previously unavailable)
3. New product development – Virgin Ice (an iced tea available in existing markets)
4. Diversification – Virgin Vines and Virgin Vodka (diversification into the alcoholic market)

5 SWOT analysis

SWOT analysis is a commonly used technique to assess the current situation of the business. It is an essential component of the marketing plan. Often SWOT is used as a start to marketing audits when in reality it should always be used as a means of summarising and drawing together audit findings. Strengths and weaknesses are features of the organisation and its product or service range; opportunities and threats are features of the environment, particularly the immediate competitive or task environment. The completed analysis allows companies to pin down real issues which should be addressed as a priority and developed into objectives.

The current situation faced by the organisation is broken down into strengths, weaknesses, opportunities and threats. Simply categorising factors by these labels is not enough to make this analysis effective. In each section, the factors should be ranked by importance; this can then be expanded to assess the implications of each factor to the organisation. From this, actions can be recommended in the marketing plan. Without a thorough assessment of the strengths and weaknesses, mistakes could be made in the evaluation of opportunities for the company. Solutions need to be found for weaknesses and the company needs to consider how to deal with threats.

Strengths are features from which the company may be able to derive competitive advantage. They are also known as core competences. Weaknesses are disadvantages that may have to be remedied. For example a company's growth is being hampered because its people have weak customer handling skills. A training programme could be introduced to help its people develop stronger skills.

This type of analysis is often criticised for being subjective and simplistic. It could be considered as the point of view of the creator and factors could easily be missed or not considered important. Information should be drawn from the marketing audit and should be objective and based on solid data from marketing research, external analysts or internal experts. Competitors should also be covered in the analysis.

Managers will produce an overall SWOT and also ones for major business units, product groups, brands and key target markets. They may also produce them for key competitors and separate markets.

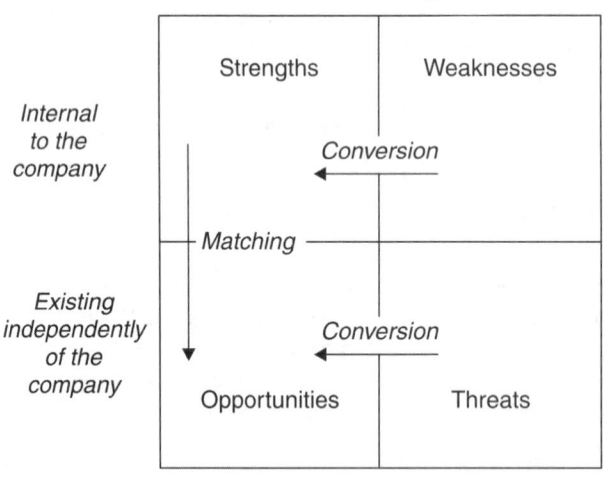

SWOT Analysis

	Strengths	Weaknesses
Internal to the company		← Conversion
	— Matching —	
Existing independently of the company		← Conversion
	Opportunities	Threats

ACTIVITY 4.3

application

Go through around five back copies of a marketing news publication and identify examples of:

1. Market penetration
2. Market development or extension
3. New product development
4. Diversification

Give examples of political, economic, social and technological factors which might offer opportunities or be sources or threats.

The analysis of internal strengths and weaknesses according to Dibb and Simkin (2008) should focus on the following:

(a) **Marketing**

    (i) Product
    (ii) Pricing
    (iii) Promotion
    (iv) Marketing information / intelligence
    (v) Service / people
    (vi) Distribution / distributors
    (vii) Branding and positioning
    (viii) Resources

(b) **Engineering and product development**

(c) **Operations**

    (i) Production / engineering
    (ii) Sales and marketing
    (iii) Processing orders / transactions
    (iv) Economies of scale

(d) **People**

    (i) R&D
    (ii) Distributors
    (iii) Marketing
    (iv) Sales
    (v) After sales / service
    (vi) Processing / customer service.

It can also look at the skills of staff, wages and benefits, training and development, motivation, conditions and turnover. These are all factors which affect the successful implementation of a customer-focused marketing philosophy and the marketing strategy.

(e) **Management**

    (i) Structures, behaviours and philosophies may need altering to help the implementation of the marketing strategy. These can be raised in the SWOT.
    (ii) Strategic alliances, partnerships, mergers and other structural issues should be cited.

(f) **Company resources**

    (i) People and skills
    (ii) Finance (budgets)
    (iii) Scheduling

(g) For the external environment looking at threats and opportunities, Dibb and Simkin (2008) say the areas to examine are:

    (i) Social / cultural

    (ii) Regulatory / legal / political

    (iii) Technological

    (iv) Economic conditions

    (v) Competition: global players; international versus national versus local; the intensity of rivalry; ability; threat of entry; pressure from substitutions; market's customer needs; bargaining power of buyers, distributors and suppliers.

SWOT analysis enables organisations to review their core competences, their areas of competitive advantage, customer needs, how they fit with the competition and requirements for the product portfolio. This should lead companies to the next stage where strategies can be set to harness or remedy findings from these factors. A successful strategy is one that exploits strengths and seizes opportunities, while remedying weaknesses and dealing effectively with threats.

Unfortunately, it is unusual for a company to possess all the strengths it needs to exploit its chosen opportunities and overcome the immediate threats. It is very common, therefore, for companies to undertake programmes of corporate development in which they attempt to overcome crucial weaknesses and build new strengths. There may also be attempts to convert threats into opportunities by the same process, eg buying out a rival group of companies.

Additional useful reading will include:

McDonald (2009) Chapters 4 and 5. This text generally would be highly useful for you to read.

Dibb and Simkin (2005) Chapters 4 and 10 covers marketing planning.

Learning objective review

Learning objectives	Covered
1. Understand the purpose and practicalities of undertaking a marketing audit.	☑ Assess current situation ☑ Systematic and periodic
2. Conduct a marketing audit.	☑ Business economic environment ☑ Market and market characteristics ☑ Competition
3. Understand and utilise the planning gap model.	☑ Assists strategic goal fulfilment ☑ Quantities size of gap between targets and forecasts ☑ Gap filled new strategies
4. Conduct SWOT analysis.	☑ Summarises audit findings ☑ Should quantify rather than simply categorise ☑ Enables core competency identification

Quick quiz

1. What is a marketing audit?
2. What is the business environment?
3. State four economic influences on business.
4. Summarise the effect of technological change on business.
5. What main factors determine the intensity of competition?
6. What are the five competitive forces?
7. What is a SWOT analysis?

Activity debriefs

Worksheet activity 4.1

If you find it difficult to obtain a copy, contact a local small charity and ask if they have one which you could help to refine. It would be a great learning experience.

Worksheet activity 4.2

This will depend on research within your own organisation. Try discussing your research and results with colleagues. Are their views similar to yours?

Worksheet activity 4.3

This will depend on the publications that you chose but should be similar to the following examples:

Market penetration – recruitment of additional sales staff, the use of a promotional team.

Market development or extension – entering a new market, eg news about organisations entering your home market, eg Frappuccino entering China.

New product development – you will possibly have found multiple examples of new or improved products in the press.

Diversification – these new items are not so common as due to the costs and risks associated with diversification they tend not to be frequent strategies for organisation. Coca-cola diversifying into the ready to drink coffee market in Japan is one example of related diversification.

Quiz answers

1. A detailed analysis of marketing capacity and practice, which enables plans to be made with the aim of improving company performance.

2. All the factors that act on the company's markets, including its suppliers, competitors and customers.

3. Examples include:

   - Inflation rate
   - Interest rates
   - Tax regime
   - Unemployment rate
   - Exchange rates
   - Availability of credit

   You may think of others.

4. - New products and services
   - New methods and processes
   - New means of delivering services
   - New ways to identify markets

5. - A market with a large number of rivals is likely to be more competitive than one with a few.
   - A fast rate of industry growth reduces competition; stagnation increases it.
   - High fixed costs require high volumes and promote competition on price.

6. The threat of new entrants
   The threat of substitutes
   Bargaining power of customers
   Bargaining power of suppliers
   Rivalry amongst current competition

7. The analysis of the current situation into strengths, weaknesses, opportunities and threats.

References

Dibb, S. & Simkin, L., (2008) Marketing Planning – A Workbook for Marketing Managers. Cengage Learning, London.

Drummond, G., Ensor, J. & Ashford, R.,(2008) Strategic Marketing Planning & Control. (3rd ed.), Butterworth-Heinemann, Oxford.

Friend, G. & Zehle, S.,(2004) The Economist Guide to Business Planning. The Economist in assoc. with Profile Books, London.

Kotler, P. Armstrong, G. Wong, V. & Saunders, J.,(2008) Principles of Marketing. (5th European ed.), Pearson Education, Harlow.

Lancaster, G. Massingham, L. & Ashford, R.,(2002) Essentials of Marketing. (4th ed.), McGraw-Hill Education, Maidenhead.

McDonald, M., (2007) Marketing Plans – How to Prepare Them, How to Use Them. (6th ed.), Butterworth-Heinemann, Oxford.

Chapter 5

Appraising the external marketing environment

Topic list

1. The nature of environmental change
2. Environmental scanning
3. Environmental analysis frameworks
4. Impact of external forces and issues
5. External audit tools

Introduction

Environmental analysis helps us understand the factors that will directly face organisations and have a major impact upon the way that they operate. External and internal analysis forms part of the strategic analysis framework and guides the formulation of strategies and the strategic marketing plan. This chapter looks at the external marketing environment and the nature of external change. Specific tools that are of use in assessing factors arising in the organisation's environment will be examined, including environmental scanning and external audit tools such as PEST, Porter's Five Forces and Strategic Group Mapping.

Syllabus-linked learning objectives

By the end of the chapter you will be able to:

Learning objectives	Syllabus link
1. Understand the need for external analysis and the changing nature of environmental change.	2.4
2. Employ key environmental analysis frameworks and external audit tools.	2.4

1 The nature of environmental change

KEY CONCEPT

The **marketing environment** is the actors and forces outside marketing that affect marketing management's ability to develop and maintain successful relationships with its target customers.

Kotler, et al. (2008)

Organisations must deal with factors that are controllable or uncontrollable. It is an on-going challenge to stay one step ahead of the competition while trying to deal with forces that may hinder efforts to satisfy target customer needs and build relationships and retention levels. Environmental analysis is the process of predicting the environment in which the organisation has to operate. An organisation that is informed about the challenges it may shortly have to face is more likely to be prepared with workable strategies.

External analysis is split into two components: the macro- and the micro-environment. Both of these elements are external to the organisation. The macro-environment looks at forces that would impact upon all organisations operating in a particular market and are not controllable. These forces include economic, political, technological and socio-cultural factors. Key examples would be the level of inflation, interest or exchange rates. A company cannot directly affect the passing of laws, although undertaking lobbying activities or joining a trade organisation may bring about positive changes. The micro-environment is more specific to the firm and looks at the forces that directly impact its ability to fulfil its function, such as competitors, customers, distribution channels, suppliers and the general public. The company has more influence over the micro-environment. Effective external environmental analysis involves assessing which of these macro and micro factors will have an impact upon the organisation, now or in the near future, and understanding the likely impacts of this.

Environmental change can happen during different time frames and this enables some factors to be easily accounted for in marketing plans. **Cyclical change** is temporary, repetitive and can be predictable, eg seasonal variation in demand. It can also account for fluctuations in the economy such as inflation or changing interest rates. This lack of permanence means that long-term initiatives should not be based on the patterns of cyclical change. Factors arising from these phases should be dealt with flexibly to enable the organisation to change direction when the cycle begins to end.

Evolutionary or **structural change** is more critical. This type of change is long-term and permanent. It could occur due to a sudden innovation or a gradual process but is likely to be irreversible. Innovations and developments in information technology is an example of evolutionary change. Evolutionary change can have a major impact on strategic development for an organisation.

The speed of environmental change is also a consideration for companies when undertaking planning. There are three types to consider: stable, dynamic and turbulent. In a stable market, a strategic plan can be developed with ease but in markets that are exceptionally turbulent, this would be a more difficult process. In some cases, strategic decisions may have to be made when uncertainty reduces.

Stable markets enjoy little or no change in their environment. They may be typified by a mature market. Any change that does occur is likely to be slow and easily identified. Relationships between suppliers, customers, distributors and manufacturers will have been established over time and will be unlikely to change in the near future.

Dynamic markets will experience change but at a moderate pace. The changing factors may not always be predictable. There may be new entrants to the market but also some existing competitors exiting. The market may be typified by low levels of mergers and acquisitions but businesses will still have to adapt to remain competitive.

Turbulent markets are completely unpredictable and will be experiencing rapid change. There is likely to be new market entrants and high levels of technological development. They can be linked with the initial and growth phases of the product life cycle. Relationships between suppliers, manufacturers, distributors and customers will be continually changing.

Change is likely to be driven by customer needs which will lead to alterations in products and operation methods. It can also be driven by competitor actions and PEST factors (Political, Economic, Social, Technological). Even traditional markets can be challenged by changes in consumer habits and demographic patterns. Technology, globalisation, competition and the rise in the use of market intelligence and insight have also increased the speed and impact of change. To complicate matters further, product life cycles are becoming shorter as technologies, competitor actions and the need to add new variations and value have an effect. Finally, it is becoming increasingly difficult to predict the future, eg September 11th again being a prime example of far-reaching and wholly unpredictable change.

Change can be beneficial. It can create new opportunities for organisations that are flexible and have adopted the marketing concept. Forecasting the future success of a company based on past performance shows a lack on insight and understanding of the dynamics of the marketing environment. Companies must ensure they do not 'drift' from the true needs of the marketplace.

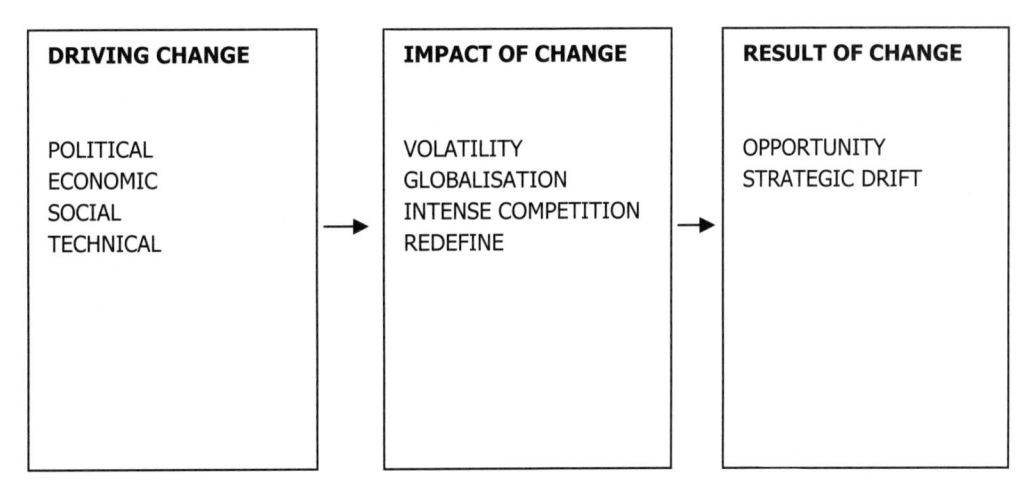

DRIVING CHANGE	IMPACT OF CHANGE	RESULT OF CHANGE
POLITICAL ECONOMIC SOCIAL TECHNICAL	VOLATILITY GLOBALISATION INTENSE COMPETITION REDEFINE	OPPORTUNITY STRATEGIC DRIFT

Drummond, et al. (2008)

2 Environmental scanning

KEY CONCEPT

Environmental scanning is the careful monitoring of a firm's internal and external environments for detecting early signs of opportunities and threats that may influence its current and future plans.

www.businessdictionary.com (2009)

Rapid and constant changes in the marketing environment mean organisations have to stay well-informed in order to be able to create effective corporate and marketing strategies based on informed analysis. To keep abreast of potential changes, companies should be scanning the environment continuously. This is the process of gathering, analysing and disseminating information for tactical or strategic purposes. Information can be taken from secondary data sources, customer databases, information services and marketing research. Factual and subjective information can be used which provides insight on the company's current or potential business environments. Environmental scanning is usually only applied to the macro-environment but can also cover industries, competitor analysis, marketing research, new product development for product innovations and the company's internal environment.

Aguilar (1967, quoted by Drummond, et al. 2008, p. 22) identifies four forms of environmental scanning.

Undirected viewing: here, there is no specific agenda to the scanning process. The marketer is seeking a general awareness of relevant factors or areas of change.

Conditional viewing: with this type of scanning, the marketer is more sensitive to information that may prove relevant in identifying changes in specific areas of activity.

Informal search: this is an organised but limited search for information supporting a particular goal.

Formal search: the search is actively pursued and designed to seek particular information.

Scanning the business environment can be done in an *ad hoc* fashion (short-term, infrequent examinations possibly initiated by a crisis), regular scanning (eg once a year), or continuous scanning on a broad range of environmental factors. Many theorists feel that continuous scanning is the most effective method in today's climate. This gives companies the opportunity to act on their findings quickly, avoiding any or further damage being done and acting in advance of competitors. Research also suggests that effective scanning and planning is linked to improved organisational learning and performance when linked with the strategic planning process.

All environmental scanning should balance the resources of the company with the benefits the process can bring. Aguilar (1967) suggests managers look for information in five key areas:

(a) **Market intelligence**: this covers market potential, structural change, competitors and industry issues, pricing, sales negotiations and customers.

(b) **Technical intelligence**: looking at new products, processes and technology as well as product problems, costs, licensing and patents.

(c) **Acquisition intelligence**: searching for leads on mergers, joint ventures or acquisitions.

(d) **Broad issues**: general conditions, government actions and policies.

(e) **Other intelligence**: suppliers and raw materials, available resources, and any other useful insight.

Chun Wei, (2001) talks about scanning behaviour being influenced by a number of factors. These include the turbulence of the market, the nature of the business, the availability and quality of information, and personal factors like the scanner's knowledge or cognitive style. Scanning as a form of information behaviour is composed of information needs (the focus and scope of scanning), information seeking, and information use. Information seeking refers to the sources that are used to scan the environment as well as the organisational methods and systems employed. Information use relates to the decision-making and strategic planning that results from the exercise.

Chun Wei also considers the point that managers who believe the environment to be more uncertain are likely to scan more – this is likely to be affected by the complexity and dynamism of the sectors in the manager's particular external environment. Senior managers are proven to scan more than lower-level managers and functional managers scan beyond the limits of their specialism.

Organisations additionally have three kinds of knowledge that can be employed in environmental scanning:

- **Tacit knowledge** is the personal knowledge of an individual and is developed over time in a job function. This learning and experience is often lost by companies when a staff member moves on or retires after a lengthy period of service.

- **Explicit knowledge** is expressed formally either through symbols such as documents or software code or in physical objects such as equipment. It can also be knowledge that is presented as rules, routines or operating procedures.

- **Cultural knowledge** is the beliefs held by the organisation based on experience, observation, reflection and its environment. It will develop shared beliefs about the nature of its business, capabilities, markets and competitors and will use this criteria to judge new ideas and proposals, etc. This could help the company answer questions such as: What knowledge would be useful to the company and worth pursuing?

ACTIVITY 5.1 — application

Identify relevant examples of tacit and explicit knowledge within your own organisation.

Next gather evidence of cultural knowledge.

Organisations may struggle with the idea of environmental scanning due to rapid changes and the vast amount of data to be analysed. Resources need to be invested to allow continuous scanning to take place and for processes and systems to be introduced to manage the results. Staff also need to be encouraged to keep abreast of environmental developments and to be aware of the implications of this new knowledge. An organisation that actively interrogates its marketing environment is more likely to succeed than a passive organisation that simply analyses the information that is easily accessible to it.

MARKETING AT WORK — application

The Environmental Scanning bulletin is a regular communication containing data relating to issues that may affect the policing of Forces in the Welsh Region (North Wales; Gwent; South Wales and Dyfed-Powys) in the future. It is designed to assist with project planning and it is for Divisional Commanders and Departmental Heads to decide to what extent they pursue the information within the document.

Scanning is focused around the following framework: political (including issues of accountability and governance), environmental (eco-terrorism and congestion charging), social (demographics, family structures), technological (communication, internet), economic (resourcing, budgetary control, increasing affluence and inequality), legal (legislative changes, growth in litigation), and ethical (Freedom of Information, Human Rights).

Its aim is to provide relevant, quality information that is up-to-date and enables the police force to be informed about new challenges and changes in advance. This means activities and actions can be brought about for the right reasons at the right time and in the right place.

3 Environmental analysis frameworks

As explained earlier in this chapter, the macro- and micro-environment are external to the organisation. Macro-marketing environment forces impact upon all organisations operating in a particular market and micro-forces are competitive issues which have a more variable or localised impact on companies.

Macro-marketing environment forces cover the following areas:

- **Legal forces** – laws affecting marketing activities such as consumer protection legislation and laws emerging from the EU.
- **Regulatory forces** – the enforcement of laws by government ministries, local government departments, non-government regulatory bodies and trade/professional associations.
- **Societal forces** – culture: groups and individuals may become affected by an organisation when it infringes their lifestyles and choices.
- **Technological forces** – the expertise required to achieve tasks and goals. Technology is quickly evolving and changing and affects how people satisfy their needs and lead their lives. Technology is changing production methods, distribution, communications and selling, affecting the products marketers can bring to marketplace and how they are presented to customers.

- **Economic conditions** – recession or boom impacts on a market as does customer demand and spending behaviour. These are important considerations for any marketer.

Micro forces are not market specific but do relate to the individual company. The organisation will still have little control over these types of forces. They cover the following areas:

- **Direct and substitute competition**: the nature and degree of competition in a product area from similar products and substitute products. The organisation can consider if the market is stable and whether new kinds of competitors are emerging.

- **Supplier influence/power**: companies want to exert control over suppliers, however, this is not always possible. It is possible for suppliers to gain the upper hand if there are few suppliers or they supply innovative or unique products.

- **Company's resource base**: supplies and materials, finances, people, time and goodwill. Trends in the marketplace and environment can strengthen or weaken the resource base, eg new industry wide working practices, legislation, altered banking policies, customer pressures and demands.

- **Customers' buying power**: requirements and perceptions should be monitored. Trends in the market can increase or decrease customer buying power. This can affect an organisation's performance.

4 Impact of external forces and issues

The analysis of marketing environment forces show the organisation which opportunities to pursue, and will impact upon the choice of markets to target, identify threats to address and indicate where products and brands should be positioned and how they should by supported by the marketing mix.

Dibb and Simkin, (2008) developed three approaches to analysing marketing environment forces:

(a) **Use external consultants**: this takes time and money and it may be difficult to find relevant experts. A number of consultants with varying expertise may be required to answer the brief.

(b) **Allocate individual forces** of the marketing environment to managers or **small teams** within the organisation. They should be given ownership of their part of the environment and be encouraged to network internally and externally with those who have knowledge, expertise or insights to aid them in this task. With this approach, intranet and database systems are of importance. Regular forums can be held to demonstrate ownership and share knowledge.

(c) **Expert opinion workshop**: cross-functional managers and decision-makers plus external industry observers and subject specialists should be invited to participate. Brainstormed issues must be themed and threats or opportunities discussed. The most important themes should be given to other work teams for exploration and analysis.

The results of the environmental analysis can be fed into the SWOT analysis. Diffenbach (1983, adapted by Drummond, et al. 2008, p. 21) highlighted the positive consequences of undertaking organised environmental analysis:

- **Awareness of environmental changes by management**. This enables them to anticipate problems in the longer term; provides the impetus to act in advance of changes; and raises the awareness of possible futures for the organisation.

- **Industry and market analysis**. Analysis allows market and product forecasts to be produced that are of higher quality; changes in buyer behaviour can be identified; as can future needs and likely new products.

- **Strategic planning and decision-making**. Flexibility and adaptability can be introduced into plans that reflect political events and economic cycles; management's perspective is broadened; and resources can be allocated to opportunities that may arise.

- **Diversification and resource allocation**. Resources can be focused in areas with long-term attractiveness; guidance can be gleaned on acquisitions; the organisation can move away from products at risk from social and political pressures.

- **Relationship with government**. This is likely to be improved through understanding and more informed relations. The company can also be proactive about forthcoming legislation.

- **Overseas business.** The company can anticipate changes in overseas markets and the way of doing business in international markets.

ACTIVITY 5.2
evaluation

Evaluate how organised environmental analysis of the external environment is within your own organisation

5 External audit tools

The following audit tools are useful in assessing factors arising in the external environment: PEST analysis, Porter's 5 Forces, Strategic Group Mapping and the Industry Life Cycle.

5.1 PEST analysis

PEST (also known as PESTEL) analysis is useful for revealing the external environmental influences on a business' performance. The organisation needs to know about the environment the business will be operating in and how this might change. Information can be collated from analysis that has already been employed for other planning purposes, as well as secondary sources such as newspapers, journals, government bodies, industry bodies, research organisations and the internet. To ensure managers do not ignore factors they are not sure about, it is important to collaborate across functions and skill sets and a PEST analysis workshop is a useful exercise. The company's objectives should first be defined before a brainstorm takes places of all the environmental factors that could affect the business' ability to achieve them, at that point in time or in the future.

5.1.1 Political and legal

Political and legal sources are numerous and include local, national and supranational (multinational political communities, eg the EU) political issues. Areas of interest are:

- Direct and indirect taxes, eg income tax and VAT
- Influence of consumer spending and market demand
- Corporate taxation (affects profitability)
- Public spending by local and central government impacts on the levels of demand in the economy
- Regional and industrial policy affects business at the micro level
- Monetary policy and level of interest rates affects demand and business' ability to service debts
- Exchange rate policy – effect on importers and exporters
- Changes in international trade creates new export markets
- Competition law says rules on what business can or cannot do
- Regulation and deregulation – impact on business environment and individual business sectors
- Local practices – corruption or bureaucracy can complicate business in certain markets
- Education and training impact on business' ability to recruit qualified staff and to compete effectively internationally
- Environmental protection measures
- Employment law
- Environmental legislation

5.1.2 Economic

Economic issues relate to local, national and global economic factors in the following areas:

- **Business cycle** – periods of faster growth then slower growth or recession
- **Employment levels** – relates to the economy's position within the business cycle and the state of the local economy. High unemployment in an area reduces demand there but makes labour easier and cheaper to hire

- **Inflation** – if the rate of increase in the price of raw materials is greater than the rate of inflation for business products then the business will experience a fall in profitability over time. Interest rates and exchange rates can affect profitability
- **House prices and stockmarket prices** – their growth or fall affects consumer confidence and spending
- **Economic development** – its position, whether underdeveloped, developing or developed influences the nature of products and services that can be marketed in a country and the level of infrastructure that exists to support the performance of business activities.

5.1.3 Social

Shifts in a country's demography and social / cultural values occurs over many years. With improvements in communication and increased employee mobility between countries, the speed of social and demographic change can be expected to increase. The impact of social and cultural change should be reviewed in relation to a specific product or service.

Population growth – the rate of growth of the population will directly impact on the size of the potential addressable market for a product or service. Population growth is typically higher in developing countries. Other areas to consider are the age structure, rural to urban immigration and labour mobility, social / cultural shifts such as attitudes towards work and leisure, levels of education, work behaviour and available labour, attitudes and values.

5.1.4 Technological

This should cover the level of experience in research and development by competitors and if any changes in technology-driven production processes should be anticipated. The introduction of new technology or processes may create a new market for a technology-based product or service. Production methods can be reviewed to see if technology can help improve them as well as whether competitors could use the technology to gain a competitive advantage. Finally, the rate of adoption of new technology can provide a gauge as to how quickly it may gain mass market appeal.

5.2 Porter's 5 Forces

Porter devised (1985) an analytical framework for examining the structural factors that affect competition within an industry. Generic competitive strategies can be suggested depending on the results. Its main purpose is to assess whether an industry is attractive for a business. It is recommended that it is conducted at strategic business unit level and not on the organisation as a whole, otherwise the range of relationships assessed could become confusing as well as the analysis losing focus.

The following diagram shows the forces driving industry competition.

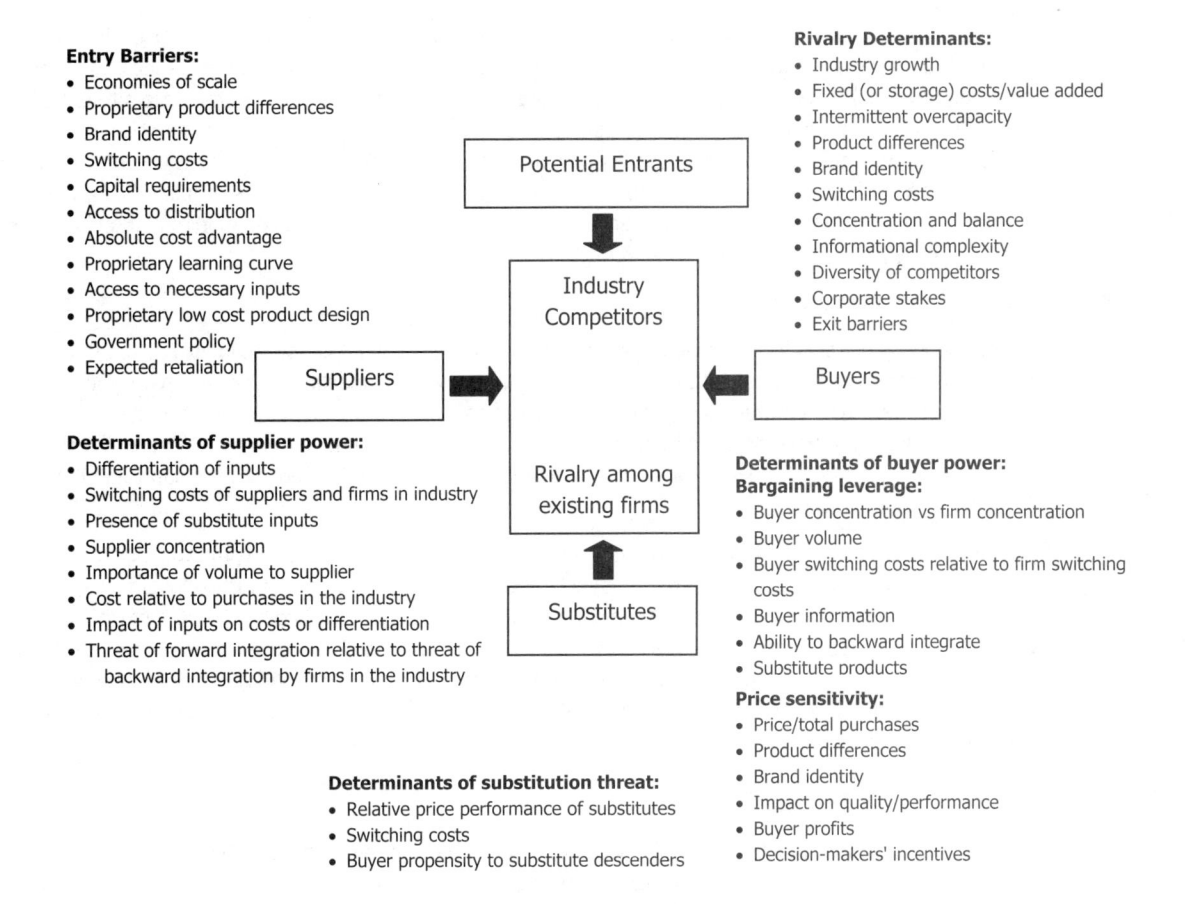

Entry Barriers:
- Economies of scale
- Proprietary product differences
- Brand identity
- Switching costs
- Capital requirements
- Access to distribution
- Absolute cost advantage
- Proprietary learning curve
- Access to necessary inputs
- Proprietary low cost product design
- Government policy
- Expected retaliation

Rivalry Determinants:
- Industry growth
- Fixed (or storage) costs/value added
- Intermittent overcapacity
- Product differences
- Brand identity
- Switching costs
- Concentration and balance
- Informational complexity
- Diversity of competitors
- Corporate stakes
- Exit barriers

Determinants of supplier power:
- Differentiation of inputs
- Switching costs of suppliers and firms in industry
- Presence of substitute inputs
- Supplier concentration
- Importance of volume to supplier
- Cost relative to purchases in the industry
- Impact of inputs on costs or differentiation
- Threat of forward integration relative to threat of backward integration by firms in the industry

Determinants of buyer power:
Bargaining leverage:
- Buyer concentration vs firm concentration
- Buyer volume
- Buyer switching costs relative to firm switching costs
- Buyer information
- Ability to backward integrate
- Substitute products

Price sensitivity:
- Price/total purchases
- Product differences
- Brand identity
- Impact on quality/performance
- Buyer profits
- Decision-makers' incentives

Determinants of substitution threat:
- Relative price performance of substitutes
- Switching costs
- Buyer propensity to substitute descenders

Porter, M. Competitive Advantage (1985)

(a) **Potential entrants**

New entrants add capacity to the market. If capacity is greater than the growth in demand for the industry's products, then profits will be reduced. The threat of new entrants is low when industries are capital intensive (a business is capital intensive if it requires heavy capital investment in buying assets relative to the level of sales or profits that those assets can generate).

The threat is also low when economies of scale are a factor. New entrants may be able to create economies of scale from their existing enterprises, or outsource manufacturing to low-cost producers possibly in other regions. Where scale economies matter, pricing is important.

Other indicators that the threat of new entrants is less likely is when access to resources is limited, access to distribution is difficult and buyers' switching costs are high (eg barriers to exiting a mortgage deal early).

Competitive strategies should be designed to deter new entrants. However, regulators may protect new entrants as the government seeks to encourage competition.

Train companies for example are capital intensive and have significant barriers to entry in the form of the rail network.

(b) **Substitutes**

Substitutes are products that perform the same function or satisfy the same need as an existing product. This threat is worse if the substitute product is cheaper or more cost effective. The threatened organisation can start making or supplying the substitute to compete. A simple example would be the DVD rental industry where substitutes are the cinema or digital downloads.

(c) **Bargaining power of suppliers**

In an industry where there are many small suppliers and few large buyers, the suppliers' bargaining power is weak. Their power is strong in an industry where there are only a few large suppliers. If there is ample availability of substitute products, and customers' switching costs are reasonable, then the ability of suppliers to raise prices is limited. The just-in-time manufacturing process increases organisations' dependency on suppliers (this is a process where stock systems trigger reordering 'just-in-time' to reduce warehouse space and costs). Porter suggests to reduce the power of suppliers, organisations should have a diverse base of suppliers or make just a few suppliers dependent on your business. Many fair trader initiatives have been launched in commodity markets to increase the bargaining power of power of poorer small farmers in developing countries.

(d) **Bargaining power of buyers**

The normal behaviour of buyers is to shop around and put downward pressure on prices. Factors that increase the power of buyers are: where switching costs are low, eg commodity products like milk which are the same no matter who produces them. The differentiation of these products can impact on price, eg if you can brand as Cravendale has done with its distinctive advertising campaign featuring animated cows and its tagline of 'filtered for purity'. The bargaining power of buyers is particularly strong when they are large compared with the supplying industry eg, Tesco purchasing farmers' goods.

Industries are not closed so it is likely that entrants will come into the market and some will execute exit strategies. Suppliers and buyers will impact upon the prospects and the profitability of the industry. Rivalry will occur amongst existing firms and the intensity of competition will affect their ability to generate adequate profit margins. The intensity of rivalry depends on a number of factors: competitors will fight for market share if the industry stops growing; when products are undifferentiated (eg when branding is not a dominant factor), competition will focus on price; and competition will be stronger in perishable markets when sales need to be made before the product expires, eg last minute summer holidays.

5.3 Strategic group mapping

Strategic group mapping seeks to plot the organisation on a map with companies who are following similar strategies and face similar strategic questions. They will be targeting groups of customers with similar profiles. There is a range of attributes which can be used to identify strategic groups such as: size of company; assets and skills; scope of the operation; breadth of the product range, choice of distribution channel; relative product quality and brand image.

For each competitor in the strategic group, a range of factors will need to be assessed: objectives; current and past strategies; capabilities; management capabilities; innovation capabilities (the ability to introduce new products, services or technologies); production capabilities; financial capabilities; future strategies and reactions; and likely reactions to the organisation's strategic moves.

Kotler, et al. (1996 quoted by Drummond, 2008, p. 32) says there are four types of response to an organisation's strategic moves:

(a) **Certain retaliation** (likely to be aggressive, particularly from the market leaders, or those with an aggressive culture).

(b) **Failure to react** (the competitor may be lulled into a false sense of security if there has been no change in the industry over time).

(c) **Specific reactions** (they may react but only to certain moves in certain areas, eg price reductions or sales promotions and may fail to respond to other moves. The more visible a competitor's move, the more likely their response.

(d) **Inconsistent reactions** (these are not predictable and can range from aggressive to a failure to react).

Strategic group mapping was developed by Michael Porter (1980) and forms part of his overall system of strategic analysis. The mapping process brings industry competitors together into meaningful groups based on at least two strategic variables. The number of groups within an industry would depend on the dimensions used to classify them. These are then placed onto a two-dimensional grid positioning firms along the two most important dimensions so direct rivals can be identified from indirect rivals. The analysis is generally based on secondary financial and accounting data.

Examples of the strategic variables that could be utilised are:

- Extent of product (or service) diversity
- Extent of geographic coverage
- Number of market segments served
- Distribution channels used
- Extent of branding
- Marketing effort
- Product (or service) quality
- Pricing policy

The analysis can help organisations identify their direct competitors and on what basis they compete; it can identify how likely or possible it is for a competitor to move from one strategic group to another; it can also help identify opportunities and strategic problems.

The agency Bluewater International provides details about creating strategic group maps.

http://www.bluewaterinternational.net/bluewater/CompetitiveAnalysis.pdf for a useful guide to creating a strategic group map.

5.4 Industry life cycle

Industries evolve in size and structurally over their life cycle. The industry's structure and competitive forces shape the environment in which businesses operate and can change throughout the life cycle. A business will need to change its strategies accordingly. The industry life cycle measures total industry sales and growth.

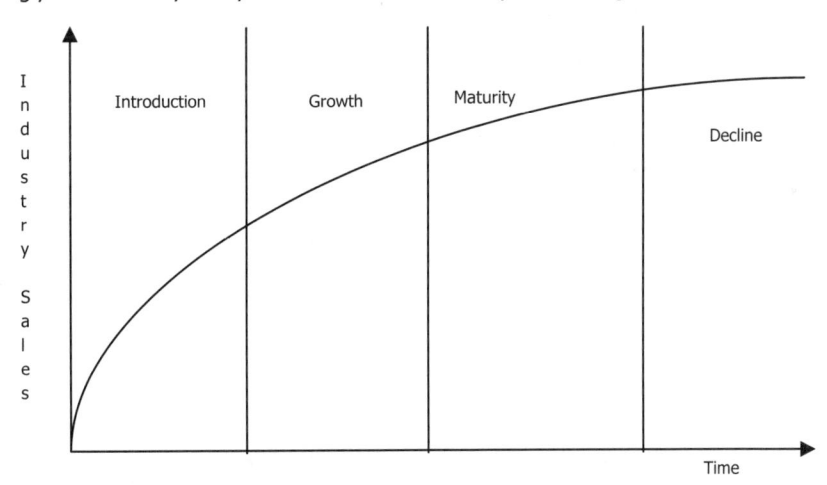

The stages of the industry life cycle break down as follows:

Introduction: At the beginning of the cycle, there are few competitors and no threat from substitutes due to the newness of the industry. The bargaining power of buyers is low; those who want the product will pay to get hold of limited supplies. Suppliers have some power because of low volumes. The industry may be relatively unimportant for suppliers.

Growth: The number of competitors increases as other firms join the growing industry. Growth in demand outstrips growth of capacity so rivalry amongst firms is checked. The bargaining power of buyers is still low because demand exceeds supply. Industry growth is associated with high profitability. Firms may be profitable but are likely to be spending on achieving market share and position.

Maturity: The bargaining power of buyers starts to increase as capacity matches or exceeds demand. The bargaining power of suppliers has declined because volumes purchased by industry is important to them. Losing a large customer could be damaging to their livelihood. The threat from substitutes is now growing. The industry will start to consolidate with mergers and acquisitions taking place. Mature industries will be settled with low risks and the opportunity to generate cash. Rivalry among competitors is fierce and falling prices pose a threat to profitability.

Decline: As capacity exceeds supply so the power of buyers increases. The weakest competitors will withdraw leading to less rivalry. Firms may combine forces to ask for government intervention or subsidies to help protect the declining industry. The threat of substitutes is now high. A slowly declining industry can produce attractive returns for investors as no new investment is required as the industry is run down and milked for cash.

5.5 Scenario planning

This is a framework that can provide a structured approach to considering the future of a marketing environment in which the organisation operates. For dynamic and turbulent markets, it may be incredibly difficult to predict the future and trying to forecast based on previous experience or performance could lead to wrong assumptions being made.

Scenario planning creates different environments in which a business may have to operate and highlights the trends and interactions that may characterise their development. It gives both a framework and a narrative for the market forecast while helping the organisation understand the forces affecting the industry and how it might evolve.

An example of the scenario planning impact / uncertainty matrix is shown in the following diagram:

	Business Impact	
	LOW	HIGH
Uncertainty HIGH		
Uncertainty LOW		

There are 4 stages to this process:

Stage 1 Identify factors of high uncertainty and high impact. A list of environmental factors from previously conducted PEST analysis can be allocated across the four quadrants of an impact / uncertainty matrix. Uncertainty relates to how easy it is to predict the future behaviour of a factor. Impact relates to how significantly a factor influences business performance. Factors that are certain and benign may become highly volatile and influential in the future.

Stage 2 Next, alternative behaviour patterns for those factors should be described. The top right quadrant contains the environmental factors that have the greatest potential impact on the business and highest level of future uncertainty. Around two to three different development paths for each of the factors in the quadrant should be described, the paths should be contrasting but realistic.

Stage 3 Select three to four of most informative scenarios to form the basis of market demand forecasts and strategy formulation.

Stage 4 Write scenario descriptions – each scenario should be given an appropriate name and a vivid description. A description of how they develop over time should be prepared. Additional factors from the quadrants can be included.

ACTIVITY 5.3

application

Think of how the future marketing environment might impact your organisation using a scenario planning matrix as above. You will need to consider all possible PESTEL issues.

Learning objective review

Learning objectives	Covered
1. Understand the need for external analysis and the changing nature of environmental change.	☑ Controllable and uncontrollable factors ☑ Environmental change in different time frames ☑ Uncertainty in markets
2. Employ key environmental analysis frameworks and external audit tools.	☑ Environmental scanning ☑ Environmental analysis framework ☑ Macro and micro forces ☑ PESTEL analysis ☑ Porter's 5 forces ☑ Strategic group mapping ☑ Industry life cycle ☑ Scenario planning

Quick quiz

1. Identify some 'controllable' factors that marketers face.
2. Cyclical change is long term and permanent. True or False?
3. What is environmental scanning?
4. What are the four forms of environmental scanning according to Drummond?
5. What is strategic group mapping?

Activity debriefs

Worksheet activity 5.1

This will depend on your own research.

Worksheet activity 5.2

This will depend on your own research. Use Drummond's List as a starting point if you are finding this a difficult activity to complete.

Worksheet activity 5.3

This will depend on your own research. You should have created quite an extensive table. Even thinking of one development such as the growth of social networking you will possibly consider the business impact as high because:

- in order to protect your brand(s) it will be important to register your claims before others can
- your customers and clients may be established users of social media and expect you to also use it.

In terms of uncertainty however, it is likely to also be high (unless you are working in the IT industry and have a high level of expertise) because how it is likely to be developed in the future is difficult to anticipate.

Quiz answers

1. Controllable factors can include:

    The marketing mix plans, marketing spend, agency selection etc

2. False. Structural change is long term and permanent while cyclical change is temporary and often seasonal.

3. The careful monitoring of a firm's internal and external environments for detecting early signs of opportunities and threats that may influence its current and future plans.

4. Undirected viewing, conditional viewing, informal search and formal search.

5. A method of plotting the organisation on a map with companies who are following similar strategies and face similar strategic questions.

References

Bluewater International. (2005). *'Competitive Analysis'*. [Online] Updated 2005. Available at http://www.bluewaterinternational.net/bluewater/CompetitiveAnalysis.pdf [Accessed 16 Apr 2009].

BusinessDictionary.com. (2009). *Definition – environmental scanning'*. [Online] Copyright 2007-2009. Available at http://www.businessdictionary.com/definition/environmental-scanning.html [Accessed 19 Apr 2009].

Chun Wei, C. (2001). *'Environmental scanning as information seeking and organisational learning.'* [Online] Updated 24 Sep 2001. Available at http://InformationR.net/ir/7-1/paper112.html [Accessed 16 Apr 2009].

Dibb, S. & Simkin, L., (2008) Marketing Planning – A Workbook for Marketing Managers. Cengage Learning, London.

Drummond, G., Ensor, J. & Ashford, R., (2008) Strategic Marketing Planning & Control. (3rd ed.), Butterworth-Heinemann, Oxford.

Friend, G. & Zehle, S.,(2004) The Economist Guide to Business Planning. The Economist in assoc. with Profile Books, London.

Kotler, P. Armstrong, G. Wong, V. & Saunders, J.,(2008.) Principles of Marketing. (5th European ed.), Harlow: Pearson Education, Harlow.

Lancaster, G. Massingham, L. & Ashford, R., (2002). Essentials of Marketing. (4th ed.). Maidenhead:. McGraw-Hill Education, Maidenhead.

Local Government Association, (2007). *'All Wales Environmental Scanning Bulletin'*. [Online] Updated Oct 2007. Available at http://www.lga.gov.uk/lga/aio/1098312 [Accessed 19 Apr 2009].

McDonald, M., (2007) Marketing Plans – How to Prepare Them, How to Use Them. (6th ed.), Butterworth-Heinemann, Oxford.

Porter, M. (1985) Competitive Advantage, The Free Press, New York.

Chapter 6
Appraising the internal marketing environment

Topic list

1 Resource-based planning and strategy
2 Internal environmental analysis frameworks

Introduction

As we saw in the previous chapter, environmental analysis helps us understand the factors that will directly face organisations and have a major impact upon the way that they operate. External and internal analysis forms part of the strategic analysis framework and guides the formulation of strategies and the strategic marketing plan. This chapter looks at the internal marketing environment. It looks at the nature of organisational change and how the organisation can exploit its assets and competences in gaining competitive advantage. We will then examine a range of frameworks and internal audit tools that enable the assessment of the internal environment, including the product life cycle, value chain and some of the important portfolio models.

Syllabus-linked learning objectives

By the end of the chapter you will be able to:

Learning objectives	Syllabus link
1. Understand the nature of internal organisational change and the concept of resource-based planning.	2.5
2. Undertake internal environmental analysis using a variety of frameworks and models.	2.5

Examining the internal environment of an organisation and assessing its resources is the final stage of the auditing process. This tells the company the information and analysis it needs to identify its key assets and competences upon which a strategic position can be firmly built. An organisation is looking for the ability to compete and satisfy its customers' needs in attractive market areas and to develop a competitive position that matches its capabilities to the needs of its consumers.

1 Resource-based planning and strategy

The planning process aims to maximise the use of the business' resources (internal factors) while taking into consideration the environment (external factors). Analysing both these factors helps management when it comes to setting or reviewing their objectives and strategies and considering alternative options.

A resource-based view of an organisation is very different to that of the marketing concept. With a resource-based concept, the company seeks to exploit its distinctive capabilities whereas with a market orientation, responsiveness to market needs is key.

KEY CONCEPT

What are resources? **Resources** refer to the assets and competences of an organisation.

Assets can be described as the tangible and intangible capital of the company. These can be financial or non-financial.

Competences are the skills that lie within the organisation. These skills are applied in order to deploy the assets to deliver the organisation's strategic capabilities in the market of their choice. Corporate capabilities are the combination of assets and competencies that demonstrate the organisation's competitive capacity.

Assets according to Drummond, et al. (2008) can be broken down to include the following:

(a) Financial assets – working capital, access to investment finance, creditworthiness.

(b) Physical assets – ownership or control of facilities and property.

(c) Operational assets – production plant, machinery and process technologies.

(d) People assets – quantity of human resources available and the quality of this resource.

(e) Legally enforceable assets – ownership of copyrights and patents, franchise and licensing agreements.

(f) Systems – management information systems and databases, general infrastructure for supporting decision-making activities.

(g) Marketing assets – these can be split into four categories:

    (i) **Customer-based assets** – these are assets that the customer perceives as important:

- Image and reputation of the company.
- Brand franchises – effective brands have high customer loyalty, defendable competitive positions and higher margins because customers feel the higher price is merited by the added value the brand provides.
- Market leadership – provides benefits such as market coverage, widespread distribution and good shelf positioning.
- Country of origin – customers associate specific attributes with different countries.
- Unique products and services – eg price, quality, design or level of innovation.

    (ii) **Distribution-based assets** – the size and quality of the distribution network (geographical spread, intensity of coverage, fitness for purpose) and the level of control over distribution channels (can stop competitors getting a hold in a region).

    (iii) **Internally-based assets** – cost structure (may have higher capacity utilisation, better economies of scale, new or more innovative technology enabling the organisation to set lower prices with the asset being the manufacturing cost base. Information systems – can be used to collect and analyse customer, competitor and market information and create customer databases which can be exploited as a powerful marketing asset. Innovatory culture – advantages can be created in marketing activities through innovation, eg the new product development process is supported and front line customer service staff can develop creative solutions to customer' issues. Production skills – eg more flexibility, higher quality, shorter lead times.

    (iv) **Alliance-based assets** – links to formal or informal external relationships. Agreement with third parties can give the organisation access to markets (through local distributors), management expertise (from outside agencies), access to technological developments or processes (licensing or joint ventures), and exclusive agreements (third parties that exclude competitors).

Organisational competences are the abilities and skills to enable the exploitation of a company's assets. Competences can be found at the three decision-making tiers: strategic, functional and operational and at three levels of the organisation's structure: corporate, team and individual level according to Hooley, et al. (1998 quoted by Drummond, et al. 2008, p. 93).

Drummond, et al. break down competences into six areas:

(a) **Strategic competences**: relating to management skills, the drive and strategic direction of the organisation, and the ability to create a strategic vision, communicate, motivate, implement strategy, assess changing circumstances, learn and innovate.

(b) **Functional competences**: the skills to manage activities in functional areas such as finance, operations and marketing. The marketing function is also assessed on skills like handling customer relationships, channel management, product management, product innovation and NPD.

(c) **Operational competences**: skills relating to the running of day-to-day operations. In marketing, this relates to co-ordinating and implementing sales force activities, promotional campaigns, PR, special offers and discounts, updating product packaging and labelling, co-ordinating and controlling external relationships for suppliers like ad agencies, etc.

(d) **Individual competences**: the skills of individual staff to execute tasks in their area of responsibility, at a strategic, functional or operational level.

(e) **Team competences**: formal or informal teams, need the skills to work together and manage projects effectively.

(f) **Corporate-level competences** – skills which apply to the organisation and its ability to execute tasks at the three levels: strategic, functional and operational, eg by fostering innovation, exploiting and updating the company knowledge base.

Once an organisation has identified its key assets and competences, these can be mapped to uncover key relationships and assess whether some assets are more important than others.

ACTIVITY 6.1 — Application

Using Drummond's six areas of competence, evaluate our own organisation's competences.

2 Internal environmental analysis frameworks

It is important to identify assets and competences that can be used by the marketing function to excel in the industry. Assets and competences can also be found in other functions within the organisation so Hooley (1998) recommends firms undertake a full audit. This should cover five categories:

- Financial resources
- Managerial skills
- Technical sources
- Organisation
- Information systems

Once this is completed, analysis can move on to examining specific marketing activities undertaken by the organisation with an internal marketing audit.

Kotler, et al. (2008) also highlight five areas of coverage for the internal marketing audit:

(a) **Marketing strategy audit** – current corporate and marketing objectives. Are they relevant and explicit? Does the strategy fit with the objectives? Are there adequate resources to implement the strategy?

(b) **Marketing structures audit** – marketing function and its relationship with other areas. Examine the profile of the marketing function. Is there communication between marketing itself and other functions? Are marketing activities carried out efficiently?

(c) **Marketing systems audit** – looks at planning systems, control measures, NPD processes and information systems to support these activities.

(d) **Productivity audit** – uses financial criteria such as profitability and cost effectiveness to assess relative productivity of products, market sectors, distribution channels and geographic markets.

(e) **Marketing functions audit** – covers all aspects of the marketing mix: products and services, pricing policy, distribution arrangements, organisation of the sales team, advertising policy, PR and other promotions.

The organisation can also examine its activities in the area of innovation which is becoming increasing important to companies who wish to stand out from the crowd and grow their market leadership status.

2.1 The innovation audit

Innovation is increasingly becoming a method of achieving competitive advantage. The organisation needs to be able to assess how effective it is in delivering the levels of innovation required to create new products, services, implementing technology and finding better ways of undertaking marketing activities. Innovative practice means companies must find ways of harnessing creativity in their staff at all levels of the business. Staff at Google spend 80% of their week on core projects and 20% on innovation activities that 'speak to their personal interests and passions'. These may be activities that benefit the company's bottom line but they are also concerned about stimulating employees, keeping them motivated and inspired, and helping them to learn and grow (The Mama Bee, 2009).

The innovation audit assesses whether assets and competences are available from a number of perspectives.

2.1.1 The current organisation climate with regard to innovation

Drummond, et al. (2008) recommend conducting an attitude survey of key areas of the organisation's climate that affect creativity. There are eight influential factors that support innovation and four areas of constraints as highlighted by Burnside, (1990, quoted by Drummond, et al. (2008), p. 96).

Influential factors break down as:

- **Teamwork**: level of employees' commitment to work, the level of trust between members and their willingness to help each other.
- **Resources**: access to resources in terms of facilities, staff, finance and innovation.
- **Challenge**: of work in terms of importance and nature of task.
- **Freedom**: the amount of control individuals have over their own work and ideas.
- **Supervisor**: managerial support in terms of clear goals, good communication and building moral.
- **Creativity infrastructure**: level of senior management support and encouragement of creativity, having the structures in place that are necessary for developing creative ideas.
- **Recognition**: recognition and rewards given for innovative ideas.
- **Unity and co-operation**: collaborative and co-operative atmosphere and the amount of shared vision in the organisation.

Constraints are:

- **Insufficient time**: to consider alternative approaches to work.
- **Status quo**: taking the traditional approach, or managers and staff unwilling to change the way we do things.
- **Political problems**: battles over areas of responsibility and a lack of co-operation between different areas of organisation.
- **Evaluation pressure**: evaluation or feedback systems may be inappropriate. An environment that is focused on criticism and external evaluation.

Two other areas which can be included when assessing staffs' perception of the organisation's climate are:

(a) **Creativity**: their overall perception of how creative the organisation is.
(b) **Productivity**: how productive the organisation is perceived to be.

2.1.2 Metaphorical description techniques

The technique of metaphorical description was developed by Morgan (1993, quoted by Drummond, et al. (2008), p. 97) and was designed to overcome the limitations of literal language. Metaphorical description describes more complex relationships and connections within the organisation. Individuals undertaking this analysis should describe the organisation in terms of a metaphor. These metaphorical descriptions can then be analysed. They can show a more rounded view of the organisational climate and are likely to be either positive or negative and based around seven organisational practices:

- Managerial skills
- Organisational structure
- Operations
- Organisational life cycle
- Strategic orientation
- People orientation
- Power orientation

2.1.3 Hard measures of organisation's current performance in innovation

Hard measures that can be reviewed include the rate of new product development in the last three years, customer satisfaction ratings and staff turnover figures. Innovation / value portfolio analysis can also be conducted on strategic business units or specific products to see if they are 'settlers' (products or businesses that offer normal value), 'migrators' (products or businesses that offer value improvements over their competitors), or 'pioneers' (products or businesses that offer value innovations).

2.1.4 Organisation's policies and practices currently used to support innovation

A review can be made of current policies to see if structures and procedures have been developed to foster creativity and innovation. Sometimes policies are too detailed and bureaucratic meaning that innovation is stifled. An FMCG organisation for example had 60 different lines of 'sign of' to be completed when developing a new confectionary product.

2.1.5 Balance of cognitive styles of the senior management team

Cognitive styles is a term from psychology that explains the way individuals think, perceive and remember information, or their preferred approach to using information to solve problems. It is important to have a mix of cognitive styles amongst the senior management team in order to ensure the organisation will lean towards creativity and innovative practices.

Management can employ a range of cognitive styles as seen in this framework, adapted from Hurst, et al. (1989) by Drummond, et al. (2008) p. 100.

Cognitive preference	Concerned with...	Handles these with...	Tends to be...
Intuition	Possibilities, patterns and ideas	Metaphors and symbols	Ingenious and integrative
Feeling	People and values	Force of personality	Enthusiastic and insightful
Thinking	Cause and effect things	Regulations and language	Reliable and orderly
Sensation	Activities, events	Spontaneity and action	Adaptable and practical

Interestingly, theorists say that team members with similar cognitive styles will feel more positive about their participation in a team. Matching cognitive styles will make individuals feel more comfortable working together but cannot guarantee a positive outcome.

2.2 Innovative companies

In the 2009 annual survey of top business executives by the Boston Consulting Group (BCG) (in conjunction with BusinessWeek magazine), more respondents said that innovation spending will be flat or down than since the ranking began in 2005. However, companies that strive to be innovative are still making returns on their innovation investments. IBM is shifting jobs to low-cost centres of manufacturing and service such as India as well as broadening its services through acquisitions. The Chief Executive, Samuel Palmisano, was quoted by BusinessWeek as saying: *'Some may be tempted to hunker down, to scale back their investment in innovation. While that might make sense during a cyclical downturn, it's a mistake when you're going through a major shift in the global economy.'*

2.2.1 The world's most innovative companies

(Taken from the BusinessWeek's 25 Most Innovative Companies List 2009 compiled from a survey of top executives by the Boston Consulting Group.)

2009 Rank	2008 Rank	Company	HQ Country	Known for its Most Innovative... (% who think so in top executive survey)
1	1	APPLE	USA	PRODUCT 47%
2	2	GOOGLE	USA	CUSTOMER EXPERIENCE 26%
3	3	TOYOTA MOTOR	JAPAN	PROCESS 35%
4	5	MICROSOFT	USA	PROCESS 26%
5	7	NINTENDO	JAPAN	PRODUCT 48%
6	12	IBM	USA	PROCESS 31%
7	15	HEWLETT-PACKARD	USA	PROCESS 39%
8	13	RESEARCH IN MOTION	CANADA	PRODUCT 53%
9	10	NOKIA	FINLAND	PRODUCT 38%
10	23	WAL-MART STORES	USA	PROCESS 49%

MARKETING AT WORK   application

The Department for Innovation, Universities and Skills was set up in June 2007 with the brief of serving learners and businesses (including the public sector) and helping the UK to foster innovation.

It aims to do this by creating an 'excellent, accessible education system' to provide individuals with the skills they need to prosper, especially those who may be moving from welfare into work, or from unskilled jobs towards a more rewarding career. The Department also assists businesses in helping develop skills in their staff for today and the future, as well as creating an environment in which researchers and businesses can work together to turn their ideas into high-value products and services.

The DIUS wants to ensure Britain is the best place in the world to run an innovative business or service. It sees this as critical to the UK's future prosperity, quality of life and future job prospects. It is believed that boosting and focusing investment in innovation in areas where the UK has strength and potential for future competitive advantage must be a key element of government action during the downturn to ensure a successful recovery.

2.3 Internal audit tools

Products and services should be able to maximise an organisation's opportunities and to fit customers' needs. In order to do this, a company must be able to assess which are the most profitable and which should be divested (when a company sells off a business unit in order to focus on more profitable areas).

There are a number of portfolio analysis models which will be looked at here. They are particularly useful for existing, larger businesses with multiple products. They can help make strategic decisions about the allocation of cash resources amongst a portfolio. Some may need cash injection, some generate cash and others may need to be divested. This type of analysis can also be done for competitors and can help the company make strategic comparisons between their business and key competitors.

2.3.1 Product life cycle

Product life cycles are becoming shorter due to fast-moving customer requirements and competitor activity. This can make it hard for firms to recover the high cost of NPD and R&D during a product's life cycle. Therefore, this model can be used as a control mechanism to assist with the planning of marketing activities and sales forecasting. It can also identify the main challenges facing a product and should be done on a product-by-product, and market-by-market basis. The implications of the PLC analysis can be used to develop more effective marketing strategies and programmes for the implementation of the marketing mix.

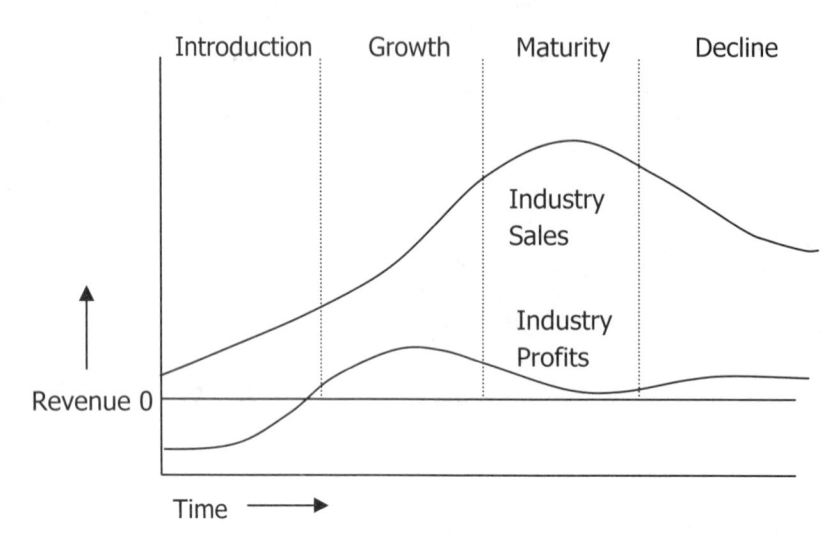

Attributed to Dibb, et al. (2006) taken from Dibb and Simkin (2008, p. 65)

The stages of the product life cycle break down as follows:

(a) **Introduction**

This is the early stage of the product's life before sales start to increase. It is a risky stage and needs a great deal of management input as start-up and research costs will already have been invested. It is still possible to fine tune the marketing mix or relaunch the product. If there are early signs of success and the resources are available, then the firm can opt for penetration pricing in order to drive up volume and capture market share before competitors enter the market. This will increase the risk involved. Penetration pricing is a technique where the price is set at a low initial entry price to attract new customers. It relies on customers switching to the new lower priced brand.

(b) **Growth**

The start of the growth stage is characterised by an acceleration in the level of sales. As volume increases, demand for the product is proven and competitors enter the market. This leads to more investment in capacity and working capital. This early growth stage may be when most funding is needed. The beginning of the stage is all about winning new customers and as it progresses, it moves to customer retention. This stage is also marked by the point of inflection on the s-shaped PLC curve where growth stops accelerating and starts decelerating.

(c) **Maturity**

This stage can be sub-divided into growth maturity, stable maturity and decaying maturity. Growth objectives remain, but companies will be looking to increase their sales through higher repeat purchasing, increased frequency and finding new uses for the existing product. There will be a fight for market share and cost reduction. Some competitors may consolidate their offerings or offer an improved version of the product with new marketing mix activities, eg stimulating sales through changing pricing, promotions, service or distribution. The aim in the maturity stage is to seek differentiation or competitive advantage for the product.

(d) **Decline**

At this stage, the least efficient competitors will start to exit the market. There will be a strong focus on cost reduction to maintain profitability despite declining sales. Assets may be reallocated. It is common to see re-organisation and a change of management style. Demand for some products may remain but will settle at a lower level. Sales may fall due to customer tastes, competing substitute products, social concerns, legislation, media coverage or corporate policies. Despite this, a declining product can still provide a profitable niche business.

2.3.2 Portfolio models: the value chain

Porter describes the organisation as a series of processes that generate value for customers and other stakeholders. By examining each value creating activity, sources of potential cost leadership and differentiation can be identified. The links between the activities are critical to ensure continuation of the value chain. The final value generated is the margin of value.

This model, shown in the diagrams below, helps analyse competitive advantage, the key skills and processes involved and the linkages between them that can be improved to generate success. A useful exercise would be to link the value chains of manufacturers involved in the same production process to show common support activities and to find ways of reducing overall costs and improve co-ordination between the companies.

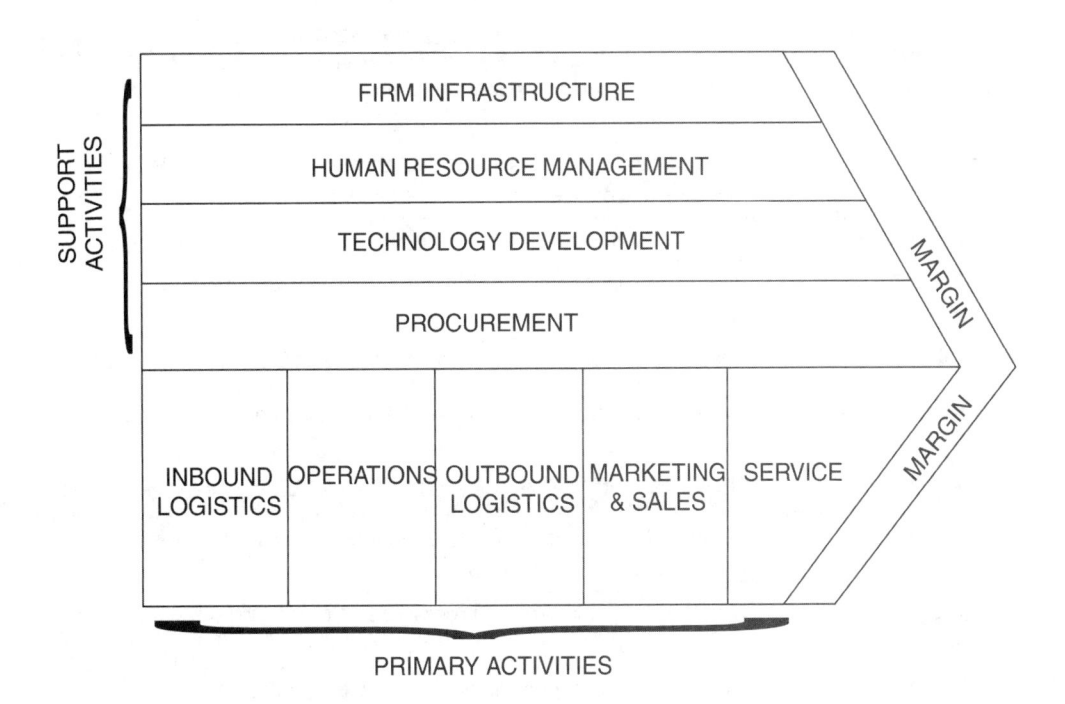

SUPPORT ACTIVITIES	FIRM INFRASTRUCTURE				
	HUMAN RESOURCE MANAGEMENT				
	TECHNOLOGY DEVELOPMENT				
	PROCUREMENT				
	INBOUND LOGISTICS	OPERATIONS	OUTBOUND LOGISTICS	MARKETING & SALES	SERVICE

PRIMARY ACTIVITIES — MARGIN

	Secondary Activities			
	Firm's infrastructure			
	Technology development			
	Human resource management			
	Procurement			
In-bound logistics	Operations	Out-bound logistics	Marketing and sales	Service

Primary Activities

Margin of value

The **margin** is the excess the customer is prepared to **pay** over the **cost** to the firm of obtaining resource inputs and providing value activities.

Primary activities are directly related to production, sales, marketing, delivery and service.

Activity	Comment
Inbound logistics	Receiving, handling and storing inputs to the production system: warehousing, transport, stock control.
Operations	Convert resource inputs into a final product. Resource inputs are not only materials. People are a resource especially in service industries.
Outbound logistics	Storing the product and its distribution to customers: packaging, warehousing, testing.
Marketing and sales	Informing customers about the product, persuading them to buy it, and enabling them to do so: advertising, promotion.
After-sales service	Installing products, repairing them, upgrading them, providing spare parts and so forth.

Support activities provide purchased inputs, human resources, technology and infrastructural functions to support the primary activities.

Activity	Comment
Procurement	Acquire the resource inputs to the primary activities (eg purchase of materials, subcomponents equipment).
Technology development	Product design, improving processes and/or resource utilisation.
Human resource management	Recruiting, training, developing and rewarding people.
Management planning	Planning, finance, quality control: Porter believes they are crucially important to an organisation's strategic capability in all primary activities.

Linkages connect the activities of the value chain.

(a) **Activities in the value chain affect one another**. For example, more costly product design or better quality production might reduce the need for after-sales service.

(b) **Linkages require co-ordination**. For example, just-in-time requires smooth functioning of operations, outbound logistics and service activities such as installation.

KEY CONCEPT

concept

Value activities are the means by which a firm creates value in its products.

Activities incur costs, and, in combination with other activities, provide a product or service that earns revenue. 'Firms create value for their buyers by performing these activities.'

MARKETING AT WORK

application

Let us explain this point by using the example of a **restaurant**. A restaurant's activities can be divided into buying food, cooking it, and serving it (to customers). There is no reason, in theory, why the customers should not do all these things themselves, at home. The customer however, is not only prepared to **pay for someone else** to do all this but also **pays more than the cost of** the resources. The ultimate value a firm creates is measured by the amount customers are willing to pay for its products or services above the cost of carrying out value activities. A firm is profitable if the realised value to customers exceeds the collective cost of performing the activities.

(a) Customers **purchase value**, which they measure by comparing a firm's products and services with similar offerings by competitors.

(b) The business creates value by carrying out its activities either more efficiently than other businesses, or combining them in such a way as to provide a unique product or service.

ACTIVITY 6.2

application

Outline different ways in which the restaurant described in the example above can create value.

The examples below are based on two supermarket chains, one concentrating on low prices, the other differentiated on quality and service. See if you can tell which is which.

(a)

Firm infrastructure	Central control of operations and credit control				
Human resource management	Recruitment of mature staff	Client care training	Flexible staff to help with packing		
Technology development		Recipe research	Electronic point of sale	Consumer research & tests	Itemised bills
Procurement	Own label products	Prime retail positions		Adverts in quality magazines & poster sites	
	Dedicated refrigerated transport	In store food halls Modern store design Open front refrigerators Tight control of sell-by dates	Collect by car service	No price discounts on food past sell-by dates	No quibble refunds
	INBOUND LOGISTICS	OPERATIONS	OUTBOUND LOGISTICS	MARKETING & SALES	SERVICE

6: Appraising the internal marketing environment 113

(b)

Firm infrastructure	Minimum corporate HQ				
Human resource management		De-skilled store-ops	Dismissal for checkout error		
Technology development	Computerised warehousing		Checkouts simple		
Procurement	Branded only purchases big discounts	Low cost sites			Use of concessions
	Bulk warehousing	Limited range Price points Basic store design		Low price promotion Local focus	Nil
	INBOUND LOGISTICS	OPERATIONS	OUTBOUND LOGISTICS	MARKETING & SALES	SERVICE

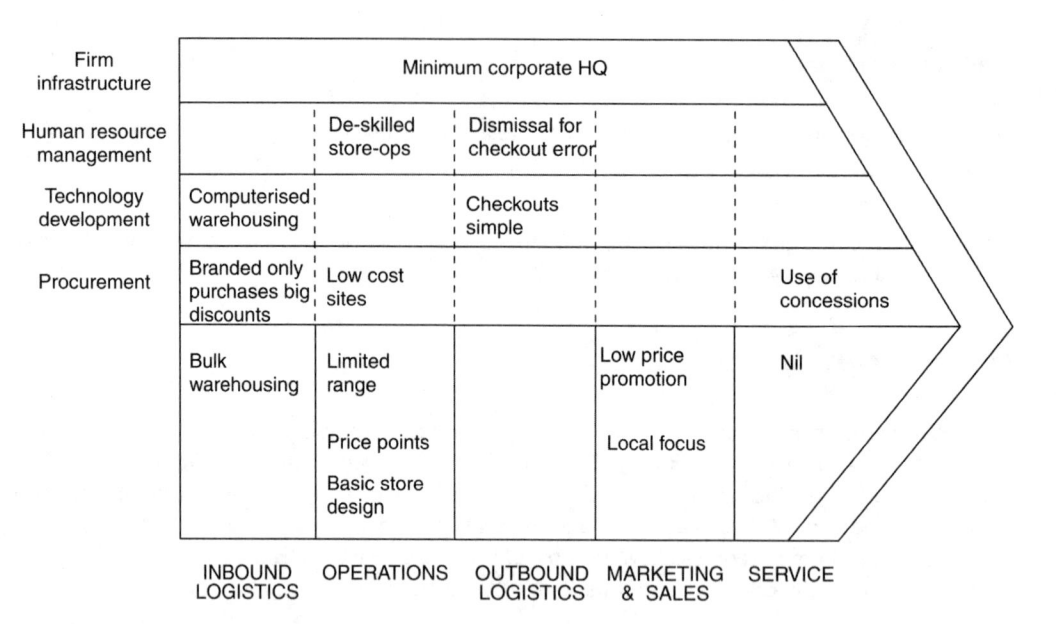

2.3.3 Portfolio models: the Boston Matrix

The Boston Matrix was created in the 1970s by the Boston Consulting Group to help companies decide on an appropriate strategy for their future. The matrix looks at how different products or parts of a company can be compared in terms of market growth and share. A company's ability to develop its product portfolio relies on its cash flow and this matrix classifies products according to cash usage and generation on those two dimensions of market growth rate and market share using a scatter graph.

Products or business units fall into four quadrants:

(a) **Cash cow**: A product or business unit with a large share of the market that is no longer growing. It is a revenue generator but this can be invested in other areas of the company. Further investment in the cash cow would be unlikely to produce more profit.

(b) **Star**: A product or business unit with a large share of the market. Unlike the cash cow, it is growing rapidly. It requires more investment to grow further which it might be able to fund from its own profits. When it stops growing, a star may become a cash cow.

(c) **Problem child/Question mark**: A product or business unit with a small share of a growing market. Considerable investment is required to make it grow.

(d) **Dog**: A product or business unit with a small share of a market that is not growing. This sector is of little value to a company and divestment may be the way forward.

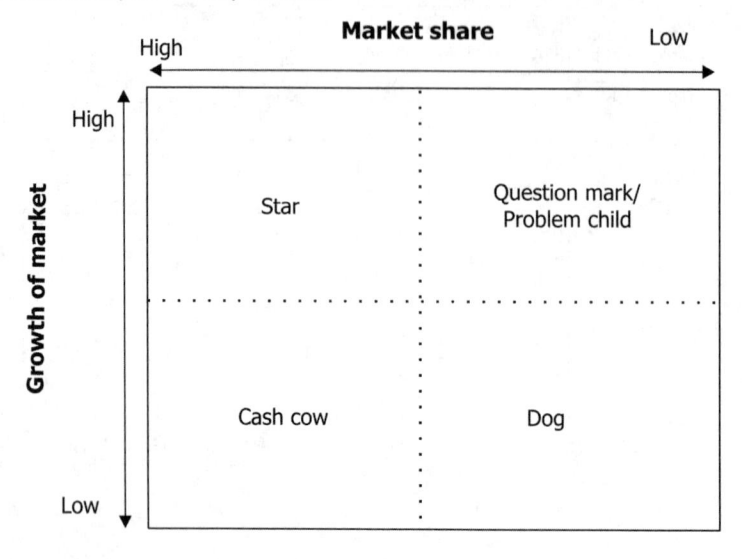

	Market share	
	High ← → Low	
High ↑ Growth of market Low ↓	Star Cash cow	Question mark/ Problem child Dog

The natural cycle in an industry is for business units to start as question marks, then turn into stars. When the market stops growing, the unit will become a cash cow. At the end of the cycle, the cash cow turns into a dog. Analysts can decide from these findings whether to fund parts of their business and by how much, and also which units to divest.

The BCG stated in 1970 that: Only a diversified company with a balanced portfolio can use its strengths to truly capitalise on its growth opportunities. The balanced portfolio has:

- Stars whose high share and high growth assure the future;
- Cash cows that supply funds for that future growth; and
- Question marks to be converted into stars with the added funds.

2.3.4 Portfolio models: Directional Policy Matrix

The Directional Policy Matrix is a more complex model which assesses business strength and market attractiveness. It looks at the worth of investing in particular areas to determine strategic planning goals, funding and human resources. It can be used for strategic business units, product groups, individual products or brands, target markets or market segments.

The performance of each unit is reviewed and the 'health' of each in the context of the overall portfolio will help the company to decide which to build (develop and increase market share), maintain (invest resources to keep at a certain level of market share), harvest (sell-off or pull out after taking the last potential sales) or divest (drop immediately).

The analysis is broken down into six stages:

Stage 1 **Decide which variables are most appropriate for assessing market attractiveness.** It should be a cross-functional team who select these variables not just marketers. Some long-term factors and market-facing factors should be included as well as current profitability.

Stage 2 **Decide which criteria are appropriate for examining the business position in relation to the leading competitor.** Around 10-12 variables should be selected which are industry-specific, focusing on strengths that major players emphasise and which customers are looking for, eg product sales, industry sales, profitability, customer retention rate, etc.

Stage 3 Two lists of variables will now have been produced for market attractiveness and business position. Next, the importance of each variable relative to the others is decided. A weighting is allocated. This should add up to 100 in each list. These lists and weightings can remain constant over time to allow for the monitoring of trends.

Stage 4 A score is now given to each variable reflecting how the product shapes up relative to the others being assessed. A 5 or 7 point scale can be used, eg 0.0 = low/poor, 0.5 = medium/average and 1.0 = high/good.

Stage 5 Then the weightings are multiplied by the score to give a ranking for each variable. The sum of the rankings for each product group will then be calculated. This gives a total out of 100 for market attractiveness and another score for business position.

Stage 6 The two totals are plotted for each item (product, etc) on the matrix using a circle. The diameter reflects sales volume or proportion of total company income from the unit. If the market size is known, an area of the circle can be shaded to show it. Otherwise small circles might be divested even though you have dominant market share and little outlay.

Example of Directional Policy Matrix Analysis, Dibb and Simkin (2008):

Market attractiveness – example analysis for a strategic business unit.

Variable	Agreed weighting	Agreed scoring	Final ranking
Industry sales	5	0	0
Product sales	10	0.5	5
Market share	25	0.5	12.5
Profitability	25	1	25
Competitor intensity	10	0.5	5
Customer retention rate	10	0.5	5
Future growth prospects	10	1	10
Ability to differentiate	5	0	0
			62.5

Business position/Competitive position – example analysis for a strategic business unit.

Variable	Agreed weighting	Agreed scoring	Final ranking
Product quality	25	1	25
New technology	5	0.5	2.5
Sales force coverage	15	0.5	7.5
Service back-up	15	0.5	7.5
Manufacturing skills	20	1	20
Distribution proficiency	20	1	20
			82.5

Those units appearing in the top left are 'star' products (or markets etc). Those in the bottom left are 'cash cows' where the bulk of the company's income will be generated. In the centre and top right are those with an uncertain future. Further analysis and scenario planning may be required to see whether the firm should cut its losses. In the bottom right are 'dogs' with little potential who will be loss-makers. A common approach is for the marketing director to analyse the strategic business units for all segments and individual marketing managers to examine the portfolio at product level.

Go to www.market-modelling.co.uk/matrix to view an example of a software package building matrix.

When it come to using the matrix in order to make strategic decisions, the theoretical framework shown below assists.

	Business Position / Strengths		
	High		Low
High (Market Attractiveness)	Highly desirable /protect descenders	Significant potential	Caution/ Selectivity
	Caution/ Selectivity	Manage for £s	Harvest/ Withdraw
Low	Protect/Invest elsewhere	Take the money	Kill off/Divest

Source: adapted from Dibb and Simkin (2008)

Drummond, et al. (2008) Chapter 5 covers portfolio analysis

Learning objective review

Learning objectives	Covered
1. Understand the nature of internal organisational change and the concept of resource-based planning.	☑ Types of assets ☑ Competences
2. Undertake internal environmental analysis using a variety of frameworks and models.	☑ Innovation audit ☑ Innovative companies ☑ Product life cycle ☑ The value chain ☑ The Boston matrix ☑ Directional policy matrix

Quick quiz

1. State six areas of marketing activity that would be examined during an internal appraisal.
2. What are the five categories that should be used to conduct an internal audit according to Hooley (2008).
3. What is the value chain?
4. What are the four categories of marketing assets?
5. What are hard measures of innovation?
6. At what point on the product life cycle would a product be at if the marketing objectives involve trying to win new customers.

Activity debriefs

Worksheet activity 6.1

This will depend on your own research.

Worksheet activity 6.2

Here are some ideas.

(a) It can become more efficient, by automating the production of food, as in a fast food chain.

(b) The chef can develop commercial relationships with growers, so he or she can obtain the best quality fresh produce.

(c) The chef can specialise in a particular type of cuisine (eg Nepalese, Korean).

(d) The restaurant can be sumptuously decorated for those customers who value atmosphere and a sense of occasion, in addition to a restaurant's purely gastronomic pleasures.

(e) The restaurant can serve a particular type of customer (eg celebrities).

Each of these options is a way of organising the activities of buying, cooking and serving food in a way that customers or chosen customers will value.

Quiz answers

1. Six from:
   - Market specifics, eg advertising and customer care
   - Products
   - Distribution
   - R&D
   - Finance
   - Plant and equipment
   - Management and staff
   - Organisation
   - Stocks

2. Five categories include:
   - Financial resources
   - Managerial skills
   - Technical sources
   - Organisation
   - Information systems

3. A comprehensive model of marketing activities

4. Customer-based assets
   Distributor-based assets
   Internally-based assets
   Alliance-based assets

5. Hard measures include:
   (a) Rate of NPD
   (b) Customer satisfaction ratings
   (c) Staff turnover figures

6. The growth stage.

References

Dibb, S. & Simkin, L., (2008) <u>Marketing Planning – A Workbook for Marketing Managers.</u> Cengage Learning, London.

DIUS. (2009). *'What we do'.* [Online] Updated 2009. Available at http://www.dius.gov.uk/about_DIUS/what_we_do.aspx [Accessed 17 Apr 2009].

Drummond, G., Ensor, J. & Ashford, R.,(2008) <u>Strategic Marketing Planning & Control.</u> (3rd ed.), Butterworth-Heinemann, Oxford.

Friend, G. & Zehle, S.,(2004) <u>The Economist Guide to Business Planning</u>. The Economist in assoc. with Profile Books, London.

Jana, R. (2009). *'Is innovation too costly in hard times?'* [Online] Updated 09 Apr 2009, 5:00pm. Available at http://www.businessweek.com/magazine/content/09_16/b4127046252968.htm?chan=magazine+channel_in%3A+inside+innovation [Accessed 16 Apr 2009].

Kotler, P. Armstrong, G. Wong, V. & Saunders, J.,(2008) <u>Principles of Marketing.</u> (5th European ed.), Pearson Education, Harlow.

McDonald, M., (2007) <u>Marketing Plans – How to Prepare Them, How to Use Them</u>. (6th ed.), Butterworth-Heinemann, Oxford.

Market Modelling Ltd. (2009). *'Directional Policy Matrix Software Demo'.* [Online] Updated 2009. Available at http://www.market-modelling.co.uk/MATRIX/MATRIX_Step09_1.htm [Accessed 20 Apr 2009].

The Mama Bee. (2009). *'Google's 80/20 Innovation Model'.* [Online] Updated 27 Mar 2009. Available at http://themamabee.wordpress.com/2009/03/27/management-friday-googles-8020-innovation-model/ [Accessed 20 Apr 2009].

Wikipedia. (2009). *'Cognitive Style'.* [Online] Updated 09 Feb 2009, 07:22. Available at http://en.wikipedia.org/wiki/Cognitive_style [Accessed 20 Apr 2009]

Chapter 7
Market segmentation

Topic list

1. Marketing strategies
2. Market segmentation
3. Segmentation variables
4. Benefits of market segmentation
5. Potential costs associated with market segmentation
6. Conditions for successful segmentation
7. Contemporary methods of segmentation

Introduction

This chapter begins the discussion of marketing strategy by examining market segmentation. As will become apparent, companies have several choices: they can attempt to reach all buyers in a given market, go after smaller groups or segments of the market, or even individual buyers. Irrespective of whether a company aims for the entire market or smaller market segments, the aim of marketing strategy is to identify specific customer needs and then to design a marketing programme that can satisfy those needs. For companies to do this effectively, an in-depth understanding of customers (both current and potential) is required, including their needs, wants, expectations, motivations and behaviours.

Market segmentation has become crucial to the success of most companies. Segmentation enables marketers to define and understand customer needs and affords the opportunity to create tailored products to better suit those needs.

Segmentation has also been said to improve customers' standards of living, having resulted in the vast array of products available nowadays. Increasingly, customers have come to expect companies to identify and profile their needs and wants and to create tailored products accordingly. For this reason, market segmentation is a vital part of marketing strategy. It should be borne in mind that unless a company has segmented the market and selected and analysed an appropriate target market, no decisions can be made with regard to other elements of the marketing strategy and the marketing mix.

Syllabus-linked learning objectives

By the end of the chapter you will be able to:

Learning objectives	Syllabus link
1. Critically evaluate the role of marketing strategies and demonstrate how they can be used to develop competitive advantage, market share and growth.	3.1
2. Assess the importance of market segmentation as a basis of selecting markets to achieve the organisation's business and marketing objectives via customer satisfaction.	3.2
3. Critically evaluate the different segmentation approaches available to organisations in different organisational contexts and sectors and make recommendations for their use.	3.3

1 Marketing strategies

1.1 Marketing strategies, marketing objectives and customer satisfaction

So far in this study text we have discussed the marketing orientation as a philosophy of business and contrasted it with production and selling orientations. You will recall that the marketing orientation (or 'marketing concept') holds that a business is most likely to achieve its goals and objectives when it is organised to meet current and potential needs of customers more effectively than the competition.

The customer-led organisation thus places the satisfaction of customer requirements at the heart of its decisions, tasks and activities. Such an organisation knows that profit, growth and stability all depend on management's ability to meet the need of customers and to do this better than the competition. Consequently, all marketing strategies and tactics are geared towards this objective. The marketing strategies of segmentation, targeting and positioning which are discussed in this and the subsequent chapters are thus all designed in keeping with the overarching goal of satisfying customer requirements, and to do this in a way that is superior to competitors.

We have already looked at the concept of marketing objectives and have seen that they can be expressed in terms of sales target/turnover, market share etc. The marketing strategies designed to achieve these objectives are built around two essential foundations: the choice of target market segment(s) and the choice of differential advantage. Taken together, these comprise the positioning strategy of the brand.

In the marketing plan, this will be expressed as follows:

(a) **Target market segment(s)**. In this section, the plan will specify the types of customers to be targeted. This will include an analysis of customer needs and profiles, such as who the customers are, where they are, when they buy, how frequently they buy, how they use the product, and so on.

(b) **Differential advantage.** Also known as a 'competitive edge', the differential advantage outlines how the company serves customer targets better than the competition. A sustainable differential advantage is a perceived difference that induces customers in the target segment to prefer one company's offering to that of others. Sources of differential advantage can include offering a superior product, better service, or a lower price. The key issue is that the differential advantage needs to be grounded in an understanding of what customers value (ie provide satisfaction of customer requirements), should be unique or substantially different from competitor offerings, difficult to copy (ie sustainable) and should be profitable.

The positioning strategy is crucial and needs to be clearly defined, as it provides the framework for all subsequent marketing mix decisions.

This chapter and the next discuss the issues and strategies associated with market segmentation, target marketing and positioning. We will examine different approaches to market segmentation and look at target marketing in both consumer and business markets. Effective segmentation and target marketing sets the stage for the development of the product offering, its positioning, and the design of a marketing programme that can effectively deliver the offering to the targeted customers.

2 Market segmentation

2.1 Principles of market segmentation, targeting and positioning

Market segmentation, targeting and positioning are an essential aspect of marketing strategy. In this context, Kotler and Keller (2006) note that *'the formula segmentation, targeting and positioning (STP) is the essence of strategic marketing'.*

Market segmentation can be defined as *'the art of discerning and defining meaningful differences between groups of customers to form the foundations of a more focused marketing effort'* (Brassington and Pettitt, 2006). The principle underlying market segmentation is straightforward: companies should not be 'all things to all men' (ie aim their products at all possible buyers in a given market place), but should identify specific groups of customers, also known as customer segments, whose requirements they can serve well. It is argued that by segmenting markets, companies are not only able to serve the interests of their customers well, and potentially better than the competition, but they are also likely to fare better in the marketplace, due to the focused nature of their efforts.

Segmentation rests on the insight that customers in a given market are never homogenous: customers differ in terms of the benefits they seek from products, their ability or willingness to spend, their media preferences, and so on. As we have seen in earlier chapters, customers have different needs, wants and preferences and exhibit different types of buying behaviour and decision-making processes. Thus it makes sense for marketers to segment the market and target one or more segments with specialised, tailored, offerings.

According to Kotler (1991), the process of market segmentation entails the subdivision of a market into distinct subsets of customers, where any subset may conceivably be selected as a target market to be reached with a distinct marketing mix.

KEY CONCEPT

Segmentation is the process of splitting customers into different groups, or segments, within which customers with similar characteristics have similar needs. By doing this, each one can be targeted and reached with a distinct marketing mix.

In terms of the above, then, a market segment can be defined as a customer group that exhibits a shared set of specific needs, wants, buying behaviour and other characteristics, which distinguish it from other customer groups.

MARKETING AT WORK

A good way to understand market segmentation is by using the concept of mass marketing as your starting point. In mass marketing a seller targets one product at all buyers, engaging in the mass production, mass distribution and mass promotion of the one product to all buyers. Coca-Cola is a very good example of this. For many years it sold only one kind of Coke in a 6.5 ounce bottle. The original Coke was introduced in 1886 and for many years this was the only coke product sold by the company. Then, due to shifting consumer demands, Coca-Cola introduced Diet Coke in 1982, and later caffeine-free Diet Coke. In 2006 the company launched Coke Zero (without any sugar), and followed by the introduction of Diet Coke plus vitamins and Diet Coke plus antioxidants. These products are now targeted at different segments of the market, ie at a group of consumers who share a similar set of needs and wants which the company wants to satisfy.

As markets become more competitive, there are increasing constraints on budgets. At the same time, consumers having more choice. How can resources be used more efficiently and effectively to ensure consumers make the 'right' choices? Segmentation achieves this by identifying target groups for marketing purposes.

Successful segmentation can be a key source of **competitive advantage**. It forms the basis of identifying and selecting appropriate and attractive target markets that the organisation can serve best, so as to enable the achievement of business and marketing objectives via customer satisfaction. Unfortunately, of those businesses that do bother to segment their markets, few consciously adopt an approach that maximises their competitive advantage, opting instead for traditional methods of segmentation.

Once the market has been segmented and profiles of the resultant segments have been developed, marketers need to analyse and evaluate the attractiveness of each segment in terms of profit and growth and select those offering the best potential to the firm. This process is known as **targeting**. Various factors will need to be considered in assessing the attractiveness of segments and management has several strategic options in developing a targeting strategy. All these will be discussed in more detail in Chapter 8.

Following selection of a suitable target segment or segments, the firm will need to develop a **positioning** strategy: this will entail building a differential advantage that will set its offer apart from competitors and developing a marketing mix to implement its positioning strategy. Positioning is explored further in Chapter 9 of this study text.

Steps in segmentation, targeting and positioning identified by Kotler

(a)   Identify **segmentation** variables and segment the market
(b)   Develop segment profiles
(c)   Evaluate the attractiveness of each segment
(d)   Select the **target** segment(s)
(e)   Identify **positioning** concepts for each target segment
(f)   Select, develop and communicate the chosen concept

ACTIVITY 7.1

concept

Market segmentation holds obvious implications for the marketing mix of a product.

Taking the example of Coca-Cola in 'Marketing at Work' above, consider the influence of segmentation, targeting and positioning on product design and communication.

To assist you in your task, type 'Diet Coke advertising' into the Google search engine and look at the images. Then repeat the process by using the search term 'Coke Zero advertising'. What is immediately apparent? Also look at other Coca-Cola web sites to ascertain how segmentation leads to definite communications choices.

3 Segmentation variables

In order to arrive at suitable market segments, marketers subdivide a market by applying a range of criteria, also known as segmentation variables or bases. The choice of appropriate criteria for subdividing the market is very important and different variables are used for consumer and business markets.

3.1 Segmenting consumer markets

In consumer markets, the four major segmentation variables are geographic, demographic, psychographic and behavioural.

3.1.1 Geographic segmentation

Geographic segmentation defines customers according to their location. For instance, the market can be divided into regions, countries, counties, cities or neighbourhoods. This is often a useful starting point. For example, small businesses in the service or retail sector, may initially wish to target customers within their immediate neighbourhood. Many multinationals also segment geographically, targeting specific regions or countries with specific products.

Geographic segments are easy to define and measure, and information is often freely available from public sources. However, on its own, geographic segmentation is not enough. By dividing a consumer market purely on the basis of geography an oversimplified picture of the consumer emerges. Even in a relatively small geographical area, consumers exhibit a wide range of different needs and wants and geographic segmentation alone will not provide any relevant information on consumer characteristics to the marketer. For this reason, marketers need to ensure the application of additional variables to a given market, so as to arrive at a more complete and relevant profile of customers. While geographic segmentation provides a useful foundation, it is therefore supplemented by other, more customer-focused segmentation methods, such as those described in the ensuing sections.

Example: hairdressers usually attract business from their surrounding catchment area. However, hairdressers do not segment merely on geography alone, but segment further on other criteria, such as gender, age, fashion-consciousness, etc.

3.1.2 Demographic segmentation

With demographic segmentation, the market is divided into segments based on variables such as age, gender, income, occupation, family size, family life cycle and socioeconomic status. One of the key benefits of demographics is that they can provide a good profile of customers on criteria that can be easily translated into marketing strategies. For instance, segmenting consumers according to age offers useful guidelines for choice of advertising media and creative strategy. A case in point is magazines, which carefully segment their readers according to gender, age, and socioeconomic profile.

3.1.3 Social class

Variables such as age and gender, income, and so on present few problems but social class has always been one of the most dubious areas of marketing research investigation. Class is a highly personal and subjective phenomenon, to the extent that some people are class conscious or class aware and have a sense of belonging to a particular group.

JICNAR's social grade definitions (A-E), which correspond closely to what are called Social Classes I-V on the Registrar General's Scale, are often used in quota setting.

Registrar General's Social classes	JICNAR Social grades	Social status	Characteristics of occupation (of head of household)
I	A	Upper middle class	Higher managerial/professional, eg lawyers, directors
II	B	Middle class	Intermediate managerial/administrative/professional, eg foremen, shop assistants
III (i) non-manual	C_1	Lower middle class	Supervisory, clerical, junior managerial/administrative/professional, eg foremen, shop assistants
(ii) manual	C_2	Skilled working class	Skilled manual labour, eg electricians, mechanics
IV	D	Working class	Semi skilled labour, eg machine operators
			Unskilled labour, eg cleaning, waiting tables, assembly
V	E	Lowest level of subsistence	State pensioners, widows (no other earner), casual workers

From 2001 UK Office for National Statistics used the categorisation system, reflecting recent changes in the UK population.

New social class	Occupations	Examples
1	Higher managerial and professional occupations	
1.1	Employers and managers in larger organisations	Bank managers, company directors
1.2	Higher professional	Doctors, lawyers
2	Lower managerial and professional occupations	Police officers
3	Intermediate occupations	Secretaries/Pas, clerical workers
4	Small employers and own-account workers	
5	Lower supervisory, craft and related occupations	Electricians
6	Semi-routine occupations	Drivers, hairdressers, bricklayers
7	Routine occupations	Cark park attendants, cleaners

As noted above, using social class as a segmentation variable can be problematic. In particular, a major problem lies in the fact that social class has been used as an indicator of individuals' lifestyles and has been fraught with many assumptions, which may not hold true in practice. It is quite possible that members of the same social class or socioeconomic group exhibit very different types of buying behaviour and purchase motivations.

3.1.4 The family life cycle

The family life cycle (FLC) is a summary demographic variable that combines the effects of age, marital status, career status (income) and the presence or absence of children. It is able to identify the various stages through which households progress. The table below shows features of the family at various stages of its life cycle. Particular products and services can be target-marketed at specific stages in the life cycle of families.

It is important to remember that the model of the family life cycle shown in the table displays the classic route from young single to older unmarried. In contemporary society, characterised by divorce and what may be the declining importance of marriage as an institution, this picture can vary. It is possible and not uncommon to be young, childless and divorced, or young and unmarried with children. Some people go through life without marrying or having children at all. Individuals may go through the life cycle belonging to more than one family group. At each stage, whether on the classic route or an alternative path, needs and disposable income will change. Family groupings are, however, a key feature of society.

(a) It is modelled on the demographic patterns of industrialised Western nations – and particularly America.

(b) As noted above, while the FLC model was once typical of the overwhelming majority of American families, there are now important potential variations from that pattern, including:

    (i) Childless couples – because of choice, career-oriented women and delayed marriage

    (ii) Later marriages – because of greater career-orientation and non-marital relationships: likely to have fewer children

    (iii) Later children – say in late 30s. Likely to have fewer children, but to stress the quality of life

    (iv) Single parents – (especially mothers) because of divorce

    (v) Fluctuating labour status – not just in work or retired, but redundancy, career change, dual-income

    (vi) Extended parenting – young, single adults returning home while they establish careers/financial independence; divorced children returning to parents; elderly parents requiring care; newly-weds living with in-laws

    (vii) Non-family households
- unmarried (homosexual or heterosexual) couples
- divorced persons with no children
- single persons (often due to delaying of first marriage and the fact that there are more women than men in the population)
- widowed persons (especially women, because of longer-life expectancy)

	I	II	III	IV	V	VI	VII	VIII	IX
	Bachelor stage	Newly married couples	Full nest I	Full nest II	Full nest III	Empty nest I	Empty nest II	Solitary survivor on labour force	Solitary survivor(s) retired
	Young single people not living at home	Young, no children	Youngest child under six	Youngest child six or over	Older married couples with dependent children	Older married couples, no children living with them, head of family still in labour force	Older married couples, no children living at home head of family retired		
	Few technical burdens. Fashion/opinion leader led. Recreation oriented. Buy basic, kitchen equipment, basic furniture, cars, equipment for the mating game, holidays. Experiment with patterns of personal financial management and control	Better off financially than they will be in the near future. High levels of purchase of homes and consumer durable goods. Buy cars, fridges, cookers, life assurance, durable furniture, holidays. Establish patterns of personal financial management and control.	Home purchasing at peak. Liquid assets/savings low. Dissatisfied with financial position and amount of money saved. Reliance on credit finance, credit cards, overdraft etc. Child dominated household. Buy necessities washers, dryers, baby food and clothes, vitamins, toys, books etc.	Financial position better. Some wives return to work. Child dominated household. Buy necessities foods, cleaning material, clothes, bicycles, sports gear, music lessons, pianos, holiday etc.	Financial position still better. More wives work. School and examination dominated household. Some children get first jobs; others in further/higher education. Expenditure to support children's further/higher education. Buy new, more tasteful furniture, non-necessary appliances, boats etc. holidays.	Home ownership at peak. More satisfied with financial position and money saved. Interested in travel, recreation, self-education. Make financial gifts and contributions. Childcare gain qualifications; move to Stage 1. Buy luxuries, home improvements e.g. fitted kitchen etc.	Significant cut in income. Keep home. Buy medical appliances or medical care products which aid health, sleep and digestion. Assist children. Concern with level of savings and pension. Some expenditure on hobbies and pastimes.	Income still adequate but likely to sell family home and purchase a smaller accommodation. Concern with level of savings and pension. Some expenditure on hobbies and pastimes. Worries about security and dependence.	Significant cut in income. Additional medical requirements. Special need for attention, affection and security. May seek sheltered accommodation. Possible dependence on others for personal financial management and control.

There has been some criticism of the traditional FLC model as a basis for market segmentation in recent years. (See, for example, Lawson, R. 'The Family Life Cycle: a demographic analysis', Journal of Marketing Management, *Summer 1988).*

An alternative or modified FLC model is needed to take account of consumption variables such as:

(a) Spontaneous changes in brand preference when a household undergoes a change of status (divorce, redundancy, death of a spouse, change in membership of a non-family household)

(b) Different economic circumstances and extent of consumption planning in single-parent families, households where there is a redundancy, dual-income households

(c) Different buying and consumption roles to compensate/adjust in households where the woman works. Women can be segmented into at least four categories – each of which may represent a distinct market for goods and services:

　　(i)　Stay-at-home homemaker
　　(ii)　Plan-to-work homemaker
　　(iii)　'Just-a-job' working woman
　　(iv)　Career-oriented working woman

In summary, demographics, like the geographics, are easy to define and measure and information can be easily obtained from public sources. On the down side, however, their major drawback, in keeping with demographics, is that they are too general and descriptive in nature. While both of these segmentation categories describe *who* the consumer is, they do not attempt to uncover *why* the consumer behaves as he does.

Additional drawbacks associated with demographic segmentation are that they may fail to account for the following:

(a) Individuals within the same demographic segment may exhibit quite different behavioural patterns and may be motivated by substantially different needs and wants run the risk of assuming that all consumers in a given demographic group share the same needs and wants

(b) There may be significant similarities in motivations and behaviour between individuals in different demographic segments

Despite these disadvantages, the relative ease of measurement associated with demographics accounts for their popularity among marketing practitioners.

3.1.5 Geodemographic segmentation

Geodemographics has been defined as 'the analysis of people by where they live' (Sleight, 1997). It combines geographic information with demographics and lifestyle data about specific neighbourhoods. Geodemographics are useful in that they help companies understand not only *where* their customers live, but also *how* they live and therefore enable the development of a clearer and more detailed profile of customers.

Several UK companies offer geodemographic databases useful to the marketer. These include Mosaic ™ (provided by Experian) and ACORN ('A Classification of Residential Neighbourhoods'), offered by CACI. These databases are valuable to marketers in many areas of consumer marketing, for instance in planning sampling areas for market research studies, finding suitable locations for direct mail campaigns or evaluating specific geographic areas for new retail outlets. For retailers, in particular, geodemographics are invaluable, as they help to evaluate and monitor important variables such as the catchment, shopper profiles and competition in particular trading areas.

As an example, the ACORN system divides the UK into 17 groups which together comprise a total of 54 different types of areas, which share common socio-economic characteristics.

(a) The 17 ACORN groups are as follows.

The ACORN targeting classification: abbreviated list		% of population
A	*Thriving (19.7%)*	
A1	Wealthy achievers, suburban areas	15.0
A2	Affluent greys, rural communities	2.3
A3	Prosperous pensioners, retirement areas	2.4

The ACORN targeting classification: abbreviated list cont'd		% of population
B	Expanding (11.6%)	
B4	Affluent executives family areas	3.8
B5	Well-off workers, family areas	7.8
C	Rising (7.8%)	
C6	Affluent urbanites, town and city areas	2.3
C7	Prosperous professionals, metropolitan areas	2.1
C8	Better-off executives, inner city areas	3.4

3.1.6 Psychographic segmentation

This is also known as 'lifestyle segmentation'. It is concerned with people's opinions, attitudes, beliefs and aspirations hence provides much deeper and richer insights into the consumer than the methods discussed thus far. By defining consumers' lifestyles, marketers are able to sell products in terms of psychological benefits that can potentially enhance the consumer's lifestyle.

Joseph Plummer (1974), an early proponent of lifestyle segmentation, broke this category down into four major dimensions: activities, interests, opinions and demographics.

Lifestyle dimensions			
Activities	**Interests**	**Opinions**	**Demographics**
Work	Family	Themselves	Age
Hobbies	Home	Social issues	Education
Social events	Job	Politics	Income
Vacation	Community	Business	Occupation
Entertainment	Recreation economics	Economics	Family size
Club membership	Fashion	Education	Dwelling
Community	Food	Products	Geography
Shopping	Media	Future	City size
Sports	Achievements	Culture	Stage in lifecycle

Source: Joseph Plummer

Marketers can build a comprehensive profile of the consumer by researching each of these categories. When applied over large groups of individuals, marketers are able to aggregate consumers with significant profile similarities into specific lifestyle segments.

Over the years, variations on the lifestyle or psychographic approach have been developed, analysing more precisely people's attitudes towards certain goods or services. The value of this approach is that it isolates potential consumer responses to particular product offerings.

MARKETING AT WORK

concept

The Henley Centre for Forecasting has outlined four different kinds of consumers in the market for technological and media products.

(a) **Technophiles** (24% of the population) 'are enthusiastic about technology in a general sense and also show a high level of interest in applications of new technology. They are concentrated among the under-35s, are more likely to be male than female, and are more likely to belong to social grade C1 than AB'.

(b) **Aspirational technophiles** (22% of the population) 'are excited in a general sense about technology but are much less interested in its applications. They are more likely to be male than female, and are concentrated in the AB social grade'.

(c) **Functionals** (25% of the population) 'claim to be uninterested in technology but are not hostile to its applications, especially those areas which offer an enhancement of existing services. These consumers are more likely to be family ... and are most numerous among the over 45s'.

(d) **Technophobes** (28% of the population) 'are hostile to technology at all levels and are sceptical about whether technology can offer anything new. Technophobes are concentrated in the over-60 age group, are more likely to be female than male, and are distributed fairly evenly through the social grades'..

3.1.7 The VALS™ ('Values and Life Style') framework

This framework was the result of a survey in the USA, identifying nine lifestyle groups in the population passing through various developmental stages, as presented below.

Development stage	Grouping (% of population)
Need driven	**Survivors**. This is a disadvantaged group who are likely to be withdrawn, despairing and depressed (4%).
	Sustainers are another disadvantaged group, but they are working hard to escape poverty (7%).
	These groups have relatively little purchasing power.
Outer-directed	**Belongers** are characterised as being conventional, nostalgic, reluctant to try new ideas and generally conservative (33%).
	Emulators are upwardly mobile, ambitious and status conscious (10%).
	Achievers. This group enjoys life and makes things happen (23%).
	These groups are affluent and interested in status products.
Inner-directed	**'I-am-me'** tend to be young, self-engrossed and act on whims (5%).
	Experientials wish to enjoy as wide a range of life as possible (7%).
	Societally conscious have a clear sense of social responsibility and wish to improve society (9%).
	These groups are more concerned with individual needs.
Nirvanna	**Integrateds** are completely mature psychologically and combine the positive elements of outer and inner directness (2%). Very few individuals reach this stage.

There are several advantages and disadvantages associated with psychographic segmentation. On the plus side, they enable marketers to create more specific, tailored offerings to consumers with regard to all elements of the marketing mix. This can result in greater customer loyalty towards a given product and can also help defend against competitors. On the down side, however, psychographic segments can be difficult and expensive to measure and define and, in contrast to the other types of segmentation, information is unlikely to be available via public sources.

Psychographic segmentation is of particular relevance to products that entail greater psychological rather than functional benefits for customers, such as cars, perfumes, designer clothing, and so on. With such products, marketers attempt to create specific images in terms of which consumers will feel that the product can either help them to achieve their aspirations or enhance their current lifestyles.

The key value of psychographic segmentation lies in its ability to (Solomon, 1994):

- Define target markets
- Position the product
- Communicate product attributes to consumers
- Help identify opportunities and trends, which in turn can help develop overall strategy

3.1.8 Behavioural segmentation

The segmentation approaches discussed thus far have centred on the customer, with the aim of establishing as detailed a customer profile as possible. Behavioural segmentation, by contrast, focuses on the customer's relationship with the product. This is important, as even individuals with similar demographic and/or psychographic profiles can interact quite differently with the same product.

Behavioural segmentation segments buyers into groups based on their attitudes to and use of the product, and the benefits they expect to receive.

Markets can be segmented according to the following behavioural variables:

3.1.9 Benefits sought

Consumers can be classified according to the benefits they seek. An example of benefit segmentation in the toothpaste market is provided below.

Benefit segmentation of the toothpaste market

Segment name	Principle benefit sought	Demographic strengths	Special behavioural characteristics	Brand disproportionately favoured	Personality characteristics	Lifestyle characteristics
The sensory segment	Flavour, product appearance	Children	Users of spearmint flavoured toothpaste	Colgate Strip	High self-involvement	Hedonistic
The Sociables	Brightness of teeth	Teens, young people	Smokers	Macleans, Ultra-Brite	High sociability	Active
The Worriers	Decay prevention	Large families	Heavy users	Crest	High hypochondriasis	Conservative
The Independent	Price	Men	Heavy users	Brands on sale	High autonomy	Value-oriented

Benefit segmentation is concerned with the underlying reasons why customers are attracted to various product offerings and is thus highly relevant to marketing decisions. However, this approach can be difficult to execute in practice. The research required to identify behavioural segments is also expensive and time consuming. The key to successful behavioural segmentation is to have clear insights into basic customer needs and benefits sought by different customer groups. This information can then subsequently be combined with demographic, geographic and psychographic segmentation to arrive at complete consumer profiles.

ACTIVITY 7.2
application

The snack food market can be segmented in many ways. One study has broken the market down into the following segments: nutritional snackers, weight watchers, guilty snackers, party snackers, indiscriminant snackers and economical snackers. List the benefit/s you would think each segment is looking for, and what type of snacks would appeal to the different segments?

3.1.10 Usage rate

Consumers can be segmented into light, medium and heavy product-users. An examination of usage patterns and volumes can pinpoint where to focus marketing activity.

Heavy users frequently account for only a small percentage of the total market but account for a high percentage of total consumption.

3.1.11 End-use

This variable concerns the question of what a given product is used for. For instance, soup as a meal is associated with a variety of different end-uses, each of which appeals to a different usage segment. For instance, it may be used as an easy office lunch, a dinner party starter, a warming snack or a meal replacement. Consequently, soup manufacturers have developed a broad range of brands and product lines to cater for the various end-uses associated with this product.

3.1.12 Loyalty

Consumers can be divided into different groups according to brand loyalty status.

- 'Hard core loyals': consumers who only buy one brand, all the time
- 'Split loyals': consumers who display loyalty to two or three brands
- 'Shifting loyals': consumers who shift their loyalty from one brand to another
- 'Switchers': consumers who show no loyalty to any given brand, but switch between different brands

Analysing the various degrees of brand loyalty can lead to very interesting insights: thus, a company can learn a great deal about its products' strengths by studying its hard-core loyals. Split loyals, on the other hand, can reveal those brands which are most competitive with the company's own. An investigation of consumers who are shifting between brands can point out particular marketing weaknesses and may act as a useful impetus to correct such weaknesses. Finally, a company that operates in a market dominated by 'switchers', will frequently need to rely on price-cutting.

It is important to remember that what may, at first glance, appear to be brand-loyal buying behaviour, can often be the result of something altogether different. It could well be a sign of indifference, habit, a low price, non-availability of other brands, or high switching costs.

Consumers' brand loyalty is increasingly under threat, in part as a result of a greater number of alternative brands available in the marketplace and in part due to manufacturers' increasing propensity to use incentives and promotions to undermine customer loyalty towards competitors' brands. In the UK grocery retail sector, a major threat to manufacturers' brands comes from supermarkets' own brands, which increasingly offer the same levels of quality, but at a much lower price.

3.1.13 Attitude

Segmenting consumers according to their attitudes towards a given product or organisation is said to result in one of five attitude groups: enthusiastic, positive, indifferent, negative or hostile. Consumers who are enthusiastic about a product require different handling by the marketer than those who are hostile towards the product. For instance, a hostile group might need persuasion and should be given opportunity to sample a product, together with an advertising campaign geared towards addressing the causes of their hostility. Attitude-based segmentation is important in cause-related marketing, the marketing of charities and health education. For instance, 'stop smoking' campaigns frequently segment smokers according to attitude. As can be imagined, targeting hostile smokers requires very different approaches to those aimed at smokers who are already positive and committed to giving up smoking.

3.1.14 Buyer readiness stage

Markets usually consist of consumers in different stages of readiness to buy a product. Thinking back to the AIDA model introduced in an earlier chapter, the consumer may either be aware or unaware of the product, may be informed and interested, may have a desire to purchase the product, and may even intend to buy it.

Buyer readiness is an important variable to the marketer, particularly in terms of decisions relating to the communications mix. For instance, at the early stages of buyer readiness, consumers may be unaware of a given product, indicating the need to generate *awareness* of the product. Then, there will be a need to provide information to generate *interest* in the product. This interest may then lead to a *desire* to purchase the product, which in turn will frequently stimulate *action* leading to purchase.

ACTIVITY 7.3

application

Consider possible segmentation variables for adult education, magazines, and sports facilities.

3.1.15 Multivariable segmentation

In concluding our discussion of consumer segmentation bases, it is important to point out that it is highly uncommon for marketers to use only one type of segmentation variable. Instead, a number of different segmentation variables are used in practice (known as 'multivariable segmentation'), yielding a richer profile of potential customer group to be targeted.

Geodemographics, discussed in section 3.1.3 above, is representative of the multivariable approach to segmentation, entailing demographics alongside geographics and psychographics. As data collection methods and database creation and maintenance become increasingly sophisticated, multivariable segmentation is becoming easier and more affordable. A case in point is the growth in loyalty store cards provided by UK supermarkets, which enable retailers to gather highly detailed information and thus build a comprehensive profile of individual shoppers. Information gathered reveals important information about how individual consumers shop, when they shop, what they buy, how much they buy, where they buy, and so on. This information is used by the supermarkets to identify and define useful segments within their customer base, to provide individually tailored offers to specific customer groups and to further improve their overall marketing mix.

MARKETING AT WORK

concept

Regarded by many as a pioneer of its kind, the Tesco Clubcard, introduced in 1995, has enabled Tesco to take information from every shopping basket processed by its checkouts and use it to make marketing and management decisions. Tesco realised early on that the shortcoming with the purely geodemographic model of customer targeting is that it is based on the premise of you are where you live. This was clearly not the case, even neighbours differed significantly.

The Tesco model, by contrast, is based on individual particularities: you are what you buy. It creates like-minded groups of people with similar tastes and activities, according to their purchases. Rather than forcing a profile onto households using generalised data from their postcode, the customer behavioural approach starts with their distinctive actions.

Segmenting users enabled Tesco to target its vouchers and coupons at people who really wanted them. Redemption rates for coupons varied from 3% (the sort of rate Tesco expected from a pre-Clubcard, untargeted mailing) to 70%. But, as it became better at modelling customer behaviour, the target reached an unprecedented 20% within a year.

Tesco also took a majority share in the research consultancy DunnHumby, who were tasked with making marketing sense of all the transactional data, and this company has in latter years become very successful at segmenting groups of consumers and selling the profiles on to brand companies eager to make use of this incredibly powerful tool.

3.2 Segmenting business markets

The principles of segmentation apply equally to consumer and business markets. While there are some common variables, such as geography, usage rate and benefits sought, most of the variables used to segment business markets differ from those utilised in the segmentation of consumer markets.

According to Wind and Cardozo (1974), business markets should be segmented by employing the following two-stage framework:

(a) Stage 1:   Identification of subgroups with common characteristics within the market as a whole. These are known as macro segments and are discussed further below.

(b) Stage 2:   Selection of target segments from within the macro segments, based on differences in buying characteristics. These are known as micro segments and are discussed in section 3.2.2 below.

3.2.1 Macro segmentation variables

Macro segments are based on characteristics of organisations and the wider purchasing context within which they function. Macro segments consist of organisations which share specific requirements and other patterns, which are said to result in similar buying behaviour and responses to marketing approaches. Macro segmentation employs the following three organisational characteristics as variables: size, location and usage rate. Data relevant to these variables can be easily obtained from published sources.

3.2.2 Size

Company size is typically measured by such factors as number of employees and sales turnover and can be a very significant variable. For instance, small companies frequently have different needs and buying preferences than larger organisations. The size of an organisation also impacts on its relationships with suppliers and purchasing behaviour. A large company may well have many different people involved in decision-making, may have very complex and formalised decision-making processes and procedures and may also have specific requirements in terms of level of service or technical co-operation required. Conversely, a small organisation may have simpler decision-making structures and purchasing routines, involving a relatively small number of decision-makers.

The size of an organisation also impacts on volume requirements, average order size, distribution and sales costs and their bargaining power as customers, which in turn may impact on the attractiveness of different segments as potential targets.

3.2.3 Location

The geographic location of organisations can be a useful way of segmenting the market for a business product. For instance, potential customers in different parts of the same country, as well as in different countries, may have varying product requirements, specifications and distribution arrangements. Location will also influence the cost of sales and distribution and the extent of competitive intensity, all of which may influence the attractiveness of a given segment as a potential target market.

3.2.4 Usage rate

Similar to segmentation in consumer markets, usage rate can be a useful way of categorising potential customers. Thus, organisations may be classified as 'heavy', 'medium' or 'light' users of a given product. 'Heavy users', for instance, may have specific requirements in terms of prices (including price discounts) and delivery arrangements. In general, it may be better to cultivate a relationship with a single heavy user, rather than trying to attract several light users.

3.2.5 Product or service application

Products and services can be used in many different ways. By applying this variable, customer groupings with specific requirements can be identified.

Standard industrial classification (SIC) codes can help identify specific industry sectors using specific products for different applications. For instance, glass has many different industrial uses, ranging from architecture to the car industry to packaging. Each of these sectors exhibits different buyer behaviour patterns and requirements, for instance, as relates to price sensitivity or quality and performance specifications.

The macro level variables discussed thus far can be useful starting points for defining broad market and segment boundaries, but requires further refinement to allow for a more customer-focused analysis. This is provided by micro level segmentation, which is discussed further below.

3.2.6 Micro segmentation variables

Several different micro segments may exist within one macro segment. Some common bases for micro segmentation in business markets are outlined below.

Micro segmentation variables in business markets	Comment
Technology	The business customer's stage of technology development impacts on its manufacturing and product technology, and thus on its demand for different types of product. High technology firms increasingly demand suppliers to be integrated to their computer systems for all stages of the purchasing process.
Purchasing policies	Business customers approaches to purchasing can be a useful segmentation variable. Examples include: customers preferring lease-based deals versus those wanting to purchase, companies demanding single supply sources versus multiple sources, or public sector organisations requiring obligatory bidding versus companies preferring to negotiate the price.
DMU structure and decision-making processes	Many business purchase decisions are made by a group of individuals, also known as a decision-making unit (DMU). As different members of the DMU frequently have different perceptions and requirements, the market may be segmented according to DMU configuration and the processes involved in reaching purchasing decisions.
Buyer-Seller relationships	Corporate customers differ in terms of their requirements of their suppliers. While some have higher expectations and require long-term relationships, others may have lesser demands of suppliers. The type of relationship required can thus be a useful basis for segmentation business customers.

4 Benefits of market segmentation

Benefit	Comment
Better satisfaction of customer needs	By segmenting the market and creating different offers based on the needs of each segment allows for a higher level of customer satisfaction.
Growth in profits	Some customer segments are willing to pay more than others for certain benefits, thereby raising average prices and profits.
Revenue growth	Segmenting the market according to customer needs means that more customers may be attracted by what is on offer, in preference to competing products.
Customer retention	As customers' circumstances change (due to age, income and family life cycle), purchasing patterns change. By creating offerings suitable to each life cycle stage, marketers can retain customers who might otherwise defect to competitors.
Targeted communications	For communications to be effective, they need to meet and reflect the relevant needs, wants, and preferences of customers. Segmenting the market enables marketers to do this and to create clear communications designed to meet the target segments' specific needs, wants and preferences.
Innovation	By identifying unmet needs through segmentation, companies can innovate to satisfy them. Thus, segmentation can be said to stimulate innovation.
Segment share	Small or new companies need to aim for leadership in a given segment in order to stay competitive (focus strategy). Segmentation enables a firm to implement a focus strategy successfully.

5 Potential costs associated with market segmentation

Despite the potential benefits outlined above, companies often fail to successfully implement segmentation strategies. Young (1996) points out that two of the most common reasons for failure lie in (a) little or no use of appropriate data to support appropriate segmentation choice and (b) segmentation approaches that are not suitable to corporate objectives.

Piercy and Morgan (1993) note that segmentation should not be focused only on applying the range of the variables discussed thus far, but should take into account the role and capabilities of the organisation itself. According to the authors, an understanding of the organisation, its culture, operating processes and structure is vital, as they all influence the organisation's view of the market and how it should be segmented.

Another risk inherent in segmentation lies in the fact that, where markets are segmented into a large number of segments, this can lead to market fragmentation, which in turn can result in a loss of economies of scale in production and purchasing.

Finally, in markets where several organisations compete for the same customer segments, the proliferation of brands can be very confusing for consumers, while also entailing extensive administrative and marketing costs for brand owners in getting their brands to the consumer.

6 Conditions for successful segmentation

For segmentation to be successful and to be a strategic tool to the organisation, it needs to meet several essential criteria. The following questions are commonly asked to decide whether or not the segment can be used for developing marketing plans.

Criteria	Comment
Can the segment be measured?	It might be possible to conceive of a market segment, but it is not necessarily easy to measure it. For example for a segment based on people with a conservative outlook to life, can conservatism of outlook be measured by market research?
Is the segment large enough?	The potential market has to be of sufficient size in order to be profitable.
Can the segment be reached?	There has to be a way of getting to the potential customers via the organisation's promotion and distribution channels.
Do segments respond differently?	If two or more segments are identified by marketing planners but each segment responds in the same way to a marketing mix, the segments are effectively one and the same and there is no point in distinguishing them from each other.
Can the segment be reached profitably?	Do the identified customer needs cost less to satisfy than the revenue they earn?
Is the segment suitably stable?	The stability of the segment is important, if the organisation is to commit huge production and marketing resources to serve it. The firm does not want the segment to 'disappear' next year. Of course, this may not matter in some industries.

Steps in the analysis of segmentation are as follows.

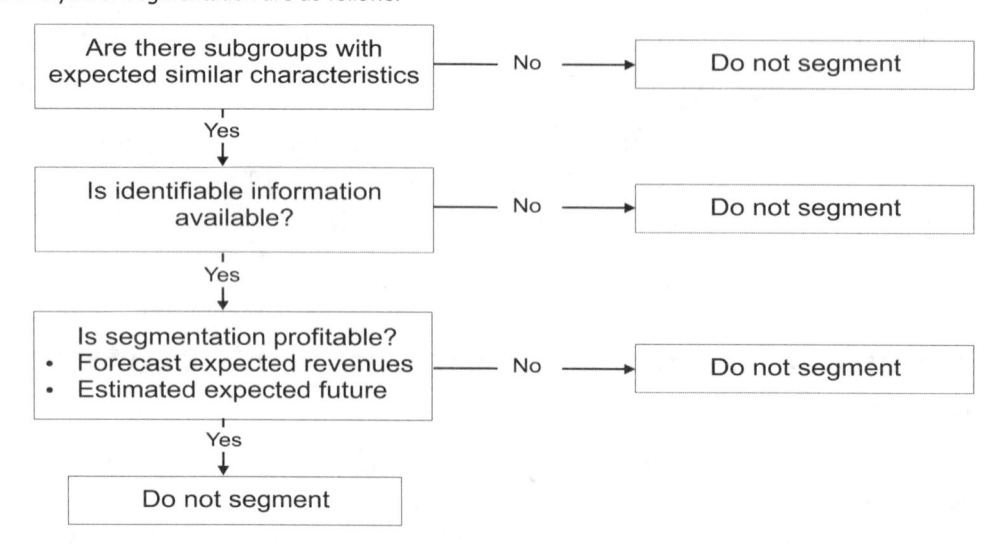

```
    Are there subgroups with           No
    expected similar characteristics  ─────▶  Do not segment
              │
             Yes
              ▼
    Is identifiable information        No
    available?                        ─────▶  Do not segment
              │
             Yes
              ▼
    Is segmentation profitable?
    • Forecast expected revenues       No
    • Estimated expected future       ─────▶  Do not segment
              │
             Yes
              ▼
    Do not segment
```

> **ACTIVITY 7.4** — *evaluation*
>
> What are some of the mistakes companies can make when segmenting markets?

7 Contemporary methods of segmentation

Further to the more traditional approaches to segmentation discussed in the course of this chapter, recent years have seen the rise of additional approaches to segmentation.

7.1 Relationship-based approaches to segmentation

Reflecting the move towards relationship marketing, there has recently been an emphasis on relationship-based approaches, focusing on the relationship requirements of customers as a variable for segmentation. According to these approaches, customers' relationship-seeking behaviours differ in terms of the type of relationships they require with suppliers (for instance, short term versus long term, as alluded to previously) and the type of 'intimacy' they desire from the relationship (eg distant or close). According to Hooley, Saunders and Piercy (2004), markets can be segmented into the following groups:

(a) **Relationship seekers** – customers desiring a close and long-term relationship with suppliers or retailers

(b) **Relationship exploiters** – buyers interested only in short-term relationship with suppliers, but not averse to a close relationship, which can be exploited for any potential advantages on offer

(c) **Loyal buyers** – customers requiring a long-term relationship, but at a distance

(d) **Arm's-length transaction buyers** – buyers who do not desire close or long-term relationships with suppliers, but prefer to shop around for the best deal

7.2 Critical event segmentation

A relatively recent addition to behavioural segmentation approaches is known as 'critical events segmentation' (CES). This approach is based on the idea that major events in an individual's life generate specific needs, which can be satisfied by providing a particular set of products and services. Examples of such critical events include marriage, the birth of children, unemployment, retirement, illness, moving home or death. Financial services, including insurance and pension funds, private healthcare and legal services are all examples of service-providers who have seen the benefits of critical event segmentation and are employing CES to provide tailored offerings to relevant consumer segments. Additional examples include suppliers of greeting cards (eg Hallmark) who use marketing approaches based on the idea of critical events, such as Birthdays, Weddings, Illnesses, Bereavement, and so on. Similarly, chocolate companies, such as Thorntons, also employ CES segmentation by promoting such special events as Valentine's Day and Mother's Day.

7.3 Online behaviours as bases for segmentation

Technological advances have led to changes in the ways in which companies segment and target markets. For instance, many companies analyse clickstream data in online transactions, allowing them to target specific segments with product offers or promotional messages. Companies such as Amazon, for example, have developed systems that enable them to track online consumer behaviour, resulting in a wealth of information concerning customers' browsing behaviour, purchases of specific products such as books and CDs, and so on. This information is then utilised to design product offerings tailored to the customer's specific requirements and preferences.

MARKETING AT WORK

Marketers are increasingly targeting young consumers via online networking sites. MySpace, for instance, reaches over 70 million registered users, mostly in the 12-17 year old age group. In addition to the sheer numbers of a similar demographic involved who share the same basic interests in music, movies and the internet in general, social networking also allows firms to collect a striking amount of information on users and this enables them to carefully target promotions to the right audience. Music and film companies regularly use MySpace and Procter & Gamble launched Secret Sparkle to 16-24 year-old woman using MySpace.

Learning objective review

Learning objectives	Covered
1. Critically evaluate the role of marketing strategies and demonstrate how they can be used to develop competitive advantage, market share and growth.	☑ Marketing strategies, marketing objectives and customer satisfaction ☑ Principles of market segmentation, targeting and positioning ☑ Benefits of market segmentation ☑ Potential costs associated with market segmentation
2. Assess the importance of market segmentation as a basis of selecting markets to achieve the organisation's business and marketing objectives via customer satisfaction.	☑ Marketing strategies, marketing objectives and customer satisfaction ☑ Principles of market segmentation, targeting and positioning ☑ Benefits of market segmentation ☑ Potential costs associated with market segmentation ☑ Conditions for successful segmentation
3. Critically evaluate the different segmentation approaches available to organisations in different organisational contexts and sectors and make recommendations for their use.	☑ Segmenting consumer markets ☑ Segmenting business markets ☑ Contemporary methods of segmentation

Quick quiz

1. Upon which two essential foundations are marketing strategies built to achieve stated marketing objectives?
2. Provide a definition of market segmentation.
3. List Kotler's six steps to effective segmentation, targeting and positioning.
4. List the four major groups of segmentation variables.
5. Name the four major dimensions of 'lifestyle segmentation' according to Plummer.
6. What is 'behavioural segmentation' and how does it segment buyers?
7. According to Wind and Cardozo (1974), business markets should be segmented by employing a two-stage framework. Identifying macro segments and then selecting micro segments within them, list the segmentation variables within each group.
8. What are the benefits of market segmentation?
9. Name three contemporary methods of segmentation.
10. What is critical event segmentation?

7: Market segmentation

Activity debriefs

Worksheet activity 7.1

Whereas Coca-Cola, the mother brand, follows a broad targeting strategy and ties itself to football and music, Diet Coke seems to be specifically targeted at females and Coke Zero, although more subtle, has an adult male target in mind. Diet Coke has a definite association with female health and style and fashion (witness the give-away of a diamond and ruby encrusted red dress in one promotion). Coke Zero, as can immediately be ascertained from the rather masculine packaging design, is targeted at males. Coke Zero is a sugar free copy of the original, and communicates the fact that it is calorie free, rather than a diet drink, as young males associate diet drinks with females. Coke Zero advertising reflects the male as hero surrounded by beautiful women, and also witness the use of Wayne Rooney, certainly no shrinking violet, in the advertising. It is immediately apparent that Diet Coke is most definitely feminine when its advertising images are viewed.

Worksheet activity 7.2

Segment name	Nutritional snackers	Weight watchers	Guilty snackers	Party snackers	Indiscriminate snackers	Economical snackers
Benefits sought	Nutritional. All-natural ingredients	Low calorie, quick energy	Low calorie, quick energy	Can be served to guests, goes well with beverages	Good tasting, satisfies hunger cravings	Low price, best value
Types of snacks eaten	Fruits, vegetables, cheeses	Yoghurt, vegetables	Yoghurt, cookies, crackers, candy	Potato chips, nuts, crackers, pretzels	Candy, ice cream, cookies, potato chips, pretzels, popcorn	No specific products

Worksheet activity 7.3

(a) Adult education
- Age
- Sex
- Occupation
- Income
- Social class
- Education
- Family life cycle
- Lifestyle
- Leisure interests and hobbies

(b) Magazines and periodicals
- Sex (Woman's Own)
- Social class (Country Life)
- Income and class aspirations (Ideal Home)
- Occupation (Marketing Week, Computer Weekly)
- Leisure interests (Railway Modeller)
- Political ideology (Spectator, New Statesman)
- Age

(c) Sporting facilities
- Geographical area (rugby in Wales, skiing in parts of Scotland, sailing in coastal towns)
- Population density (squash clubs in cities, riding in country areas)
- Occupation (gyms for office workers)
- Education (there may be a demand for facilities for sports taught at certain schools, such as rowing)
- Family life cycle or age (parents may want facilities for their children, young single or married people may want facilities for themselves)
- Gender
- User status

Worksheet activity 7.4

Two of the most common reasons for the failure of segmentation strategies are that (a) there are little or no appropriate data to support the choices of segments that companies have made and (b) the segments chosen are not suitable to company objectives. With regard to the latter it is important that segmentation strategies take into account the role and capabilities of the company. Companies should also avoid markets that have become fragmented, ie where the market has been segmented into such a large number of segments that it leads to a loss of economies of scale in terms of production and purchasing.

Quiz answers

1. The essential foundations of marketing strategy are the choice of target market segment(s), and the choice of differential advantage. Taken together, they comprise the positioning strategy of the brand.

2. Market segmentation is the process of splitting customers into different groups, or segments, within which customers with similar characteristics have similar needs. By doing this, each segment can be targeted and reached with a distinct marketing mix.

3. Kotler outlines the six steps of effective STP as follows: Identify segmentation variables and segment the market; Develop segment profiles; Evaluate the attractiveness of each segment; Select the target segments; Identify positioning concepts for each segment; Select, develop and communicate the chosen concept.

4. The four major groups of consumer segmentation variables are geographic, demographic, psychographic and behavioural.

5. Plummer breaks down lifestyle segmentation into the dimensions of activities, interests, opinions and demographics.

6. Behavioural segmentation focuses on the customer's relationship with the product. This is important, as even individuals with similar demographic and/or psychographic profiles can interact quite differently with the same product. Behavioural segmentation segments buyers into groups based on their attitudes to and use of the product, and the benefits they expect to receive.

7. Macro segmentation variables within business markets are: size, location, usage rate and product or service application. Micro segmentation variables are technology, purchasing policies, decision-making unit (DMU) structure and process, and buyer-seller relationships.

8. The benefits of market segmentation can be summarised as follows: Better satisfaction of customer needs; growth in profits; revenue growth; customer retention; targeted communications; innovation; and increased segment share.

9. Further to the more traditional approaches to segmentation discussed in the course of this chapter, recent years have seen the rise of additional approaches to segmentation. These are relationship-based approaches to segmentation, critical event segmentation, and segmentation based on online behaviours.

10. A relatively recent addition to behavioural segmentation approaches is known as 'critical events segmentation' (CES). This approach is based on the idea that major events in an individual's life generate specific needs, which can be satisfied by providing a particular set of products and services. Examples of such critical events include marriage, the birth of children, unemployment, retirement, illness, moving home or death.

References

Brassington, F. and Pettitt, S. (2006), Principles of Marketing (4th Ed.), Pearson Education, London.

Hooley, G., Saunders, J. and Piercy, N. (2004), Marketing Strategy and Competitive Positioning (3rd Ed.), Pearson Education, London.

Kotler, P. and Keller, K.L. (2006), Marketing Management (12th Ed.), Pearson Education, London.

Kotler, P. (1991), Marketing Management, Prentice Hall, Harlow.

Lawson, R. 'The Family Life Cycle: A Demographic Analysis', Journal of Marketing Management, Summer 1988

Piercy, N.F. and Morgan, N.A. (1993), 'Strategic and Operational Market Segmentation: A Managerial Analysis', Journal of Strategic Marketing, 1, pp. 123-40

Plummer, J. 'The Concept and Application of Lifestyle Segmentation', Journal of Marketing (January 1994), pp. 33-37

Sleight, P. (1997), Targeting Customers: How to Use Geodemographic and Lifestyle Data in Your Business (2nd Ed.), NTC Publications, New York.

Solomon, M.R. (1994), Consumer Behaviour (2nd Ed.), Allyn and Bacon

Wind, Y. and Cardozo, R. (1974), 'Industrial Marketing Segmentation', Industrial Marketing Management, 3 (March), pp.153-66

Young, D. (1996), 'The Politics behind Market Segmentation', Marketing News, 21 October, 17

Chapter 8
Targeting

Topic list

1. The value of targeting markets
2. Evaluating market segment attractiveness
3. The segment evaluation process
4. Target coverage strategies

Introduction

Once the market has been segmented and profiles of the segments have been developed, marketers need to evaluate the attractiveness of each segment and ascertain whether it offers opportunities that match the firm's capabilities and resources. Selecting the right target market from a range of possible alternatives is an essential ingredient in developing a good marketing strategy and involves careful investigation of a range of specific criteria. Until a company's target market has been clearly identified and its requirements and motivation fully explored, it is not possible to develop a robust positioning strategy or, indeed, a relevant and compelling marketing programme.

Syllabus-linked learning objectives

By the end of the chapter you will be able to:

Learning objectives	Syllabus link
1. Assess the value of targeting markets as an approach to achieving customer satisfaction, competitive advantage and retention.	3.4
2. Critically evaluate a range of targeting coverage strategies for different organisational contexts and sectors.	3.5
3. Assess the attractiveness and value of selected market segments.	3.6

1 The value of targeting markets

In Chapter 7 it was pointed out that market segmentation has become an essential ingredient in corporate success. Segmentation enables marketers to **define and understand customer needs** and affords the opportunity to **create tailored products to better suit those needs**. As we shall see in the course of this chapter, the process of targeting forms the next step in marketing strategy development and consists of **evaluating the attractiveness of different target segments** and **selecting the most suitable ones** as targets for marketing programmes. Targeting focuses the company's efforts and avoids wastage by selecting only those segments that the company can serve well and potentially better than the competition. In this way, it enables companies to **effectively use their resources** and eliminate wastage – as marketing **efforts are focused on specific target segments**, rather than going after the market as a whole, only those customer groups that can be effectively served form the target of company efforts.

KEY CONCEPT

A **target market** is a market or segment selected for special attention by an organisation (possibly served with a distinct marketing mix).

Furthermore, as the choice of target market(s) involves the selection of only those segments where the company is able to serve customer needs in a potentially **more effective way than competitors**, targeting is not only a useful vehicle for achieving **customer satisfaction**, but also offers scope for the company to differentiate itself from competitors and thereby offers **potential for achieving competitive advantage**. The potential for creating sustainable competitive advantage in target markets via effective **positioning strategies** is explored in more detail in Chapter 8.

2 Evaluating market segment attractiveness

Once segments have been identified, each segment needs to be evaluated in terms of market attractiveness and company capability, or potential capability, in the given market segment. In addition to criteria such as size, growth, profitability, low risk and scale economies, the firm needs to consider whether investing in the segment presents a viable option in light of the company's objectives, competences and resources. Some segments may well be attractive, but may not meet with the company's longer-term objectives. Similarly, the company may not possess the requisite competences to offer superior value to its customers.

A range of factors are considered in assessing market segment attractiveness and they tend to be conveniently grouped into external and internal criteria for evaluation.

2.1 External criteria for evaluation

Hooley et. al. (2004) provide a comprehensive discussion of external evaluation criteria including market factors, competitive factors, economic and technological factors and business environment factors. These are addressed in more detail below.

Market factors	Comment
Segment size	Size is an obvious factor in determining segment attractiveness; the larger the segment, the greater the potential for achieving economies of scale in marketing and production and hence operating efficiencies. Segments offering potentially high volumes of sales are very attractive for achieving strategic objectives such as sales expansion.
Segment growth rate	The growth rate of segments is particularly attractive for companies pursuing growth objectives. Growing markets tend to offer attractive opportunities for achieving company sales growth.
Bargaining power of customers	Markets where negotiating power of buyers (either distribution chain intermediaries or consumers) is high incline to be less attractive than those where suppliers tend to have the upper hand. A key example is the highly concentrated UK grocery sector, which is dominated by four major retail chains with considerable purchasing power.
Stage of industry life cycle	Different stages in the market's life cycle or evolution hold different levels of attractiveness for companies, depending on company objectives. Markets in the growth phase require more investment, resulting in lesser short-term returns, whereas mature markets are more attractive for companies seeking more immediate cash and profit contribution, as lower levels of investment are required.
Price elasticity and sensitivity	Markets that are price-sensitive are generally less attractive, as they tend to be characterised by price wars (specifically in the mature stage of industry evolution).
	Markets that are less price-sensitive and where price elasticity of demand is low, are more attractive to companies, unless the company has a major cost advantage over its competitors.
Seasonality and cyclicality of demand	Fluctuations in demand due to seasonality or cycle affect the attractiveness of potential segments, particularly where companies serve highly seasonal markets. Identifying new segments to serve when demand in existing segments is low due to seasonality, can present an attractive option. Companies manufacturing highly seasonal items such as suntan products have found it useful to target segments in the southern hemisphere, where seasonal demand exists for their products when it is winter in the northern hemisphere.
Predictability	The more predictable and stable a given market segment, the more attractive it is likely to be, as marketers will find it easier to predict the potential value of that segment. For the same reason markets characterised by turbulence and unpredictability are likely to be less attractive and should be avoided.

The extent and nature of competition in a given market segment is another key consideration in evaluating a segment's attractiveness. The following factors, in particular, need to be considered when assessing the competitive environment.

Competitive factors	Comment
Intensity of competition	Markets dominated by one or a few large competitors are usually difficult to enter and may be unattractive, unless the company is able to provide some competitive edge over its rivals.
	In markets characterised by many smaller players offering competitively similar products, there is likely to be extensive price competition. These segments will only be attractive if the company has a distinct cost advantage or is able to provide a highly differentiated or unique offering that will be valued by customers.
Quality of competition	Market segments are more attractive if the existing competitors are stable and committed to the market. Conversely, segments characterised by volatile and less predictable competitors are more difficult to serve and control and are thus less attractive as potential targets.
Degree of differentiation	Markets with little differentiation between competitive product offerings tend to offer significant opportunities and may therefore be attractive to companies who can offer such differentiation.
Threat of substitution	The emergence of substitute products to current offerings in a given market can be a considerable threat, as they can make the existing offerings obsolete. Consider, for instance, the emergence of PCs rendering typewriters obsolete, or the more recent advent of the digital camera which has come to replace conventional cameras.
	While all markets are potentially vulnerable to new substitutes, those experiencing a real threat of substitution or those where substitution is imminent, should best be avoided as targets.

Factors in the market's broader economic and technological environments which should be considered in evaluating segment attractiveness include the following:

Economic and technological factors	Comment
Barriers to entry	Markets with considerable barriers to entry, such as high switching costs for customers or protected technology, are notoriously difficult to enter. Even where companies may attempt entry, the exorbitant costs involved act as a formidable barrier, making these markets unattractive for selection and thus should be avoided.
Barriers to exit	Some markets have high exit barriers, where existing companies are locked into untenable positions. These markets are equally unattractive. Some potential target markets may have both high entry barriers (ie substantial investment requirements) and high exit barriers, as once entry has taken place, the company may be locked into a situation where it is forced to continue using its existing facilities so as to achieve some form of return on capital employed.
Bargaining power of suppliers	Markets where suppliers have extensive bargaining power, for instance, in cases where suppliers have a monopoly or duopoly over the supply of raw materials or other inputs, are considerably less attractive than those where there are many competing suppliers.
Investment required	The attractiveness of potential target markets is also affected by the financial commitments required in gaining entry and serving the market. Where such costs are prohibitive, this will deter entry by making the market target unattainable.
Margins available	Margins available differ from one market to the next, influenced by such factors as competitive rivalry and price sensitivity. Generally speaking, the margins to be attained influence that market's attractiveness. However, as discussed earlier, other mitigating factors, such as the company's objectives, will help determine whether this will act as a deterrent against targeting that market.
Level of technology	For technologically advanced companies, a high level and usage of technology will make a market more attractive than those where this is not the case. Conversely, companies where advanced technology is not an issue, for example, where competences and skills lie in areas such as people, markets with a lower use and level of technology may be more suitable.

The general business environment is another key determinant of market segment attractiveness. According to Hooley, et al. (2004), key issues to be considered in this category include the political and legal environments, economic factors and issues concerning socially acceptable and environmentally considerate practices.

Business environment factors	Comment
Exposure to economic fluctuations	Some markets are more susceptible to economic fluctuations than others. Commodity markets are a case in point, as they are often subject to wider economic change.
Exposure to political and legal factors	Markets vulnerable to political or legal factors tend to be less attractive than those which are not.
Extent of regulation	Degree of regulation in a market will impact on companies' freedom of action. Generally speaking, a less regulated market offers more potential for innovative players than tightly controlled markets.
Social and environmental acceptability	With increasing concern for the social and ecological environment, companies are increasingly required to behave in socially and environmentally responsible ways.

The following table provides a convenient summary of the external factors impacting on market segment attractiveness.

Market factors	Competitive factors
Size; growth rate; bargaining power of buyers; life cycle stage; price elasticity; seasonality and cyclicality of demand; predictability	Intensity; quality; degree of differentiation; threat of substitution
Economic and technological factors	**Business environment factors**
Barriers to entry and exit; bargaining power of suppliers; investment required; margins; level of technology	Economic fluctuations; political and legal; regulation; social and environmental acceptability

Adapted from Hooley, et al. (2004)

MARKETING AT WORK — application

Small- or medium-sized international wine producers might want to think carefully before entering the UK wine market. Although one of the largest wine importing countries in the world, the UK is a notoriously difficult market to enter, and the pitfalls are many.

Market factors: First of all, the bargaining power of customers is very high (five supermarket chains are responsible for more than 80% of all the wine sold in the UK). Consumers are also very price sensitive in that they have become used to the discounted wine prices in the supermarkets and often look to buy at the bargain or 'on-offer' price.

Competitive factors: Competition is intense in this sector. A number of big wine corporations and many smaller- and medium-sized producers are competing in this market, where often differentiation can only be built on the back of a very large advertising budget. Consumer tastes are also not that developed and entrenched, so it is easy to substitute one product for another. Very often competing wines are very similar to one another in taste.

Economic and technological factors: Due mainly to an oversupply of wine on the world market, suppliers have very little bargaining power and are sometimes desperate to make a sale and get rid of some of their wine. Costs for smaller companies are prohibitively high, especially with regard to marketing and advertising, but also in terms of customs and excise duties that have to be paid upfront. Many of the factors above combine to impact very negatively on margins.

Business environment factors: Due to a perceived drinking problem amongst the youth, politicians are taking steps to regulate the market for alcoholic beverages in the UK. The introduction of minimum prices in stores and higher taxes are some of the measures currently being discussed.

For the small- to medium-sized producer, the UK market does not rate very highly in terms of market attractiveness and many have turned away from this market to focus their efforts elsewhere.

2.2 Internal factors for evaluation: determining current and potential company strengths

In evaluating market segments, external factors are just one side of the coin. We also need to assess the company's resources, competences and capabilities and how they can be deployed to serve a particular market segment. This involves determining both the current and potential strengths of the company.

As part of this evaluation process, the firm needs to consider the following issues:

(a) Its current market position
(b) Its economic and technological position
(c) Its capability profile

In evaluating its strengths in a particular market or segment in which the company currently operates, attention needs to be paid to the following:

Current market position	Comment
Relative market share	Market share in markets already targeted by the company serves as a barometer of how well the company is currently serving its target. The higher the share, the better its performance. High market share also aids further penetration of the market, as it is accompanied by high levels of customer awareness and extensive distribution coverage. Hence, share of market is a vital marketing asset that can be harnessed to further develop the company's position.
Rate of change in market share	Rapidly increasing market share reflects a company's ability to serve the market better than competitors. Even where current share of market is low, a growing share sends positive signals to the market – for instance, distributors are made aware of the need to stock and display larger quantities of the product.
Unique and valued products	The ability to offer superior and differentiated products (in both current and potential markets) valued by consumers is a key source of competitive advantage and thus enables a stronger competitive position.
Exploitable marketing resources	Where a company has marketing assets such as a favourable image, strong brand name(s), customer relationships and distribution networks in one target market, these can often be exploited and built upon in other target markets.

The next set of factors refers to the resources that can be utilised to exploit opportunities in the marketplace.

Capability profile	Comment
Management strength	This is a key asset of the company. The skills and competences of a firm's management staff are important strengths which can be deployed in the market.
Marketing strength	Superior marketing skills are another key source of corporate strength. For instance, a company's marketing strengths in new product development and brand building can successfully be leveraged and exploited in entering new target markets.
Forward and backward integration	Current or potential strength in serving a given target market is also affected by the extent of control the company has over raw material supply (ie via backward integration) and distribution channels (forward integration). High integration, particularly in markets characterised by high supplier and buyer power, can result in considerable strength *vis à vis* competitors.

Further to the above, the company's economic and technological characteristics and resources relative to competitors will also require evaluation.

Economic and technological position	Comment
Relative cost position	A company's cost structure in relation to competitors can be a marketing asset. Relatively low production and marketing costs can provide the company with an edge over rivals in a given target market.
Capacity utilisation	The level of capacity utilisation is a major factor in the cost structure of most companies. This is particularly the case for small- and medium-sized businesses.
Technological position	Companies who possess a technological edge relevant to a particular target segment will have an advantage over others who do not possess such capabilities.

In summary, the factors impacting on the company's current and potential strengths are presented below.

Current position

Relative market share; change in market share; unique and valued market offerings; exploitable marketing resources

Capability profile

Management strength; marketing strength; forward and backward integration

Economic and technological position

Relative cost; capacity utilisation; technology

Adapted from Hooley, et al. (2004)

In closing, it is important to remember that company or business strength in a given segment is always relative to (a) other competitors serving the market segment and (b) the requirements of customers in that segment.

3 The segment evaluation process

In section 2 above, we discussed a range of factors that need to be considered in evaluating segment attractiveness. But how do marketers actually utilise this knowledge to make market segment choices? Put differently, how does the actual process of evaluation and selection take place?

Portfolio matrices have been found very useful in the selection of target segments. There are several steps involved in using this approach (Hooley, 2004):

Step 1 **Identify factors relevant to the market** (select from list of factors provided above, in section 2)

Step 2 **Assign weights to each factor based on each factor's perceived importance**

Step 3 **Evaluate and each potential market segment on a scale from 1 (='poor') to 5 (='excellent') and compute a summary score on the two main dimensions of 'market segment attractiveness' and 'company business strength in serving that segment' using the weightings** (see table below)

The subjective choice and weighting of factors used in the analysis ensure that the model is customised to the needs of the specific company. Where appropriate, factors can be more objectively assessed through the use of marketing research or economic analysis (Hooley, 2004).

This approach will result in a portfolio model, such as the one below, a hypothetical company. This model allows for an easy assessment and objective discussion of the various alternatives.

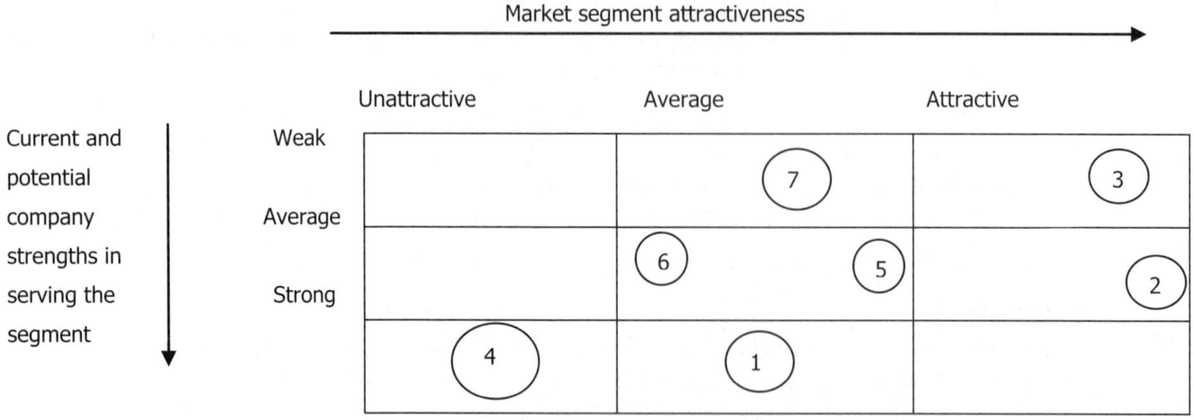

	Market segment attractiveness		
	Unattractive	Average	Attractive
Weak		7	3
Average	6	5	2
Strong	4	1	

(Current and potential company strengths in serving the segment — vertical axis)

Ideally, companies will be looking for target markets in the bottom right-hand corner of the figure above. However, as these kind of opportunities are rare, trade-offs will frequently need to be made. For instance, one possibility might be to select segments where the company is currently strong, or can potentially become so, but which are less attractive (for example, target opportunity 1 in the above figure). Alternatively, the company may consider going into segments that are more attractive, but where its current or potential strength is average (ie target opportunity 2 above).

In order to develop a defensible position in the marketplace, focusing on areas of current or potential strength usually makes most sense. Generally speaking, the advice would be to select an apparently less attractive market where a company can exploit strengths than to go after a market segment which may appear attractive, but where the company may, at best, be only an average or weak player. However, sometimes attractive segments can be pursued despite current weaknesses in business strength, when such strengths could either be built or bought-in through mergers or acquisitions (Hooley, 2004).

Market segments of medium attractiveness where the company has medium strength should be invested in selectively (target opportunities 5 and 6). Average or unattractive markets where business strength is weak (such as in target opportunity 7 above) should be avoided.

This is summarised in the figure below.

	Market segment attractiveness		
	Unattractive	Average	Attractive
Weak	Strongly avoid	Avoid	Possibilities
Average	Avoid	Possibilities	Secondary targets
Strong	Possibilities	Secondary targets	Prime targets

(Current and potential company strengths in serving the segment — vertical axis)

ACTIVITY 8.1

evaluation

What are the main two main dimensions on a portfolio matrix that a company needs to investigate and quantify to help it come to decisions regarding the choice of target markets?

Finally, a company should also consider the **overall portfolio of businesses or markets** it is currently operating in. Companies will typically try to build a **balanced portfolio** of activities, seeking balance in such factors as cash use and generation, risk and return and focus on present versus future activities (Hooley, 2004).

4 Target coverage strategies

Having evaluated and selected appropriate market segments to target, utilising the steps outlined above, the company is then in a position to decide *how* to target the chosen segments. Traditional approaches to market coverage (ie targeting strategies) include:

(a) Undifferentiated targeting
(b) Differentiated targeting
(c) Concentrated targeting

These are addressed below.

Targeting strategy	Comment
Undifferentiated	This policy is to produce a single product and hope to get as many customers as possible to buy it; segmentation is ignored entirely. This is sometimes called **mass marketing**.
Differentiated	The company attempts to provide different products aimed at a different market segment (for example, shampoo manufacturers develop different types of shampoo for different market segments, ie consumers with dry and damaged hair, coloured hair, greasy hair, flat hair, dandruff, etc).
Concentrated	The company attempts to produce the ideal product for a single segment of the market (for example, Rolls Royce cars, Mothercare mother and baby shops).

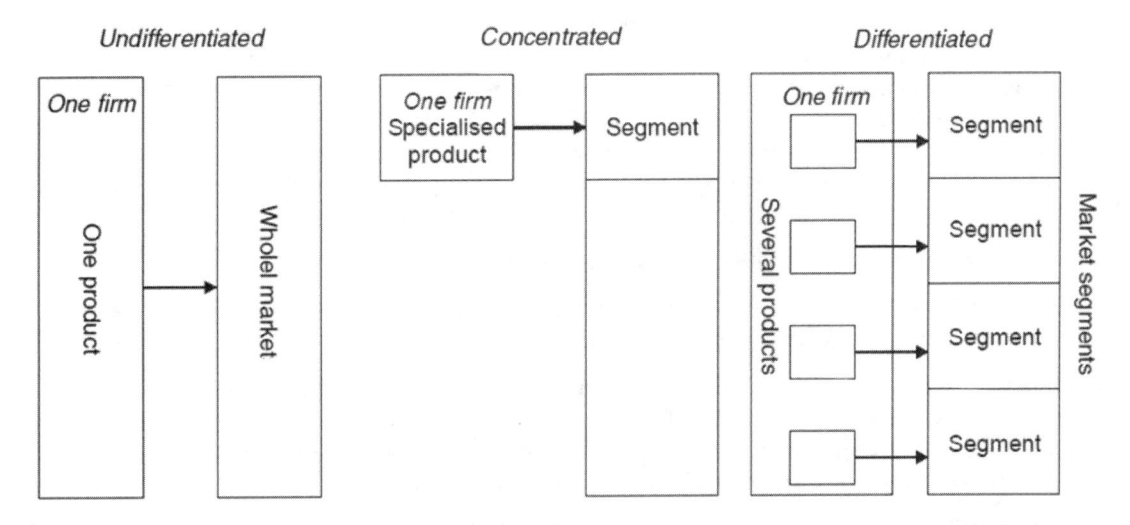

Undifferentiated: One firm / One product → Whole market

Concentrated: One firm Specialised product → Segment

Differentiated: One firm / Several products → Segment, Segment, Segment, Segment (Market segments)

The **undifferentiated** targeting approach assumes that the market is one homogenous unit, with no significant differences between individual customers within that market. Therefore, this approach ignores any segment differences and goes after the whole market with one offering. It uses a single marketing mix that serves the needs of the entire market and is likely to involve mass distribution and mass communication, with the aim of having as broad an appeal as possible. The major **disadvantage** with this approach is that it ignores the existence of segments naturally occurring in the market. As we have seen in our earlier discussion on segmentation (Chapter 7), people do differ in their needs, wants and benefits sought, so it is unlikely that one offering aimed at the entire market will meet all individual buyers' requirements. Therefore, as the product offering has not been tailored to specific segments, specific segments in the market are likely to be unsatisfied by the current 'mass' offering and can easily defect to offerings of competitors who more closely match their needs and requirements. Undifferentiated approaches are best suited for products with limited psychological appeal. An often cited example is that of petrol, although even in this category changes are afoot, with petrol retailers increasingly starting to differentiate their offerings (via unleaded petrol or petrol with extra additives). As can be imagined, the undifferentiated approach to marketing is becoming increasingly rare, due to the realisation of inherent differences between individual buyers, which underscores the need for segmentation in the first instance.

Despite these obvious shortcomings, there are distinct **advantages** associated with this approach. Undifferentiated marketing can yield significant economies of scale (one single product aimed at a potentially large market) and keeps down costs, specifically in terms of research and development (R & D), production, inventory, transportation, advertising and product management. These lower costs can then also be turned into lower prices to appeal to price-sensitive segments of the market.

Differentiated targeting holds a range of **advantages**, not least of all because this approach allows marketers to tailor their offerings to individual segments, thereby enabling customer satisfaction due to better meeting of their needs. Differentiation can be a distinct source of competitive advantage and it furthermore also allows the company to spread risk, so that if a given segment becomes unattractive or declines, there are still other segments that can generate revenue for the company.

For differentiation to be implemented effectively a detailed understanding of the market is required, including how it is developing (remembering that markets are never static, but evolve, and are thus subject to constant change). Detailed market knowledge enables the company to identify new opportunities and emerging segments on an ongoing basis.

The major **disadvantage** of differentiated marketing is the additional costs this approach entails in terms of marketing and production (more product design and development costs, potential loss of economies of scale in production and storage, additional promotion costs and administrative costs and so on). When the costs of differentiation of the market exceed the benefits from further segmentation and target marketing, a firm is said to have over-differentiated.

On the whole, a differentiated strategy can be said to dilute the company's efforts as resources are spread thinly. It is thus important for the organisation not to overstretch itself in the number of segments it attempts to cover. Nevertheless, the differentiated strategy is a very useful one, in particular in highly competitive markets.

MARKETING AT WORK

application

Differentiated marketing is adopted by companies seeking to offer **a distinct product** or service **to each chosen segment of the market**. Depending on a company's resources, differentiated marketing can help in achieving total market domination. The strategy pursued by **Van den Berghs** (a subsidiary of Unilever) in the yellow fats market is a good example. The company segmented the market into five different segments on the basis of benefits sought by consumers and launched brands into four of the segments. Central to the success of the company was its unwillingness to accept the segmentation in the market adopted by others.

The five benefit segments identified by Van den Berghs were as follows:

Segment 1 consisted of consumers seeking a 'real butter taste' and would not forego that taste at almost any price. This segment chose butter. Van den Berghs deliberately did not target this segment.

Segment 2 consumers wanted the taste, feel and texture of butter but were concerned about the price. These consumers would typically buy the cheapest butter. Into this segment the company launched Krona Dairy Crest, a block margarine with butter taste and a premium margarine price. This was to attract customers trading down from butter. This was followed by the successful launches of Clover and 'I Can't Believe It's Not Butter'.

Segment 3 were former butter users prepared to accept existing margarines as a butter substitute, and who appreciated margarine's additional benefits over butter, such as easy spreading and tub packaging. The company's Stork brand was the market leader in this segment.

Segment 4 were concerned with diet and weight control. Here the company's Outline brand was a leading brand and subsequently St Ivel Gold was successfully launched to appeal to this segment.

Segment 5 was concerned with health in general and cholesterol in particular. Consumers in this segment were particularly interested in spreads with low cholesterol and high in polyunsaturated fats. The market leader in this section was Flora, another Van den Bergh company brand.

The **concentrated** targeting approach is the most focused of the three strategies discussed thus far. As it involves specialisation in serving one specific segment, it can obtain highly detailed insights into the target segment's needs, wants and requirements. However, a major disadvantage associated with concentrated marketing is the business risk of relying on a single segment of a single market. Having all its eggs in one basket can be risky, as if that segment should fail, there will be no other segments to fall back on. Furthermore, the company's success in the segment might attract the attention of rivals and can thus make the company vulnerable to entry by competitors into that segment. On the other hand, specialisation in a particular market segment can give a firm a profitable, although perhaps temporary, competitive edge over rival firms.

Another attraction of the concentrated approach is that it keeps costs down, as only one marketing mix needs to be managed. There is also the potential to achieve economies of scale. Strategically speaking, as resources are concentrated into only one segment, this can allow the company to achieve a stronger and more defendable position than can potentially be attained by competitors who are operating in more than one segment and are thus spreading their efforts more thinly. On the down side, however, being a niche specialist in only one segment can make it more difficult for companies to diversify into other segments. On the one hand, this can be due to strong association by consumers of the company with its original niche; on the other hand, difficulties may arise from lack of experience of operating in more than one segment.

The **choice between undifferentiated, differentiated or concentrated marketing** as a marketing strategy will depend on the following factors:

(a) **The extent to which the product and/or the market may be considered homogeneous**. Mass marketing may be sufficient if the market is largely homogeneous (for example, for safety matches)

(b) **The company's resources must not be over-extended by differentiated marketing**. Small firms may better succeed by concentrating on one segment only

(c) **The product must be sufficiently advanced in its life cycle** to have attracted a substantial total market; otherwise segmentation and target marketing is unlikely to be profitable, because each segment would be too small in size

Finally, it should also be remembered that strategic decisions should never be taken in isolation, but should be considered in light of **competitors' activities**. In particular, if competitors are already implementing clearly differentiated strategies, it would be dangerous for a company to adopt an undifferentiated approach. In such cases, it would be wiser to either (a) identify segments in which competitors are strong and assess whether it might be possible to attack them head-on in those segments or (b) to identify an entirely different niche that can be successfully served by the company.

MARKETING AT WORK — application

Organisations with limited resources often practise concentrated marketing focusing on one segment, to enable them to build a strong position in that segment. A downside of this approach is that, with time, the segment may become less attractive to the organisation. Such was the case with Lucozade, developed in the 1920s and marketed successfully for many years as a tonic (a forerunner of the energy drink) to people recovering from illness. By the 1970s sales has dropped significantly due to lower levels of illness and the company then decided that it was time to reposition the brand. A series of evolutionary positioning shifts were orchestrated with little effect. It was not until Lucozade realised the potential of the sports market for energy drinks that the product really started taking off. In the early 1980s a new positioning was developed around the theme 'Lucozade is not only delicious and refreshing but can quickly replace lost energy'. Using Daley Thompson, the Olympic decathlete and heavy metal music from Iron Maiden, the company launched an advertising campaign that appealed to younger consumers. In the first year of the new campaign, sales volume increased by 40%.

Source: Hooley, et al. (2004)

ACTIVITY 8.2

application

Identify one disadvantage of adopting a concentrated marketing approach and one disadvantage of pursuing a differentiated marketing strategy.

4.1 Customised marketing

In addition to the more traditional approaches outlined above, recent advances in communications and internet technology have given rise to new individualised approaches to targeting, which allow companies to customise their marketing programmes so as to precisely meet customers' needs, wants and preferences. Three categories of such customised approaches can be identified:

Customised marketing strategies	Comment
One-to-one marketing	This approach entails creating a unique product or marketing programme for each customer in the target segment. For example, Amazon tracks customers who browse and buy from its web site and uses this information to customise product offerings, which are tailored to individual customers' specific preferences and requirements.
Mass customisation	This involves creating unique products to individual customers on a mass scale. A typical example is Dell, who creates thousands of custom-made computers on a daily basis.
Permission marketing	Although similar to one-to-one marketing, this approach differs in that customers give companies permission to specifically target them. Examples include opt-in e-mail lists, where consumers allow companies to send e-mails to inform them about products they might be interested in purchasing.

One-to-one marketing is characterised by **personalisation**, where every element of the marketing programme is customised to meet the specific needs of a particular customer. As noted, this approach has grown rapidly in e-commerce, where customers can be precisely targeted. Additionally, one-to-one marketing is popular in luxury or custom-made products such as airplanes, luxury boats and yachts and custom-made houses. Similarly, many service firms such as solicitors, doctors and hairdressers use customised approaches in their marketing programmes to match individual needs.

An extension of one-to-one marketing, **mass customisation** enables companies to provide individual customers with unique offerings, on a mass scale. With this approach, not only can the specific needs of customers be met in a tailored fashion, but companies can also incur significant cost savings due to economies of scale.

Permission marketing entails a major advantage over other individualised approaches: by virtue of the fact that customers have already opted in to a firm's targeting efforts, it is highly likely that these are customers are interested in the firm's offering. Consequently, a great deal of potential waste (in terms of marketing expense and efforts) can be avoided, as the company is targeting an already captive audience. Contrast, for example, traditional mass media advertising where only a small percentage of the audience has any real interest with a company's product, with the permission marketing approaches of, for example, airlines, who have been requested by customers to e-mail periodic information pertaining to airfare and other specials. Clearly, the marketing approach of the latter will be much more focused and effective in terms of marketing resources than that adopted by the former.

All of the customised marketing strategies discussed thus far are predicted to grow considerably in future, because their focus on the individual customer makes them indispensable to the development and maintenance of long-term customer relationships. Put simply, customers prefer to maintain relationships with those companies that best meet their needs.

Despite their obvious advantages, customised marketing strategies are notoriously expensive. To make their adoption viable, Ferrell & Hartline (2008) propose that companies should ensure the following:

(a) The delivery of the marketing programme should be automated as far as possible, so as to become **cost efficient**. A key example is the internet, which makes this possible by enabling individual customisation in real time.

(b) Despite the presence of automation, the programme should also entail **personalisation**. This means providing customers with choices, not just in terms of the product itself, but throughout the marketing programme. Dell and

Amazon are indicative of this approach, by combining automatisation with extensive personalisation: customers can choose specific delivery locations, payment and shipping terms, other features such as gift wrapping and whether to opt in to e-mail promotions. By monitoring clickstream information in real time, these firms are able to offer product suggestions while customers visit their web sites. In addition to increasing sales, this customised information also better fulfils customer needs, thereby increasing the potential for establishing long-term customer relationships

MARKETING AT WORK — application

SWIG (www.swig.co.uk) is a UK retailer specialising in premium wines. The company describes its business as supplying 'artisan wines from around the world'. The company targets top-end consumers with busy lifestyles who are interested in wine and wine culture, but do not always have the time to find special and unique products from interesting producers. The web site is a major driver of business and has facilities for browsing and purchasing, arranging delivery, and sharing in the experiences of the owners who have personally visited producers of the wines on offer and supply anecdotes and other stories from around the world. The company also produces a web newsletter to which members sign up, and occasionally organises wine tasting evenings where members can connect with one other, meet the wine makers from around the world, network, taste wine and purchase.

The company has thus circumnavigated some of the pitfalls associated with entering the UK wine market mentioned in the earlier Marketing at Work example in this chapter. By targeting a niche segment and then using a powerful combination of one-to-one marketing, permission marketing and even mass customisation, they have been able to avoid the problems of low margins and high promotional cost associated with dealing with supermarkets to reach their target market..

ACTIVITY 8.3 — concept

What are the major characteristics of permission-based marketing?

ACTIVITY 8.4 — concept

What is one-to-one marketing?

Learning objective review

Learning objectives	Covered
1. Assess the value of targeting markets as an approach to achieving customer satisfaction, competitive advantage and retention.	☑ The value of targeting markets
2. Critically evaluate a range of targeting coverage strategies for different organisational contexts and sectors.	☑ Target coverage strategies: undifferentiated, differentiated, concentrated and customised marketing
3. Assess the attractiveness and value of selected market segments.	☑ Evaluating market segment attractiveness: external and internal criteria for evaluation ☑ The segment evaluation process

Quick quiz

1. What are the four sets of external evaluation criteria that need to be applied when assessing market segment attractiveness?

2. List six factors in the market's broader economic and technological environments which should be considered in evaluating segment attractiveness.

3. Name three issues a firm needs to consider in determining its current and potential company strengths.

4. Name three traditional approaches to targeting strategies or market coverage.

5. List three customised marketing approaches.

6. What is the major advantage of permission marketing?

7. In the discussion of market segment attractiveness and competitive forces, what is meant by 'the threat of substitution'?

8. How does the 'bargaining powers of suppliers' impact on a decision to enter into a particular market segment?

9. Which factors govern the choice of undifferentiated, differentiated or concentrated marketing strategies?

10. What is meant by mass customisation?

Activity debriefs

Worksheet activity 8.1

The two dimensions on a portfolio matrix are 'market segment attractiveness' and 'current and potential company strengths in serving the segment'.

Worksheet activity 8.2

A major disadvantage associated with *concentrated marketing* is the business risk of relying on a single segment of a single market. Having all its eggs in one basket can be risky, as if that segment should fail, there will be no other segments to fall back on. Furthermore, the company's success in the segment might attract the attention of rivals and can thus make the company vulnerable to entry by competitors into that segment. On the other hand, specialisation in a particular market segment can give a firm a profitable, although perhaps temporary, competitive edge over rival firms.

The main disadvantage of *differentiated marketing* is the additional cost of marketing and production (extra product design, the loss of economies of scale in production and storage, extra promotion and administrative costs). When the costs exceed the benefits of further segmentation and target marketing, the firm is said to have over-differentiated.

Worksheet activity 8.3

Permission marketing is different from the other customised approaches discussed in this section in that customers make a conscious choice to become part of the firm's target market.

This approach is commonly executed via an opt-in e-mail or mobile telephone list where consumers are informed, via periodic messages about goods and services they might be interested in buying.

Permission-based marketing has a big advantage in that customers opting-in already have an interest in the products offered by the firm.

It also allows a business to target individual consumers, thereby not wasting marketing resources and expense.

Worksheet activity 8.4

One-to-one marketing is characterised by personalisation, where every element of the marketing programme is customised to meet the specific needs of a particular customer. As noted, this approach has grown rapidly in e-commerce, where customers can be precisely targeted. Additionally, one-to-one marketing is popular in luxury or custom-made products such as airplanes, luxury boats and yachts and custom-made houses.

Quiz answers

1. The four main categories of external evaluation criteria are: market factors, competitive factors, economic and technological factors and business environment factors.

2. The six factors within the broader economic and technological environments are: barriers to entry, barriers to exit, bargaining powers of suppliers, investment required, margins available, and level of technology.

3. In determining its current and potential company strengths a firm needs to consider its current market position, its economic and technological position, and its capability profile.

4. The three approaches are: undifferentiated targeting, differentiated targeting and concentrated targeting.

5. The three approaches to customised marketing strategy are: one-to-one marketing, mass customisation and permission marketing.

6. Permission marketing entails a major advantage over other individualised approaches: by virtue of the fact that customers have already opted in to a firm's targeting efforts, it is highly likely that these are customers that are interested in the firm's offering. Consequently, a great deal of potential waste (in terms of marketing expense and efforts) can be avoided, as the company is targeting an already captive audience.

7. The emergence of substitute products to current offerings in a given market can be a considerable threat, as they can make the existing offerings obsolete. Consider, for instance, the emergence of PCs rendering typewriters obsolete, or the more recent advent of the digital camera which has come to replace conventional cameras.

   While all markets are potentially vulnerable to new substitutes, those experiencing a real threat of substitution or those where substitution is imminent, should best be avoided as targets.

8. Markets where suppliers have extensive bargaining power, for instance, in cases where suppliers have a monopoly or duopoly over the supply of raw materials or other inputs, are considerably less attractive than those where there are many competing suppliers.

9. The factors are:

   - The extent to which the product and/or the market may be considered homogeneous. Mass marketing may be sufficient if the market is largely homogeneous (for example, for safety matches).

   - The company's resources must not be over-extended by differentiated marketing. Small firms may succeed better by concentrating on one segment only.

   The product must be sufficiently advanced in its life cycle to have attracted a substantial total market otherwise segmentation and target marketing is unlikely to be profitable, because each segment would be too small in size.

10. This involves creating unique products to individual customers on a mass scale. A typical example is Dell, who creates thousands of custom-made computers on a daily basis.

References

Ferrell, O.C. and Hartline, M.D. (2008), Marketing Strategy (4th Ed.), Thomson Southwestern, London.

Hooley, G., Saunders, J. and Piercy, N. (2004), Marketing Strategy and Competitive Positioning (3rd Ed.), Pearson Education, London.

Chapter 9
Positioning

Topic list

1. Marketing positioning strategy and the organisation's value proposition
2. Positioning options and their implementation within the context of the organisation and its markets

Introduction

As we have seen in the preceding chapters, all marketing strategy is built on segmentation, targeting and positioning. A company discovers different needs and groups in the marketplace, targets those needs and groups it can satisfy in a way that is superior to the competition, and then positions its offering so that the target market recognises the company's distinctive offering and image.

Kotler and Keller (2006) note that if the company does a poor job of positioning, the market will be confused. If the company does an excellent job of positioning, then it can work out the rest of its marketing planning and differentiation from its positioning strategy.

This chapter will investigate ways in which effective positioning may be achieved.

Syllabus-linked learning objectives

By the end of the chapter you will be able to:

Learning objectives	Syllabus link
1. Examine the concept of marketing positioning strategy and how it can be used to convey the organisation's value proposition.	3.7
2. Critically evaluate positioning options and their implementation within the context of the organisation and its markets.	3.8

1 Marketing positioning strategy and the organisation's value proposition

1.1 Distinction between positioning and differentiation

KEY CONCEPT

Positioning is the act of designing the company's offer and image so that it achieves a distinct and valued place in the target customer's mind'. The firm is thus attempting to **differentiate** *and* **position** *its product offering relative to competitive offerings.*

Differentiation and positioning are complex and sometimes confusing terms that can be clarified as follows:

Product differentiation entails **creating differences in a company's product** offering that set it apart from those of competitors.

Positioning refers to **the creation of a mental image** of the product offering and its distinct features in the **mind of the targeted consumers**.

Differentiation is thus about **the product itself**, while **positioning** is about the **customer's perception of the benefits** the product possesses.

1.2 Differential advantage

As the previous chapter illustrated, the choice of target market segments indicates where a company will compete. There will, however, be **other firms competing in the same segments** and customers will be faced with a decision of whom to support. Consequently, a key strategic task of management is to create a sustainable **differential advantage** designed to attract consumer choices.

> **KEY CONCEPT**
>
> A **sustainable differential advantage** is a perceived difference that leads customers in the target segment to prefer one company's offer above those of others. The difference may be based on a product that is seen as superior, has a lower price or better service support.
>
> When a company is successfully able to create a sustainable competitive advantage this often leads to a higher market share and **profits**, as well as making the company less vulnerable to attack from competitors.

1.3 Customer value and organisational profit

Any attempt to be successful at creating a **sustainable differential advantage** must start with a solid understanding of **what it is that customers value**.

> **KEY CONCEPT**
>
> According to Doyle and Stern (2006), **customer value** is the total satisfaction customers perceive the product is offering, less the price to be paid for it (including operating or running costs over the life of the product). Economists refer to the perceived satisfaction using the term '**utility**'.

For example, for a customer buying a car, the utility that any model is seen to offer would be a function of the car's size, standard of the fittings, performance, perceived image and so on. Also taken into account would be the price of alternatives and the amount the customer is able to afford. The customer is also likely to compare maintenance, labour, insurance and other running costs. A car manufacturer can **create value** for the customer by **increasing the utility** of the vehicle (by offering features that are perceived as superior), **lowering the price** or by **cutting other operational or running costs**.

This definition is expressed in the following equation: **Value = Utility – Price**

At the same time as offering superior value to the customer, the differential advantage must also be of benefit to the firm, in the form of profit, expressed by the following equation:

Profit = Price – Cost

These equations show that there are three fundamental ways of creating sustainable differential advantage:

1. **Increase utility** without disproportionately increasing cost
2. **Lower cost** without disproportionately lowering utility
3. Seek a **new positioning in the market** with different levels of both utility and price.

1.4 Creating differential advantage

Perceived customer satisfaction, or utility, is always a combination of rational, economic factors and subjective image dimensions.

Doyle and Stern (2006) note that the factors that drive product differentiation can be grouped into four categories: product, service, personnel and image.

1.4.1 Product drivers

The **physical product** can be differentiated by design so it is perceived as better than competitive products or cheaper to operate.

Product drivers	Description
Performance	The level of a product's primary operating characteristics, eg speed, capacity, accuracy
Features	Characteristics added to the primary function, eg a car augmented by satellite navigation, climate control or entertainment system
Reliability	Is the product reliable or will the customer have problems with it?
Conformance	Do the design and operating systems of the product meet expected specifications?
Durability	This refers to the expected working life of the product
Operating costs	The operating costs over the product's life cycle, eg installation, energy consumption, labour, insurance
Serviceability	This refers to the facility with which a product can be repaired
Aesthetics	How the product looks and feels to the buyer

1.4.2 Service drivers

It is very difficult to achieve significant product differences in very competitive markets. Strong rivals often have similar capabilities to compete and copy each other very quickly. In these circumstances, differences in **service quality** can play a very big role in differentiating a product or company.

The following table lists some of the service elements that can be utilised to augment and differentiate a product.

Service drivers	Comment
Credit and finance	Grants, loans, terms and conditions can add to a product's appeal
Ordering facilities	The ease or efficiency with which customers can order the product
Delivery	The speed and reliability with which the product is delivered
Installation	How effectively or easily can the product be put into working order for the customer
Training and consulting	Additional help and support offered to the customer
After-sales service	The quality of the product's maintenance and back-up support
Guarantees	Comprehensive guarantees may eliminate perceived purchase risks
Operational support	A variety of services that can be offered to reduce a customer's cost structure or enhance its marketing effectiveness

1.4.3 Personal drivers

Company **personnel** have become a very big driver of differential advantage, especially in service-oriented markets. High-quality personal service is difficult to copy. The key attributes of people who add value are listed in the table below.

Personnel drivers	Comment
Professionalism	Training is needed to equip staff with the required skills and knowledge
Courtesy	Customers expect politeness and consideration
Trustworthiness	Staff should be honest and credible
Reliability	Customers want service that is accurate and consistent
Positivity	People want to deal with staff who believe they can overcome most difficulties
Responsiveness	Staff should respond quickly to customer requests and problems
Initiative	Staff should use initiative in solving customer problems and not have to refer small matters to superiors
Communication	Staff should be able to understand customers and provide information to them effectively

1.4.4 Image drivers

The **image** of a company or brand should be a major source of differential advantage. Experiments in different product fields have shown that in blind product tests customers cannot differentiate between alternatives. Once a well-known company or brand name is attached, they will not only choose this brand, but also be willing to pay more for it.

Image drivers	Comment
Strong positive image supporting customer confidence in the product	A strong positive image gives a customer confidence in the product
Socio-psychological confidence	Socio-psychological confidence is created when customers perceive the brand as enabling them to make a positive personal or social statement.
Economic confidence	Economic confidence is achieved when a brand or company name engenders an image of value, performance or reliability

1.4.5 The Role of cost

The drivers listed above achieve differential advantage by increasing utility. However, as noted in section 1.2 above, differential advantage can also be created by lowering costs.

As mentioned earlier, perceived customer satisfaction is always a combination of rational economic factors and subjective image factors. In business markets, the former are especially important while the latter are particularly relevant in consumer markets. Whatever the case, **competition based on cost** and **competition based on differentiation** are two alternatives open to the firm.

Doyle and Stern (2006) claim that this is an **artificial choice** and that today **companies need both low cost and utility enhancing differentiation**, as low costs permit the firm to create a differential advantage by either cutting price to the consumer, or by investing more in product, services, personnel and image improvements, thereby **increasing value**.

1.5 Alternative positioning strategies

We have seen that a company can offer superior value by differentiating strategies that **add value** or **reduce costs**. A third way of enhancing its competitiveness is by **positioning itself and its products more effectively**. Positioning strategy thus refers to the choice a company makes with regard to the segment it wants to target and the choice it makes with regard to how it wants to compete in a targeted segment, ie how it wants to establish a differential advantage.

As mentioned before, firms can **design their marketing programmes to position and enhance the image of a product offering in the minds of consumers**.

To do this, a firm can choose amongst several positioning strategies that revolve around strengthening the brand, repositioning the brand or repositioning the competition (Ferrell and Hartline, 2008).

A company can choose to make **real changes** to a product, or can choose to make a psychological shift in the way it **presents** the brand to the target market. The following are some alternative positioning strategies that can be considered when a company finds that it needs to make changes in order to strengthen the position of its offering.

Alternative positioning strategies	Example
Change existing brand	To compete in a personal computer market where prices were falling rapidly in the 1990s, Compaq cut its prices and simplified its features to maintain it foothold in this market.
Introduce a new brand	The reaction of IBM to the same problem in the personal computer market was to introduce a new, cheaper brand under another brand name with components sourced from the Far East.
Alter brand beliefs	Jameson Irish whiskey successfully positioned itself from a whiskey ingredient in an Irish coffee to an aspirational product competing in a premium segment above standard price whiskies.

Alternative positioning strategies	Example
Alter beliefs about competitive brands	We are all familiar with the ongoing duel between Pepsi and Coke to bring consumers to differing viewpoints about each other's brands.
Alter the importance of certain attributes	Volvo raised the importance of safety in choosing a car, and so increased the value of its differentiation.
Introduce new or neglected attributes	Unilever was successful in introducing a benefit not previously considered important by consumers – it introduced Radion, a new detergent that eliminated odours.
Find a new market segment	Dunhill went from the smoking accessories business into the men's clothing market, creating a new luxury segment of very expensive, high quality ready-to-wear suits.

ACTIVITY 9.1

concept

What is a sustainable competitive advantage and why is it important?

1.6 Competitive positioning strategies

As was alluded to above, competitive positioning is about making choices that ensure a fit between target segments and the competences and assets a firm can deploy to serve these target segments better than competitors.

There are a myriad of positioning alternatives and these can be summarised along six dimensions of differentiation. Positioning can be based on price, technical quality, service, customisation, benefit differentiation, or innovation (Hooley, et al. 2004).

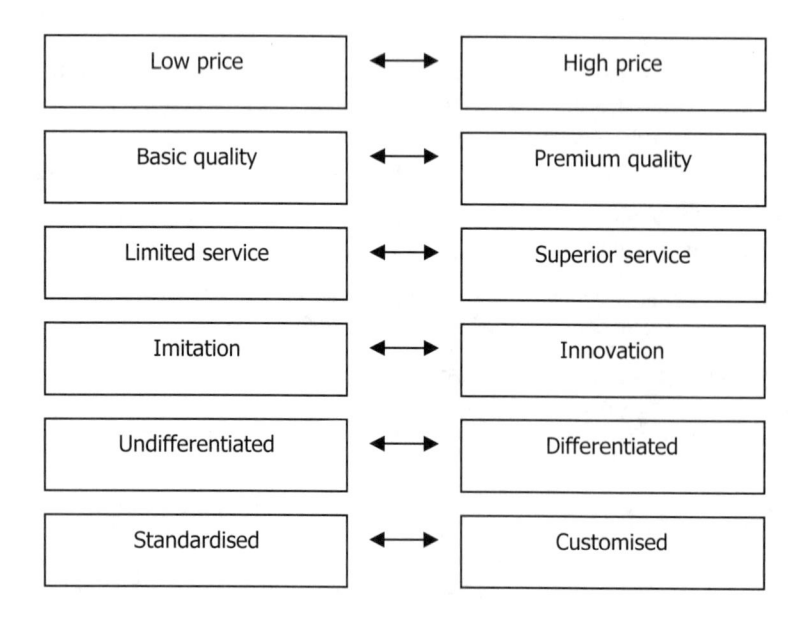

Low price	High price
Basic quality	Premium quality
Limited service	Superior service
Imitation	Innovation
Undifferentiated	Differentiated
Standardised	Customised

Source: adapted from Hooley, et al. (2004)

Let's now take a closer look at each of these positioning strategies.

1.6.1 Price positioning

For a low price position to be sustainable it is essential that a company is able to **keep its costs in check**, better than or at least as good as competitors. If no real cost advantage exists, a company might find itself vulnerable in a price war.

Positioning as a **low cost supplier** requires **strong capabilities at cost controlling**, from the procurement of raw materials to the distribution logistics and all input costs in between.

Another requirement for a successful low price positioning strategy is the existence of a **price-sensitive customer segment**.

MARKETING AT WORK — application

The success of the Skoda Felicia car in the UK, on sale at a price of £5,999, is a good example illustrating the strategy of positioning at a low cost to a price-sensitive segment. Consumer research had clearly identified a segment that had no interest in buying cars to impress others and believed that cars were over-hyped and overpriced.

The success of both Ryanair and Easyjet are further examples of successful low price positioning aimed at price sensitive consumers.

Many firms position their offerings at the other extreme, ie the more **premium end of the market**. Cosmetics and designer fashion are two examples. To support this positioning, it is essential that the brand has established an **exclusive image** that customers are willing to pay a **premium** for in the first place. Very often brand assets are built through the creative use of promotional campaigns.

1.6.2 Quality positioning

Positioning as a high technical quality supplier also needs effective **control systems**, especially of **quality assessment** and **assurance**. It also requires technical competence and a clear idea of what the consumer values as 'quality'. German car-makers have been very successful at positioning their products at the higher end of the quality scale. Often critical to a quality positioning are the marketing assets of brand image and reputation, which can take years to create, and which companies should take care to protect.

1.6.3 Innovation positioning

Rapidly changing markets, especially where **rapid technological developments** are involved, often present an **opportunity to position on the basis of innovation**, or speed to market. In the car and PC markets it has been shown that **constant innovation** is a significant characteristic of market leading firms. **Speed to market** is also becoming increasingly important for success. Recent studies have shown that for many companies a more successful strategy is to be a **fast follower**, thereby cutting out the mistakes and development cost of first movers. The Dyson company is a very good example of a firm with an innovation positioning, not only in product design and engineering, but also in terms of its marketing and sales processes.

1.6.4 Service positioning

Service positioning is becoming increasingly important due to the **variations in the level of service** on offer and **customer expectations**. Crucial to effective service delivery are **market sensing skills** to identify the level and type of service required, **customer bonding skills** to build relationships, **service systems** that assist the service-providers in delivering service to customers, and **monitoring skills** to assess customer satisfaction. Most critical of all to providing a superior service are the people or staff who provide the service. Selection, training, motivating and reward of service staff should receive high priority in service organisations wanting to establish a **competitive edge through superior service delivery**.

1.6.5 Differentiated benefits positioning

Differentiated benefits positioning revolves around **identifying alternative benefits within markets** and then focusing on providing for these. Success here depends on a set of **well developed skills in segmentation**, and effective **new product development skills** to actually deliver the benefits sought by the customers. One example of this is the marketing of Boddingtons Draught Bitter on the basis of 'smoothness' and not in terms of 'sociability' as with most other beers.

MARKETING AT WORK
application

Another example of differentiated benefits positioning is the success of the Scope mouthwash brand from Procter and Gamble. Until Scope was launched, Listerine was the undisputed market leader in the mouthwash sector in the US. Up until that moment it was assumed that mouthwashes should taste bad, a perception that was in part reinforced by the Listerine campaign of 'the taste you hate two times a day'. Scope was launched with a pleasant taste and successfully challenged Listerine offering the additional benefit of good taste ('a mouthwash doesn't have to taste bad to be effective'). Within a few years Scope was rivalling Listerine in market share.

1.6.6 Customised positioning (one-to-one marketing)

Offering products and services tailored to individual customers is perhaps the pinnacle of targeting and positioning. The Smart car is a classic example, in terms of which customers can choose individual fittings and colours. Porsche manufactures only 150 cars a day, with customers choosing from a myriad of combinations to suit their particular tastes and requirements. Flexible production processes are of course central to the success of this strategy.

Mass customisation makes it possible for firms to enjoy cost and efficiency advantages, while at the same time tailoring offers to individuals. Amazon.com is a good example of a company which, despite having over five million customers, manages to practise one-to-one marketing. The company's click-through technology enables it to identify each individual customer's specific interests and requirements, which in turn allows the company to target the customer with tailored offerings of similar products for future purchase. Levi Strauss now offers customised denim jeans by taking measurements in store and relaying them to the factory to produce a unique garment for customers.

From the discussion above it should have become clear that positioning needs to be based soundly on the marketing assets and competences of the company to deliver superior customer value. Companies need to monitor and respond to changing market requirements, but will also need to build and develop their resources and capabilities to meet the challenges ahead.

Hooley et al. (2004) note that, going forward, we can expect firms to become more selective in their choice of target markets and customers to serve and to concentrate on building longer-term relationships to ensure long-term value creation.

ACTIVITY 9.2
evaluation

Why would you want to be a fast follower?

1.7 Relationship positioning strategies

There has been a realisation recently by many companies that successful positioning is increasingly about creating ongoing relationships with target customers. We have already seen that superior service can be a driver of differentiation. Many markets, especially in developed countries, are now mature or growing slowly and there are fewer customers to compete for. In addition it has been calculated that attracting new customers can cost as much as five times more than simply retaining current customers through servicing them adequately. Customer retention, and the bigger prize of customer loyalty that it can bring, requires companies to develop strategies focused on delivering these goals. It increasingly involves emphasis on the service activities that augment the basic product offering.

To retain customers by building bonds and ties between them and the organisation, companies are turning to the techniques involved in relationship marketing. These techniques are designed to improve two-way communication between customer and company, and to ultimately result in customer loyalty. It is important to note that while customer retention is essentially a measure of repeat purchase behaviour, even if the company had failed to provide a high level of satisfaction; customer loyalty has more to do with positive feelings customers have towards a company, ie the level to which they trust and value the company and the extent to which they actively want to do business with the organisation, and recommend it to others. Customer loyalty is more closely related to customer satisfaction.

KEY CONCEPT

Relationship marketing has been variously defined as:

- *'The process whereby both parties – the buyer and provider – establish an effective, efficient, enjoyable, enthusiastic and ethical relationship: one that is personally, professionally and profitability rewarding to both parties'*
(Porter, 1993, p. 14)

- *'The process of creating, maintaining and enhancing strong, value-laden relationships with customers and other stakeholders'*
(Kotler et al. 1999, p. 11)

- *'All marketing activities directed towards establishing, developing and maintaining successful relational exchanges'*
(Morgan & Hunt, 1994, p. 22)

- *'To identify and establish, maintain and enhance, and when necessary terminate relationships with customers (and other parties) so that the objectives regarding economic and other variables of all parties are met. This is achieved through a mutual exchange and fulfilment of promises.'*
(Grönroos, 2000, p. 242)

Relationship marketing seeks to build **long-term relationships** with selected sufficient-value customers, moving them up the relationship marketing ladder (shown below) from mere customers to clients and supporters, and eventually to advocates and partners. Each step represents a closer and potentially more **profitable relationship for the business**, and of finding ways of **enhancing the value both parties get from the relationship**. The increasingly important area of relationship marketing is discussed in more detail in Chapter 11 of this study text.

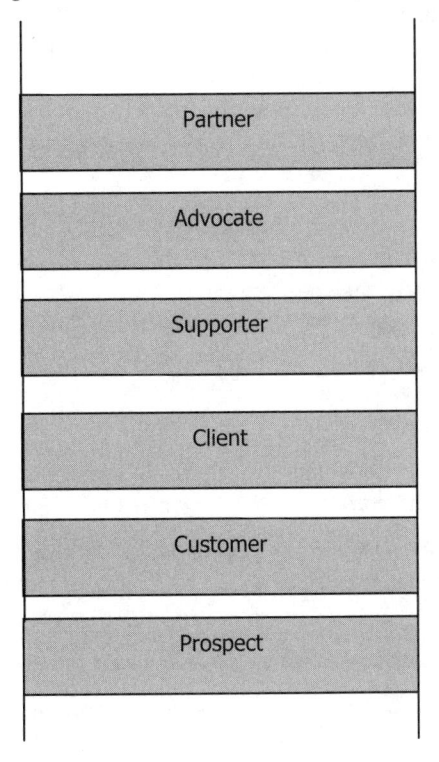

Partner
Advocate
Supporter
Client
Customer
Prospect

Source: Payne, et al. (1995)

MARKETING AT WORK

application

Customer retention and loyalty are crucial to any business. Loyalty is not easily gained and frequently firms may think that they are implementing customer loyalty programmes when at the very best they are simply mechanisms to buy customer loyalty. Take for example the use of supermarket loyalty cards. Customers very often hold a number of cards from different supermarkets and do not necessarily behave loyally to any supermarket. The result is that the 'loyalty' programme does not deliver loyalty, and many supermarket organisations now feel they need the programme simply to stay competitive. In the end the loyalty that the card was supposed to deliver, did not materialise.

Another example in the same vein is the loyalty cards issued by airlines for free miles. It has been shown that customers very often hold two or three cards from competing airlines. As more and more airlines issued 'loyalty' cards, it simply became a necessity for airlines to have one to stay competitive.

Three main methods that have been suggested for building closer links with customers and moving them up the relationship marketing ladder:

1.7.1 Building enhanced benefits of loyalty

Building relationships might entail the development of enhanced financial or social benefits for customers.

Financial benefits give the customer a financial reason to remain loyal to a company. Examples might include the collection of air miles through use of a specific credit card, or a store loyalty card where shoppers build credits towards a free purchase.

Social benefits might include corporate hospitality at social or sports events.

1.7.2 Creating structural ties and bonds

Sometimes companies create structural ties with customers that make it difficult or costly for customers to break. For instance medical equipment companies provide hospital surgeons with equipment designed to perform hip and knee transplants with their own make of implant. The equipment does not work so well with competitive makes of implants. So surgeons remain loyal. The medical supply company will then sponsor symposia to enable surgeons to keep up-to-date with medical advance and this also helps to build corporate goodwill and customer supplier relationship.

1.7.3 Creating delighted customers

When customers get more from the relationship than they were looking for they tend to move up the relationship ladder. To improve the probability of customer retention it is very often necessary to go beyond what was expected and deliver even greater value to customers. Retention rates are significantly higher amongst very satisfied or delighted customers, and they are more likely to become advocates, telling others about their good experiences.

1.7.4 The 3 Ss of customer service

According to Hooley, et al. (2004), there are three critical elements in successful service provision. Termed the 3 Ss of customer service, these are: **strategy**, **systems** and **staff**.

First, in order for a firm to deliver superior customer service, it has to have a clear **service strategy** in place that forms part of the basic fabric of the organisation. All parts of the organisation should be familiar with the role they need to play in the delivery process.

Second, the company should put in place **systems of operation** to enable the staff to deliver the promised service.

Finally, and perhaps most importantly, **staff** need to be trained, committed and empowered to deliver the levels of service that will create customer delight.

1.7.5 Providing superior service

In the process of delivering superior service, firms need to understand exactly what superior service means in the context of their business. They need to know precisely what constitutes a 'delighted customer' by identifying gaps between customer experiences and their expectations, and then going about fixing any shortcomings.

This implies a dedication to the process of managing and exceeding customer expectations, constant monitoring of customer satisfaction, and systematic gap analysis to identify and eliminate causes of dissatisfaction.

1.8 Selecting target markets and points of difference

As we have seen before, the aim of positioning is to successfully create a customer-focused value proposition, a compelling reason why a target customer should choose a particular product above another. The goal is to position the brand in the minds of consumers to maximise the potential benefit to the company. Nearly all positioning approaches require that the similarities and differences between competing brands be defined and communicated. Deciding on a positioning will entail a frame of reference by the identification of a target market and the competition, and then identifying the ideal points-of-parity and points-of-difference.

In positioning a product one needs to define a **competitive frame of reference**. A first step in doing this would be to determine the **category membership** of the product, that is, the set of products against which a brand will compete, and which can be said to be close substitutes for the given product. Target market decisions are often a key indicator of the competitive frame of reference.

1.8.1 Points-of-difference and points-of-parity

Once a competitive frame of reference for positioning has been fixed by defining the customer target market and nature of a product's competition, marketers can define appropriate points-of-difference and points-of-parity associations.

Points-of-difference are attributes or benefits that consumers strongly associate with a particular brand, which they evaluate positively and believe cannot be found to the same extent in any other brand. **Favourable and unique brand associations** that constitute points of difference can be based on virtually any type of attribute or benefit. Examples are Nike (performance) and Lexus (quality).

According to Kotler and Keller (2006), **points-of-parity** are not unique to the brand and are most probably **shared with other brands in the category**. They come in two forms. **Category points-of-parity** are associations that consumers see as essential for a certain category. They represent necessary but not sufficient conditions for brand choice. For example, a travel agency will not be regarded as truly a travel agency if it is unable to make air and hotel reservations, provide advice about leisure packages, and offer ticket payment and delivery options. Customers expect this from all travel agents.

Competitive points-of-parity are associations designed to negate competitor's points-of-difference. In the Marketing at Work example below Miller Lite promised, as all beers do, 'taste', and then went on to deliver a point-of-difference that other beers did not have.

If a product is able to achieve the latter, and offer a unique point-of-difference, it is likely to be in a very strong competitive position within a given target segment.

MARKETING AT WORK — application

When Miller Lite beer was introduced to the market, the advertising strategy had two objectives. It carried the message of 'great taste', and the told the consumer that because it contained one-third less calories, it was 'less filling'.

The point-of-parity in the beer category was taste. Beer consumers wanted taste and Miller Lite promised this. At the same time it created a point-of-difference through less calories and being less filling. The company cleverly used ex-professional athletes who presumably would not drink a beer that did not taste great. The ad ended with the clever tagline 'Everything you always wanted in a beer... And Less'.

1.9 Positioning and perceptual maps

1.9.1 Relative position

As we have seen, differentiation is about the product itself and positioning is about the perceptions that customers have of the **real or imaginary benefit of the product**. Although differentiation and positioning can be based on actual product features, the important task for the company is to develop a **relative position** for the product in the targeted customers' mind.

The concept of positioning is based on a **customer led perspective** and has important **implications for product design**, but will also be reflected in a whole range of the product's characteristics, including **brand image, packaging and quality**, and in the **price** and **communications** elements.

The process of creating a **favourable relative positioning** involves **several steps** (Ferrell and Hartline, 2008).

(a) By conducting market research, identify **attributes desired by the target market**. At this stage the research will focus on the **class of products** being studied rather than on an individual product.

(b) Examine the **differentiating attributes** and relative position of all potential competitors in the product class.

(c) **Compare** the position of your product offering against the positions of the competitors **for each key attribute** (needs, wants, benefit desired).

(d) **Identify a unique position** that focuses on attributes that your product can offer customers that current products do not.

(e) **Develop and implement a marketing plan** that will take advantage of the firm's position and **persuade customers** that the **company's product offering will best meet their needs**.

(f) **Continually monitor the whole process** to make sure the firm's marketing programme stays on track and to identify emerging positioning opportunities.

1.9.2 Perceptual maps

Once the positioning process has been completed for each attribute, it is useful to use a research technique that makes it easier to visualise the whole process, called **perceptual mapping**. The perceptual map below shows the mapping of toilet tissue on two dimensions, price and softness, which represent two attributes that might be important for buyers of toilet tissue. It can be seen that Brand A serves the bottom end of the market with a cheap functional offering, while those in segment 2 are willing to pay a bit more for Brand B which offers a softer, gentler experience. Brand C is closer to segment 1, while Brand D is drifting and seems to offer nothing particular that is appealing to either segment 1 or 2 consumers.

KEY CONCEPT

concept

A **perceptual map** represents customer perceptions and preferences spatially by means of a visual display.

Here is a perceptual map of the toilet tissue market.

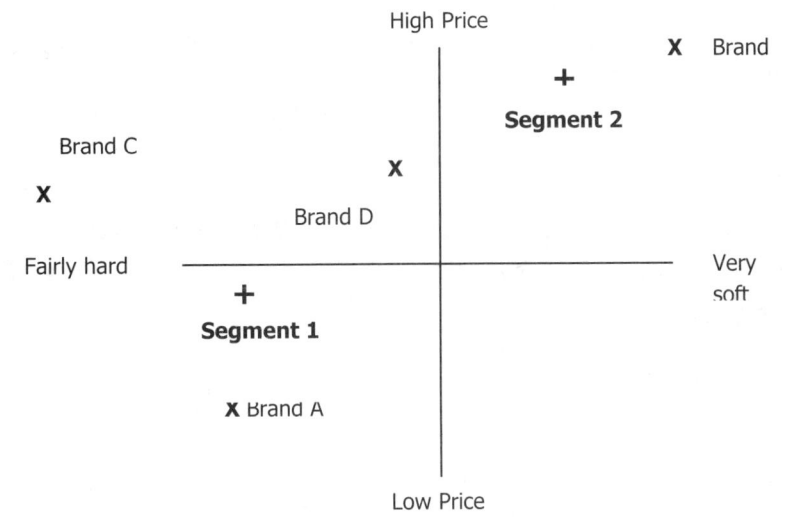

```
                        High Price
                            |
                            |         X  Brand
                            |      +
                            |     Segment 2
    Brand C                 |
      X              X      |
                   Brand D  |
                            |
  Fairly hard ───────────────────────────── Very
                    +       |              soft
                 Segment 1  |
                            |
                 X Brand A  |
                            |
                        Low Price
```

Source: Brassington, F. and Pettitt, S. (2006)

Using multidimensional scaling techniques it is possible to map any number of dimensions. This is necessary as two dimensions or attributes are normally insufficient to represent the complexities of target market opinion. Using the example of toilet tissue again, it is clear on the multidimensional map below that certain attributes tend to cluster together. In the example below it can be deduced that for segment 2, Brand E might be in a position to expand its colour range and appeal to consumers in this segment without alienating its own consumers. Brand F seems to be poorly positioned to serve any segment. Brand G is well positioned in segment 4 that seems to have more of an environmental conscience.

A multidimensional map of the toilet tissue market is shown below.

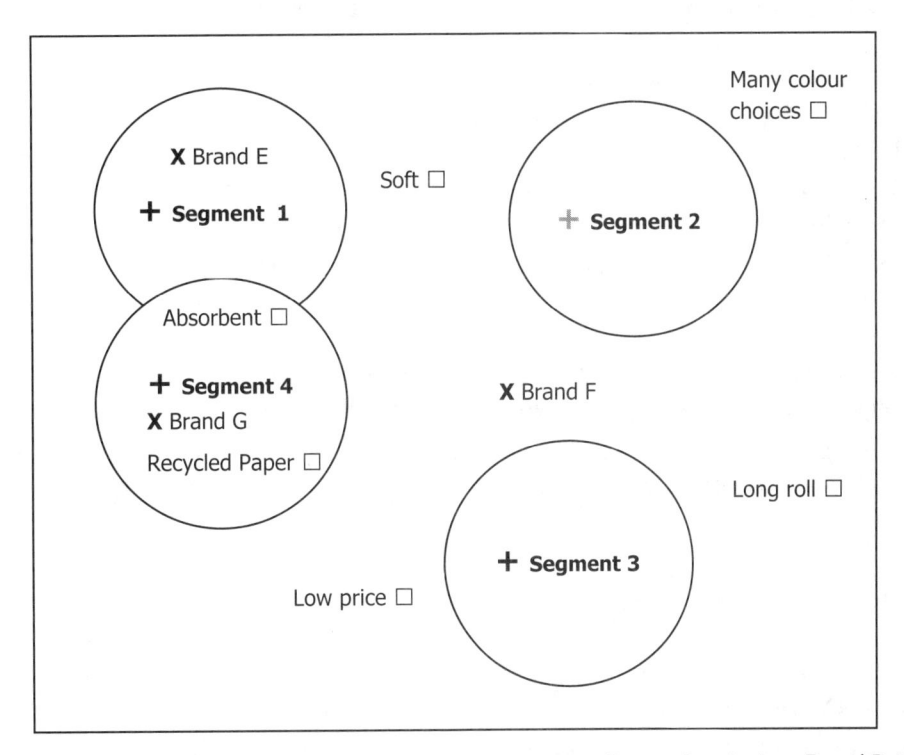

```
┌─────────────────────────────────────────────────────┐
│                                      Many colour    │
│                                      choices □      │
│       ╭─────────╮                                   │
│       │ X Brand E│    Soft □     ╭─────────╮        │
│       │         │                │          │       │
│       │+ Segment 1│               │+ Segment 2│      │
│       ╰─────────╯                ╰─────────╯        │
│                                                     │
│       Absorbent □                                   │
│       ╭─────────╮                                   │
│       │+ Segment 4│                                 │
│       │ X Brand G│        X Brand F                 │
│       │Recycled Paper □│                            │
│       ╰─────────╯                                   │
│                                          Long roll □│
│                                                     │
│                              ╭─────────╮            │
│                              │+ Segment 3│           │
│                              ╰─────────╯            │
│                   Low price □                       │
└─────────────────────────────────────────────────────┘
```

Source: Brassington, F. and Pettitt, S. (2006)

Perceptual maps illustrate two important issues. First, they indicate products that are similar in terms of the relative position they hold in the customer's mind. Second, they indicate voids in the current mindscape for a product category, which may hold promise of a potential opportunity in terms of a product's positioning (it might however also indicate that customers have no need for such a product). Further research will be necessary to ascertain if this space represents a viable unmet segment of the market.

Perceptual maps help a company to determine an appropriate course of competitive action. A perceptual map can help to decide whether you take on the competition head on, or how far away from the competition to differentiate, or where your product's weaknesses lie, or for that matter what the weaknesses of competing products are. It will lead to an understanding of the marketing tasks that need to be embarked on to improve the product offering.

2 Positioning options and their implementation within the context of the organisation and its markets

2.1 Criteria for effective positioning and competitive advantage

Based on a thorough analysis of the data, a company will finally decide on a particular positioning option to differentiate its product in the minds of consumers. There are, however, **two important considerations** that will impact on whether the positioning will be successful or not (Kotler and Keller, 2006):

(a) Will consumers **find the promised positioning desirable**?
(b) **Has the firm the capabilities** to deliver the positioning promised?

2.1.1 Consumer desirability criteria

Relevance: Will consumers find the positioning and, especially, the point-of-difference, **relevant and important**?

Distinctiveness: Consumers must find the point-of-difference **distinctive and superior**.

Believability: Consumers must find the point-of-difference **believable and credible**, and a brand must offer a **compelling substantiation** why consumers should choose it above others.

2.1.2 Company deliverability criteria

Feasibility: The company must be able to actually **deliver and create** the point-of-difference and the product design and marketing offering must support the desired association. The positioning might entail real changes to the product itself, or just perceptual ones that need to be communicated to the target consumer (for example, General Motors worked hard to change public perception that Cadillac was not a young and contemporary brand).

Communicability: Consumers must be given a **compelling substantiation** as to why a brand can deliver promised benefits. It is very difficult to create an association that is not consistent with current consumer knowledge or that consumers may have trouble believing in.

Sustainability: Is the positioning **defensible and difficult to attack**. Will the company be able to **reinforce and strengthen the brand association over time**? If yes, the positioning is likely to be enduring.

We can add another important criterion to those outlined above, namely, that of **profitability**. The firm must be able to deliver the product offering at a price, cost and volume structure that makes it sustainably **profitable** to produce (Doyle, 2006).

MARKETING AT WORK

application

Positioning strategies can be created around product attributes, benefits, users, use/application, product category, and quality/price. Here follows an example of a positioning strategy for each.

Attributes – ads for PCs that emphasise speed and what sort of chip they have, eg Pentium 111.

Benefits – holidays are advertised as offering relaxation and excitement.

Use/application – 'easy to use' products (eg hair tints that can be washed in).

User – reflect user characteristics to appeal to the target market and confirm their choice. May use celebrity endorsements such as David Beckham in the Vodaphone ads.

Product category – The Natural History Museum is fundamentally educational, but is moving towards a 'theme park' image for the schools market.

Quality/price – as in 'value for money' advertisements.

ACTIVITY 9.3 — evaluation

The process of creating a favourable relative positioning involves several steps (Ferrell and Hartline, 2008). Discuss this process.

2.2 Positioning and its impact on the marketing mix

The **marketing mix** refers to the set of marketing decisions that management has to take to **implement the positioning strategy** that has been decided upon and that will ensure that it achieves its **objectives**. These decisions are a set of tactics that have to be actioned around the 4 Ps of product, price, promotion and place.

Each of the elements in the mix should be designed to execute the required positioning. It is thus crucial that **decisions relating to elements of the mix are taken to support the positioning strategy**. For example, a premium positioning should manifest itself in a premium product quality and a premium price (a low price might just destroy the premium positioning). Marketing communications should also deliver the superior quality claimed, and advertising media and distribution channels should also be of a more high-end nature to reflect the intended premium positioning.

All parts of the mix need to be **consistent with the positioning** and not pull in different directions. If mix elements contradict each other, the clarity of the positioning will suffer and customers will be left confused. All these touch points with the target customer must be executed in a consistent manner that result in the company achieving an advantage over its competitors.

2.3 Positioning and repositioning

So far in this chapter we have explored the different facets of differentiation and positioning and have had a good look at the processes involved. Next we will take a look at the **practical implications of positioning**, and indeed **repositioning**. As part of this discussion, we will also be addressing the concept of **product life cycle** which can influence the positioning of a brand and move the company to explore and implement **positioning changes**, ie **repositioning**.

2.3.1 Repositioning, revitalisation and rationalisation

Over time there may be many **factors that can erode a brand's franchise and profitability**. Markets may decline, new technology introduced, consumer tastes may change, costs may rise or new competition may enter the market. Under these circumstances it may be necessary to **revitalise and reposition** a brand. Doyle and Stern (2006) state that a company is faced with two broad alternatives when such a situation arises:

(a) Increase volume, or

(b) Increase the brand's productivity (ie increasing profit by increasing prices, or cutting costs or by elimination altogether from the portfolio of the company – rationalisation).

The first option should be to increase brand sales performance. This can be done by **expanding the market for a brand (revitalisation)** or by **enhancing its competitive position in the market it is operating in (repositioning)**.

2.3.2 Revitalisation

There are four ways to revitalise a brand:

(a) **Find new markets** – this will frequently involve international expansion.

(b) **Enter new segments** – Johnson & Johnson baby shampoo was not performing very well until the company started targeting adults who needed a mild shampoo because they washed their hair regularly.

(c) **Find new applications** – by identifying new customer needs a brand can sometimes dramatically increase its potential market, as in the case of a branded baking soda which found new application as a deodoriser for refrigerators, sinks and animals.

(d) **Increase brand usage** – by making the product easier and more convenient to use (eg the introduction of tea bags), providing regular incentives (discounts), or finding ways to increase the quantity used (eg by introducing larger pack sizes).

2.3.3 Repositioning

The focus of repositioning is to increase volume by winning/increasing market share.

There are a number of alternatives to consider.

(a) **Real repositioning** – A brand may need to be updated by tangibly incorporating the latest technology, functions and design. This is quite evident in the mobile phone market.

(b) **Psychological repositioning** – A company might try to change buyers' beliefs about the competitiveness of a brand. In other words, it is not changing the product, but is attempting to change the perceptions that consumers have about the product. A few years ago Tesco advertised competitive prices and emphasised their high quality merchandise when it wanted to change customer perception as to the quality of the goods on sale in its stores.

(c) **Competitive repositioning** – this entails altering customers' beliefs about competitors. Coke and Pepsi have regularly used comparative advertising in the past to achieve this.

(d) **Reweighting values** – Persuade buyers to attach greater importance to certain values at which the brand is good at. Volvo introduced safety as a criterion for buying a car and was the first car manufacturer to recognise and exploit the value of safety as a differentiator when other manufacturers were concentrating on other attributes.

(e) **Neglected values** – Sometimes new choice criteria can be introduced. The Times introduced a tabloid newspaper format in addition to its broadsheet version since its readers valued an easier-to-read format (particularly while commuting).

(f) **Changing preferences** – Switch buyer preferences. For instance switch the preference of buyers from low price to higher quality/economic value.

(g) **Augmenting the brand** – this entails enhancing the competitive position of a brand by adding additional products and services to the core product, such as after-sales service and guarantees.

2.3.4 Positioning and repositioning during the product life cycle

Decisions about products, product lines, branding, differentiation, and positioning, are ongoing strategic issues, and brands need to be managed differently over time.

Ferrell and Hartline (2008) note that the product life cycle, despite its limitations, is a useful framework for discussing product strategy over time.

	Introduction	Growth	Maturity	Decline
Overall marketing goals	Stimulate product awareness and trial	Increase market share by acquiring new customers; discover new needs and market segments	Maximise profit by defending market share or stealing it from competitors	Reduce expenses and marketing efforts to maximise the last opportunity for profit
Product strategy	Introduce limited models with limited features; frequent product changes	Introduce new models with new features; pursue continuous innovation	Full-model line; increase supplemental product offerings to aid in product differentiation	Eliminate unprofitable models and brands

	Introduction	Growth	Maturity	Decline
Pricing strategy	Penetration pricing to establish a market presence or price skimming to recoup development costs	Prices fall due to competition; price to match or beat the competition	Prices continue to fall; price to beat the competition	Prices stabilise at a low level
Distribution strategy	Gradually roll out product to expand availability; get channel intermediaries on board	Intensify efforts to expand product reach and availability	Extensive product availability; retain shelf space; phase out unprofitable outlets or channels	Maintain a level necessary to keep brand loyal customers; continue phasing out unprofitable channels
Promotion strategy	Advertising and personal selling to build awareness; heavy sales promotion to stimulate product trial	Aggressive brand advertising, selling, and sales promotion to encourage brand switching and continued trial	Stress brand differences and benefits; encourage brand switching; keep the brand/product fresh	Reduce to a minimal level or phase out entirely

Source: Ferrell and Hartline (2008)

The table above illustrates the **four stages of the product life cycle** and the **strategic marketing considerations associated with each stage**. A stage not represented here, but crucially important, is the pre-launch or development stage, a time when the product is designed and the marketing strategy devised.

Strategic imperatives regarding the 4 Ps change over the life of a product, and new tactics are often employed to suit the changing environment. We will pay particular attention to **the role of positioning in this process**.

(a) **The development stage**

It is imperative that companies identify target market needs before developing a product strategy. New products that closely match consumer's needs and have strong advantages over competing products (reflected in the product's differentiation and positioning) are much easier to market in the introductory phase of its life cycle.

(b) **Introductory stage**

In this phase the marketing strategy devised should be tightly integrated with the firm's competitive advantage(s) and strategic focus. Marketing strategy goals at this phase include attracting customers by raising awareness and interest, promoting trial, strengthening and expanding supply chain relationships and engaging in consumer education.

(c) **Growth stage**

During this phase the firm has two overriding priorities: establishing a strong defensible market position and achieving financial objectives. To accomplish this there are a number of important marketing strategy goals:

(i) Leverage the perceived differential advantages of the product through branding, price, value and secure a strong market position

(ii) Establish a clear product and brand identity

(iii) Create a unique positioning through the use of advertising and promotion that emphasises the benefits for target consumers

(iv) Control product quality to ensure satisfaction

(v) Always keep abreast of what competitors are doing

During this stage the emphasis shifts from customer acquisition to retention.

Consumer and trade relationships are very important at this stage to ensure a long maturity stage and the maximisation of profit.

This phase will also see new competitors entering the market. The firm must protect itself by building a defensible position which could be based on image, price, quality, or some technological standard.

(d) **Maturity stage**

Growth in the market now slows. Firms generally need to hold on to their market share, steal share from competitors or increase their share of customer (see Marketing at Work below). To do this the firm could choose from four general options:

(i) Develop a new product image
(ii) Find and attract new users
(iii) Discover new applications and uses for the product
(iv) Apply new technology to the product.

(e) **Decline stage**

A firm may want to attempt to postpone the decline stage, in which case the demand for the product may need to be renewed through **repositioning**, develop new uses or features for the product or apply new technology.

It is commonly acknowledged that postponing decline is a **very expensive exercise**, and many companies accept the inevitable and change to a **harvesting strategy**, gradually reducing marketing expenditure and investing its increased cash flow into the development of new products.

MARKETING AT WORK

application

Banks are particularly adept at increasing their share of customer by offering a range of products to their existing customer base. A student might become a customer of the bank through opening a savings account, and this might quickly develop as the bank offers a student loan. On completion of studies the student would start working and the bank would offer a credit card, or a home loan a little while later, together with loan protection insurance or life insurance. Then there might be share portfolio services, investment advice, etc. Likewise many large grocery chains are increasing share of customer by adding additional features such as restaurants, video rental, dry cleaning services, and even banking and insurance services in an attempt to create a one stop shop for family needs.

Learning objective review

Learning objectives	Covered
1. Examine the concept of marketing positioning strategy and how it can be used to convey the organisation's value proposition.	☑ Marketing positioning strategy and the organisation's value proposition: ☑ Distinction between positioning and differentiation ☑ Differential advantage ☑ Customer value and organisational profit ☑ Creating differential advantage ☑ Alternative positioning strategies ☑ Competitive positioning strategies ☑ Relationship positioning strategies ☑ Selecting target markets and points of differences ☑ Positioning and perceptual maps
2. Critically evaluate positioning options and their implementation within the context of the organisation and its markets.	☑ Positioning options and their implementation within the context of the organisation and its markets ☑ Criteria for effective positioning and competitive advantage ☑ Positioning and its impact on the marketing mix ☑ Positioning and repositioning

Quick quiz

1. What is the distinction between positioning and differentiation?
2. What is it that needs to be understood before attempting to create a sustainable differential advantage?
3. List the four drivers of differentiation.
4. According to Hooley, et al. (2004), there is a myriad of positioning alternatives that can be summarised along six dimensions of differentiation. Briefly list these.
5. Provide two requirements of successful low price positioning strategies.
6. What are the four essential requirements for a successful service positioning strategy?
7. Why is it so important for companies to build ongoing relationships with customers?
8. Why might it be necessary to reposition a brand?
9. Explain psychological repositioning.
10. What is meant by a harvesting strategy in the decline phase of a product's life cycle?

Activity debriefs

Worksheet activity 9.1

The choice of target market segments indicates where a company will compete. There will, however, be other firms competing in the same segments and customers will be faced with a decision of whom to support. Consequently, a key strategic task of management is to create a sustainable differential advantage designed to attract consumer choices.

A sustainable differential advantage is a perceived difference that leads customers in the target segment to prefer one company's offer above those of others. The difference may be based on a product that is seen as superior, has a lower price or better service support. When a company is successfully able to create a sustainable competitive advantage this often leads to a higher market share and profits, as well as making the company less vulnerable to attack from competitors.

Worksheet activity 9.2

Rapidly changing markets, especially where rapid technological developments are involved, often present an opportunity to position on the basis of innovation, or speed to market. In the car and PC markets it has been shown that constant innovation is a significant characteristic of market leading firms. Speed to market is also becoming increasingly important for success. Recent studies have shown that for many companies a more successful strategy is to be a fast follower, thereby cutting out the mistakes and development cost of first movers.

Worksheet activity 9.3

The concept of positioning is based on a customer led perspective and has important implications for product design, but will also be reflected in a whole range of the product's characteristics, including brand image, packaging and quality, and in the price and communications elements.

The process of creating a favourable relative positioning involves several steps (Ferrell and Hartline, 2008):

- By conducting market research, identify attributes desired by the target market. At this stage the research will focus on the class of products being studied rather than on an individual product.

- Examine the differentiating attributes and relative position of all potential competitors in the product class.

- Compare the position of your product offering against the positions of the competitors for each key attribute (needs, wants, benefit desired).

- Identify a unique position that focuses on attributes that your product can offer customers that current products do not.

- Develop and implement a marketing plan that will take advantage of the firm's position and persuade customers that the company's product offering will best meet their needs.

- Continually monitor the whole process to make sure the firm's marketing programme stays on track and to identify emerging positioning opportunities.

Quiz answers

1. Product differentiation entails creating differences in a company's product offering that set it apart from those of competitors. Positioning refers to the creation of a mental image of the product offering and its distinct features in the mind of the targeted consumers. Differentiation is thus about the product itself, while positioning is about the customer's perception of the benefits the product possesses.

2. Any attempt to be successful at creating a sustainable differential advantage must start with a solid understanding of what it is that customers value.

3. The four drivers of differentiation are: product drivers, service drivers, personnel drivers, and image drivers.

4. The six dimensions of differentiation are: price, quality, service, innovation, benefit differentiation and customisation.

5. Positioning as a low cost supplier requires strong capabilities at cost controlling, from the procurement of raw materials to the distribution logistics and all input costs in between. Another requirement for a successful low price positioning strategy is the existence of a price-sensitive customer segment.

6. Crucial to effective service delivery are market sensing skills to identify the level and type of service required, customer bonding skills to build relationships, service systems that assist the service-providers in delivering service to customers, and monitoring skills to assess customer satisfaction. Most critical of all to providing a superior service are the people or staff who provide the service. Selection, training, motivating and reward of service staff should receive high priority in service organisations wanting to establish a competitive edge through superior service delivery.

7. Many markets, especially in developed countries, are now mature or growing slowly and there are fewer customers to compete for. In addition it has been calculated that attracting new customers can cost as much as five times more than simply retaining current customers through servicing them adequately. Customer retention, and the bigger prize of customer loyalty that it can bring, requires companies to develop strategies focused on delivering these goals. It increasingly involves emphasis on the service activities that augment the basic product offering.

8. Over time there may be many factors that can erode a brand's franchise and profitability. Markets may decline, new technology introduced, consumer tastes may change, costs may rise or new competition may enter the market. Under these circumstances it may be necessary to revitalise and reposition a brand.

9. A company might try to change buyers' beliefs about the competitiveness of a brand. In other words, it is not changing the product, but is attempting to change the *perceptions* that consumers have about the product. A few years ago Tesco advertised competitive prices and emphasised their high quality merchandise when it wanted to change customer perceptions regarding the quality of the goods on sale in its stores.

10. It is commonly acknowledged that postponing decline is a very expensive exercise, and many companies accept the inevitable and change to a harvesting strategy, gradually reducing marketing expenditure and investing its increased cash flow into the development of new products.

Brassington, F. and Pettitt, S. (2006), Principles of Marketing (4th Ed.), Pearson Education, London.

Doyle, P. and Stern, P. (2006), Marketing Management and Strategy (4th Ed.), Pearson Education, London.

Ferrell, O.C. and Hartline, M.D. (2008), Marketing Strategy (4th Ed.), Thomson, London.

Grönroos, C. (2000), Service Management and Marketing, Wiley, London

Hooley, G., Saunders, J. and Piercy, N. (2004), Marketing Strategy and Competitive Positioning (3rd Ed.), Pearson Education, London.

Kotler P., Armstrong G., Meggs D., Bradbury E. and Grech J. (1999), Marketing: An Introduction, Prentice Hall, Harlow.

Kotler, P. and Keller, K.L. (2006), Marketing Management (12th Ed.), Pearson Education, London.

Morgan, R.M. & Hunt, S.D. (1994), *'The commitment-trust theory of relationship marketing'* in Journal of Marketing, Vol. 58, no 3, pp 20-38

Payne, A., Christopher, M., Clark, M. and Peck, H. (1995), Relationship Marketing for Competitive Advantage, Oxford: Butterworth-Heinemann as cited in Hooley, G., Saunders, J. and Piercy, N. (2004), Marketing Strategy and Competitive Positioning *(3rd Edition)*, Pearson Education, London

Porter, C. (1993) quoted in The Marketing Strategy Letter, May 1993, p 14.

Chapter 10
Implementing marketing planning

Topic list

1. Integrated marketing
2. Forecasting
3. Budgeting
4. Scheduling marketing activities: time scales and responsibilities
5. Barriers and constraints to implementing marketing planning and ways to address them

Introduction

Many a marketing manager has come to the realisation that good strategic planning without effective implementation is a recipe for disaster. Poor implementation can negate all the hard work that has gone into marketing planning, resulting in failure to reach corporate and marketing objectives, often leading to customer dissatisfaction and frustration within the firm.

Despite this, strategic planning has often been emphasised at the expense of strategic implementation. Crucial to the success of the company, marketing implementation is the process of turning marketing plans into a series of actions that will ensure achievement of the firm's objectives. A brilliant strategic plan will count for nothing if it cannot be implemented properly. In this section, therefore, we will provide guidelines on the organisational structures, systems and processes needed to implement marketing planning effectively.

Syllabus-linked learning objectives

By the end of the chapter you will be able to:

Learning objectives	Syllabus link
1. Assess the significance of the key dimensions of implementing marketing planning in practice.	4.1
2. Critically evaluate the barriers and constraints to implementing marketing planning, and consider how they may be addressed by organisations.	4.2

1 Integrated marketing

In Chapter 1 we discussed the organisation and role of marketing. Organising the structure of the marketing department was covered together with a brief consideration of cross-functional relationships. Successfully managing relationships between teams is essential for successfully integrating marketing.

Modern businesses are likely to organise themselves in an **integrated fashion** in order to provide customers with an efficient and effective service. Integrated marketing is achieved when departments **work together to satisfy the needs of customers**.

Integrated marketing takes place at all **levels within an organisation**:

Within the **marketing function itself** – where market research, promotion, customer service, planning, and product management must work together towards the **central goal of satisfying the customer**.

Within **all other functions in the organisation** – all other departments need to recognise the importance of the marketing functions in **enhancing customers' experiences of the company**.

The following diagram demonstrates the differences in priority given to customers by a traditional organisation chart, and a customer-oriented organisation chart.

(a) Traditional organisation chart **(b) Modern customer-oriented organisation chart**

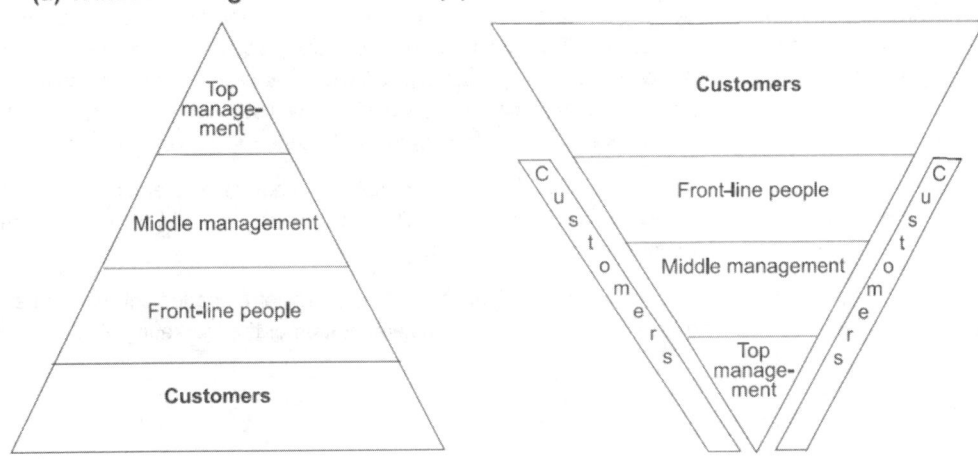

[Diagram (a): Pyramid with Top management at apex, Middle management, Front-line people, Customers at base]

[Diagram (b): Inverted pyramid with Customers at top, Front-line people, Middle management, Top management at bottom, with Customers along the sides]

1.1 The boundaryless organisation

A boundaryless organisation facilitates **cross-functional team working** and a **customer-focused service approach**. This is a very **contemporary approach** to designing an organisation. Robbins and Coutler (2004) define a boundaryless organisation as follows:

'**An organisation whose design is not defined by**, or limited to, **the horizontal, vertical, or external boundaries imposed by a predefined structure**'.

This approach was championed by Jack Welch, the former CEO of General Electric, when he was regenerating that organisation. He felt that boundaries were divisive.

- **Vertical boundaries** divided workers from managers
- **Horizontal boundaries** separated the various functions from each other

The boundaryless organisation **avoids inflexible structures** and chains of command, preferring instead to encourage a more **open and trusting environment** where **information and ideas flow freely**. This enabled Welch and GE to introduce **cross-functional team working**, serve their customers better and **improve the performance of the business**.

1.2 Internal marketing

From Chapter 1 you should remember that many modern organisations have adopted an **internal marketing approach** to facilitate marketing implementation. The practice of internal marketing derives from the service industries where it was first used as a means of **making employees aware of the need for customer satisfaction**. Internal marketing refers to **the use of marketing techniques to motivate and integrate employees to facilitate the implementation of the firm's marketing strategy**. Today this approach is regarded as **central to the success of marketing-led organisations** and **places the responsibility for implementation on all employees, regardless of level**. We will be looking at internal marketing in more detail in section 5 of this chapter and in Chapter 11 of this Study Text.

1.3 Other factors influencing the implementation of marketing planning in practice

Having an appropriate organisational structure for the effective delivery of the marketing plan is but one facet of marketing implementation. There are a number of other interrelated elements that must work together to achieve successful implementation.

Shared goals and values – these stimulate organisational commitment whereby all employees are motivated to achieve the firm's goals and objectives and work together to achieve implementation of the marketing plan.

Systems and processes – examples include information systems, strategic planning, capital budgeting, procurement, manufacturing, quality control and performance measurement. Both the inputs and outputs of these systems and processes have to be designed so as to facilitate the effective implementation of marketing plans.

Resources – a firm's resources might include a wide variety of assets that can be brought together during marketing implementation. These assets might be tangible resources, such as financial resources, facilities, equipment and manufacturing capacity and intangible resources, such as marketing expertise, brand equity, external relationships and goodwill towards the organisation. An honest and critical evaluation of available resources during the planning phase is necessary to help ensure that strategy and marketing implementation are within the realms of possibility. Once the marketing plan has been completed, the planner needs to seek the approval of needed resources from top management.

People – the quality, diversity and skill of a firm's human resources can make or break the implementation of its marketing strategy. Their selection and training, compensation and commitment all need constant attention with the objective of maximising the ability of the company to implement its marketing plan.

Leadership – it is the responsibility of the organisation's leadership, such as its senior management team, to establish a corporate culture that is favourable to, and facilitates, the effective implementation of the marketing plan.

2 Forecasting

A marketing plan needs to stipulate and schedule all **financial and other resource requirements** to enable managers to accomplish the tasks set within the document. This is partly about **costs**, and partly about **forecasting expected revenues**. Fundamental to the success of implementing a marketing plan is the ability to **predict** the market, and then make an accurate assessment of company sales going forward.

2.1 Market forecasts and sales forecasts

Market forecasts and sales forecasts **complement each other**. The **market forecast** should be carried out first of all and should cover a **longer period of time**.

As its name implies, the market forecast is an estimate or forecast for **the market as a whole**. It mainly involves the **assessment of environmental factors**, outside the organisation's control, which will affect the **demand for its products and/or services**.

KEY CONCEPT

The **market forecast** is a forecast for the market as a whole. It is mainly involved in the assessment of environmental factors, outside the organisation's control, which will affect the demand for its products/services.

2.1.1 Components of a market forecast

The following are typical components of a market forecast:

(a) **The economic review** (assessing the national economy, government policy, covering forecasts on investment, population, gross national product, and so on).

(b) **Specific market research** (to obtain data about specific markets and forecasts concerning total market demand).

(c) **Evaluation of total market demand for the firm's and similar products** (for example in terms of profitability and market potential).

2.1.2 Sales forecasts

Sales forecasts are **estimates of sales** (in volume, value and profit terms) of a product in a **future period** for a given marketing mix.

Sales potential is an estimate of the part of the market that is within the possible reach of a product.

Factors governing sales potential

(a) The price of the product
(b) The amount of money spent on sales promotion
(c) How essential the product is to consumers

(d) Whether it is a durable commodity whose purchase the customer is able to postpone
(e) The overall size of the possible market
(f) The competition and their capabilities

Whether sales potential is worth exploiting will depend on the **cost** which must be incurred **to realise the potential**.

2.1.3 Estimating market demand

Estimating market demand is not necessarily as straightforward as might be thought. Imagine you are the marketing manager of a company producing sports footwear. What is your market demand? Is it the volume of shoes purchased in the UK, or Europe, or the whole world? Should you be considering tennis shoes as well as running shoes? Shoes for children or only adults? And should you be forecasting demand for the next year or over the next five years? The permutations seem endless.

A **demand function** is simply an expression denoting that **sales demand for a product is dependent on several factors**. These demand variables can be grouped into two broad categories.

(a) **Controllable or strategic variables**. These are factors over which the firm's management should have some degree of control, and which they can change if they wish. Controllable variables are essentially the marketing mix.

(b) **Uncontrollable variables**. These are factors over which the firm's management has no control. These include consumer variables and competitor variables.

Consumer variables depend on decisions by consumers, or the circumstances of consumers (for example, their wealth).

Competitor variables depend on decisions and actions by other competing firms.

There are also other variables outside the organisation's control. These include **decisions by other organisations** (including government organisations) or factors which are outside the control of anyone (for example weather conditions, or the total size of the population).

2.2 Forecasting methods

Conventionally, forecasting techniques are used to **predict demand in the short- to medium-term**. However, such techniques depend on the **reliability of past data**.

Forecasting methods fall into two main groups. **Qualitative methods** are often used in the earlier stages of forecasting and are an aid to describing likely changes ahead and assumptions used. **Quantitative techniques** tend to be used in later stages when production and financial plans require more accurate numbers.

2.2.1 Qualitative forecasts

We can distinguish between the following types of qualitative forecasts:

Management judgement

A company might forecast sales on the basis of the judgement of one or more executives or experts within the organisation. The major disadvantage is that the individuals are too close to the organisation to be truly objective.

Panels of experts

Panels of experts from the ranks of industrialists, economists, academics or management consultants are chosen for their sound knowledge and opinion on the market. The panel is presented with forecasts and views of the future and asked to comment. The panel should be balanced to represent a range of opinion. Consensus is then reached on the result.

Sales force surveys

Sales forces are a valuable source of information as they are very close to the customers, dealers, accounts, etc. On the down side, however, a number of factors might influence the objectivity of sales force surveys. For example, a sales person with his or her own agenda, or an overly optimistic or naïve sales person will each bias the forecast in a certain way.

Genius forecasting

An individual with expert judgement might be asked for advice. This could for instance happen in the fashion industry where the ability to understand specific customer trends and preferences will be very useful.

Scenario planning techniques

These methods aim to provide a complete picture of trends and events to **create a view of alternative situations**. The main method used tends to be the **Delphi technique**.

This technique was originally developed to overcome problems relying on known experts or personalities in the jury.

In its application as a qualitative forecasting technique, the Delphi technique retains anonymity of participants, who remain known only to the organiser. Participants respond to a questionnaire containing tightly-defined questions. The results are collated and statistically analysed, and are related by the organiser back to each expert who then responds again. In this way the organiser is able to build an 'uncontaminated' report or forecast.

The main disadvantages associated with this technique are that it is time consuming, and evidence seems to be emerging to suggest that experts are universally optimistic.

ACTIVITY 10.1

application

Define 'sales potential' and name the factors governing it.

2.2.2 Quantitative or statistical techniques

Statistical forecasts rely on **past data to predict the future**, assuming that patterns or relationships which held in the past will continue to do so. Many statistical techniques aim to **reduce the uncertainty** managers face (such as rapidly changing environmental conditions and the competitive environment). While in static conditions the past can be a relatively good guide to the future, it needs to be pointed out that the business environment is neither static nor simple, so these methods should be used with a good **degree of caution**.

Time series analysis

With this method, data for a number of months or years are obtained and analysed.

The aim of time series analysis is to identify

- Seasonal and other cyclical fluctuations
- Long-term underlying trends

For example, the UK's monthly unemployment statistics show a **headline figure** and the **underlying trend**.

Regression analysis

This technique aims to ascertain whether there are underlying correlations between two variables (eg sales of ice cream and the weather). Remember that the relationship between two variables may only hold between certain values. (You would expect ice cream consumption to rise as the temperature becomes hotter, but there is a maximum number of ice creams an individual can consume in a day, no matter how hot it is.)

Econometrics is the study of **economic variables and their interrelationships**, using computer models. Short-term or medium-term econometric models might be used for forecasting.

Leading indicators are indicators which change **before** market demand changes. For example, a sudden increase in the birth rate would be an indicator of future demand for children's clothes. Similarly, a fall in retail sales would be an indicator to manufacturers that demand from retailers for their products will soon fall.

The firm needs the ability to **predict the span of time between a change in the indicator and a change in market demand**.

Market tests

These can give an insight into **real behaviour** rather than making assumptions about intentions. Managers need to be sure that the structure of the test and the area in which it takes place are truly **representative of the target market and planned marketing mix**.

2.2.3 Problems with statistical forecasts

- Past relationships do not necessarily hold for the future.
- Data can be misinterpreted, and relationships assumed where none exist. For example, sales of ice cream rise in the summer, and sales of umbrellas fall – the link is the weather, not any correlation between them.
- Forecasts do not account for special events (eg wars), the likely response of competitors and so on.
- The variation and depth of business cycles fluctuate.
- In practice statistical forecasters underestimate uncertainty.

2.2.4 Statistical versus judgemental forecasts

The relative advantages and disadvantages of each method can be summarised as follows.

Use of forecasts	Statistical	Judgement
Changes in established patterns	Past data is no guide	Can be predicted but could be ignored
Using available data	Not all past data is used	Personal biases and preferences obscure data
Objectivity	Based on specific criteria for selection	Personal propensity to optimism/pessimism
Uncertainty	Underestimated	Underestimated, with a tendency to over-optimism
Cost	Inexpensive	Expensive

Use of both quantitative and qualitative techniques

In reality, the more cross-checking of forecasts that takes place using a variety of techniques, the more the techniques are suited to a specific industry, the better and more reliable the forecast will be.

MARKETING AT WORK — application

Many small enterprises have been found to lack even the most basic marketing skills, with seven out of ten start-ups failing to identify their market and potential customers. But simple marketing techniques can make the difference between failure and success.

Some of Britain's most innovative entrepreneurs started their businesses as little more than cottage industries. Richard Branson founded his business empire – which now stretches from air travel to personal equity plans – by selling records to his school friends, and Anita Roddick started *The Body Shop* by bottling potions and lotions on her kitchen table. Both have eschewed the text book marketing techniques and the jargon favoured by their competitors because they are intuitive marketers and, crucially, they carefully identified their target markets. Inevitably, not all those starting-up a new enterprise have the innate talent of a Branson or a Roddick and some fail to embrace even the most basic marketing principles. John Stubbs, chief executive of the Marketing Council, says: 'Marketing for some remains obscure and is perceived as an expensive luxury.' Research from *Barclays Bank* indicated that only three in ten start-up businesses carry out initial research to identify their market and potential customers, increasing the likelihood of one of the most common causes of business failure: loss of market and sales.

3 Budgeting

> **KEY CONCEPT**
>
> A **budget** is a consolidated statement of the resources required to achieve desired objectives, or to implement planned activities. It is a planning and control tool relevant to all aspects of management activities.

3.1 Budgets and forecasts

- A forecast is an estimate of what might happen in the future.
- By contrast, a budget is a plan of what the organisation would like to happen, and what it has set as a target, although it should be realistic and so it will be based to some extent on the forecasts prepared.
- However, in formulating a budget, management will be trying to establish some control over the conditions that will apply in the future. (For example, in setting a sales budget, management must decide on the prices to be charged and the advertising expenditure budget, even though they might have no control over other market factors.)
    - Management might be able to take **control action** to bring forecasts back into line with the budget.
    - Alternatively, management will have to accept that the budget will not be achieved, or it will be exceeded, depending on what the current forecasts include.

Budgets perform a dual role. They **incorporate forecasting** and planning information. They **incorporate control measures**, in that they plan how resources are to be used to achieve the targets, and they can be flexed for corrective action.

3.2 Budgets and targets

A **budget** is a plan expressed in monetary terms, representing the resources needed to achieve the objective.

In terms of strategic marketing management, **planned** results often comprise:

- Targets for the overall **financial objective**, for each year over the planning period, and other financial strategy objectives such as productivity targets.
- Subsidiary **financial targets**.
- Financial targets in the annual budget (including the sales budget and marketing expenditures budget).
- Product-market strategy targets.
- Targets for each element of the **marketing mix**.

3.3 Setting targets

The organisation's objectives provide the basis for setting targets and standards. Each manager's targets will be directed towards achieving the company objectives. Targets or standards do two things.

- They tell managers what they are **required to accomplish**, given the authority to make appropriate decisions.
- They indicate to managers **how well their actual results** measure up against their targets, so that control action can be taken where it is needed.

It follows that in setting standards for performance, **it is important to distinguish between controllable or manageable variables and uncontrollable ones**. Any matters which cannot be controlled by an individual manager should be excluded from their standards for performance.

3.4 Setting budgets

The **principal budget factor** should be identified at the beginning of the budgetary process. It is often sales volume and so the sales budget has to be produced before all the others.

A **budget** is a consolidated statement of the resources required to achieve objectives or to implement planned activities. It is a planning and control tool relevant to all aspects of management activities.

3.5 Purposes of a budget

- **Co-ordinates** the activities of all the different departments of an organisation; in addition, through participation by employees in preparing a budget, it may be possible to motivate them to raise their targets and standards and to achieve better results.
- **Communicates** the policies and targets to every manager in the organisation responsible for carrying out a part of that plan.
- **Control** by having a plan against which actual results can be progressively compared.

3.6 Preparing budgets

Procedures for preparing the budget are contained in the **budget manual**, which indicates:

- People responsible for preparing budgets
- The order in which they must be prepared
- Deadlines for preparation
- Standard forms

The preparation and administration of budgets is usually the responsibility of a **budget committee**. Every part of the organisation should be represented on the committee. The preparation of a budget may take weeks or months, and the budget committee may meet several times before the master budget is finally agreed. Functional budgets and cost centre budgets prepared in draft may need to be amended many times over as a consequence of discussions between departments, changes in market conditions, reversals of decisions by management, etc during the course of budget preparation.

3.7 The budget period

A budget does not necessarily have to be restricted to a one-year planning horizon. The factors which should influence the **budget period** are as follows.

- **Lead times**. A plan decided upon now might need a **considerable time** to be put into operation. Many companies expect growth in market share to take a number of years.
- **In the short-term some resources are fixed**. The fixed nature of these resources, and the length of time which must elapse before they become variable, might therefore determine the planning horizon for budgeting.
- All budgets involve some element of **forecasting and even guesswork**, since future events cannot be quantified with accuracy.
- Since **unforeseen events** cannot be planned for, it would be a waste of time to plan in detail too far ahead.
- Most budgets are prepared over a one-year period to enable managers to plan and control **financial results for the purposes of the annual accounts**.

3.8 The principal budget factor

The first task in budgeting is to identify the principal (key, limiting) budget factor. This is the **factor which puts constraints on growth**. The principal budget factor could be:

- **Sales demand**, ie a company is restricted from making and selling more of its products because there would be no sales demand for the increased output at a price which would be acceptable/profitable to the company.

- **Resources**, such as machine capacity, distribution and selling resources, the availability of key raw materials or the availability of cash.

Once the principal budget factor is defined then the rest of the budget can be prepared.

ACTIVITY 10.2
evaluation

What do you think is the crucial difference between the principal budget factors of an organisation producing confectionery and a non-profit-oriented organisation such as a hospital?

3.9 Problems in constructing budgets

- Difficulties in identifying **principal budget factors**:
  - Sales demand may not be known
  - Resources may not be known
- **Unpredictability** in economic conditions or prices of inputs.
- Because of **inflation**, it might be difficult to estimate future price levels for materials, expenses, wages and salaries.
- **Managers might be reluctant to budget accurately**.
  - **Slack**. They may overstate their expected expenditure, so that by having a budget which is larger than necessary, they will be unlikely to overspend the budget allowance. (They will then not be held accountable in control reports for excess spending.)
  - They may **compete** with other departments for the available resources, by trying to expand their budgeted expenditure. Budget planning might well intensify inter-departmental rivalry and the problems of 'empire building'.
- **Inter-departmental rivalries** might ruin the efforts towards co-ordination in a budget.
- **Employees might resist budget plans** either because the plans are not properly communicated to them, or because they feel that the budget puts them 'under pressure' from senior managers to achieve better results.

3.10 Sales budget

A **preliminary sales estimate** will include:

- A study of normal business growth
- A forecast of general business conditions
- A knowledge of potential markets for each product
- The practical judgement of sales and management staff
- A realisation of the effect on sales of basic changes in company policy

The **adjustment of the above preliminary sales estimate will be impacted by**:

- Seasonal nature of the business
- The viewpoint of optimum selling prices
- Overall production or purchasing capacity
- Viewpoint of securing even manufacturing loads
- Overall selling expenses and net profits
- The financial capacity of the business

The **adjusted anticipated sales** by value and quantity contained in the sales budget should then be classified by commodities, departments, customers, salesmen, countries, terms of sale, methods of sale, methods of delivery and urgency of delivery (rush or normal).

An example of expense budgeting items related to marketing is provided below.

Budget category	Item
Selling expenses budget	Salaries and commission
	Materials, literature, samples
	Travelling (car cost, petrol, insurance) and entertaining
	Staff recruitment and selection and training
	Telephones and telegrams, postage
	After-sales service
	Royalties/patents
	Office rent and rates, lighting, heating etc
	Office equipment
	Credit costs, bad debts etc
Advertising budget	Trade journal – space
	Prestige media – space
	PR space (costs of releases, entertainment etc)
	Blocks and artwork
	Advertising agents commission
	Staff salaries, office costs, etc
	Posters
	Cinema
	TV
	Signs
Sales promotion budget	Exhibitions: space, equipment, staff, transport, hotels, etc
	Literature: leaflets, catalogues
	Samples/working models
	Point of sale display, window or showroom displays
	Special offers
	Direct mail shots – enclosure, postage, design costs
Research and Development (R & D) budget	Market research – design and development and analysis costs
	Packaging and product research – departmental costs, materials, equipment
	Pure research – departmental costs materials, equipment
	Sales analysis and research
	Economic surveys
	Product planning
	Patents
Distribution budget	Warehouse/deposits – rent, rates, lighting, heating
	Transport – capital costs
	Fuel – running costs
	Warehouse/depot and transport staff wages
	Packing (as opposed to packaging)

3.11 A note on marketing communication

The theory behind setting an advertising budget is the theory of diminishing returns, ie for every extra £1 of advertising spent, the company will earn an extra £x of profit. Further expenditure on advertising is justified until the marginal return £x diminishes to the point where £x < £1. Unfortunately, the **marginal return from additional advertising cannot be measured easily in practice** for the following reasons.

- Advertising is only one aspect of the overall marketing mix, and only one element of the promotions mix.
- Advertising has some long-term effect, which goes beyond the limits of a measurable accounting period.
- Where the advertising budget is fixed as a percentage of sales, advertising costs tend to follow sales levels and not *vice versa*.

3.12 Methods for setting the marketing budget

Method	Comment
Competitive parity	Fixing promotional expenditure in relation to the expenditure incurred by competitors. (This is unsatisfactory because it presupposes that the competitor's decision must be a good one.)
The task method (or objective and task method)	The marketing task for the organisation is set and a promotional budget is prepared which will help to ensure that this objective is achieved. A problem occurs if the objective is achieved only by paying out more on promotion than the extra profits obtained would justify.
Communication stage models	These are based on the idea that the link between promotion and sales cannot be measured directly, but can be measured by means or intermediate stages (for example) increase in awareness, comprehension, and then intention to buy).
Al you can afford	Crude and unscientific, but commonly used. The firm simply takes a view on what it thinks it can afford to spend on promotion given that it would like to spend as much as it can.
Investment	The advertising and promotions budget can thus be designed around the amount felt necessary to maintain a certain brand value.
Rule-of-thumb, non-scientific methods	These include the percentage of sales, profits, etc.

4 Scheduling marketing activities: time scales and responsibilities

Successful implementation requires that all employees know the specific activities for which they are responsible, and the timetable for completing each activity. Creating a master schedule is not always easy due to the wide variety and sequence of activities needed to complete a plan. Ferrell and Hartline (2008) stipulate some basic steps to achieve a schedule and timeline for implementation:

- Identify the specific activities to be performed
- Determine the time required to complete each activity
- Determine the sequence of activities
- Arrange the proper sequence and timing of activities
- Assign responsibility

It is also very helpful to create a master schedule as outlined in the following example of a hypothetical marketing implementation schedule.

Activities	Month	June				July				August			
	Week	1	2	3	4	1	2	3	4	1	2	3	4
Product activities		x											
Finalise packaging changes													
Production runs		x	x			x	x			x	x		
Pricing activities													
Hold 10% off sale at retail							x					x	
Hold 25% off sale at retail													
Promotion activities													
Informational web site operational		x											
Television advertising			x	x		x	x			x	x		
Newspaper advertising			x		x	x	x			x	x		x
Coupon in newspaper insert				x			x						
In-store point-of-purchase (p-o-p) displays			x	x	x	x							
In-store signage					x	x	x	x				x	x
Distribution activities													
Shipments to warehouses		x		x		x		x		x		x	
Shipments to retail stores			x		x		x		x		x		x
10% volume discount to the trade		x	x	x	x	x	x	x	x	x	x	x	x

Source: adapted from Ferrell, O.C. and Hartline, M.D. (2008)

Scheduling is a crucial and sometimes difficult task. Many firms use sophisticated project management tools such as a PERT (programme evaluation and review technique), CPM (critical path method) or other computerised planning programs to schedule the timing of marketing activities.

A note on time scales: marketing plans may be **short**-, **medium**-, or **long-term** in focus.

Short-term normally refers to the shortest period of time appropriate to the operations of the organisation. This is normally one year, but may be even shorter, as is the case of the fashion industry (one season). Short-term plans are normally about implementation, achieving set objectives and allocating deadlines and responsibilities.

Medium-term plans would normally cover a one-to-three year period, and would focus not so much on implementation, but more on ongoing strategic issues, such as maintaining a winning strategy. This could include new product development or opening up a new market or repositioning a product.

Long-term plans are nearly always strategic and often involve large capital projects such as building a major plant. These plans could be anything from three to 20 years.

5 Barriers and constraints to implementing marketing planning and ways to address them

5.1 Managerial, organisational and cultural shortcomings

Not all businesses use a formal marketing planning approach. Many businesses survive and some seem to prosper by processes such as 'muddling through' and 'freewheeling opportunism'. Even in quite large and successful organisations, including some that claim to be market- or customer-oriented, the marketing planning process is of limited effectiveness. There are a number of reasons for this: these are sometimes called barriers to marketing planning or barriers to implementation. McDonald (2002) discusses these problems in some detail.

- **Weak support from the top**. Much of the planning process depends on internal information. Where this is controlled by heads of functional departments, those department heads must co-operate with marketing. There needs to be support from the top in this.

- **Poorly managed introduction.** Marketing planning must be introduced with care. The purpose and nature of the concept must be communicated and training must be provided in the necessary techniques. Management support must be obtained at all levels.

- **Lack of line management support.** Marketing planning will fail if there is hostility, lack of skill or lack of information among line managers. These can arise as a result of poor structure or processes, or for cultural reasons such as the absence of a marketing orientation.

- **Simplistic forecasting.** Line managers are accustomed to forecasting in numerical terms for budgetary purposes; they tend to do it by extrapolating current conditions. They are less used to exploring underlying causes and exploring key issues such as strengths and weaknesses.

- **Too much detail.** A linked problem is that even where a planning process exists, it is often unable to produce effective summaries. The result is huge and indigestible volumes of data. These are not only useless for planning, they also have a de-motivating effect.

- **The annual ritual.** When the marketing planning process fails to deliver results, managers see it as a chore to be completed as soon as possible and with as little effort as possible.

5.2 Skills needed for effective implementation of marketing programmes

Bonoma (1985) has identified four sets of skills needed for implementing marketing programmes:

- **Diagnostic skills** – To clearly analyse the reason for marketing programmes failing. Was it poor strategy or poor implementation? If the latter, identify what went wrong.

- **Identification of company level** – Problems can occur on three levels: the marketing function, the marketing programme, and the marketing policy level.

- **Implementation skills** – Marketers need a range of skills if implementation is to be effective: allocating skills for budgeting resources; organising skills to develop an effective organisation; and interaction skills to motivate others to get things done.

- **Evaluation skills** – Marketers also need evaluation skills to monitor and evaluate marketing actions.

5.3 Planning inadequacies

According to Dibb and Simkin (2000), the major causes of inadequate planning stem from a combination of managerial, cultural and organisational issues, as outlined in the table below.

Dibb and Simkin's observed barriers hindering marketing planning
Poor grasp of the marketing concept
Little or no marketing analyses undertaken
Strategy determined in isolation of analysis or formulation of tactical programmes
Blinkered view of the external environment
Poor and inadequate marketing intelligence
Little internal sharing of marketing intelligence
Inadequate understanding and support from senior management
Poor internal communications in marketing between functions/tiers
Planning activity fades out
Planning and personnel overtaken by events
Lack of confidence/conviction
Little opportunity for lateral thinking

Source: Dibb, S. and Simkin, L. (2000)

In order to address these inadequacies and ensure effective implementation of marketing planning, the authors suggest a number of remedies or core implementation requirements, categorised as cultural foundations and process requisites, followed by a specific key actions:

Core implementation requirements	
Cultural foundations	**Process requisites**
Corporate: Vision, mission, marketing fit, receptiveness to change	**Participants**: Orientation, managing, expectations, involvement
Marketing: Ethos, culture, skills, role	**Progress management**: Schedules, reviews, performance monitoring, remedial action
Leadership: Abilities, understanding, participation, control	**Requisite resources**: Creation and allocation, personnel schedules, budgets, marketing information, IT, time
Realism: Capabilities, resources, operational constraints and implentability	**Skills**: Concept comprehension, training, external support, facilitation
Awareness: Impact of new strategic initiatives and planning	**Personnel**: Team selection, skills, functions, hierarchy, senior support
Facilitation: Strategy initiatives, operationalisation	**Communications**: Internal and external, channels, processes, target audiences, schedule
Communication: Internal channels, intra-team/site co-operation	**Budgets**: Process and implementation costs

Key actions
Audits: Corporate vision/history of projects, information, people skills, marketing tool skills, communication channels.
Task specification: Scope, involvement, process time points, communication procedures, external support, resources, roll-out requirements.
Orientation: Up-front orientation workshops (senior and participants), skill training, progress reviews, implementation strategies and tactics.
Task authorisations: Team selection, budgets, information and personnel access, timeframes, process stages, deliverables
Reviews: Progress meetings, senior management progress assessments, evolving, findings, emerging problems, determination of final recommendations.

Source: Dibb, S. and Simkin, L. (2000)

5.4 Corporate strategy and organisational resources

From previous chapters you should be aware that corporate strategy entails the central scheme or means for allocation of the resources within the organisation to achieve its business and corporate objectives. It is here where the **allocation of resources** is prioritised and the integration of these resources in the areas of finance, production, human resources, research and development and marketing are controlled and co-ordinated. Organisations have many priorities, and so it follows that if the firm is not particularly marketing led, or consumer focused, the **allocation of resources to the marketing plan and marketing activities might not be sufficient**. This could possibly lead to an inability to meet with marketing objectives.

Central to the success of the marketing implementation plan would be the **commitment of all its employees**, and this is another area which should be driven from the top of the organisation and **addressed in the formulation of its corporate strategy**. It is thus crucially important that marketing planning and implementation is prioritised and integrated into corporate strategy to ensure adequate organisational resources are put in place to achieve marketing objectives.

5.5 The role of innovation in the company

Innovation is a major responsibility of modern management, particularly in commercial organisations. This is because both technology and society are developing extremely rapidly; new products must be matched with new market opportunities if businesses are to survive and prosper. Innovation in marketing is particularly important, since **marketing** provides much of the **interface** between the **organisation** and its **rapidly changing environment**.

It is an important part of the marketing manager's job to innovate, to recognise innovative ideas when they appear and to develop and manage the conditions and processes that support innovation.

It is important to remember that **the need for innovation does not just relate to products and services**: internal business processes are likely to be fertile ground for innovation and improvement. Innovation responses to the demands made of the marketing function will also be required and may prove to be particularly rewarding.

To encourage innovation the objective for management should be to create a more **outward-looking organisation**. People should be encouraged to **use their initiative** to look for new products, markets, processes, designs and ways to improve productivity.

Innovation thrives best in an organisation when it is supported by its culture. Attwood (1990) suggests the following steps to encourage innovation.

- Ensure management and staff know what innovation is and how it happens
- Ensure that senior managers welcome, and are seen to welcome, changes for the better
- Stimulate and motivate management and staff to think and act innovatively
- Understand people in the organisation and their needs
- Recognise and encourage potential 'entrepreneurs'

5.6 Encouraging innovation

Companies can be organised and run in a way that stimulates innovation. In addition to the need for cultural support outlined above, this also depends in large part on **practical measures**.

An innovation strategy calls for a management policy of **giving encouragement to innovative ideas**. This will require positive action.

- **Financial backing to innovation**, by spending on R & D and market research and risking capital on new ideas.

- **Giving employees the opportunity to work in an environment where the exchange of ideas for innovation can take place**. Management style and organisation structure can help here. Management can actively encourage employees and customers to put forward new ideas. Participation by subordinates in development decisions might encourage employees to become more involved with development projects and committed to their success. Development teams can be set-up and an organisation built-up on project team-work.

- Where appropriate, recruitment policy should be directed towards appointing employees with the necessary skills for doing innovative work. Employees should be trained and kept up-to-date.

- Certain managers should be made responsible for obtaining information from outside the organisation about innovative ideas, and for communicating this information throughout the organisation.

- Strategic planning should result in targets being set for innovation, and successful achievements by employees should be rewarded.

5.7 Overcoming lack of innovation: building a creative marketing capability within the organisation

To meet with the demands of a very competitive environment, not only is it crucial for a company to be customer-oriented, but it also needs to be creative and innovative. Companies are quick to cancel out each others' advantage, differentiation is increasingly harder to achieve. Therefore the only answer is for a firm to build its capabilities in strategic innovation and imagination, in processes and skills better able to generate new ideas. Some steps that can be taken to effect this are

- Get external help and ideas, through consulting firms
- Appoint a marketing task force
- Hire strong marketing talent, consider mixing into the marketing department individuals who are clearly lateral thinkers
- Develop strong in-house marketing training programmes
- Install a modern marketing planning system
- Establish an annual marketing excellence recognition programme
- Empower employees
- Shift from department focus to process outcomes focus

5.8 Monitoring performance metrics and control mechanisms.

KEY CONCEPT

Control is the process of monitoring the performance of individuals and units, and taking whatever actions may be necessary to bring performance into line with plans, by adjusting performance or, possibly, the plans themselves.

5.8.1 Stages in the marketing control process

To control is to measure results against targets and take any action necessary to adjust performance.

The **marketing control process** can be broken down into four stages.

(a) **Development of objectives and strategies.** As we have seen, strategic marketing planning culminates in a marketing plan with a detailed explanation necessary to execute the marketing programme. The marketing plan will include specific strategies, and marketing goals and objectives (while goals are broad, motivational and somewhat vague, an objective must contain a specific and measurable outcome).

(b) **Establishment of standards (critical success factors).** This stage refers to the types of output controls that will be used to measure marketing performance and compare it to stated marketing objectives during and after the execution of the marketing plan. These standards will include overall performance standards such as sales value, volume, market share, profitability, customer retention, etc. They will also include performance standards relating to product performance (quality, branding, and innovation), price performance (eg revenue targets, price elasticity), supply chain performance, and promotional performance.

(c) **Evaluation of performance.** This stage is concerned with the process of comparing actual performance with set standards. There should be an essential flow of information that enables performance to be measured as well as highlighting emerging problem areas. As soon as the control mechanism shows that a gap is opening between proposed targets and actual achievement, managers should start looking for the reasons for this happening.

(d) **Corrective action.** Only once the reasons for the performance being off-target have been identified can the firm devise a programme of minor or major changes to bring the marketing strategy and objectives back on track.

Part of the corrective action stage may well be to **adjust objectives and strategies** in the light of experience.

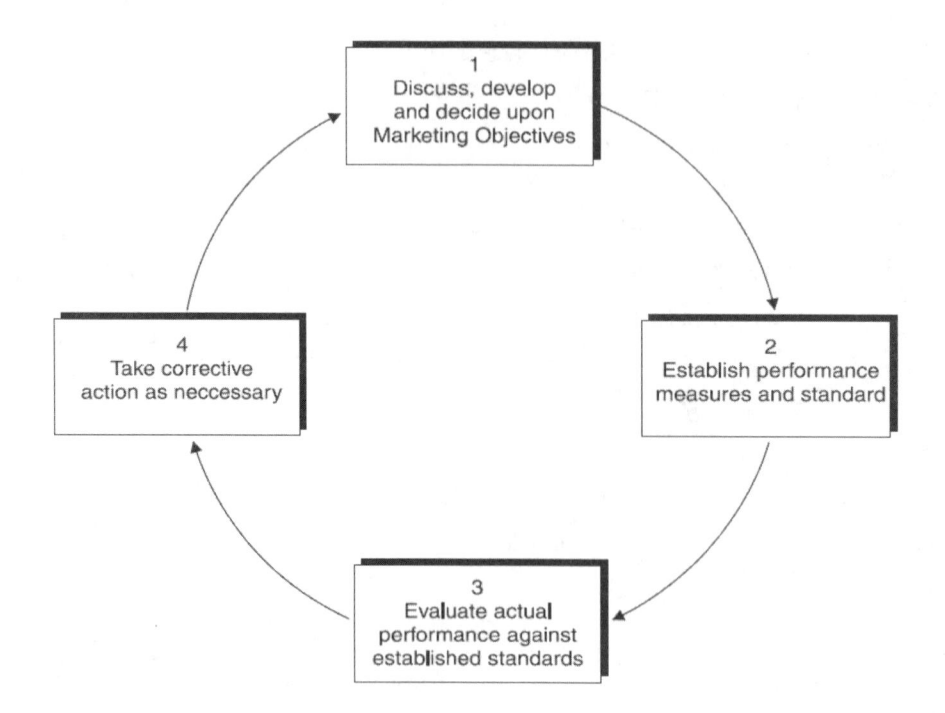

```
        1
Discuss, develop
and decide upon
Marketing Objectives

4                                   2
Take corrective              Establish performance
action as neccessary         measures and standard

        3
Evaluate actual
performance against
established standards
```

ACTIVITY 10.3

application

What are some of the steps management can take to build a creative marketing capability within an organisation?

5.8.2 Examples of marketing measures

Feedback information	Standards	Control actions
Sales figures	Against budget	Simulate or dampen down demand
Complaints	Number, frequency, seriousness	Correct action
Competitors	Relative to us	Attack/defence strategies
Costs/profitability	Ratios	Cost cutting exercises
Corporate image	Attitude measures	Internal/external communications

Because marketing is essentially concerned with people, **controlling marketing activities is particularly problematic**. Difficulties arise with information, timing and the cost aspects of marketing plans.

5.8.3 Measures relating to the marketing mix

There are a number of ways of measuring the elements of the marketing mix. The table below carries a number of **critical success factors (CSFs)**, which are also relevant to controlling various elements of the marketing implementation plan.

Activity	CSF
New product development	Trail rate
	Repurchase rate
Sakes programmes	Contribution by region, salesperson
	Controllable margin as percentage of sales
	Number of new accounts
	Travel costs
Advertising programmes	Awareness levels
	Attitude ratings
	Cost levels
Pricing programmes	Price relative to industry average
	Price elasticity of demand
Distribution programmes	Number of distributors carrying the product

As was stated above, corrective action might have to follow measurement. Part of the corrective action stage may well be to **adjust objectives and strategies** in the light of experience.

5.8.4 Benchmarking and the market environment

Benchmarks may be established (using marketing research and competitor intelligence) **to provide external targets of achievable performance**.

Benchmark = an external target of performance against which a firm measures its activities.

Benchmarks can be set against, say, the leading competitor on a variety of key performance indicators, as an objective form of control. In this case, marketing research and competitor intelligence would be needed to establish benchmarks and to monitor progress.

5.8.5 Monitoring competitor performance

When an organisation operates in a competitive environment, it should try to obtain information about the **financial performance of competitors**, to make a comparison with the organisation's own results. It might not be possible to obtain reliable competitor information, but if the competitor is a public company it will publish an annual report and accounts.

- Financial information which might be obtainable about a competitor
- Total profits, sales and capital employed
- ROCE, profit/sales ratio, cost/sales ratios and asset turnover ratios
- The increase in profits and sales over the course of the past 12 months (and prospects for the future, which will probably be mentioned in the chairman's statement in the report and accounts)
- Sales and profits in each major business segment that the company operates in
- Dividend per share
- Gearing and interest rates on debt
- Share price, and P/E ratio (stock exchange information)

Benchmarking focuses on improvement in key areas and sets **targets** which are challenging but achievable. What is really achievable can be discovered by examining what others have achieved: managers are thus able to accept that they are not being asked to perform miracles. Benchmarking is, however, **reactive**; rather than imitating a competitor, another competitive strategy may be preferable. Furthermore, it is **not focused on the customer**. The firm should set itself targets that customers value.

5.8.6 Market share performance

KEY CONCEPT

Market share is 'one entity's sales of a product or service in a specified market expressed as a percentage of total sales by all entities offering that product or service'. Thus, a company may have a 30% share of a total market, meaning that 30% of all sales in the market are made by that company.

Another useful measure of performance is the **market share** obtained by the organisation's product. A market share performance report should draw attention to the following.

- The link between cost and profit and market performance in both the short-term and the long-term
- The performance of the product or market segment in the context of the product life cycle
- Whether or not the product is gaining or losing ground

Changes in market share have to be considered against the change in the **market as a whole**, since the product might be increasing its share simply because the market is declining, with the competition losing sales even more quickly. The reverse may also be true. The market could be expanding, and a declining market share might not represent a decline in absolute sales volume, but indicates a failure to grab more of the growing market.

5.8.7 Monitoring customers

Key customer analysis may be employed in industrial markets. In some industrial markets or reseller markets, a producer might sell to a small number of key customers.

The performance of these customers would therefore be of some importance to the producer: if the customer prospers, he will probably buy more and if he does badly, he will probably buy less. It may also be worthwhile monitoring the level of profitability of selling to the customer. Key customer analysis calls for **seven main areas of investigation**.

- Key customer identity
- Customer history
- Relationship of customer to product
- Relationship of customer to potential market
- Customer attitudes and behaviour
- The financial performance of the customer
- The profitability of selling to the customer

5.8.8 Targets, budgets and ratios

In terms of strategic marketing management, planned results often comprise:

- Targets for the overall financial objective, for each year over the planning period, and other financial strategy objectives such as productivity targets.
- Subsidiary financial targets.
- Financial targets in the annual budget (including the sales budget and marketing expenditure budget).
- Product-market strategy targets.
- Targets for each element of the marketing mix.

5.8.9 Economy, efficiency and effectiveness

Economy, efficiency and effectiveness are all generally desirable features of organisational performance. **Economy** lies in operating at minimum cost. However, an over-parsimonious approach will reduce effectiveness.

Efficiency consists of attaining desired results at minimum cost. It therefore combines effectiveness with economy.

Effectiveness is achieving established objectives. There are usually several ways to achieve objectives, some more costly than others. Some people use the word efficiency in a more restricted sense than that explained above, to mean the same thing as productivity; that is, the ratio of output to input. It is possible to be very productive in doing the wrong thing: no amount of efficiency will make a company profitable if it brings the wrong products to market.

5.8.10 Quantitative and qualitative targets

Performance can be measured in quantitative or qualitative terms.

Quantitative measurements are expressed in figures, such as cost levels, units produced per week, delay in delivery time and market penetration per product.

Qualitative targets, although not directly measurable in quantitative terms, may still be verified by judgement and observation. Where possible, performance should be measured in quantitative terms because these are less subjective and liable to bias. Qualitative factors such as employee welfare and motivation, protection of the environment against pollution, and product quality might all be gauged by quantitative measures (such as employee pay levels, labour turnover rates, the level of toxicity in industrial waste, reject and scrap rates).

ACTIVITY 10.4   evaluation

What are the disadvantages of using money as a measure when collecting management control information?

5.8.11 Marketing performance standards

The most common measures by which marketing performance is judged are **sales levels**, **costs** and **market share**. However, responsible companies will also have **ethical and social responsibility standards**. The most marketing-oriented organisations will be likely to pursue **relationship marketing** which entails a high degree of customer care. Thus, in addition to sales measures, many companies will seek to **measure customer satisfaction**.

Performance standards could thus be set at sales of £X for the period, Y% market share and Z% profit, all set against a maximum number of customer complaints.

The organisation monitors performance at given time intervals **by comparing actual results with the standards set** to determine whether it is on, above or below these targets.

ACTIVITY 10.5   application

Give examples of measures by which performance can be judged.

5.9 Corrective action and contingency plans

Where performance against standard is below a tolerable level then remedial action needs to be taken. This may mean invoking **contingency plans** previously drawn up for this purpose or taking *ad hoc* actions such as initiating sales promotions. On reflection, it may be decided that the original target was, in fact, unattainable.

5.9.1 Contingency planning

Events in the real world very rarely go according to plan. It is necessary for planners to consider problems that might arise and take appropriate steps once they occur. There are several requirements for contingency planning.

- The organisation must have the **capability to adapt** to new circumstances. This will almost certainly imply financial reserves, but may require more specific resources, such as management and productive capacity.
- There is a range of possible responses to any given contingency. The organisation should **consider its options** in advance of needing to put them into action.

A **prompt response** will normally be appropriate. Achieving this depends to some extent on having the resources and having done the planning mentioned above, but it will also depend on a kind of organisational agility. In particular, decision-making processes need to be rapid and effective.

5.10 Internal marketing

> **KEY CONCEPT** — concept
>
> **Internal marketing** has a range of meanings, but the most useful relates to the promotion of a high level of customer awareness throughout the organisation, using marketing communication techniques to change culture and deliver training.

Internal marketing has a range of meanings, but the most useful relates to the promotion of a high level of customer awareness throughout the organisation, using marketing communication techniques to change culture and deliver training.

The term internal marketing has been used in a variety of ways. It has, for instance, been adopted in the field of quality management where the concept of the internal customer is used to motivate staff towards achieving quality objectives. In its most common usage, internal marketing means the promotion of a marketing orientation throughout the organisation and, in particular, creating customer awareness among staff who are not primarily concerned with selling. Hotel housekeeping staff, for instance, may rarely be seen by the guests, but their work makes a major contribution to guest perceptions.

The achievement of a widespread marketing orientation may involve major changes in working practices and organisational culture. The successful management of organisational change depends to a great extent upon successful communication (a major marketing activity). 'Internal marketing' has therefore come to mean the communication aspect of any programme of change and, even more simply, the presentation by management to staff of any information at all.

5.10.1 Internal marketing as part of marketing management

If we concentrate on the use of the term to mean the use of marketing approaches and techniques to gain the support and co-operation of other departments and managers for the marketing plan, we will see that a number of challenges may exist. The first is that we may well be looking at a **major cultural shift**. Even in businesses which have highly skilled and motivated sales teams, **there may be areas of the organisation whose culture, aims and practices have nothing to do with customer satisfaction**.

> **MARKETING AT WORK** — application
>
> Engineering is a good example. The old nationalised industries like British Railways and Post Office Telecommunications saw engineering effectiveness as their major goal, with customer service nowhere.
>
> These nationalised industries were hidebound by tightly drawn job descriptions and task demarcations. The concepts of **flexible rostering** and **team working** were introduced with some difficulty.

5.10.2 Internal marketing and organisational change

Measuring activities against contribution to customer satisfaction means that some areas of the organisation are likely to shrink. The process of **delayering** may be necessary to streamline the organisation, make it **more flexible** and bring the personnel much **closer to the customer**. Many middle managers have company-facing jobs doing administrative and scheduling tasks that in reality require little supervision if the relevant employees are properly empowered to get on with the job. A Total Quality approach can also lead to staff reductions: if the organisation succeeds in improving initial quality, the need for people to handle complaints, claims and rework is much diminished.

At the same time as these changes are being made, **front-line sales and marketing capability will probably have to be enhanced**. This is likely to involve more than just an increase in numbers. **New working practices** are likely to be introduced, including **working in cross-functional teams**. In particular, the natural partner of delayering is **empowerment**. Front line staff will take **greater responsibility for delivering customer satisfaction** and will be given the necessary authority to do so. **Relationship marketing databases and staff** will be installed and key account managers appointed. Such restructuring of the organisation has important human resources management (HRM) implications. Contemporary business practice is to set up a Human Resources (HR) model which is aligned with the overall business strategy. An HR model provides a coherent framework covering all aspects of HR management, so that the organisation selects, develops and rewards the appropriate people to ensure that its mission, strategy and objectives are delivered.

Sometimes, a great deal of management effort is devoted to setting-up **policies, procedures and plans** but **insufficient attention is paid to people, their attitudes, skills and behaviours**. The importance of developing top-class employees to serve the company's clients and customers can often be underestimated.

Research suggests that although the principles involved may be acknowledged by a large number of companies, **formalised internal marketing programmes in the UK are still fairly uncommon**. Initial findings make several other suggestions.

- Internal marketing is **implicit in other strategies** such as quality programmes and customer care initiatives, rather than standing alone as an explicit policy in its own right.

- Where it is practised, internal marketing tends to involve a **core of structured activities** surrounded by less rigorously defined *ad hoc* practices.

- To operate successfully, internal marketing relies heavily on **good communication** networks. Internal marketing is a key factor in **competitive differentiation**.

- **Conflicts** between functional areas are significantly **reduced** by internal marketing.

- Internal marketing depends heavily on **commitment at the highest level of management**, on general, active, widespread **co-operation**, and on the presence of an **open management style**.

MARKETING AT WORK — application

'Virgin Atlantic has long recognised the critical role internal marketing plays in its success. One of the secrets of the airline's success has been enthusiastic empowered, motivated employees. Sir Richard Branson has said: 'I want employees in the airline to feel that it is *they* who can make the difference, and influence what passengers get.' 'We aren't interested in having just happy employees. We want employees who feel involved and prepared to express dissatisfaction when necessary. In fact, we think that the constructively dissatisfied employee is an asset we should encourage and we need an organisation that allows us to do this – and that encourages employees to take responsibility, since I don't believe it is enough for us simply to give it.' Virgin Atlantic's philosophy has been to stimulate the individual, to encourage staff to take initiatives and to empower them to do so.'

Christopher et al. (2002), p. 111

You might like to check out Virgin Atlantic's web site to see the kinds of statements it makes about how it values its employees, the expectations it has of them, and the values it tries to encourage in them. Link: Virgin Atlantic http://www.virgin-atlantic.com/en/gb.

Follow the Careers link to the dedicated recruitment site, and click on 'Working for Us'.

5.10.3 The marketing mix for internal marketing

The **product** under the internal marketing concept is the changing nature of the job. **Price** is the balance of psychological costs and benefits involved in adopting the new orientation, plus those things which have to be given up in order to carry out the new tasks. Difficulties here relate to the problem of arriving at an accurate and adequate evaluation of psychological costs.

Many of the methods used for communication and **promotion** in external marketing may be employed to motivate employees and influence attitudes and behaviour. HRM practice is beginning to employ techniques, such as multi-media presentations and in-house publications. Presentational skills are borrowed from personal selling techniques, while incentive schemes are being employed to generate changes in employee behaviour.

Advertising is increasingly used to generate a favourable corporate image amongst employees as well as external customers.

Distribution for internal marketing means e-mails, meetings, conferences and physical means such as notice boards which can be used to announce policies and deliver training programmes.

Physical evidence refers to tangible items which facilitate delivery or communication of the product. Quality standards such as BS 5750/ISO 9000, for instance, place great emphasis on documentation. Other tangible elements might involve training sessions, which would constitute commitment to standards or policies.

Process, which refers to how a customer actually receives a product, is linked to communication and the medium of training which may be used to promote customer consciousness.

People are the **participants** involved in producing and delivering the product. Those receiving the product, who may influence the customer's perceptions, are clearly important within the internal marketing process. Communications must be delivered by someone of the right level of authority. The way in which employees act is strongly influenced by fellow employees, particularly their immediate superiors.

Segmentation and marketing research can also be used in internal marketing. Employees may be grouped according to their service characteristics, needs, wants or tasks. Research will monitor the needs and wants of employees, and identify the impact of corporate policies.

5.10.4 Issues concerning the internal marketing concept

Even effective use of inwardly directed marketing techniques cannot solve all employee-related quality and customer satisfaction problems. Research clearly shows that actions by the human resources department, or effective programmes of human resources selection and training, are likely to be more effective than marketing-based activities.

Learning objective review

Learning objectives	Covered
1. Assess the significance of the key dimensions of implementing marketing planning in practice.	☑ Organising marketing activities ☑ Forecasting ☑ Budgeting ☑ Scheduling marketing activities: time scales and responsibilities
2. Critically evaluate the barriers and constraints to implementing marketing planning, and consider how they may be addressed by organisations.	☑ Barriers and constraints to implementing marketing and ways to address them ☑ Managerial, organisational and cultural shortcomings ☑ Skills needed for effective implementation of marketing programmes ☑ Planning inadequacies ☑ Corporate strategy and organisational resources ☑ The role of innovation in the company ☑ Encouraging innovation ☑ Overcoming lack of innovation: building a creative marketing capability within the organisation ☑ Monitoring performance metrics and control mechanisms ☑ Corrective action and contingency plans ☑ Internal marketing

Quick quiz

1. What are the four key areas that marketing departments need to take responsibility for, and which frequently provide the basis for organising marketing departments?
2. Provide a definition of a 'boundaryless organisation'.
3. What are the three components of a market forecast?
4. Distinguish between sales forecasts and sales potential.
5. Provide a short explanation of the difference between budgets and forecasts.
6. List the different approaches to setting a marketing budget.
7. What are the basics steps to achieving a schedule and timeline for marketing activities according to Ferrell and Hartline (2008)?
8. What are the four stages of the marketing control process?
9. Name three critical success factors of an advertising programme.
10. Provide a short definition of 'internal marketing'.

Activity debriefs

Worksheet activity 10.1

Sales potential is an estimate of the part of the market that is within the possible reach of a product.

Factors governing sales potential:

- The price of the product
- The amount of money spent on sales promotion
- How essential the product is to consumers
- Whether it is a durable commodity whose purchase the customer is able to postpone
- The overall size of the possible market
- The competition and their capabilities
- Whether sales potential is worth exploiting will depend on the cost which must be incurred to realise the potential.

Worksheet activity 10.2

A sweet company's principal budget factor is likely to be demand, as expressed in sales forecasts. A hospital's principal budget factor is almost certainly going to be the funding allocation from the government.

Worksheet activity 10.3

Some steps that can be taken to build a creative marketing capability are:

- Get external help and ideas, through consulting firms
- Appoint a marketing task force
- Hire strong marketing talent, consider mixing into the marketing department individuals who are clearly lateral thinkers
- Develop strong in-house marketing training programmes
- Install a modern marketing planning system
- Establish an annual marketing excellence recognition programme
- Empower employees
- Shift from department focus to process outcomes focus

Worksheet activity 10.4

Costs and profits may not be the best way of comparing the results of different parts of a business. Some managers may prefer to quantify information in non-monetary terms.

The sales manager may look at sales volume in units, size of market share, speed of delivery, volume of sales per sales representative or per call. A stores manager might look at stock turnover periods for each item, volume of demand, the speed of materials handling, breakages, obsolescence.

Where qualitative factors (notably human behaviour and attitudes) are important, monetary information is less relevant. This is one reason why strategic planning information, which relies more heavily on both external and qualitative factors, is generally more imprecise and not necessarily expressed in money terms.

Worksheet activity 10.5

Possible performance measures are:

- Sales levels
- Market share
- Marketing costs
- Profitability
- Customer satisfaction

Quiz answers

1. Irrespective of the way it is organised, every marketing department must take responsibility for four key areas. These frequently also provide the basis for the department's organisation. They are: functions (eg promotion, pricing), geographical areas (domestic, EU, international), products (research, development, support, innovations), and markets (personal, corporate).

2. The 'boundaryless organisation' avoids inflexible structures and chains of command, preferring instead to encourage a more open and trusting environment where information and ideas flow freely. This enabled Welch and GE to introduce cross-functional team, working to serve their customers better and improve the performance of the business.

3. The following are the three typical components of a market forecast: the economic review (assessing the national economy, government policy, covering forecasts on investment, population, gross national product, and so on); specific market research (to obtain data about specific markets and forecasts concerning total market demand); evaluation of total market demand for the firm's and similar products (for example in terms of profitability and market potential).

4. Sales forecasts are estimates of sales (in volume, value and profit terms) of a product in a future period for a given marketing mix. Sales potential is an estimate of the part of the market that is within the possible reach of a product.

5. A forecast is an estimate of what might happen in the future. By contrast, a budget is a plan of what the organisation would like to happen, and what it has set as a target, although it should be realistic and so it will be based to some extent on the forecasts prepared.

6. The different approaches to setting a marketing budget are as follows: competitive parity, the task method, communication stage models, 'all you can afford', investment, and rule of thumb.

7. Ferrell and Hartline (2008) stipulate some basic steps to achieve a schedule and timeline for implementation: identify the specific activities to be performed; determine the time required to complete each activity; determine the sequence of activities; arrange the proper sequence and timing of activities; assign responsibility.

8. To control is to measure results against targets and take any action necessary to adjust performance. The marketing control process can be broken down into four stages: development of objectives and strategies; establishment of standards (critical success factors); evaluation of performance; corrective action.

9. Three important critical success factors of an advertising programme are: awareness levels, attitude ratings and cost levels.

10. In its most common usage, internal marketing means the promotion of a marketing orientation throughout the organisation and, in particular, creating customer awareness among staff who are not primarily concerned with selling. Hotel housekeeping staff, for instance, may rarely be seen by the guests, but their work makes a major contribution to guest perceptions.

References

Attwood, T (1990), *'Corporate culture: for or against you'*, Management Accounting (UK); Issue: 1; Jan 90 (68/1).

Bonoma, T. (1985), <u>The Marketing Edge: Making Strategies Work</u>, New York, The Free Press.

Dibb, S. and Simkin, L. (2000), *'Pre-Empting Implementation Barriers: Foundations, Processes and Actions – The Need for Internal Relationships'*, Journal of Marketing Management, 16, pp.483-503.

Ferrell, O.C. and Hartline, M.D. (2008), <u>Marketing Strategy</u> (4th Ed.), Thomson, London.

McDonald, M. (2002), <u>Marketing Plans: How to Prepare Them, How to Use Them</u>, Butterworth Heinemann, Oxford.

Payne, A., Christopher, M., Clark, M. and Peck, H. (1995), <u>Relationship Marketing for Competitive Advantage</u>, Oxford: Butterworth-Heinemann as cited in Hooley, G., Saunders, J. and Piercy, N. (2004), <u>Marketing Strategy and Competitive Positioning</u> (3rd Ed.), Pearson Education, London

Robbins, S. and Coulter, M. (2004). <u>Management</u> (8th Edition). Prentice-Hall, London

Chapter 11
Marketing planning in different contexts

Topic list

1. Marketing planning for different stakeholder groups
2. Planning in consumer and business-to-business markets
3. Services marketing
4. Marketing planning in large and small organisations
5. Marketing planning in non-profit organisations
6. Internal marketing and internal marketing segmentation
7. The international and global dimension of marketing planning
8. Planning marketing in the virtual marketplace
9. Relationship-based marketing planning and customer retention
10. Marketing planning in highly competitive markets

Introduction

This chapter investigates marketing planning in a variety of different contexts and sectors. While many of the principles and techniques discussed in this Study Text can equally be applied to many of the contextual settings addressed in this chapter, you will find that each area has its own particular characteristics, idiosyncrasies and requirements that require some form of adaptation of marketing planning.

In what follows, we shall be addressing ways in which marketing planning finds its application in a wide range of contexts ranging from marketing planning for different stakeholder groups to planning marketing in the virtual marketplace.

Syllabus-linked learning objectives

By the end of the chapter you will be able to:

Learning objectives	Syllabus link
1. Propose and justify approaches to implementing the process of marketing planning in different contextual settings.	4.3

1 Marketing planning for different stakeholder groups

1.1 What are stakeholders?

For any given organisation, there will be a number of individuals and groups who have some kind of a relationship with it, or have invested in it in some way, or are affected by its activities – and who therefore have a legitimate interest or 'stake' in it.

These parties are called **stakeholders**.

KEY CONCEPT

'Stakeholders are those individuals or groups who depend on the organisation to fulfil their own goals and on whom, in turn, the organisation depends.'
(Johnson & Scholes, 2005, p. 179)

'Stakeholders are individuals and/or groups who are affected by or affect the performance of the organisation in which they have an interest. Typically they would include employees, managers, creditors, suppliers, shareholders (if appropriate) and society at large.'
(Worthington & Britton, 2006, p. 220)

'A stakeholder of a company is an individual or group that either is harmed by, or benefits from, the company or whose rights can be violated, or have to be respected, by the company. Other groups, besides shareholders, who typically would be considered stakeholders are communities associated with the company, employees, customers of the company's products, and suppliers.'
(Jobber, 2007, p. 201)

1.2 Categories of stakeholders

There are three broad categories of stakeholder in an organisation.

- **Internal** stakeholders, who are members of the organisation. Key examples include the directors, managers and employees of a company – or the members of a club or association, or the volunteer workers in a charity. They may also include other functions of the organisation (eg marketing, production or finance) which have a stake in marketing activity, and/or separate units of the organisation (eg regional or product divisions) which have a stake in its plans.

- **Connected** stakeholders (or primary stakeholders), who have an economic or contractual relationship with the organisation. Key examples include the shareholders in a business; the customers of a business or beneficiaries of a charity; distributors and intermediaries; suppliers of goods and services; and financiers/funders of the organisation.
- **External** stakeholders (or secondary stakeholders), who are not directly connected to the organisation, but who have an interest in its activities, or are impacted by them in some way. Examples include the government, pressure and interest groups (including professional bodies and trade unions), the news media, the local community and wider society.

Here is a quick visual snapshot of the total stakeholder environment:

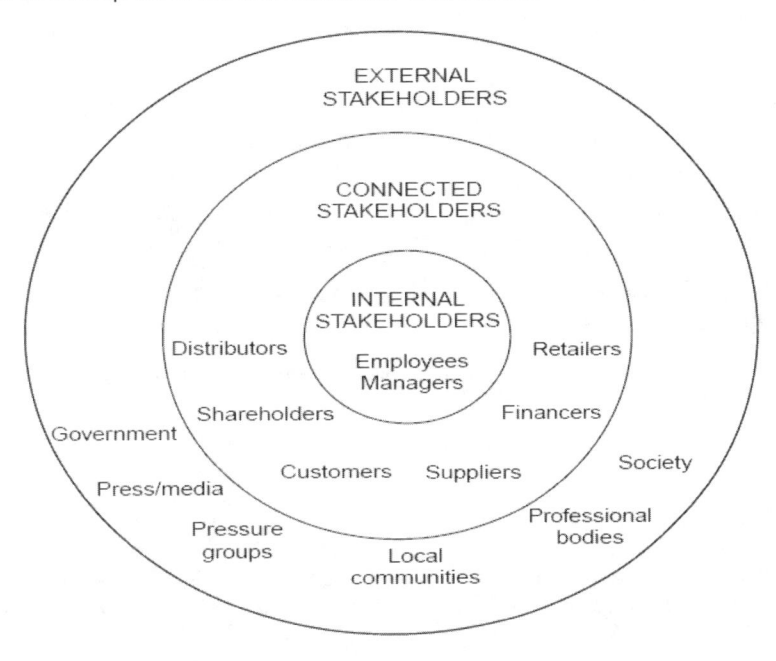

[Diagram: Three concentric circles labelled from innermost to outermost: INTERNAL STAKEHOLDERS (Employees, Managers); CONNECTED STAKEHOLDERS (Distributors, Shareholders, Customers, Suppliers, Retailers, Financers); EXTERNAL STAKEHOLDERS (Government, Press/media, Pressure groups, Local communities, Society, Professional bodies).]

While it is useful to categorise stakeholders in this way, it would be a mistake to think of them as entirely separate groups. Customers are also members of the wider community, and may be shareholders in the company and/or members of a consumer or environmental protection group, for example. Employees of the organisation may also be customers, shareholders and perhaps members of a trade union which can bring influence to bear on their behalf with the management of the organisation. So there are always areas in which membership and interests intertwine.

The key point of stakeholder theory is that an organisation affects its environment and is affected by its environment. The boundaries of the organisation are highly permeable: influence flows from internal stakeholders outwards (eg through marketing) and from external stakeholders inwards (eg if a major customer pressures sales staff to represent its interests within the organisation, or more generally if a marketing-oriented organisation seeks to listen to its customers and meet their needs).

MARKETING AT WORK

application

Cadbury Schweppes is an international confectionery and beverages company, selling chocolate, sweets, gum and beverages around the world. It uses different ways to communicate with different stakeholder groups.

Shareowners – Cadbury Schweppes has over 60,000 registered shareowners. These include private individuals as well as large institutional investors, such as pension funds and banks. All shareowners are entitled to attend the Annual General Meeting, at which they have the opportunity to ask questions, discuss the company's performance and vote on certain issues.

Consumers – Consumers can contact the company by various means and Cadbury Schweppes deals with consumer enquiries on a daily basis. It performs market research to track changing consumer trends. Many parts of the business also use survey and market research panels to find out what consumers think of products.

Customers – The company has ongoing discussions with its customers. Wholesalers and retailers (intermediaries) provide the vital link to consumers and it is they who make Cadbury Schweppes' brands widely available.

Employees – Managers hold regular individual and team meetings to inform colleagues about the business and hear their views. The company also conducts surveys to check how its employees feel about working at Cadbury Schweppes. Internal newsletters, a group web site and many local web sites help employees keep up-to-date with what is going on.

Society – The company enters into regular dialogue with organisations such as national governments and international bodies such as the World Health Organisation (WHO), to discuss issues that affect the company. These issues can be anything from agricultural policy to education and skills.

ACTIVITY 11.1 application

It is worth bearing in mind that organisations in the public and not-for-profit and voluntary sectors have similar stakeholder groups to private sector commercial firms – even if their 'customers' are more difficult to define. Consider the cases of:

- A local council which provides services and amenities to the surrounding area.
- A charitable organisation which raises funds and volunteer support for environmental 'clean up' activities nationwide.

Who are the customers of these organisations? To what other stakeholder groups will they need to address marketing messages?

1.3 Stakeholders in marketing

As we noted earlier, each function, unit and project of an organisation may be said to have stakeholders, whose needs and influence may need to be taken into account. For any given marketing activity or decision, it should be possible to identify relevant stakeholder groups.

- The **owners or sponsor** of the project or activity, who puts authority behind it, initiates it and sets its objectives (for example, the marketing manager or director).
- **Customers, users or beneficiaries** of the activity or its outputs: for example, internal departments who receive marketing advice or input, and external customers at whom products/services are targeted.
- The various **target audiences** of marketing messages: the customer base, consumer or industrial markets, the press, the recruitment and financial markets and so on.
- **Other functions** of the organisation, who may share marketing's overall aims (profitable and competitive business) but may have differing goals, priorities, technology, culture and timescales.
- **Suppliers** of goods and services used by marketing (eg advertising agencies and media, research consultants, intermediaries) – and suppliers of goods and services to the organisation in general, since they also contribute to the products and services it offers to its customers.
- External **collaborators, partners or allies**, eg in joint promotions, sponsorship or knowledge-sharing networks.
- **Secondary stakeholders** impacted by marketing: for example, communities affected by the environmental and economic impacts of marketing plans (eg waste packaging or price changes) or interest groups concerned with the environment, trading practices, consumer rights, advertising standards and so on.

1.4 The nature of the 'stake'

We suggested earlier that the 'stake' or interest of a stakeholder group might arise from a number of sources. It is important to think about what the nature of the stake is, to decide:

- Whether the stakeholder's interest is legitimate, and therefore entitled to consideration and response

- How important the stakeholder is: how much power it has to influence, support or constrain plans and activities; what contributions it may make (if its goals coincide with those of the organisation); and what risks it may pose (if its goals conflict with those of the organisation)
- What kind of response may be required to satisfy the stakeholder, in order to gain or maintain its support – or minimise its resistance – to marketing plans.

Some broad types of stake that you might use when analysing stakeholder groups include the following.

Nature of stake	Comment
Market or contractual relationships	Employees, suppliers, distributors and intermediaries, customers and clients have formal economic or legal relations with the organisation. They directly participate in the organisation's activity, as part of the value creation system. Mutual rights, obligations and interdependencies apply, often protected by law (for example, on the fulfilment of contracts for the sale of goods, or fair terms and conditions for employees).
Participation and contribution	Stakeholders participate in an organisation's activity, and in the creation of value for the customer. Suppliers, for example, may contribute quality materials, efficient delivery, reliable availability and perhaps ideas for on-going product improvements – all of which may add value to the total offering to the end consumer. Different organisational functions may contribute to marketing (eg by supplying information on product features or allocating marketing budgets). Other stakeholders may participate less directly: for example, advisory bodies (such as the Health & Safety Executive) may help the organisation to develop best practice and compliance with regulations.
Influence	Stakeholder groups may influence a marketing organisation in various ways. Some, like managers and regulatory bodies, have direct authority to shape decisions. Others, like major customers or suppliers, may be actively consulted or involved. Others may exercise indirect forms of influence, by: <ul><li>Supporting or resisting plans – or mobilising others to do so</li><li>Providing information or skills which shape marketing decisions</li><li>Imposing constraints (eg limiting the budget)</li><li>Imposing or threatening sanctions if concerns are not met (eg withdrawing custom or co-operation).</li></ul>
Interests	Groups may be said to have an 'interest' when their goals are bound up with those of the organisation or marketing function. For example: <ul><li>The activities of the organisation (or marketing function) impact on them, or their ability to fulfil their own goals. This would apply most obviously to employees, other functions, customers, suppliers and competitors, for example – but also to wider communities affected by, say, higher prices or environmental damage</li><li>They have invested resources (finance, skills, time) in the organisation – and feel entitled to some return</li><li>They are associated with the organisation in the minds of the market or public, so that its activities impact on their reputation and standing.</li></ul>

1.5 Stakeholder interests

1.5.1 Multiple interests

As we noted earlier, stakeholder groups are not discrete or separate: individuals may be members of more than one group – and may therefore bring a range of different interests and sources of influence to a given organisation or issue. Peck et al. (1999) cite several examples from stakeholder literature to make the point that some parties or individuals will have multiple stakes in an organisation.

Some employees may also be shareholders and/or customers of the organisation that employs them, and perhaps also influencers in other ways (eg as opinion leaders in their communities or as members of a trade union) Partners or allies in a business network may be each other's customers, suppliers – and even competitors.

Gummesson (1996, cited in Peck et al, *op cit*, p. 24) concludes that: 'However desirable it would be for the sake of orderliness and simplicity, there is no single dimension along which a relationship can be organised. Relationships partly overlap.'

1.5.2 Conflicting interests

One of the key points of stakeholder theory is that, inevitably, the interests of different stakeholder groups do not always coincide!

Johnson & Scholes (2005) note that: 'Since the expectations of stakeholder groups will differ, it is quite normal for conflict to exist regarding the importance or desirability of many aspects of strategy. In most situations, a compromise will need to be reached between expectations that cannot all be achieved simultaneously.'

MARKETING AT WORK

'Yes, Global US retailer Wal-Mart provides critical savings for low- and middle-income families. Yes, we can thank the company for contributing to today's low inflation and growing productivity. But the darker side of the story is how Wal-Mart achieves its fabled low prices in part by taking unfair advantage of employees and communities...

'Recent polls... show that public awareness of Wal-Mart's labour practices is growing. A company that ignores its workers and its communities will surely have trouble succeeding in today's brand-conscious world. In addition, employees and citizens are consumers too; if they are treated badly, then purchasing power will either erode or be directed elsewhere.' Garten (2004)

You might like to check out Wal-Mart's web site to see how publicly aware of environmental, community and employment issues it has become in the years since these concerns began to impact on the popularity of the brand.

Link: http://www.walmartstores.com/Sustainability

The following are just a few examples of conflicting needs and expectations of key stakeholder groups.

- In order to maximise profits (in the interests of shareholders and investors), the organisation may downsize or limit pay levels (affecting employee interests); pressure suppliers to lower their prices, or pay them late to improve cash flow (affecting supplier interests); use low-cost suppliers or enter into mass markets, which may cause a decline in quality standards (affecting customer interests); or cut corners on controlling the environmental impacts of production (affecting the interests of local communities and environmental groups).

- Marketing may aim to make strong, attractive and high-profile promises to customers about product features, quality and delivery dates. This often conflicts with the agenda of the finance function (to manage or reduce costs) and the production/operations function (which may feel the promises are unrealistic!).

- Professional bodies such as the CIM set codes of professional ethics and technical standards – but individual members may be under pressure within an organisation or business network to 'cut corners' or behave unethically (eg not reporting irregularities, or not maintaining impartiality in awarding contracts).

1.5.3 Dovetailing interests

On the bright side, stakeholder interests may also coincide or overlap, creating situations in which stakeholder groups may seek (or be willing) to support and collaborate with each other, to achieve **mutual gains**. (This is sometimes called a win-win situation: by working together, both parties achieve something they want.)

A dovetailing of interests may even create **positive synergy**: an effect whereby parties working together are able to achieve more than if they worked alone. (This is sometimes expressed by the equation 2 + 2 = 5.)

For example, a marketing-oriented organisation believes that by satisfying its customers, it can also survive, grow and maintain profitability – which is in the interests of shareholders, managers and employees, and also fulfils the needs of local communities, and society at large, for economic activity and employment.

ACTIVITY 11.2
application

R is a large high-class hotel situated in a thriving city. It is part of a worldwide hotel group owned by a large number of shareholders. The majority of the shares are held by individuals, each holding a small number of shares, and the rest are owned by financial institutions. The hotel provides full amenities, including a heated swimming pool, as well as the normal facilities of bars, restaurants and good-quality accommodation. There are many other hotels in the city, which all compete with R. The city in which R is situated is old and attracts many foreign visitors, particularly in its summer season.

Identify the main stakeholders with whom relationships need to be established and maintained by the management of R.

Explain why it is important that relationships are developed and maintained with each of these stakeholders.

1.6 Stakeholder impact on marketing

An overview of the impact of stakeholders on marketing is provided below.

- Stakeholders may seek deliberately to **influence marketing decisions** that affect them. They may have the power to do this directly (as in the case of a marketing manager, or a regulatory body) or indirectly (as in the case of consumer response or pressure group campaign).

- Stakeholders – beyond the immediate market of potential customers – may be seen as **markets** in their own right. They may be the target of marketing activity and messages intended to secure their interest, support and engagement in some kind of exchange or co-operation with the organisation. (This is the basis of trade promotions, supplier relations, public relations, media relations and corporate affairs activity, for example.)

- Stakeholders may **contribute** to marketing activity, both formally (eg suppliers of marketing services, media who carry advertising, or suppliers and distributors who are part of the process of adding customer value) and informally (eg by giving positive 'word of mouth' promotion, recommendations and endorsements, say).

- Stakeholders may **undermine or oppose** marketing activity, if their interests are threatened or damaged (eg by boycotting products, withdrawing their labour or business, spreading negative 'word of mouth' or mobilising public opinion – or even government action – against the organisation).

- Stakeholders basically **sustain marketing activity**: they represent the pool from which the organisation draws customers, contacts, suppliers and employees. If the conduct of the organisation damages or alienates them, it is effectively 'shooting itself in the foot' for sustainable future business activity.

MARKETING AT WORK
application

The Body Shop

'The **Body Shop** has never advertised but claims to get 10,000 favourable mentions in the media per year... and consumers constitute part of the sales force as voluntary 'part-time marketers'...

The official strategy is to make both the products and the packaging as environmentally friendly as feasible. Twice a year, suppliers must sign a confirmation that the ingredients or the finished product have not been tested on animals during the past five years. Companies that currently practise animal testing but cease to do so can become suppliers to The Body Shop five years later...

Every individual store has an environmental programme, a requirement in the franchise contract. The Body Shop establishes relationships with environmental organisations, among them Amnesty International and Greenpeace... Obviously there is no contradiction in marketing green products and running a profitable operation, as has been claimed by traditional companies.

'The Body Shop is, and has always been, an unashamedly green company... It was a simple expression of our core values and beliefs: values that are constantly policies by our customers and staff.' (Extracted from Gummesson, 2002 pp. 128-9)

Identify the contributions made by stakeholders to The Body Shop's marketing.

2 Planning in consumer and business-to-business markets

Consumer goods and markets have been the major focus of this Study Text, so we will not repeat issues previously addressed elsewhere.

A **marketing orientation** is just as valid within the industrial sector as it is in the consumer goods sector. Customers seek answers to their problems. Industrial products must be full of **customer benefits**, providing answers to customers' problems rather than simply being 'good products'.

However, the concerns and emphases associated with business-to-business (B2B) markets are quite different from those of consumer markets and therefore require specific investigation.

Marketing **business-to-business**, is different in nature from consumer marketing. **Target marketing** is likely to be easier in industrial marketing than in consumer marketing because of the easy availability of large amounts of analysed data.

The **business-to-business marketing mix** is likely to be very different from the consumer marketing mix, with a heavy emphasis on personal contact and product features. Industrial marketers must be prepared to seek **competitive advantage** where they can, because product differentiation may not be possible. The nature of organisational buying can be a source of competitive advantage, if it is understood.

Industrial marketing involves widely varying products and services. It is not just about raw materials, or about the selling of specialised, heavy duty machinery or equipment.

Although many of the products involved in industrial markets are the same as those bought within the ordinary consumer markets, (for example motor vehicles), **the reasons they are bought will be quite different**. Buying motivations, the criteria which customers apply, and the nature of the buying process itself will be quite different.

Organisational buyers are buying for their organisations, and what they buy is part and parcel of the business activity of the organisation involved – it is part of the process of earning a profit.

2.1 Organisational buyer behaviour

> **KEY CONCEPT**
>
> **Organisational buying behaviour** refers to the buying behaviour of organisations which buy goods and services to use in the production of other products and services that are sold, rented or supplied to others.

2.1.1 The organisational decision-making unit

The DMU of a buying organisation is often called its **buying centre**. This is not to be confused with a purchasing or procurement function or team: it is a set of buying roles exercised by different individuals and units that participate in the decision-making process. As Kotler et al. (1999) note, *'the buying centre concept presents a major marketing challenge. The business marketer must learn who participates in the decision, each participant's relative influence and what evaluation criteria each decision participant uses.'*

The buying centre will involve those formally involved in purchase decisions, such as department managers, purchasing managers and accountants. It may also involve less obvious, informal participants who may initiate or influence the buying process.

MARKETING AT WORK — application

Post-It Notes

'Surprisingly, Post-It Notes failed in concept, prototype and launch testing. In a last ditch effort, 3M sent the product to the secretaries/PAs of CEOs in large companies. They were asked to use the product and give feedback. In this case, the connectors were the secretaries/PAs and the consumer-brand connection came from allowing consumers to use the product. Now just count the number of Post-It-Notes on your desk today!'

Rob Smithson, 'Sowing the Seeds for Success', *AdNews*, 25 March 2005

As in consumer marketing, it is helpful to consider the information needs of different roles (and individuals, if known, within a corporate buying centre).

- **Users** may be targeted with information on the technical characteristics, reliability, performance and service contracts pertaining to a product, since this will be relevant to their desired outcomes – and they may have influence in this area.

- **Influencers** may have technical expertise, or may be concerned with rational criteria such as cost/benefit analysis and competitor comparison. Influencers are a particularly useful contact where the purchase relies on technical knowledge: the sales person can become a respected technical adviser. Trade journals, professional bodies and consultants are also used as a source of influential information, so trade/public/media relations will be an important component of the promotional mix.

- **Deciders/buyers/financers** are likely to be powerful individuals or teams: the marketer may need to take into account a variety of personal, organisational and task objectives. Buying centres may be politically complex: there may, for example, be conflict between the interests of users, influencers/deciders and financers. Marketers may need to facilitate decision-making in such situations, offering a cost/benefit analysis that will satisfy all parties.

- Even junior personnel may be **gatekeepers** for marketing information: a lesson to the marketer to use his or her relationship-building, public relations and persuasive skills at every contact with the customer.

2.1.2 The organisational buying process

A similar process to the consumer decision-making process will apply in organisational buying, but steps may be added to reflect the **formal requirements** of buying policies and criteria, and the greater **involvement** (risk and importance) of large-scale purchase contracts and supply relationships. A systematic business buying process can be shown as follows:

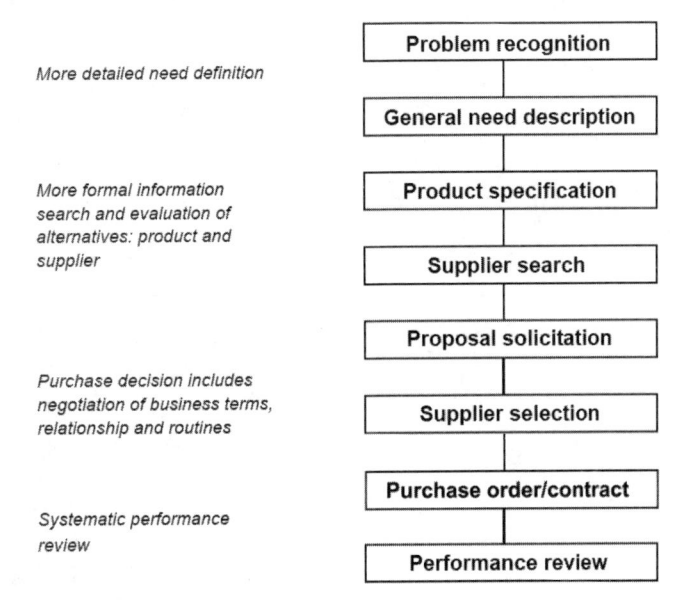

More detailed need definition	**Problem recognition**
	↓
	General need description
	↓
More formal information search and evaluation of alternatives: product and supplier	**Product specification**
	↓
	Supplier search
	↓
	Proposal solicitation
	↓
Purchase decision includes negotiation of business terms, relationship and routines	**Supplier selection**
	↓
	Purchase order/contract
	↓
Systematic performance review	**Performance review**

Whether the organisation will go through all these stages in a given case will depend on the nature of the **buying situation**.

- Some purchases will be a **straight re-buy** or the routine topping-up of stocks without changing supplier or product specifications: for example, the re-ordering of stationery supplies. (This may be done on an automatic re-ordering system by the purchasing department, or even by the supplier, requiring only post-purchase review to ensure satisfaction.)
- Some purchases will be a **modified re-buy**: the organisation wants to change product specifications, prices, terms or suppliers (which should stimulate competitive offerings from existing and alternative suppliers). Any or all stages of the buying decision may be revisited.
- Some purchases will be a **new task** situation: the organisation is buying a product or service for the first time. In such circumstances, an extensive and systematic decision-making process may take place. This is an opportunity to each key member of the buying centre and to offer support and information in making the decision.

2.1.3 Influences on organisational buyers

Webster and Wind (1972) identify four main groups of influences on business buyers.

Environmental factors	• Health and prospects of the economy and market sector in which the business operates (affecting ability to invest)
	• Scarcity of materials (affecting importance of secure supply)
	• Cultural factors (eg ethics and customs)
	• Legal/political influences (eg obligation to seek tenders)
	• Technological factors (eg use of e-procurement, e-auctions)
Organisational factors	• Objectives of the organisation (requiring cost efficiency, long-term supply continuity, risk management quality)
	• Policies, procedure and systems (buying policies, quality assurance, authorisation requirements)
	• Structure (purchasing responsibilities, communication and decision-making channels, cross-functional procurement teams or projects)
Interpersonal factors	• Nature and distribution of influence within the buying centre (based on authority, status, expertise, control over resources? Who 'really' makes the decision?)
	• Flow of information into and within the buying centre (who are the gatekeepers?)
	• Interpersonal skills of buyers (negotiating, persuading, conflict resolution, networking)
Personal factors	• Personal needs, preferences and perceptions of the buyer (authority, expertise, values, professionalism, attitudes to risk and cost and so on).

2.2 Differences between B2B and B2C marketing

To summarise, here is a chart showing a dozen differences between B2B (business-to-business) and B2C (business-to-consumer) marketing, drawn from Powers (1991). Note especially the different emphases in the marketing mix elements.

Area	B2B marketing	B2C marketing
Purchase motivation	Multiple buying influences and stakeholders	Individual family need
	Support company operations	
Emphasis of seller	Long-term economic needs	Immediate satisfaction
Customer needs	Each customer has different needs for complex total offering	Groups of customers (market segments) have similar needs

Area	B2B marketing	B2C marketing
Nature of buyer	Group decisions	Purchase by individual or family unit
Time effects	Long-term relationships	Often, short-term relationships
Product details	Technically sophisticated	Lower technical content
Promotional decisions	Emphasis on personal selling	Emphasis on mass media advertising, sales promotion
Price decisions	Price negotiated Terms are also important	Prices are substantially fixed Discounts are also important
Place decisions	Limited number of large buyers: short channels	Large number of small buyers: complex channels
Customer service	Critical to success	Arguably, less important in some markets
Legal factors	Contractual arrangements	Contracts only on major purchases
Environmental factors	Affect sales both directly and indirectly	Affect demand directly

2.3 Marketing mix differences in business-to-business marketing

The industrial marketing mix differs from the marketing mix for consumer products. Often industrial products are not packaged for resale, prices tend to be negotiated with the buyer and distribution tends to be more direct. The promotional mix is also generally different in that consumer goods are often advertised heavily on TV and in mass media, whereas industrial marketing companies tend to restrict advertising to trade magazines.

Much more reliance is placed on personal selling. An industrial buyer purchases off the page, especially where capital goods are concerned. Whereas most FMCG are purchased on a self-service basis, industrial goods involve a great deal more personal contact. Industrial marketers also use **exhibitions and demonstrations** to quite a high degree when promoting their products.

2.3.1 Product

Most business-to-business marketing mixes will include **elements of service** as well as product. Pre-sales services may involve technical advice, quotations, opportunities to see products in action and free trials. After-sales service will include Just-in-Time delivery, service and maintenance and guarantees. Products will also be custom-built to a much greater degree than for consumer marketing mixes. Frequently, products will have to be tested to laid down conditions. Packing will be for protection rather than for self-service. Some of these elements can comprise a powerful differential competitive advantage. For example, ICI offers laboratory testing of various metals so that industrial customers can be assured of the one most suitable for given corrosive conditions.

When buying machine tools, **efficiency features** can be the most powerful buying motive. Other product-unique features may be the ease of or safety of operation. If an operator can manage two machines rather than one, his potential output is doubled. Training of operators is another service often provided by manufacturers of industrial equipment.

2.3.2 Price

Price is not normally fixed to the same degree as in consumer markets. Particularly where products or services are customised, price is a function of buyer specification. Price is negotiable to a much greater extent and may depend upon the quantity, add-on services and features and sometimes the total business placed per year. Retrospective annual discounts act as loyalty incentives. Mark-downs and special offers as used in consumer markets have spread to industrial market pricing.

Trade discounts can apply in those cases where industrial and commercial goods are marketed through middlemen (see section below on distribution). In some industrial markets, especially construction, prices are set under a **tendering system**.

2.3.3 Promotion

Within the promotional mix, **personal selling** is very important in business-to-business marketing. Some industrial products are quite complex and need explaining in a flexible way to non-technical people involved in the buying process.

Buying in business-to-business marketing is often a group activity and, equally, selling can be a team effort. Salespeople are expected to follow-up to ensure that the products are working properly and that the business buyer is perfectly satisfied. Where an industrial equipment manufacturer markets through an industrial dealer, the manufacturer's sales force may be required to train the dealer sales force in product knowledge.

The partnership approach is present to a much greater degree in industrial selling, where the buyer needs information and services and the seller is seeking repeat business in the long term.

The types of **media** used for advertising differ greatly from those in consumer markets. Mass media are rarely used. Advertising is usually confined to **trade magazines**, which reach more precise targets. Direct mail is used to supplement personal selling.

Industrial exhibitions are popular as a means of personal contact with particular target markets, and factory visits are used as a means of engendering confidence in the manufacturer's abilities and standards. More industrial marketers are using PR, through agencies, as a means of gaining favourable publicity in the trade media and to build up their corporate images.

2.3.4 Place

Industrial marketers tend to deliver direct where agents are used, as in international markets. UK manufacturers will usually deliver direct to overseas business clients.

Sometimes, however, business-to-business distributors are employed, particularly for consumable and lower-value goods. **Business-to-business channels** are:

Manufacturer → Business buyer

Manufacturer → Agents → Business buyer

Manufacturer → Business distributor → Business buyer

Manufacturer → Agents → Business distributor → Business buyer

On-time delivery can be an extremely important requirement in industrial markets, especially where valuable contracts can be held up for want of a relatively small piece of equipment. In such circumstances, the premium on delivery is so great that penalty clauses for lateness are invoked.

2.3.5 Services

Business organisations are also significant buyers of services, for example insurance, banking, management consultancy and information technology, payroll services and office cleaning. The growth of outsourcing means that suppliers and customers need to establish good relationships and each need to know exactly what is expected of the relationship. The quality of the people and process elements of the service marketing mix are probably more important than physical evidence.

3 Services marketing

KEY CONCEPT

A **service** may be defined as ' ... any activity of benefit that one party can offer to another that is essentially intangible and does not result in the ownership of anything. Its production may or may not be tied to a physical product.' (Kotler 2002)

The extension of the service sector, and the application of market principles across many public sector and ex-public sector organisations, has made a large number of service-providers much more marketing-conscious.

Services are an important area of the British economy and account for more employment than the manufacturing sector. There are a number of reasons why services marketing is more important today than in the past. These include the following.

(a) **The growth of service sectors in advanced industrial societies**. More people now work in the service sector than in all other sectors of the economy and the major contributors to national output are the public and private service sectors. Invisible earnings from abroad are of increasing significance for Britain's balance of trade. In fact about 80% of the UK's economy is made up of services of one kind or another.

(b) **An increasingly market-oriented trend within service-providing organisation**. This has been particularly apparent within the public sector with the advent of internal markets, market testing and the chartermark. The public sector in Britain includes service provision in the legal, medical, educational, military, employment, transportation, leisure and information fields. Increasingly, there is a focus on profits in many of these areas. The private sector embraces not-for-profit areas such as the arts, charities and religious and educational organisations and includes business and professional services in travel, finance, insurance, management, the law, building, commerce and entertainment.

3.1 Characteristics of services marketing

Services differ from physical products in that they cannot be owned, are intangible, perishable and inherently variable, and their consumption cannot be separated in time from their production.

These five characteristics, which are unique to service markets, can be summarised as:

- Intangibility
- Inseparability
- Heterogeneity
- Perishability
- Lack of ownership

Characteristic	Comment
Intangibility	A service cannot be seen, touched or displayed. The heart of the service is the experience created for the customer, for example, a haircut or a flight. The service experience is intangible and is only delivered after the customer has committed himself to the purchase.
Inseparability	In general, it is impossible to separate the production and consumption of a service. (For example, a theatrical event is consumed when it is produced.)
Heterogeneity	Each service experience is likely to be different, depending on the interaction between the customer and other customers, service staff, and other factors such as time, location and the operating procedures.
Perishability	Services are perishable. They cannot be stored, they must be produced on demand and often can only be produced in the presence of the customer. A bus journey or concert cannot be 'stored'.
Lack of ownership	With services there is no transfer of ownership. For instance, a train seat can be reserved for a journey, but it cannot be owned. Services are experiences and are reflective of 'temporary use' (such as a holiday in Ibiza or a visit to the cinema) but they do not confer ownership to the consumer.

3.2 Marketing implications of services characteristics

These unique characteristics of services present challenges to the marketer, who needs to find ways to address them.

The specific marketing implications are as follows:

3.2.1 Intangibility

Dealing with the problems associated with this intangible nature of services may involve strategies to **enhance tangibility**.

(a) **Increasing the level of tangibility**. When dealing with the customer, staff can use physical representations or illustrations to make the customer feel more confident as to what it is that the service is delivering.

(b) **Focusing the attention of the customer on the principal benefits of consumption**. This could take the form of communicating the benefits of purchasing the service so that the customer visualises its appropriateness. Promotion and sales material could provide images or records of previous customers' experience.

(c) **Differentiating the service and reputation-building**. This is achieved by enhancing perceptions of service and value through offering excellence in the delivery of the service and by promoting values of quality, service reliability and value for money. These must be attached as **values** to brands, which must then be managed to secure and enhance their market position.

3.2.2 Inseparability

The provision of a service cannot be separated from the provider. Consequently, increasing importance is attached to **values of quality and reliability** and a customer service ethic which can be transferred to the service provision. This emphasises the need for customer orientation, high quality staff in the service provision and high quality training for them.

3.2.3 Heterogeneity

Many services face a problem of **maintaining consistency in the standard of output**. Variability of quality in delivery is inevitable, because of the number of factors which may influence it. This may create problems of operations management. For example, it may be difficult or impossible to attain:

(a) **Precise standardisation of the service offered**. The quality of the service may depend heavily on who delivers the service and when it takes place. Booking a holiday may well be quite different on a quiet winter afternoon than on a hectic spring weekend, and will vary according to the staff member dealing with the client.

(b) **Influence or control over perceptions of what is good or bad customer service**. From the customer's perspective, it is very difficult to obtain an idea of the quality of service in advance of purchase.

As a result, it is necessary to monitor customer reactions constantly and to maintain an attitude and organisational culture which emphasises three things.

- Consistency of quality control
- Consistency of customer service
- Effective staff selection, training and motivation

3.2.4 Perishability

The fact that services cannot be stored and are innately perishable presents specific marketing problems. **Meeting customer needs in these operations depends on staff being available when they are needed**. This must be balanced against the need to minimise unnecessary expenditure on staff wages. Anticipating and responding to levels of demand is, therefore, a key planning priority. There are two risks.

- Low level of demand will be accompanied by substantial fixed cost.
- Excess demand may result in lost custom through inadequate service provision.

Policies must seek to match demand with supply by price variations and promotions to stimulate off-peak demand.

3.2.5 Lack of ownership

Services do not result in the transfer of property. In the case of purchasing a product, there is permanent transfer of title and control over the use of an item. An item of service provision is often defined by the length of time it is available. This may very well lessen the perceived customer value of a service, and consequently make for unfavourable comparisons with **tangible** alternatives. Attempts have been made to overcome this problem by providing **symbolic** tangible items which can be taken away and kept. Car brochures, theatre programmes and the plethora of corporate gift wares such as golf umbrellas, pens and keyrings, are all examples of this.

3.3 The extended marketing mix for services

The traditional marketing mix, consisting of the 4 Ps, has been addressed throughout this Study Text. For service products, however, additional elements of the marketing mix are necessary to reflect the special characteristics of services marketing. These are as follows:

(a) **People**: these include both service-providers and customers who participate in the production and delivery of the service experience

(b) **Physical evidence**: this refers to the tangible clues that support the main service product. These include facilities, the infrastructure and the products used to deliver the service

(c) **Processes**: this relates to the operating processes that take the customer though from initial order to the manufacture and delivery of the service

3.3.1 People

Services depend on people as well as the interaction between people. This includes the service provider's staff, the customer, and other customers. As the customer is frequently a participant in the creation and delivery of the service, there are implications for service quality, productivity and staff training. Of vital concern to the service-provider is the ability of its staff to provide friendly and effective customer interactions, to deliver the service to the required standard and also to present an image that is consistent with the one adopted by the organisation.

3.3.2 Physical evidence

Physical evidence refers to the tangible elements that support the service delivery and that offer clues about the positioning of the service product. Remember that a key challenge faced by the services marketer is how to make the intangible more tangible. Physical evidence can be manifested in a service provider's environment, including such issues as furnishings, colours, layout of furniture and general ambience (consider for instance how these elements can be manifested in very different ways in a bank or a restaurant, in order to provide a tangible evidence of the specific type of service on offer. Physical evidence can also consist of facilities, such as vans, vehicles and aeroplanes, or it can be reflected via staff's uniforms or other tangible evidence, such as logos, labels, brochures or tickets. It can thus also include tangible items that are given to customers to take away with them, which serve to symbolise the intangible benefits they have received.

3.3.3 Processes

As the creation and consumption of services occurs usually simultaneously, the production of the service is an important part of its marketing, since the customer either witnesses it or is directly involved in it. For this reason, service providers require efficient, smooth and customer-friendly procedures. Efficient processes can become a **marketing advantage** in their own right. For example, if an airline develops a sophisticated ticketing system, it can encourage customers to take connecting flights offered by allied airlines. Efficient processing of purchase orders received from customers can decrease the time it takes to satisfy them. Efficient procedures in the long-term save money.

4 Marketing planning in large and small organisations

Much of the discussion in this Study Text has addressed marketing in the larger organisation, with many of the principles and concepts of marketing planning discussed with the larger organisation in mind. Larger organisations tend to be rich in management resources and are likely to possess levels of expertise, resources and flexibility to a much higher level than is possible with the smaller organisation.

Small organisations face a range of specific challenges, which can act as barriers to the full implementation of marketing possibilities. With limited management resources, small businesses frequently only have one or two managers who are tasked with carrying out a wide range of managerial functions. As managers' time and efforts tend to be consumed with managing the day-to-day operations of the company, they are frequently unable to engage in strategic marketing planning. Furthermore, due to their limited financial resources, they are likely to be unable to invest in researching new markets and developing new products ahead of the competition. As small businesses frequently also come about as a result of their owner/manager's manufacturing skills, they often tend to be characterised by a production rather than a marketing orientation.

4.1 Challenges faced by small organisations

Small organisations have their special problems of cost, cash flow, marketing and management.

(a) **Lack of economies of scale**. A small business will not qualify for the best purchasing terms from suppliers; will probably have to pay a higher rate of interest on its bank borrowings; and will not be able to afford to employ specialist staff, instead having to buy-in their services at very high hourly rates.

(b) **External factors**. It is a constant complaint from businesses in the UK that there is an ever-increasing **burden of regulation and compliance** upon them. To the extent that this is true, this burden is likely to weigh most heavily on the small, owner-managed business, with its very limited administrative capacity.

(c) **Over-reliance on a few key individuals** can cause catastrophe if one of them leaves or is sick for a prolonged period.

(d) **Small market areas or a restricted range of products** mean that small businesses are particularly vulnerable to environmental changes. They tend to have all their eggs in one basket.

(e) **Cannot raise money**. Many small businesses complain they are unable to raise finance and rely heavily on bank loans. (Many proprietors, however, are unwilling to sacrifice control in order to raise bank finance.)

(f) Strategic decision-making is likely to be **heavily influenced by the experience and priorities of the owner(s)** of small- and medium-sized businesses. These people not only tend to retain ultimate control of their businesses but tend to exert firm control over their more junior managers, partly by their recruitment policies and partly by their expressed preference.

4.2 The start-up business

In addition to the problems that can affect small businesses generally, the start-up business has its own particular weaknesses.

(a) **Lack of profit**. A new venture is unlikely to turn an accounting profit for two to three years because significant investment has to be made in such things as premises, stocks, recruitment and business development before turnover starts to build up. It is essential, therefore, that start-ups have the financial resources to run at a loss for several years.

(b) **Poor cash flow.** Managing cash flow is a demanding job: many owner-managers do not possess the necessary skills. The problem is exacerbated when the business is undercapitalised, which is often the case with start-ups. A further problem is that large firms often fail to pay their small business suppliers on time.

(c) New owner-managers are often **deficient in other skills** besides financial ones. New businesses are often founded by a person, or group of people, with expertise in only one or two business disciplines. Typically, these will be selling and/or technological expertise. Knowledge of procurement, logistics, personnel management, production engineering, marketing techniques and the essential detail of administration will often be missing. As a result, the aspiring sole trader or partnership is likely to find that unforeseen problems arise and consume an inordinate amount of time, hampering the deployment of the skills the managers do possess.

(d) **Marketing expertise** is a particularly crucial requirement for the new business. Where the business is founded to exploit a new technical development, there is a long journey from the initial idea to market success. A fertile target market must be discovered by market research or created by promotional techniques; distribution systems must be set-up and, perhaps most important of all, a suitable price must be set. Where distribution is to be through agents or wholesalers, as will often be the case, important discounts must be conceded without undermining either immediate cash flow or ultimate profitability.

(e) Another important area of skill that is frequently lacking in new businesses is **personnel management**. Information technology applications have reduced the requirement for staff in terms of overall numbers but have increased the requirement for staff with a high level of specialised skills. Whether staff are engaged in large or small numbers, they must be managed carefully if they are to be motivated to support the firm's efforts. All too frequently, staff are taken for granted, poorly organised and even abused.

(f) The effect of the **business cycle** should not be overlooked. A business started-up at the peak of the cycle is likely to have only three or four years in which to establish itself and secure its position before the economic trend starts to decline. When times are hard, it will be difficult for most businesses even to maintain turnover and expansion will be a remote dream. Larger customers are likely to be merciless in their exploitation of small business's unwillingness to press them for payment, while suppliers will be equally merciless in demanding payment. During the trough of the cycle, larger businesses will cut costs by reducing their headcounts. The option of self-employment is likely to be quite attractive to some of those made redundant, but their prospects are not good: they will be starting-up in a sluggish market and in the face of increased competition – from each other.

5 Marketing planning in non-profit organisations

The objectives of charities and other not-for-profit organisations are different from those of most other commercial organisations. While they may carry out economic activities, their main purpose is not profit maximisation. Although the marketing concept does involve profit, marketing techniques such as segmentation and targeting, can be applied by non-profit sectors to further their objectives. Note that, in the discussion that follows, we will be using the terms 'non-profit' and 'not-for-profit' interchangeably.

KEY CONCEPT

Not-for-profit (NFP) organisations might be defined as organisations which do not have increasing the wealth of the owners as a primary objective, though the larger co-operative and mutual societies probably do not count as NFP bodies. Also, many NFP bodies undertake clearly commercial ventures, such as shops and concerts, in order to generate revenue.

We could define **not-for-profit** enterprises by recognising that their first objective is to be 'non-loss' operations in order to cover their costs and that profits are only made as a means to an end such as providing a service, or accomplishing some socially or morally worthy objective.

5.1 The relevance of marketing to the not-for-profit sector

MARKETING AT WORK

The **public sector** has recently needed marketing skills to cope with changes in funding and increased competition as a result of compulsory competitive tendering for council services. The Army struggles to recruit able employees often attracted by higher salaries in the commercial sector. Many NFP organisations have introduced initiatives to raise money, such as hospitals selling paramedical services to local industry, and universities developing commercial centres to sell research and consultancy skills.

Marketing management is now recognised as equally valuable to both profit-oriented and NFP organisations. The tasks of marketing audit, setting objectives, developing strategies and marketing mixes and controls for their implementation can all help in improving the performance of charities and NFP organisations.

5.2 Distinctive characteristics of the not-for-profit sector

Four key differences can be identified that distinguish not-for-profit marketing from marketing approaches found in for-profit organisations. They relate to **objectives**, **target markets**, **marketing mixes** and controlling **marketing activities**.

(a) **Objectives** will not be based on profit achievement but rather on **achieving a particular response from target markets**. This has implications for reporting of results. The organisation will need to be open and honest in showing how it has managed its budget and allocated funds raised. Efficiency and effectiveness are particularly important in the use of donated funds.

(b) **The concept of target marketing** is different in the not-for-profit sector. There are no buyers but rather **a number of different audiences**. A target public is a group of individuals who have an interest or concern about the charity. Those benefiting from the organisation's activities are known as the client public. Relationships are vital with donors and volunteers from the general public. In addition, there may also be a need to lobby local and national government and businesses for support.

There are four types of customers for charities.

(i) **Beneficiaries** include not only those who receive tangible support, but also those who benefit from lobbying and publicity.

(ii) **Supporters** provide money, time and skill. Voluntary workers form an important group of supporters. Those who choose to buy from charities are supporters, as are those who advocate their causes.

(iii) **Regulators** include both formal bodies, such as the Charities Commission and local authorities, and less formal groups such as residents' associations.

(iv) **Stakeholders** have rights and responsibilities in connection with charities and include trustees, managers, staff and representatives of beneficiaries.

(c) Charities and NFP organisations often deal more with services than products. In this sense the **extended marketing mix of people**, **process and physical evidence** is important.

(i) **Appearance** should be business-like rather than appearing extravagant.

(ii) **Process** is increasingly important; for example, the use of direct debit to pay council tax, reduces administration costs, thus leaving more budget for community services.

(iii) **People**, whether employed or volunteers, must offer good service and be caring in their dealings with their clients.

(iv) **Distribution channels** are often shorter with fewer intermediaries than in the profit-making sector. Wholesalers and distributors available to business organisations do not exist in most non-business contexts.

(v) **Promotion is often dominated by personal selling** with street corner and door-to-door collections. Advertising is often limited to public service announcements due to limited budgets. Direct marketing is growing due to the ease of developing databases. Sponsorship, competitions and special events are also widely used.

(vi) **Pricing** is probably the most different element in this sector. Financial price is often not a relevant concept. Rather, **opportunity cost**, where an individual is persuaded of the value of donating time or funds, is more relevant.

(d) **Controlling activities** is complicated by the difficulty of judging whether the **non-quantitative objectives** have been met. For example, assessing whether a charity has improved the situation of client publics is difficult to research. To control NFP marketing activities, managers must specify what factors need to be monitored and permissible variance levels. Statistics related to product mix, financial resources, size of budgets, number of employees, number of volunteers, number of customers serviced and number and location of facilities, may be useful.

6 Internal marketing and internal market segmentation

In the preceding chapter we noted that internal marketing refers to the use of marketing techniques to motivate and integrate employees to facilitate the implementation of the firm's marketing strategy. We also made reference to the fact that internal marketing has become central to the success of marketing-led organisations and that it places the responsibility for implementation on all employees, regardless of level.

In what follows, we will be exploring internal marketing in some more detail, and will investigate the issue of internal market segmentation, which holds important implications for planning the internal marketing mix for different segments.

6.1 Internal markets

KEY CONCEPT

The **internal market** comprises all employees, and other functions, divisions and strategic business units (SBUs) of the firm. Peck et al, (1999) identify the **internal market** as a key component of their Six Markets Model. It includes employees in all parts of an organisation with potential to contribute towards marketing effectiveness.

The concept of 'internal marketing' argues that employees and units throughout an organisation can contribute to the effectiveness of marketing to customers: most notably, through value-adding customer service and communications. It has been shown that employee satisfaction and retention (the aims of internal marketing) correlate directly with customer satisfaction and retention (the aims of customer relationship marketing) in service businesses (Schlesinger & Heskett, 1991).

6.2 Internal stakeholders

Some key considerations underpinning the importance of internal stakeholders are noted below.

- Organisations are made up of people (often referred to, these days, as the **human resources** of a business). When we talk about 'organisations' marketing to external customers/stakeholders, or establishing relationships with them, what we are really talking about is **employees of the organisation** implementing and carrying out these activities.

- Employees and their employing organisations are mutually dependent. Employees need work and its financial rewards in order to live – and organisations need employees to implement their plans and carry out their activities. Employees are therefore **key stakeholders** in the organisation, with both high interest and high (collective) power.

- According to Peck et al. (1999, p. 302) 'There are two key aspects to internal marketing. The first is concerned with how **staff work together across functional boundaries** so that their work is attuned to the company's mission, strategy and goals. The second involves the idea of the **internal customer**. That is, every person working within an organisation is both a supplier and a customer.' (Peck et al, 1999, p. 302)

- Gummesson (2002, p. 198) similarly suggests that: 'The objective of internal marketing within Relationship Marketing is to **create relationships between management and employees, and between functions**. The personnel can be viewed as an **internal market**, and this market must be reached efficiently in order to prepare the personnel for external contacts: efficient internal marketing becomes an antecedent to efficient external marketing'.

Some of the key factors in internal stakeholder groups can be summarised as follows:

Stakeholder	Interests, needs or drivers	Influence and contribution
Managers	- The organisation's survival and growth - Fulfilment of task goals and accountabilities - Fulfilment or personal goals (reward, career, development etc)	- Formal authority over planning, organisation and control - As leaders, shape the commitment, loyalty and motivation of staff - Project corporate image to the outside world - Interpersonal influence on decisions through politics, networking, influencing sills

Stakeholder	Interests, needs or drivers	Influence and contribution
Employees (and/or volunteer workers and/or members)	• The organisation's survival and growth for continued employment/prosperity • Fulfilment of personal goals (security, rewards and benefits, job satisfaction, responsibility, status, opportunity for development) • Sense of belonging and being valued • Support, information and empowerment to fulfil task goals • Health and safe working environment • Equitable treatment (equal pay, non-discrimination, employment protection)	• Key resource: ultimate source of all added value (especially in service provision) • Scarce resource: impact on bottom line, competitive edge in times of skill shortage • Negative power: threat of withdrawn or restricted labour • Potential for added value through committed, skilled, motivated performance (eg enhanced productivity, service, innovation, flexibility)

6.3 The internal customer concept

As the term suggests, the internal customer concept implies the following ideas.

- Any unit of the organisation whose task contributes to the task of other units (whether as part of a process or in an advisory or service relationship) can be regarded as a supplier of a product/service. In other words, there is an **internal supply chain** – and the 'next person to handle your work' is your internal customer.

- The objective of each unit and individual thus becomes the 'efficient and effective **identification and satisfaction of the needs, wants and expectations of customers**' (one definition of marketing) within the internal value chain – as well as outside it.

- Any given unit of the organisation must 'create, build and maintain **mutually beneficial exchanges and relationships**' (another definition of marketing) within the organisation, as well as outside it.

ACTIVITY 11.3
application

Who are the internal customers of the marketing function in your organisation, or any organisation? What are their key needs and expectations?

6.4 Internal marketing

KEY CONCEPT
concept

Internal marketing may be defined as a variety of approaches and techniques by which an organisation acquires, motivates, equips and retains customer-conscious employees (George & Grönroos, 1989), in order to help retain customers through achieving high quality service delivery and increased customer satisfaction.

Berry and Parasuraman (1991) define it as: *'attracting, developing, motivating and retaining qualified employees through job products that satisfy their needs'* – which relates it clearly to the conventional concept of the marketing exchange.

Internal marketing has been well summarised by Peck et al. (*op cit*, p. 313):

'Internal marketing is concerned with creating, developing and maintaining an internal service culture and orientation, which in turn assists and supports the organisation in the achievement of its goals. The internal service culture has a vital impact on how service-oriented and customer-oriented employees are, and, thus, how well they perform their tasks... The development and maintenance of a customer-oriented culture is a critical determinant of long-term success in relationship marketing...

'The basic premise behind the development of internal marketing is the acknowledgement of the impact of employee behaviour and attitudes on the relationship between staff and external customers. This is particularly true where employees occupy boundary-spanning positions in the organisation... The skills and customer orientation of these employees are, therefore, critical to the customers' perception of the organisation and their future loyalty to the organisation.'

In other words, it is through internal marketing that all employees can develop an understanding of how their tasks, and the way they perform them, create and deliver customer value and build relationships.

MARKETING AT WORK — application

LL Bean (US catalogue retailer)

To inspire its employees to practise the marketing concept, LL Bean has for decades displayed posters around its office that proclaim the following:

'What is a customer? A customer is the most important person ever in this company, in person or by mail. A customer is not dependent on us, we are dependent on him. A customer is not an interruption of our work, he is the purpose of it. We are not doing a favour by serving him, he is doing us a favour by giving us the opportunity to do so. A customer is not someone to argue or match wits with, nobody ever won an argument with a customer. A customer is a person who brings us his wants; it is our job to handle them profitably to him and to ourselves.'

Peck et al. (2004, p. 324) identify the following range of inter-related activities thought to be critical in implementing internal marketing.

- **Organisational design**: eg drawing key employees together in cross-functional customer service or quality teams
- **Regular staff surveys**: assessing the internal service culture and attitudes
- **Internal customer segmentation**: adapting the internal marketing mix to different employee groups
- **Personal development and training**: focused on core competences for internal marketing
- **Empowerment and involvement**: enabling staff, within defined parameters, to use their discretion to deliver better service to customers
- **Recognition and rewards**: based on employees' contribution to service excellence
- **Internal communications**: ensuring information flows to support cross-functional co-ordination, and all-employee awareness of their role and contribution to service
- **Performance measures**: evaluating each individual's and department's contribution to marketing objectives.
- **Building supportive working relationships**: creating a climate of consideration, trust and support, within which internal communications and service delivery can be continuously encouraged and improved

6.5 The internal marketing mix

Jobber (2007, p. 864) directly relates the elements of the **marketing mix** to internal customers as follows.

(a) **Product**: The **marketing plan** and strategies that are being proposed to employees or other functions, together with the values, attitudes and actions needed to make the plan successful (eg marketing budgets, extra staff).

(b) **Price**: What internal customers are being asked to **pay or sacrifice** as a result of accepting the marketing plan (eg lost resources, lower status, new ways of working or harder work).

(c) **Promotion (or communications)**: The communications **media and messages** used to inform, persuade and gain the support of internal customers for the marketing plan. The message and language will have to be adapted to the needs, concerns and understanding of the target audience (eg eliminating marketing jargon).

(d) **Place**: How the product (plan) and communications are **delivered** to internal customers: eg via meetings, committees, seminars, informal conversations and so on. This may be direct or via intermediaries (eg consultants).

6.6 Segmenting the internal market

The internal marketing mix (like the external marketing mix) will need to be adapted to the needs and drivers of the target audience. The internal market can (like the external market) be **segmented** to allow targeting to the distinctive needs of each group.

Jobber (2007) suggests segmentation of internal customers into:

- **Supporters**: those who are likely to gain from the change or plan, or are already committed to it.
- **Neutrals**: those who are likely to experience both gains and losses from the change or plan.
- **Opposers**: those who are likely to lose from the change or plan, or are traditional opponents.

The product (plan) and price may have to be modified to gain acceptance from opponents. Place decisions will be used to reach each group most effectively (eg high-involvement approaches such as consultation meetings for supporters and neutrals). Promotional objectives will also differ according to the target group, because of their different positions on issues.

Christopher et al. (2002, p. 109) suggest an alternative way of segmenting internal customers, according to **how close they are to external customers**:

(a) **Contactors** have frequent or regular customer contact and are typically heavily involved with conventional marketing activities (eg sales or customer service roles). They need to be well versed in the firm's marketing strategies, and trained, prepared and motivated to service customers on a day-to-day basis in a responsive manner.

(b) **Modifiers** are not directly involved with conventional marketing activities, but still have frequent contact with customers (eg receptionists, switchboard, the credit department). These people need a clear view of the organisation's marketing strategy and the importance of being responsive to customers' needs.

(c) **Influencers** are involved with the traditional elements of marketing, but have little or no direct customer contact (eg in product development or market research). Companies must ensure that these people develop a sense of customer responsiveness, as they influence the total value offering to the customer.

(d) **Isolateds** are support functions that have neither direct customer contact nor marketing input – but whose activities nevertheless affect the organisation's performance (eg purchasing, HR and data processing). Such staff need to be sensitive to the needs of *internal* customers as well as their role in the chain that delivers value to customers. Gummesson *(op cit)* uses the term 'part-time marketers' to describe such employees.

7 The international and global dimension of marketing planning

Organisations wishing to market internationally face a range of challenges that are likely to be very different from those encountered in domestic markets. Decisions will need to be made regarding which international markets to enter, together with identifying the best method of entering those markets. Furthermore, international marketers need to decide whether, and to which extent, the marketing mix will need to be adapted to achieve the desired positioning in the context of local needs and buyer behaviour. Marketing in the international context needs to take into account a very different environmental context, requiring in-depth analysis of the environmental forces that affect international markets. While international marketing presents many opportunities, it also entails a great deal of risk.

7.1 Reasons for marketing internationally

Companies will seek international expansion for a number of different reasons.

Reason	Comment
Small or saturated domestic market	If the domestic market is static or growth is slow, a company may seek to further growth by entering international markets
Economies of scale	Since volume of output and unit cost are related, increased volume may lead to lower costs. Expanding into international markets may provide the level of sales necessary to benefit from economies of scale.
International production	Differential labour costs in different parts of the world have become a major incentive for organisations to shift production abroad. In addition to lower labour costs, the company may also benefit from lower operating costs and save on transport and import costs. Government incentives also favour foreign investment.
Customer relationships	As customers move into international markets, their suppliers will often follow suit. Manufacturers who supply multinational firms must themselves be able to deliver worldwide and price in any currency in order to supply assembly plants in different countries.
Market diversification	The broader the range of markets served, the less likely that the firm will suffer if one market fails. For example, recessions do not happen in all countries at the same time and a truly multinational company will be able to make up losses in one market with gains in another
International competitiveness	No firm is immune from foreign competitors entering their home turf. If a firm is to remain competitive and viable in the longer term, it may need to meet foreign competitors in their own markets before having to meet them in the domestic market.

7.2 The international marketing environment

Once a decision has been made to market internationally, the organisation needs to select which foreign markets to target. The choice of foreign target market has to be made carefully and a full analysis of the international marketing environment is required in order to make an informed decision.

The table below presents a framework for comparing differences in the market environment between countries, which impact on marketing planning and strategy.

International marketing environment factors	Key elements
Political-Legal	• Type and stability of government • Government policy and attitude to overseas companies and investors • Framework and application of laws affecting marketing, eg competition, contract, agency law

Economic	• National income and wealth
	• Economic development, eg industrialisation
	• International trade:
	   – volumes, trade patterns and partners
	   – trade policies, eg tariffs, quotas
	• Economic and trade affiliations, eg EU, NAFTA, ASEAN
	• Economic and investment policies, eg taxes, incentives
	• Financial and monetary issues, eg monetary policy, financial infrastructure, currency

International marketing environment factors	Key elements
Sociocultural	- Demographic aspects, eg data on population age, education, lifestyle profiles - Social – institutions, class influences - Cultural – language, regional and customary factors; attitude to work, materialism, business protocol
Technological	- Technological level – existing facilities and infrastructure, skills and training
Geographical	- Physical features – dimensions of country/ territory, topography and climatic conditions, resources - Geo-commercial – transport, infrastructure, population dispersion/ urbanisation, land use

Source: adapted from Adcock, et al. (2001)

7.3 Market selection

Once a careful analysis of the marketing environment has taken place, the organisation needs to match opportunities and threats emerging from the market environment against its own strengths and weaknesses, skills, resources, capabilities and aspirations. The quality of this assessment will determine the success or failure of the international marketing endeavour.

Some of the key factors that need to be addressed in market selection are outlined below.

Factor	Questions to be addressed
Market factors	Is the market undeveloped, in its growth stage, or has it reached maturity? Is there sufficient potential future demand to warrant long-term commitment to the market? Are there established distribution channels? What is the length of distribution channels and how sophisticated is their infrastructure?
Competitive factors	Who are the existing competitors in the market? How well established are they? How intense and aggressive is the competition? What is the extent of their control over distribution channels? How likely are competitors to react aggressively to our entry into the market? What barriers to entry can they raise?
Trade restraint factors	What legal and regulatory factors will influence operation in the market? How will legal and regulatory factors impact on marketing mix decisions? Are there different quality and safety standards that might impact on our production? What import tariffs and quotas exist? Are there constraints on foreign companies operating in this market?
Resourcing factors	Is investment required in entering this market? Does local staff need to be recruited or existing staff be repatriated? What staff training will be required?
Entry factors	What methods of market entry are feasible in this market and what are their costs? What marketing costs will be required in establishing a market presence and developing market share? What are the cultural similarities and differences in this market and how well do we understand them?
Product fit factors	Is there a gap in the market for our product? Is there demand for it? Do we need to adapt our product to suit local requirements and conditions and, if so, to what extent?

Source: Adapted from Brassington, F. and Pettitt, S. (2006)

7.4 Market entry methods

Once a company has decided which market to enter, it needs to decide how to enter. Market entry methods (also known as 'modes of entry') consist of indirect export, direct export and overseas manufacture.

Mode of entry	Comment
Indirect export	Goods produced at home are sold abroad via intermediaries based in the home market. The goods may be sold via export houses, specialist export managers, home buying offices of foreign governments, complementary exporting and co-operative organisations.
Direct export	Goods produced at home are sold through intermediaries or sales offices based abroad.
	Direct export includes direct sales to the final user (eg via mail order), overseas agents, distributors and stockists, and company branch offices abroad.
Overseas manufacture	There are many types of overseas manufacture. The scope may cover assembly of imported components or a whole supply chain.
	Finished goods may be produced for sale to consumers or components for re-export to other group companies in an internal supply chain.
	In terms of a company's involvement, this can include contract manufacture, licensing and franchising. Wholly-owned overseas production is the most direct involvement.

7.4.1 Mode of entry selection criteria

The choice of entry method depends on a range of criteria.

Criteria	Comment
Company objectives	Companies with ambitious plans for expansion are likely to choose entry modes that will give them high levels of control in order to achieve their objectives.
	Companies with lesser ambitions are likely to select lower commitment and investment modes, such as exporting or licensing.
Resources	Where firms have limited financial resources, choice will be limited to alternatives such as exporting and licensing, which are less demanding on resources. Firms with greater resources are able to employ one of the more resource-intensive options, such as overseas production
Control needs	Companies with strong control needs over marketing activities should avoid entry modes such as joint ventures or licensing.
	The higher the need for control, the larger the resource commitments required.
Flexibility	The amount of flexibility afforded by the various entry modes varies considerably. Contractual agreements such as joint ventures or licensing often provide limited flexibility. Wholly-owned subsidiaries may be hard to divest where exit barriers are high, thereby also offering little flexibility compared to other modes of entry.
Market size and growth rate	In many cases size is the key determinant of entry choice decisions. Large markets justify major resource commitments in the form of joint ventures or wholly-owned subsidiaries.
Government regulations	Governments can impose a range of legal restrictions, thereby constraining the set of available options of market entry.
	Trade barriers also restrict the entry choice decision. When there are high trade barriers in an otherwise attractive market, direct foreign investment is often the most appropriate entry method.
Risk	This relates to the instability in the political and economic environment that may impact the company's business prospects. Generally speaking, the higher the risk factor, the less keen companies are to make major resource commitments to the country concerned

7.5 International marketing strategy

Once the organisation has analysed the characteristics of the foreign target market and has decided on a suitable mode of entry, it needs to design the marketing programme. While, in principle, this is not too different from designing the marketing mix in the domestic context, the major difference lies in the fact that the company will need to decide whether any modifications to the marketing mix are needed. Frequently the marketing mix needs to be adapted to meet the specific requirements of the foreign target market.

7.5.1 Standardisation versus adaptation

Entry into foreign markets mandates decisions about whether or not to adopt the marketing mix to local conditions. The choice is between **standardising elements of the mix** to reap advantages such as economies of scale and, on the other hand, **adaptation** which gives the advantages of flexible response to local market conditions.

Factors encouraging standardisation

(a) **Economies of scale**
    (i) Production
    (ii) Marketing/communications
    (iii) Research and development
    (iv) Stock holding

(b) **Easier management and control**

(c) **Homogeneity** of markets

(d) **Culturally insensitive** products, eg industrial components and agricultural products.

(e) **Consumer mobility**, meaning that standardisation is expected in certain products.
    (i) Camera film
    (ii) Hotel chains

(f) Where '**made in**' image is important to a product's perceived value (eg France for perfume, Italy for clothing and shoes).

(g) For a firm selling a **small proportion** of its output overseas, the incremental adaptation costs may exceed the incremental sales value.

(h) Products that are positioned at the **high end of the spectrum** in terms of price, prestige and scarcity are more likely to have a standardised mix.

Factors requiring adaptation

Adaptation may be mandatory or discretionary.

Mandatory product modification normally involves either adaptation to comply with government requirements or inevitable technical changes. An example of the former would be enhanced safety requirements, while the requirements imposed by different climatic conditions would be an example of the latter.

Discretionary modification is called for only to make the product more appealing in different markets. It results from differing customer needs, preferences and tastes. These differences become apparent from market research and analysis; and intermediary and customer feedback.

(a) Levels of customer **purchasing power**. Low incomes may make a cheap version of the product more attractive in some less developed economies.

(b) **Levels of education** and technical sophistication. Ease of use may be a crucial factor in decision-making.

(c) Standards of **maintenance and repair** facilities. Simpler, more robust versions may be needed.

(d) '**Culture-bound' products** such as clothing, food and home decoration are more likely to have an adapted marketing mix.

MARKETING AT WORK

application

Not all products are suitable for standardisation. Food products are regarded as highly culturally sensitive, ie influenced by cultural factors unique to certain countries or regions. Take the example of Cadbury-Schweppes which deals with chocolate and soft drinks.

The UK consumer's taste in chocolate is not shared by most consumers in continental Europe, who prefer a higher proportion of cocoa-butter in the final product. Marketing Cadbury's UK brands of chocolate on a Europe-wide basis would not seem to be appropriate: instead the product needs to be adapted to meet with the specific tastes of continental European consumers.

Interestingly, though, the market for soft drinks is different, with the same standardised Schweppes tonic water well established as a brand across Europe.

ACTIVITY 11.4

evaluation

Under which circumstances, both mandatory and discretionary, could a product be adapted?

7.5.2 International marketing mixes

The principles of designing marketing mixes for international markets are essentially the same as for domestic markets. Sound market analysis is required as a precursor to any decision regarding the selection of relevant marketing tools. As in domestic marketing, the segmentation and positioning strategy will be an important determinant in designing the marketing mix. However, as previously noted, the marketing strategy and programme may need to be adapted to exploit strengths and weaknesses while minimising weaknesses and threats in the local marketing environment.

8 Planning marketing in the virtual marketplace

The internet has had a significant impact on business practices and has provided new opportunities for marketers to get to know their customers better and serve their needs and wants more effectively. According to Porter (2001), the internet offers a powerful set of tools that can be used in almost any industry and as part of almost any strategy.

However, it should be noted that the internet does not change any of the fundamentals of doing business or what really creates competitive advantage (Porter, 2002). The fundamentals of business and marketing remain the same. Thus, understanding target customers' needs and wants and designing an integrated marketing programme that best meets their requirements remains just as important, regardless of whether we are dealing with conventional marketing or marketing via the internet. Porter (2002) notes that the companies that will benefit the most from the internet are those that keep a clear focus on their core strategic objectives and utilise and integrate the internet to help achieve those objectives and create and sustain competitive advantage. By contrast, companies who merely jump on the internet bandwagon to keep up with competitors or use the internet as a mere 'add-on' and separate part of their core traditional business are likely to fail.

We investigate the impact of the internet on business practice and its implications for marketing strategy, practice and planning below.

8.1 The impact of the internet on business practice

There are several features of the Internet which make it radically different from what has gone before.

(a) It **challenges traditional business models** – For example, it enables product/service suppliers to interact directly with their customers, instead of using intermediaries (like retail shops, travel agents, insurance brokers, and conventional banks). This referred to as **disintermediation**.

> **MARKETING AT WORK** — application
>
> EBay is an example of disintermediation. Customers can auction their products directly, rather than try to sell them via a specialist auction house. (Many second-hand goods would be thrown away perhaps or sold on to second-hand goods shops). EBay is also significant in that its participants can enjoy a genuinely global marketplace.

(b) Its benefits are open to both large and small companies. **Small companies** can move instantly into a global marketplace, either on their own initiative or as part of what is known as a 'consumer portal'.

(c) It offers a new **economics of information**. Much information is free. Those with internet access can view many of the world's major newspapers and periodicals without charge. However, publishers such as the Financial Times now charge for certain types of content. Some of this information might be generated by users as a co-operative exercise.

> **MARKETING AT WORK** — application
>
> Wikipedia is an online encyclopedia updated for free by users who may, or may not, be experts in the field. Users add comments and amend other people's submissions. This is, in effect, free, in direct contrast to paid-for products such as Encyclopaedia Britannica, which are authored by specialists. This does open a debate on reliability of information obtained over the internet which is after all, not peer reviewed.

(d) **It offers speed** – virtually instant access to organisations, plus the capacity (at least theoretically) to complete purchasing transactions within seconds. This velocity, of course, is only truly impressive if it is accompanied by equal speed so far as the delivery of tangible goods is concerned. This might have the effect of raising customer expectations.

(e) It has created **new networks of communication** – between organisations and their customers (either individually or collectively), between customers themselves, and between organisations and their suppliers.

(f) It stimulates the appearance of **new intermediaries** plus, correspondingly, the disappearance of some existing ones. Travel agents have had to reinvent their business in the light of online travel firms such as Expedia and eBookers, enabling consumers to buy their own flights and book hotels directly. In some important respects, the customer is in control.

(g) It promotes **transparent pricing** – because potential customers can readily compare prices not only from suppliers within any given country, but also from suppliers across the world. Some web sites offer auctions. The main threat facing companies is that prices will be driven down by consumers' ability to shop around using the internet. This phenomenon will make it harder for companies to make money using traditional business models, which assume consumers spend little time researching prices.

A relevant phenomenon is emerging in the form of **dynamic pricing**, whereby companies can rapidly change their prices to reflect the current state of demand and supply. EasyJet, and similar airlines such as RyanAir, have used the internet booking system to reduce costs.

(h) It facilitates opportunities for very **high levels of customer intimacy** between service suppliers and their clients because each client can believe that he or she is receiving personalised attention – even if such attention is actually administered through impersonal, yet highly sophisticated IT systems and customer database manipulation. Companies once had to choose between 'richness' and 'reach' in their customer relationships. 'Richness' refers to a one-to-one connection, in which customers refer to 'my' hairdresser, 'my' solicitor, 'my' accountant or 'my' bank manager. 'Reach' describes the process in which standardised approaches are made to large numbers of potential purchasers, through mail-shots and advertising. 'Richness' has traditionally been a very expensive, labour-intensive delivery mechanism, though very rewarding if applied to high-margin customers. 'Reach' can also be costly, if it calls for a mail-shot aimed at millions of possible clients. It may appear cost-effective in terms of the cost per individual targeted, yet work out to be expensive if the take-up rate is no more than two per cent (a realistic rate for many mail-shots) of recipients. With e-commerce, the distinction between 'richness' and 'reach' can be obliterated: customer intimacy can be secured without significant cost penalties.

(i) It makes possible **sophisticated market segmentation opportunities**. Visualising and approaching such segments may be one of the few ways in which e-commerce entrepreneurs can truly create competitive advantage.

(j) It **lowers barriers to entry** to certain industries, because of the speed of communication and the fact that it is a network.

(k) **Product development and market research**. The internet offers instantaneous test marketing and market research. Questionnaires can be e-mailed, completed and processed online. For software projects, users can be asked to test a 'beta' version. Entertainment, including music, humour, art, games, can be obtained over the internet in download format – legally and illegally.

(l) **Dissemination of information to all stakeholders**. For example, a corporate web site might contain details about the company's products and services for customers. It might also have data relevant to investors interested in the company's financial performance. If its business activities are controversial, it can be used to create good corporate PR. (An oil company might describe its 'environmental' policy, what it spends on development and so on). Companies can use their web sites for recruitment, for detailing standard terms with suppliers and so on.

(m) **Transaction processing**. The internet can be used to initiate and process transactions, both business-to-business and business-to-consumer. For example, accessing the web site of a delivery firm such as FedEx or DHL, enables the customer to track the progress of his or her parcel.

(n) **Relationships** between various groups of stakeholders can be improved: for example, on many help sites, users are encouraged to answer other users' questions.

8.2 The internet as a marketing tool

Internet marketing has a **wide range of uses** for organisations, including the dissemination of information, market research, PR, selling, and CRM. Internet marketing can be of great value to organisations of all types and sizes and can be very useful in **achieving marketing objectives** when integrated with more traditional marketing tools and methods. The **traditional marketing values** of customer orientation, clear differential advantage and tightly controlled marketing planning, management and control, however, remain just as important, even for companies who trade solely via the internet. A key ingredient for success in internet marketing is the ability to generate and maintain **customer trust**.

Brassington and Pettitt (2006) have grouped the many marketing uses of the internet into three broad categories, as illustrated in the table below:

Marketing uses of the internet	Examples
Research and planning tool	• Obtain market information • Conduct primary research • Analyse customer feedback and response
Distribution and customer service	• Take orders • Update product offerings frequently • Help the customer buy online • Process payments securely • Raise customer service levels • Reduce marketing and distribution costs • Distribute digital products

Marketing uses of the internet	Examples
Communication and promotion	- Generate enquiries
- Enable low cost direct communication
- Reinforce corporate identity
- Produce and display product catalogues
- Entertain, amuse and build goodwill
- Inform investors
- Detail current and old press releases
- Provide basic product and location information
- Present company in favourable light – history, mission, achievements, views, etc
- Educate customers on products, processes, etc
- Inform suppliers of developments
- Communicate with employees
- Attract new job recruits
- Answer questions about the company and its products

Source: Brassington, F. and Pettitt, S. (2006)

ACTIVITY 11.5

application

What are the uses of the internet with regard to distribution and customer service?

Research and planning

The internet provides access to a vast amount of **secondary marketing information**. While some sources are free, others can only be accessed through subscription. Many organisations offering relevant marketing information for marketing research and planning purposes, such Mintel, Financial Times and International Data Corp., offer subscription services, constantly keeping their sites up-to-date with the latest information and reports.

The internet is also a useful tool for **primary research**. Marketers can gather useful information for marketing planning purposes by analysing visitor and online ordering traffic, or via web discussion groups, feedback using structured questionnaires or via e-mail.

Distribution

Online distribution offers a range of **advantages**:

(a) Where the viewer is actively searching for products and services, every site hit could gain a potential customer, provided that interest can be maintained. 'Shopping baskets' help convey the impression of a store just like any others and help the customer to keep track of what they have bought on a particular visit. With the advent of online shopping, major categories of purchase consisted of travel, music, books, and software, but since then groceries, clothing, and electrical goods, including PCs, have become major purchases in electronic retailing. **Patterns of online shopping have changed over recent years**. Consumers are increasingly gaining **more confidence in online shopping** and are making purchases previously conceived of as high in financial risk (eg buying a high-priced PC or even a car) and psychological risk (eg buying clothing via eBay merely on the basis of verbal descriptions and two-dimensional pictures).

(b) With internet marketing, **print and mailing costs are eliminated** as no catalogue has to be produced and distributed each season. Despite the costs associated with developing and maintaining a web site, they still present a substantial saving. Web sites **increase the seller's flexibility** as they can be changed far more easily than conventionally printed pages, allowing for instant updates on prices, product availability and special offers. As an example, Amazon has many millions of users; however, the cost of communicating with them is but **a small proportion of the cost** that would be required via direct mail or media advertising.

(c) With online ordering, **order processing and handling costs are reduced**. This is because all relevant information is already in electronic form. Additionally, the customer is handling all the order entry without assistance. However, web sites providing ordering capability need to ensure that the 'behind the scenes' logistics are in place and can cope with changes in ordering patterns. Stock control and order fulfilment are essential if customer service levels are to be maintained.

(d) Real-time information flows between the customer, customer support, distribution and the supply chain can result in **cost-efficient and effective customer service and delivery**. Federal Express was one of the first to provide an integrated system that allowed customers to track the exact whereabouts of parcels on the internet. Furthermore, the company was able to turn this service into a key differential advantage against competitors.

(e) The online environment allows for **better after-sales service**. On the one hand, this is because communication is cheaper and easier, but on the other, after-sales service is also improved via feedback links, usage information, news updates on product changes and fault reporting mechanisms.

(f) **Digital products**, such as magazines, music and video, **can be easily distributed** via the internet. However, the distribution of music products that can be downloaded on to a computer is a major cause for concern for CD manufacturers, due to copyright and piracy reasons.

(g) Due to disintermediation (the removal of one or more intermediaries from the distribution channel), manufacturers are able to **get closer to the customer and reduce costs**. For example, online package holiday companies selling directly to the consumer rather than via a travel agent are bypassing the latter as an intermediary.

Communication and promotion

The internet is an effective tool for communicating with customers and target audiences. As could be seen in our earlier table outlining the major marketing uses of the internet, it has many purposes as a communications medium. Below we investigate its main uses, namely as an advertising medium, a tool for loyalty reinforcement and as a sales promotion and personal selling tool.

(a) **The internet as an advertising medium**

Despite its obvious advantages, the internet also poses a number of challenges as an advertising medium.

Advantages as an advertising medium	Disadvantages
Message can be changed quickly and easily	Limited visual presentation
Interactivity possible	Audience not guaranteed
Can create own pages cheaply	'Hits' may not represent interest – casual browsers
Can advertise on others' web pages	Relies on browsers finding page
Very low cost possible	Can create irritation
Very large audience potential	Some target groups may not use internet
Direct sales possible	Creative limitations
High information content possible	

Source: Adapted from Brassington, F. and Pettitt, S. (2006), Pickton and Broderick (2001)

Like other advertising media, the internet has its own limitations and disadvantages. This underscores the importance of **incorporating internet activities into the wider marketing plan**, as part of a coherent integrated communications strategy.

Banner advertisements remain the most common type of internet advertising. They enable the viewer to access the main information or booking page for the product or company with one click.

(b) **Loyalty reinforcement**

The organisation's web site itself is also a commanding tool for increasing the level of interaction between the customer and the brand to **reinforce loyalty**. If the viewer can be informed and entertained, and enjoys coming back to the site, this **enhances the brand values and image**.

Press releases are frequently placed automatically on the web and therefore regular updates are essential. This enables the organisation to get its message across to both members of the media and to a wider audience in a direct manner. Contact details can be provided for further press enquiries.

(c) **Sales promotion**

Since it is relatively easy to update a web page, companies **can easily create specific promotional offers over a defined period**. As an added advantage, the internet also enables organisations to **assess the response of customers to their offers**, thus enabling them to vary their offers. Price promotions, gifts and bonuses offered via the web site can all help to increase short-term sales.

(d) **Personal selling**

Since the internet is impersonal by its nature, it is more suitable for sales support and generating enquiries than for direct sales. However, the internet can be made more interactive if the customer database is able to **personalise communication** and relate it to offers that could appeal to customers, based on a customer's previous enquiries and sales history.

As we have stated previously, it is essential that organisations plan their use of the internet carefully and ensure that it is integrated into the rest of the marketing mix.

ACTIVITY 11.6

evaluation

What are the advantages of the internet as an advertising medium?

9 Relationship-based marketing planning and customer retention

One of the most important trends in marketing thinking and practice in recent years has been the shift in focus from achieving single transactions to establishing and maintaining **long-term relationships** with customers. While transactional marketing is concerned with making a single sale, relationship marketing focuses on **establishing a rapport with the customer** that will result in **repeat business** and opportunities for **further business development**.

9.1 Customer retention

It has been estimated that the costs of attracting new customers can be up to five times as high as the costs of serving existing customers in such a way that they stay with the company for the longer term. The customer needs to remain satisfied with his purchase and positive about his supplier long after the transaction has taken place. If his satisfaction is muted or grudging, future purchases may be reluctant or non-existent and he may advise others of his discontent.

Customers should be seen as potentially providing a lifetime of purchases so that **the turnover from a single individual over time might be very large indeed**. It is widely accepted that there is a non-linear relationship between customer retention and profitability in that **a fairly small amount of repeat purchasing generates significant profit**. This is because it is far more expensive in promotion and overhead costs to convert a non-buyer into an occasional buyer than to turn an occasional buyer into a frequent buyer. The repeat buyer does not have to be persuaded to give the product a try or be tempted by special deals; he needs less attention from sales staff and already has his credit account set up. New customers usually have to be won from competitors.

Today's highly competitive business environment means that customers are only retained if they are **very satisfied** with their purchasing experience. **Any lesser degree of satisfaction is likely to result in the loss of the customer**.

Companies must be active in monitoring customer satisfaction **because very few will actually complain. They will simply depart**. Businesses which use intermediaries must be particularly active, since research shows that even when complaints are made, the principals hear about only a very small proportion of them.

9.2 Relationship marketing

In improving the probability of retaining customers, companies are increasingly embracing the techniques of relationship marketing. The focus of relationship marketing is on **building bonds between the organisation and its customers**, to establish **two-way communication** between customers and the organisation and ultimately to **enhance the prospects of customer loyalty**. Relationship marketing emphasises **customer retention and satisfaction**, rather than focusing on single transactions.

Differences between transactional and relationship marketing

Transactional	Relationship
Importance of single sale	Importance of customer relation
Importance of product features	Importance of customer benefits
Short time scale	Longer time scale
Less emphasis on service	High customer service
Quality is concern of production	Quality is concern of all
Competitive commitment	High customer commitment
Persuasive communication	Regular communication

The relationship marketing ladder (Payne, et al. 1995), which you should remember from previous chapters, graphically illustrates a number of steps in relationship building.

```
Partner
Advocate
Supporter
Client
Customer
Prospect
```

Based on the relationship marketing ladder, we can describe the steps in relationship building as follows:

At the bottom of the ladder is the target customer or **prospect**. Once this individual has turned from a mere prospect into a **customer**, the intention is to establish a longer-term relationship, by turning the customer into a **client**. While a customer may have done business with the company only occasionally and may be relatively anonymous or nameless, a client is more individual and does business on a repeat basis. Having said that, clients may be relatively neutral or ambivalent towards the supplier company. Hence, the next step will be for the company to convert clients into becoming **supporters**, ie those who hold positive attitudes towards the supplier. Following on from this level in the relationship, the intention will be to create **advocates** of the company, ie those who will actively recommend the company to others. At the top rung of the ladder is the **partner**. At this stage, supplier and customer are working together in a mutually beneficial relationship. **The focus of relationship marketing is thus to move customers up the relationship ladder**, continuously trying to find ways to enhance the value for both parties in the relationship.

It must be remembered, however, that the effort involved in long-term relationship building is more appropriate in some markets than in others. Where customers are purchasing intermittently and switching costs are low, there is always a chance of business. This tends to be the pattern in commodity markets. Here, it is reasonable to take a **transactions approach** to marketing and treat each sale as unique. A **relationship marketing approach** is more appropriate where switching costs are high and a lost customer is thus probably lost for a long time. Switching costs are raised by such factors as the need for training on systems and high capital cost.

The conceptual or philosophic nature of relationship marketing leads to a simple principle, that of **enhancing satisfaction by precision in meeting the needs of individual customers**. This depends on extensive two-way communication to establish and record the customer's characteristics and preferences and build a long-term relationship. There are three important practical methods which contribute to this end.

- Building a customer database
- Developing customer-oriented service systems
- Extra direct contacts with customers

Modern **computer database systems** have enabled the rapid acquisition and retrieval of the individual customer's details, needs and preferences. Using this technology, relationship marketing enables telephone sales staff to greet the customer by name, know what he purchased last time, avoid taking his full delivery address, know what his credit status is and what he is likely to want. It enables new products to be developed that are precisely tailored to the customer's needs and new procedures to be established which enhance his satisfaction. It is the successor to **mass marketing**, which attempted to be customer-led but which could only supply a one-size-fits-all product. The end result of a relationship marketing approach is a mutually satisfactory relationship which continues indefinitely.

Relationship marketing extends the principles of **customer care**. Customer care is about providing a product which is augmented by high quality of service, so that the customer is impressed during his transaction with the company. This can be done in ignorance of any details of the customer, other than those implicit in the immediate transaction. The customer is anonymous. **Relationship marketing is about having the customer come back for further transactions**. The culture must be right; the right people must be recruited and trained; the structure, technology and processes must all be in place.

As with all relationships, it is inevitable that **problems** will arise. A positive way of dealing with errors must be designed into the customer relationship. Front line sales people cannot usually deal with the causes of mistakes as they **are built into the products**, **systems and organisation structure**. It is therefore necessary for management to promote vertical and horizontal interaction in order to spur changes to eliminate the **sources** of mistakes.

Each contact between customer and supplier organisations is an opportunity to enhance or to prejudice the relationship, so staff throughout the supplier organisation must be aware of their marketing responsibilities. Two-way communication should be encouraged so that the relationship can grow and deepen. There is a link here to the database mentioned above: extra contacts provide more information.

MARKETING AT WORK

concept

Customer loyalty

The problem with profitable customers is retaining them, because they will attract the attention of your competitors. Building customer relationships may be the answer to both types of problem.

Relationship marketing is grounded in the idea of establishing a learning relationship with customers. At the lower end, building a relationship can create cross-selling opportunities that may make the overall relationship profitable. For example, some retail banks have tried selling credit cards to less profitable customers. With valuable customers, customer relationship management may make them more loyal and willing to invest additional funds. In banking, these high-end relationships are often managed through private bankers, whose goals are not only to increase customer satisfaction and retention, but also to cross-sell and bring in investment.

In determining which customers are worth the cost of long-term relationships, it is useful to consider their lifetime value. This depends on:

- Current profitability computed at the customer level
- The propensity of those customers to stay loyal
- Expected revenues and costs of servicing such customers over the lifetime of the relationship

Building relationships makes most sense for customers whose lifetime value to the company is the highest. Thus, building relationships should focus on customers who are currently the most profitable, likely to be the most profitable in the future, or likely to remain with the company for the foreseeable future and have acceptable levels of profitability.

The goal of relationship management is to increase customer satisfaction and to minimise any problems. By engaging in 'smarter' relationships, a company can learn customers' preferences and develop trust. Every contact point with the customer can be seen as a chance to record information and learn preferences. Complaints and errors must be recorded, not just fixed and forgotten. Contact with customers in every medium, whether over the internet, through a call centre, or through personal contact, is recorded and centralised.

Many companies are beginning to achieve this goal by using customer relationship management (CRM) software. Data, once collected and centralised, can be used to customise service. In addition, the database can be analysed to detect patterns that can suggest better ways to serve customers in general. A key aspect of this dialogue is to learn and record preferences. There are two ways to determine customers' preferences: transparently and collaboratively.

Discovering preferences transparently means that the marketer learns the customers' needs without actually involving them. For example, the Ritz Carlton Hotel makes a point of observing the choices that guests make and recording them. If a guest requests extra pillows, then extra pillows will be provided every time that person visits. At upmarket retailers, personal shoppers will record customers' preferences in sizes, styles, brands, colours and price ranges and notify them when new merchandise appears or help them choose accessories. *Financial Times*.

9.3 Key account management

Key account management is one way in which relationship marketing can find a practical application in the organisation.

So far we have considered the retention of customers as an unquestionably desirable objective. **However, for many businesses a degree of discretion will be advisable**. 'Key' does not mean large. A customer's **potential** is very important. The definition of a key account depends on the circumstances. Key account management is about managing the future.

Customers can be assessed for desirability according to such criteria as the profitability of their accounts; the prestige they confer; the amount of non-value adding administrative work they generate; the cost of the selling effort they absorb; the rate of growth of their accounts and, for industrial customers, of the turnover of their own businesses; their willingness to adopt new products; and their credit history. Such analyses will almost certainly conform to a Pareto distribution and show, for instance that 80% of profit comes from 20% of the customers, while a different 20% generate most of the credit control or administrative problems. Some businesses will be very aggressive about getting rid of their problem customers, but a more positive technique would be to concentrate effort on the most desirable ones. These are the **key accounts** and the company's relationship with them can be built up by appointing **key account managers**.

Key account management is often seen as a high level selling task, but should in fact be **a business wide team effort about relationships and customer retention**. It can be seen as a form of **co-operation with the customer's supply chain management function**. The key account manager's role is to **integrate the efforts of the various parts of the organisation in order to deliver an enhanced service**. This idea has long been used by advertising agencies and was successfully introduced into aerospace manufacturing over 40 years ago. It will be the key account manager's role to **maintain communication with the customer**, note any **developments in his circumstances**, **deal with any problems arising in the relationship** and **develop the long-term business relationship**.

The key account relationship may progress through several stages.

(a) At first, there may be a typical adversarial sales-purchasing relationship with emphasis on price, delivery and so on. Attempts to widen contact with the customer organisation will be seen as a threat by its purchasing staff.

(b) Later, the sales staff may be able to foster a mutual desire to increase understanding by wider contacts. Trust may increase.

(c) A mature partnership stage may be reached in which there are contacts at all levels and information is shared. The key account manager becomes responsible for integrating the partnership business processes and contributing to the customer's supply chain management. High 'vendor ratings', stable quality, continuous improvement and fair pricing are taken for granted.

10 Marketing planning in highly competitive markets

The ability to develop robust marketing strategies to enable organisations to survive and prosper in the turbulent and highly competitive markets they face has never been more important than now. There are a number of significant changes taking place that is having a significant impact on business. These have been summarised in Hooley, et al. (2004).

10.1 The changing competitive environment

10.1.1 Changes in the business environment

Some of the major changes taking place and impacting significantly on business can be summarised as follows.

- The pace of economic change is accelerating.

- There is an explosion in innovation and new knowledge generation that is also accelerating. Every year as much new knowledge is generated through research and development as the total sum of all new knowledge up to the 1960s.

- Competitive pressures are intensifying. Computer manufacturers need to reduce costs by around 30% a year just to stay competitive.

- Manufacturing can take place almost anywhere and companies are moving production to wherever makes economic sense.

- New organisational structures are emerging as firms try to make themselves more competitive. Firms are reorganising, merging, creating alliances and partnerships in attempts to become more competitive.

- International trade is becoming liberalised through the World Trade Organisation.

- Company actions have become more visible, especially with regard to the affect they have on the environment. Customers are demanding more economically and environmentally.

No company can expect to understand and master every aspect of the macro-environment in which it operates, and many of the changes taking place are outside the control of individual firms. Most companies, however, need to understand and predict the changes going on. Encyclopaedia Britannica's losses in not grasping the technological changes brought about by computer technology is often held up as an example to illustrate that it is critical for companies to continuously 'listen' to the market, rather than be surprised by it when a competitor reinvents the business they are in.

10.1.2 Changes in markets

A number of trends can be seen in modern markets that are likely to continue into the future.

- Customers are becoming increasingly demanding of the products and services they buy. There is already evidence that without constant improvement to products and services, customers will migrate to alternative value offerings.

- Customers are less prepared than before to pay a significant premium for products that do not demonstrably offer greater value. The fact that Marlboro had to drop its price significantly to defend its market share is a good example. The implications are that differentiation needs to be based on providing a clear superior value to competitors' products.

- Competition is becoming more intense and more global in nature. Not only are markets becoming more competitive as a result of more players emerging, but the survivors are often tougher competitors. The implication of this heightened aggressive competition is that firms with unclear positionings and weak capabilities are being weeded out. Other firms are looking more closely at the scope of their organisation and targeting strategies.

10.1.3 Organisational change

Within firms the boundaries between functional areas are becoming more blurred. In leading organisations the functional boundaries have long been replaced by cross-functional process teams who view the operations of the organisation holistically. The role of marketing in companies has also come under increasing scrutiny, with critics claiming that marketing departments are not customer centric enough, are territorial and ultimately fail do create customer value. Many are advocating the rethinking of marketing as a strategic force in the business. Key to success in the future will be strategies that are responsive and adaptive, and organisational structures that are similarly inclined.

10.2 Strategic fundamentals in a changing world

A number of factors are increasingly important and essential for dealing with complex and ever changing environments:

10.2.1 The learning organisation

Within the environment as sketched above, it has been suggested that the only 'real source of sustainable competitive advantage might be the ability to learn faster than competitors' (Dickson, 1992) in Hooley, et al. (2004). A major challenge for organisations is to create the climate and culture to maximise learning. Of particular importance in the context of marketing strategy is the ability to continually develop knowledge and skills to create superior customer value.

10.2.2 A heightened market orientation and the focus on creating superior customer value

In the quest to provide superior customer value no firm can stand still. Rather than focusing on selling their own existing products, the focus of truly market-oriented firms lies in finding solutions to their customers 'problems' and thereby creating superior value for them.

10.2.3 Positioning built on marketing assets, capabilities and competences

While it is accepted that strategies need to be based on the resources and capabilities of a firm, rather than just chasing customers irrespective of the firm's ability to serve them, even resources, competences and assets need to be to be constantly improved to serve a changing market. Assets such as brand names, unique distribution systems, information and quality control systems and more, need to be deployed in the market to sustain a competitive advantage. Competences are the skills with which they are deployed. This implies, according to some resource-based theorists, that the management of a company is its most important resource.

Increasingly companies are forming alliances and networks with other organisations as they seek to create or acquire assets and competences that can be exploited in many other situations (eg extending a brand name into new markets, exploiting technology in new industries). A critical issue for the future is how different assets and competences can be combined to create new products and services.

10.2.4 Establishing closer customer relationships

What differentiates the more successful companies is their relationships with customers and suppliers. The cost (in terms of time, effort and financial resource) of creating closer relationships with all customers might, however, prove prohibitive and it is likely that multi-mode marketing, the adoption of different marketing approaches for different customers, is likely to take the place of more uniform marketing to all customers.

10.2.5 Rethinking the role of marketing

Marketing is increasingly being seen as a process within the value chain responsible for ensuring the creation of value for customers, and not as a business function. Marketing operates at two levels, strategic and operational. Operationally it is involved with the day-to-day functional marketing tasks. It is, however, at the strategic level that marketing becomes a company wide process and the 'marketing department' can no longer claim ownership of this process. Marketing needs to become flexible and responsive to change. This entails distinguishing the philosophy from the trappings and focusing on marketing skills and not titles in departments. At the strategic level everyone in the organisation should place customers at the forefront. The role and function of marketing in the organisation will need to be redefined and reasserted. Structures that facilitate rapid response will need to be created.

Learning objective review

Learning objectives	Covered
1. Propose and justify approaches to implementing the process of marketing planning in different contextual settings.	☑ Marketing planning for different stakeholder groups ☑ Planning in consumer and business-to-business markets ☑ Services marketing ☑ Marketing planning in large and small organisations ☑ Marketing planning in non-profit organisations ☑ Internal marketing and internal marketing segmentation ☑ The international and global dimension of marketing planning ☑ Planning marketing in the virtual marketplace ☑ Relationship-based marketing planning and customer retention ☑ Marketing planning in highly competitive markets

Quick quiz

1. Describe three categories of stakeholders.
2. Provide a short explanation of organisational buyer behaviour.
3. What are the major communications tools within the promotions mix for business-to-business marketing?
4. Intangibility is a characteristic of service marketing. Explain.
5. In addition to the traditional four Ps, what is meant by the extended marketing mix for services marketing?
6. List some common challenges faced by small organisations.
7. What are the three market entry methods available to firms seeking international expansion?
8. What are the three main uses of the internet as a marketing tool?
9. Briefly discuss the steps in relationship building represented by the relationship marketing ladder
10. One of the reasons for companies seeking international expansion is to benefit from economies of scale. How does this happen?

Worksheet activity 11.1

Local authority: The customers are the people who receive the services or use the amenities, especially if they also pay for them (for example, through local tax charges). Other stakeholder audiences include employees, suppliers and subcontractors, local business and not-for-profit organisations (who may benefit from, or compete with, local government initiatives for funds and provision of services), the press (especially local media) and local interest and lobbying groups.

Charity: The customers are, arguably, the beneficiaries of the services: in this case, local communities and environmental groups. However, key stakeholder audiences will include current and potential funders and volunteers (without whom the charity's activities would cease). Others will include the press and government, whom the charity will attempt to persuade of the importance of local environment issues, and other pressure groups who may support them in this attempt.

Worksheet activity 11.2

The main stakeholders in the hotel business can be identified as follows:

Hotel employees. It is important for the hotel management to develop and maintain positive working relationships with its employees for a number of reasons. At a basic level, there are legal obligations inherent in the employment relationship, so that the hotel will need to pursue 'employee relations' in various forms (such as consultation and involvement, within the EU framework, for example). More broadly, the hotel management needs to pursue constructive relations with staff in the interests of securing their commitment, loyalty and input, to support a high (and competitive) level of service to customers. Service levels are a key differentiating factor for hotels, and only committed and informed staff will be able to deliver appropriate customer care. While staff turnover is traditionally high in hotel and catering, R will benefit from staff continuity through relationship-building, because of its emphasis on high quality service and group branding.

Hotel group shareholders. Shareholders have an ultimate say in the strategic management of the group and the employment of its management – as well as providing its share capital and financial market credibility. Hotel management has legal obligations to pursue shareholder relations in the sense of reporting requirements and the referral of decisions to shareholders at statutory meetings. This may be sufficient for many of the small individual shareholders. The larger institutional shareholders, however, have greater individual power to give or withhold support from the hotel's management: they represent an important 'public' which must be co-opted to support its strategic initiatives.

Other sources of finance, such as **banks**, for example, are another important stakeholder as they provide long- and short-term loan finance for the hotels. Expansion plans (new facilities, new hotel premises) will need backing. The banks' ability to deny credit if they are not satisfied with the relationship could hamper development of both the worldwide group and the individual hotel R. If cash flow problems develop, the bank's willingness to help will be needed if the hotel is to stay in business at all.

Suppliers. The hotel 'product' is a complex bundle of product/service elements, many of which are supported and/or provided (on a contracted basis) by external suppliers. Suppliers help to ensure the smooth running of the hotels through provision of goods such as food and domestic consumables, and services such as equipment maintenance, cleaning and security. Relationships with suppliers must be maintained (eg by supplier relationship management, a good payment record and collaborative improvement planning) so that these goods and services continue to be provided. Consistency (and therefore continuity) of supply will be particularly important for a hotel with a high-quality brand to maintain. Supplier loyalty, partnership and perhaps exclusivity will also be helpful in maintaining competitive advantage, as a core resource.

Hotel customers. Customers are the raison d'être of the hotel, and the source of its continued competitive survival. As has previously been noted, it is more cost-effective to retain customers (by building mutually satisfying long-term relationships with them) than to win new ones, particularly in highly competitive markets.

It will therefore be important for R not only to provide one-off excellent experiences for customers, but relationships with them: loyalty incentives and rewards, ongoing contacts (perhaps a newsletter, special offers to returning guests and so on), and personalised service at all points of contact ('valued guest'). This should be possible not only for those who stay at the hotel, but for community users of its swimming pool (perhaps by 'winter membership' to stimulate out-of-season custom) and other facilities.

Worksheet activity 11.3

Internal customers of the marketing function include:

Senior management and shareholders, who expect the strategic objectives of the organisation to be met through effective and efficient marketing activity.

The product/operations function, which expects to be given practicable product specifications and production schedules, and expects its efforts to be justified by the success of the product in the marketplace – to feel that its output is being effectively 'sold'.

The finance/accounts/admin function, which expects clear and accurate budgets, forecasts and records of expenditure, sales and so on, for the required financial control, reporting and record-keeping systems.

The members of the organisation as a whole, who expect to be given information – and particularly 'good news' – to be able to feel pride in the organisation's image to the outside world, to identify with it and to feel that the marketing function is 'getting it right' on their behalf.

Worksheet activity 11.4

Adaptation may be **mandatory** or **discretionary**.

Mandatory product modification normally involves either adaptation to comply with government requirements or inevitable technical changes. An example of the former would be enhanced safety requirements, while the requirements imposed by different climatic conditions would be an example of the latter.

Discretionary modification is called for only to make the product more appealing in different markets. It results from differing customer needs, preferences and tastes. These differences become apparent from market research and analysis; and intermediary and customer feedback.

Levels of customer purchasing power. Low incomes may make a cheap version of the product more attractive in some less developed economies.

Levels of education and technical sophistication. Ease of use may be a crucial factor in decision-making.

Standards of maintenance and repair facilities. Simpler, more robust versions may be needed.

'Culture-bound' products such as clothing, food and home decoration are more likely to have an adapted marketing mix.

Worksheet activity 11.5

The internet can be used in the following ways to facilitate the distribution process and aid customer service:

It can be used to take orders, frequently update product offerings, help customers to buy online, process payments securely, raise customer service levels, reduce marketing and distribution costs, and distribute digital products.

Worksheet activity 11.6

The advantages of the internet as an advertising medium are as follows:

- Messages can be changed quickly and easily
- Interactivity is possible
- Own pages can be created cheaply
- Can advertise on others' web pages
- Very low cost possible
- Very large audience potential
- Direct sales possible

Quiz answers

1. There are three broad categories of stakeholders in an organisation.

   Internal stakeholders, who are members of the organisation. Key examples include the directors, managers and employees of a company – or the members of a club or association, or the volunteer workers in a charity. They may also include other functions of the organisation (eg marketing, production or finance) which have a stake in marketing activity, and/or separate units of the organisation (eg regional or product divisions) which have a stake in its plans.

   Connected stakeholders (or primary stakeholders), who have an economic or contractual relationship with the organisation. Key examples include the shareholders in a business; the customers of a business or beneficiaries of a charity; distributors and intermediaries; suppliers of goods and services; and financiers/funders of the organisation.

   External stakeholders (or secondary stakeholders), who are not directly connected to the organisation, but who have an interest in its activities, or are impacted by them in some way. Examples include the government, pressure and interest groups (including professional bodies and trade unions), the news media, the local community and wider society.

2. Organisational buying behaviour refers to the buying behaviour of organisations which buy goods and services to use in the production of other products and services that are sold, rented or supplied to others.

3. The types of media used for advertising differ greatly from those in consumer markets. Mass media are rarely used. Advertising is usually confined to trade magazines, which reach more precise targets. Direct mail is used to supplement personal selling.

4. A service cannot be seen, touched or displayed. The heart of the service is the experience created for the customer, for example, a haircut or a flight. The service experience is intangible and is only delivered after the customer has committed himself to the purchase.

5. For service products **additional elements of the marketing mix** are necessary to reflect the special characteristics of services marketing. These are as follows:

   People: these include both service-providers and customers who participate in the production and delivery of the service experience.

   Physical evidence: this refers to the tangible clues that support the main service product. These include facilities, the infrastructure and the products used to deliver the service.

   Processes: this relates to the operating processes that take the customer though from initial order to the manufacture and delivery of the service.

6. Small organisations have their special problems of cost, cash flow, marketing and management:

   Lack of economies of scale. A small business will not qualify for the best purchasing terms from suppliers; will probably have to pay a higher rate of interest on its bank borrowings; and will not be able to afford to employ specialist staff, instead having to buy-in their services at very high hourly rates.

   External factors. It is a constant complaint from businesses in the UK that there is an ever-increasing burden of regulation and compliance upon them. To the extent that this is true, this burden is likely to weigh most heavily on the small, owner-managed business, with its very limited administrative capacity.

   Over-reliance on a few key individuals can cause catastrophe if one of them leaves or is sick for a prolonged period.

   Small market areas or a restricted range of products mean that small businesses are particularly vulnerable to environmental changes. They tend to have all their eggs in one basket.

   Cannot raise money. Many small businesses complain they are unable to raise finance and rely heavily on bank loans. (Many proprietors, however, are unwilling to sacrifice control in order to raise bank finance.)

Strategic decision-making is likely to be heavily influenced by the experience and priorities of the owner(s) of small- and medium-sized businesses. These people not only tend to retain ultimate control of their businesses but tend to exert firm control over their more junior managers, partly by their recruitment policies and partly by their expressed preference.

7. They are direct export, indirect export and overseas manufacture.

8. The three main uses of the internet as marketing tool are: as a research and planning tool, to facilitate distribution and customer service, and as a vehicle for communications and promotions.

9. Based on the relationship marketing ladder, we can describe the steps in relationship building as follows:

    At the bottom of the ladder is the target customer or prospect. Once this individual has turned from a mere prospect into a customer, the intention is to establish a longer-term relationship, by turning the customer into a client. While a customer may have done business with the company only occasionally and may be relatively anonymous or nameless, a client is more individual and does business on a repeat basis. Having said that, clients may be relatively neutral or ambivalent towards the supplier company. Hence, the next step will be for the company to convert clients into becoming supporters, ie those who hold positive attitudes towards the supplier. Following on from this level in the relationship, the intention will be to create advocates of the company, ie those who will actively recommend the company to others. At the top rung of the ladder is the partner. At this stage, supplier and customer are working together in a mutually beneficial relationship. The focus of relationship marketing is thus to move customers up the relationship ladder, continuously trying to find ways to enhance the value for both parties in the relationship.

10. Since volume of output and unit cost are related, increased volume may lead to lower costs. Expanding into international markets may provide the level of sales necessary to benefit from economies of scale.

References

Adcock, D., Halborg, A., Ross, C. (2001), Marketing Principles and Practice, Pearson Education, London

Berry, L.L. & Parasuraman, A. (1991). Marketing Services: Competing through Quality. Free Press, New York.

Brassington, F. and Pettitt, S. (2006), Principles of Marketing (4th Ed.), Pearson Education

Christopher, M.G., Payne, A.F. & Ballantyne, D. (2002). Relationship Marketing: Creating Stakeholder Value. Butterworth-Heinemann, Oxford.

Dickson, P.R. (1992). *'Towards a general theory of competitive rationality'.* Journal of Marketing, 56, January, pp.69-83

Garten, J.E. (2004), *'Wal-Mart gives globalism a bad name'*, Business Week, March 8.

George, W.R. & Grönroos, C. (1989). Developing customer-conscious employees at every level – internal marketing' in Congram, C.A. & Friedman, M.L. (Eds) Handbook of Services Marketing. AMACOM, New York.

Gummesson, E. (1996), *'Towards a theoretical framework of relationship marketing'*, in Proceedings of the International Conference on Relationship Marketing, pp 5-18, Berlin.

Gummesson, E. (2002). Total Relationship Marketing. Elsevier Butterworth-Heinemann, Oxford.

Jobber, D (2007), Principles and Practice of Marketing (5th Ed.). McGraw Hill Education

Jobber, D. (2007). Principles & Practice of Marketing (5th Ed.). McGraw Hill Education, Maidenhead, Berks.

Johnson, G., Scholes K. & Whittington, R. (2005), Exploring Corporate Strategy: Text and Cases (7th Ed.), Pearson Education

Kotler, P., Armstrong, G., Meggs, D., Bradbury, E. and Grech, J. (1999), Marketing: An Introduction. Prentice Hall Australia, Sydney.

Kotler, P. (2002), Marketing Management (11th Ed.). US Imports and PHIPES

Payne, A., Christopher, M., Clark, M. and Peck, H. (1995), Relationship Marketing for Competitive Advantage, Oxford: Butterworth-Heinemann as cited in Hooley, G., Saunders, J. and Piercy, N. (2004), *Marketing Strategy and Competitive Positioning* (3rd Ed.), Pearson Education

Peck, H.L., Payne, A., Christopher, M. & Clark, M. (1999), Relationship Marketing: Strategy and Implementation. Oxford: Elsevier Butterworth-Heinemann, Oxford.

Peck H.L., Payne A., Christopher M. & Clark M. (2004). Relationship Marketing: Strategy and Implementation. Elsevier Butterworth-Heinemann, Oxford.

Pickton, D. and Broderick, A. (2001), Integrated Marketing Communications, Financial Times Prentice-Hall

Porter, M. (2001), *'Strategy and the Internet'*, Harvard Business Review, 79, pp.63-78

Porter, M. (2002) as quoted by Newing, R. (2002), *'Crucial Importance of Clear Business Goals'*, Financial Times, 5 June, p. 4

Powers, T.L. (1991), Modern Business Marketing: A strategic planning approach to business and industrial markets. West Pub Co., Saint Paul, MN.

Schlesinger, L.A. & Heskett, J.L. (1991). *'Breaking the cycle of failure in services'*. Sloan Management Review, Spring, pp 17-28.

Webster, F.E. and Wind, Y. (1972), Organisational Buying Behaviour. Englewood Cliffs, Prentice Hall: New Jersey.

Worthington, I. and Britton, C (2006), The Business Environment (5th Ed.). Pearson Education, London

Key concepts

Bargaining power 47

Controls 24, 27
Corporate audit 35
Critical success factors (CSFs) 198
Cyclical change 88

Differential advantage 123
Dynamic markets 89

Explicit knowledge 91

Legal forces 92

Marketing strategy 24, 25
Micro-environment 25, 47
Mission statement 35

Numerical forecasts 24, 26

Porter's five competitive forces 47
Product stewardship 62

Regulatory forces 92
Rivalry 47

Societal forces 138
Stable markets 89
Strategic objectives 35
Structural change 88

Tacit knowledge 91
Target market 123
Technological forces 92
Turbulent markets 89

Index

Achieving control, 22
Activities, 113
Adaptation, 235
Analysis, 21
Attitude, 132

Bargaining power, 47
Behavioural segmentation, 131
Benchmarking, 199
Boston matrix, 114
Breakeven analysis, 27
Budgeting, 188
Budgets, 188
Business-to-business marketing, 219
Buyer readiness stage, 132

Competition, 11
Competitive advantage, 173
Competitor orientation, 4
Competitor performance, 199
Consumer behaviour, 55
Consumer desirability criteria, 173
Contingency planning, 27
Control systems, 22
Control, 21
Controls, 24, 27
Core competences, 81
Corporate audit, 35
Corporate objectives, 35, 39
Corporate social responsibility, 59
Corporate strategic planning, 16
Corrective action, 201
Cost leadership, 19
Creating structural ties, 169
Critical success factors (CSFs), 198
Cross functional teams, 8
Cultural changes, 45
Cultural knowledge, 91
Culture, 56
Current situation, 16
Customer orientation, 4
Customer retention, 241
Customer service, 169
Customer value, 11
Customers, 11
Customised marketing, 154
Cyclical change, 88

Decision making unit, 216
Delighted customers, 169
Demographic segmentation, 125
Demographics, 56
Desired future position, 16
Differential advantage, 123, 160
Differentiated benefits positioning, 166
Differentiation, 19, 160
Directional policy matrix, 115
Dynamic markets, 89

Ecological (green) environment, 45
Economic conditions, 92
Economic environment, 44
Economic trends, 44
Employee markets, 12
End use, 132
Enlightened marketing, 62
Environmental Analysis Frameworks, 92
Environmental change, 88
Environmental forces, 43
Environmental scanning, 90
Environmental sustainability, 62
Environmentalism, 62
Ethical consumption, 59
Exchange, 9
Explicit knowledge, 91

Family life cycle, 126
Family, 45
Focus, 20
Forecasting methods, 185
Forecasts, 188
Functional organisation, 6

Genius forecasting, 186
Geodemographic segmentation, 128
Geographic segmentation, 125
Geographical organisation, 7
Globalisation, 57
Green concerns, 45
Green marketing, 46

Human resource management, 112

Image drivers, 163
Implementation, 21
Implementation milestones, 27
Inbound logistics, 112
Industry Life Cycle, 97
Influence markets, 12
Innovation, 54
Innovation audit, 106
Innovation positioning, 165
Inter-departmental relationships, 9
Interface, 8
Inter-functional orientation, 4
Internal analysis, 25
Internal audit tools, 109
Internal customer, 229
Internal marketing, 202
Internal markets, 12
Internal stakeholders, 65, 228
International marketing environment, 232

Key account management, 244

Legal environment, 46
Legal forces, 92
Linkages, 113
Loyalty, 132

Macro segmentation variables, 134
Management judgement, 185
Management planning, 112
Market, 11
Market entry methods, 234
Market orientation, 3
Market segmentation, 123
Market selection, 233
Market share performance, 200
Market tests, 187
Marketers as planners, 12
Marketing, 2
   audit, 74, 78
   budget, 192
   communication, 191
   objectives, 40
   performance standards, 201
   planning, 17
   plans, 74
Marketing and sales, 112
Marketing strategy, 24, 25, 122
Markets, 11
Metaphorical description, 107
Micro-environment, 25, 47
Mission, 35, 36
Mission statement, 35

Monitoring customers, 200
Multinationals, 58
Multivariable segmentation, 133

New entrants, 47
Numerical forecasts, 24, 26

Objectives, 34
One-to-one marketing, 166
Operational marketing, 14
Operations, 112
Organisation by customer, 8
Organisational buying process, 217
Organisational competencies, 105
Orientation, 3
Outbound logistics, 112

Panels of experts, 185
Perceptual maps, 170
Performance measures, 27
Personal drivers, 162
Planning inadequacies, 194
Planning, 21
Points of difference, 169
Political environment, 44
Political factors, 44
Porter's 5 Forces, 94
Porter's five competitive forces, 47
Positioning strategies, 163
Positioning, 160
Possible routes, 16
Price positioning, 165
Primary activities, 112
Procurement, 112
Product drivers, 162
Product life cycle, 110, 175
Product orientation, 3
Product stewardship, 62
Product-based organisation, 7
Production orientation, 3
Psychographic segmentation, 129
Psychological influences, 56

Qualitative forecasts, 185
Quality positioning, 165
Quantitative or statistical techniques, 186

Referral markets, 12
Regression analysis, 186
Regulatory forces, 92
Relationships, 9
Relationship marketing, 10

Relationship positioning, 166
Repositioning, 174, 175
Resource-based planning, 104
Revitalisation, 174
Rivalry, 47

Sales force surveys, 185

Sales orientation, 3
Scenario planning, 98, 186
Scheduling of plans, 23
Segment evaluation process, 149
Segmentation variables, 125
Segmenting business markets, 133
Service drivers, 162
Service positioning, 165
Services characteristics, 221
Services marketing, 220
Setting targets, 188
Situation analysis, 24
Small organisations, 224
Social class, 125
Social environment, 44
Societal forces, 92
Societal marketing concept, 3
Societal marketing, 60
Socio-economic groups, 45
Stable markets, 89
Stages of the marketing planning process, 21
Stakeholder interests, 213
Standardisation, 235
Start up business, 224
Strategic Group Mapping, 96

Strategic objectives, 35
Structural change, 88
Substitute products, 47
Supplier markets, 12
Support activities, 112
Sustainable competitive advantage, 18
Sustainable marketing orientation, 4
SWOT analysis, 81
Synergistic planning process, 16
System of exchange/b, 9

Tacit knowledge, 91

Tactical and strategic marketing plans, 20
Target market, 26, 123, 169
Technological environment, 45
Technological forces, 92
Technology development, 112
The business environment, 25
The marketing plan, 23
Time series analysis, 186
Transaction, 9, 10
Turbulent markets, 89

Value, 113

Value chain, 111
Value creation, 11
Value proposition, 11
Values and life style framework, 130
Virtual marketplace, 236
Vision, 35, 36

Notes

Notes

Notes

Notes

Notes

Notes

Notes

Notes

Notes

Notes

Notes

Review form & Free prize draw

All original review forms from the entire BPP range, completed with genuine comments, will be entered into one of two draws on 31 January 2010 and 31 July 2010. The names on the first four forms picked out on each occasion will be sent a cheque for £50.

Name: _____   **Address:** _____

_____

_____

1. How have you used this Text?
(Tick one box only)

☐ Self study (book only)
☐ On a course: college_____
☐ Other _____

2. During the past six months do you recall seeing/receiving any of the following?
(Tick as many boxes as are relevant)

☐ Our advertisement in *The Marketer*
☐ Our brochure with a letter through the post
☐ Saw website

3. Why did you decide to purchase this Text?
(Tick one box only)

☐ Have used companion Assessment workbook
☐ Have used BPP Texts in the past
☐ Recommendation by friend/colleague
☐ Recommendation by a lecturer at college
☐ Saw advertising in journals
☐ Saw website
☐ Other _____

4. Which (if any) aspects of our advertising do you find useful?
(Tick as many boxes as are relevant)

☐ Prices and publication dates of new editions
☐ Information on product content
☐ Facility to order books off-the-page
☐ None of the above

5. Have you used the companion Assessment Workbook?   Yes ☐   No ☐

6. Have you used the companion Passcards?   Yes ☐   No ☐

7. Your ratings, comments and suggestions would be appreciated on the following areas.

	Very useful	Useful	Not useful
Introductory section (How to use this text, study checklist, etc)	☐	☐	☐
Introduction	☐	☐	☐
Syllabus linked learning objectives	☐	☐	☐
Activities and Marketing at Work examples	☐	☐	☐
Learning objective reviews	☐	☐	☐
Magic Formula references	☐	☐	☐
Content of suggested answers	☐	☐	☐
Index	☐	☐	☐
Structure and presentation	☐	☐	☐

	Excellent	Good	Adequate	Poor
Overall opinion of this Text	☐	☐	☐	☐

8. Do you intend to continue using BPP CIM Range Products?   ☐ Yes   ☐ No

9. Have you visited bpp.com/lm/cim?   ☐ Yes   ☐ No

10. If you have visited bpp.com/lm/cim, please give a score out of 10 for its overall usefulness   /10

Please note any further comments and suggestions/errors on the reverse of this page.

Please return to: Dr Kellie Vincent, BPP Learning Media, FREEPOST, London, W12 8BR.

If you have any additional questions, feel free to email cimrange@bpp.com

Marketing Planning Process

Review form & Free prize draw (continued)

Please note any further comments and suggestions/errors below.

Free prize draw rules

1. Closing date for 31 January 2010 draw is 31 December 2009. Closing date for 31 July 2010 draw is 30 June 2010.

2. Restricted to entries with UK and Eire addresses only. BPP employees, their families and business associates are excluded.

3. No purchase necessary. Entry forms are available upon request from BPP Learning Media. No more than one entry per title, per person. Draw restricted to persons aged 16 and over.

4. Winners will be notified by post and receive their cheques not later than 6 weeks after the relevant draw date. List of winners will be supplied on request.

5. The decision of the promoter in all matters is final and binding. No correspondence will be entered into.